LAW, PRAGMATISM, AND DEMOCRACY

LAW,

PRAGMATISM,

AND

DEMOCRACY

❦

Richard A. Posner

HARVARD UNIVERSITY PRESS

CAMBRIDGE, MASSACHUSETTS

LONDON, ENGLAND

Second printing, 2003

Library of Congress Cataloging-in-Publication Data
Posner, Richard A.
Law, pragmatism, and democracy / Richard A. Posner
p. cm.
Includes bibliographical references and index.
ISBN 0-674-01081-7
1. Justice, Administration of—United States.
2. Rule of law—United States.   3. Democracy.
4. Pragmatism.   I. Title.

KF384 .P67 2003
340′.11—dc21   2002031877

Contents

❧

Preface

❦

Law and democracy are the twin pillars of the liberal state—representative democracy constrained by legality is what "liberal state" *means*. This book argues for a theory of pragmatic liberalism the twin halves of which are a pragmatic theory of democracy and a pragmatic theory of law. Pragmatic liberalism stands in contrast to what might be called deliberative liberalism, which is the joinder of deliberative democracy and rulebound or principle-bound adjudication. Deliberative liberalism models voting and the action of elected officials as guided by reason rather than by interest, and adjudication as guided by either rules (in the most formalistic versions of deliberative adjudication) or principles (in the legal-process and moral-philosophy versions, which are less formalistic). Pragmatic liberalism, with its unillusioned understanding of human nature and its skepticism about the constraining effect of legal, moral, and political theories on the actions of officials, emphasizes instead the institutional and material constraints on decisionmaking by officials in a democracy.[1]

The book's principal contribution to democratic theory is the revival, elaboration, and application of the theory of "elite" democracy first sketched by Joseph Schumpeter and in recent years rather thoroughly neglected. Although Schumpeter is not usually thought of as a pragmatist, his theory of democracy is pragmatic; and I argue that it provides a supe-

1. The approach is somewhat parallel to that of Russell Hardin in his recent book *Liberalism, Constitutionalism, and Democracy* (1999). See, for example, id. at 38–39.

rior normative as well as positive theory of American democracy to the political theorists' concept of deliberative democracy, on the left, and the
economists' public-choice theory, on the right. On the law side of the
book, the principal contributions are the distinction between philosophical and everyday pragmatism, an insistence on distinguishing between the
case-specific and the systemic consequences of judicial decisions, a further
insistence on distinguishing between pragmatism and consequentialism,
and an attempt at a reconciliation of legal pragmatism with legal positivism. I do not present a complete theory of pragmatic liberalism, however;
my focus is on concepts of democracy and legality rather than on the scope
and limits of government as such, though they are also crucial issues for
liberal theory.

The book builds on my earlier work but contains very little previously
published material (and that material has been extensively revised for the
book), as a sketch of its provenance will show. I presented a version of
Chapters 1 and 2 in a lecture sponsored by the George A. Miller Committee, the law school, and the philosophy department of the University of Illinois at Urbana-Champaign. I am grateful to my hosts on that occasion,
Richard Schacht and Thomas Ulen, and to the lecture audience, for helpful questions and comments. The discussion of John Marshall in the middle section of Chapter 2 is a revised version of my review of R. Kent
Newmyer, *John Marshall and the Heroic Age of the Supreme Court* (2001),
which appears in the *New Republic*, Dec. 17, 2001, p. 36 ("The Accidental
Jurist").

Chapter 3 draws on an address that I gave at the First Annual Symposium on the Foundation of the Behavioral Sciences: John Dewey: Modernism, Postmodernism and Beyond, held at Simon's Rock College of
Bard under the auspices of the Behavioral Research Council of the American Institute for Economic Research. I thank Elias Khalil, the council's di-
rector, for organizing the symposium and inviting me to give one of the
keynote addresses. I also thank Eric Posner and Cass Sunstein for their
comments on an early draft and the participants in the symposium for
their comments.

Chapters 4 through 6 draw on the Wesson Lectures in Democratic
Theory and Practice that I gave under the auspices of the Ethics in Society Program of the philosophy department of Stanford University, as well
as on presentations at the Political Theory Workshop of the University of Chicago, at the Harvard Law School Faculty Workshop, and in the

Political Economy Lecture Series (PELS) at Harvard. Lucian Bebchuk, Eamonn Callan, Kirk Greer, Thomas Grey, Jacob Levy, the audiences at my Wesson and PELS lectures, and the participants in the two workshops, as well as Jonathan Hall, made many helpful comments.

Chapter 7 is based on a draft of a lecture that I was to give at the Eighteenth Annual Meeting of the European Association for Law and Economics in Vienna on September 14, 2001. (The lecture was not delivered because the disruption of airline traffic incident to the September 11, 2001 terrorist attack on the United States prevented me from attending the conference.) I thank Wolfgang Weigel for inviting me to give the lecture and for discussion of the topic, and Albert Alschuler, Neil Duxbury, Michael Green, and Eric Posner for comments on an early draft. In a slightly different form the lecture was given at the University of Texas Law School as a Tom Sealy Law and Free Society Lecture. I thank Brian Leiter for the invitation and for a most helpful discussion of the subject of the lecture, as well as of other topics touched on in this book. Another version was given at a Stanford Law School faculty workshop, and I thank the participants in that workshop for their helpful comments; and still another at the Sorbonne—I thank Horatia Muir Watt for inviting me and for her helpful comments and those of others who attended my talk.

I tried out some of the ideas in Chapter 8 at the International Conference on the Legal Aftermath of September 11, sponsored by the New York University and Columbia Law Schools. I thank George Fletcher and Stephen Holmes, the organizers of the conference, and the participants, for helpful comments, and Anthony Arato for helpful bibliographical suggestions.

Chapter 9 originated in a paper entitled "*Bush v. Gore* as Pragmatic Adjudication," which appears in *A Badly Flawed Election: Debating* Bush v. Gore, *the Supreme Court and American Democracy* 187 (Ronald Dworkin ed. 2002). I am grateful to Ronald Dworkin for suggesting that I emphasize the pragmatic aspects of my take on the case and for his criticisms of the paper; and also to Brian Leiter for his extensive comments on the paper (which includes, incidentally, some material that appears in other chapters of the present book). I presented a version of Chapter 9, and also of Chapters 1 and 2, at the Legal Theory Workshop of Columbia Law School. Larry Kramer and the other participants in that workshop made a number of helpful comments. I presented the same trio of chapters at the Colloquium on Legal, Moral, and Political Philosophy of University College,

London. On that occasion Ronald Dworkin, Stephen Guest, Christopher Hookway, Jonathan Wolff, and other participants in the colloquium made many stimulating criticisms and suggestions.

Chapter 10 is based on "Pragmatism versus Purposivism in First Amendment Analysis," 54 *Stanford Law Review* 737 (2002), my reply to Jed Rubenfeld, "The First Amendment's Purpose," 53 *Stanford Law Review* 767 (2001). I am grateful to Michael Boudin, Frank Easterbrook, Lawrence Lessig, David Strauss, Cass Sunstein, and Adrian Vermeule for their comments on a previous draft of the reply, as well as to Professor Rubenfeld, with whom I debated our disagreements in a joint appearance in the Stanford Law Review Lecture Series. Finally, I gave lectures and workshops based on several of the chapters at Haverford College under the auspices of the William Pyle Philips Fund, and received a number of helpful comments from my host, Mark Gould, and other faculty, and student, participants.

I am indebted for very helpful research assistance to William Baude, Philip Bridwell, Tun-Yen Chiang, Bryan Dayton, Adele Grignon, Brian Grill, and Benjamin Traster; and for helpful comments on the manuscript to Michael Aronson, Peter Berkowitz, Christopher Berry, David Cohen, Neil Duxbury, Eldon Eisenach, David Estlund, Edward Glaeser, Michael Green, Thomas Grey, Stephen Guest, Russell Hardin, Mark Lilla, Larissa MacFarquhar, Eric MacGilvray, Frank Michelman, Martha Nussbaum, Richard Pildes, Charlene Posner, Eric Posner, Richard Rorty, Andrei Shleifer, Cass Sunstein, Dennis Thompson, and Donald Wittman.

LAW, PRAGMATISM, AND DEMOCRACY

Pragmatic Liberalism and the Plan of the Book

First there was the investigation and impeachment of President Clinton, and people said, yes, he's a crook but he's been an effective President and we should be pragmatic and offset his effectiveness against his misbehavior. Then came *Bush v. Gore*, where the Supreme Court handed George W. Bush the Presidency, and people said—or at least the critics of the decision, who were many, said—that the Court had acted out of an excess of pragmatism, wishing to spare the country the spectacle of a botched Presidential succession. Finally there were the September 11, 2001 terrorist attacks and in their wake people began to say that civil liberties would have to bend to pragmatic concerns about public safety. These disparate episodes (all discussed in this book) focus sharply the question of the proper role of pragmatism in law, and in government generally.

For some years now—since well before the three episodes noted in the preceding paragraph—I have been arguing that pragmatism is the best description of the American judicial ethos and also the best guide to the improvement of judicial performance—and thus the best normative as well as positive theory of the judicial role.[1] I think I've made some good points

1. See the following books of mine: *The Problems of Jurisprudence* (1990); *Cardozo: A Study in Reputation* (1990); *Overcoming Law* (1995); *The Problematics of Moral and Legal Theory*, ch. 4 (1999); *Frontiers of Legal Theory*, chs. 2–4 (2001); *Breaking the Deadlock: The 2000 Election, the Constitution, and the Courts*, ch. 4 (2001). I am not alone in urging a pragmatic approach to

and offered some telling illustrations. But I have not adequately explained the sense in which I use "pragmatism" when discussing law, which differs from the sense in which philosophers use the word, or met all the objections to my concept of pragmatic adjudication. Nor have I related legal pragmatism to legal positivism or to democracy, even though the relation between legal pragmatism and legal positivism is intimate, while that between law and democracy is inescapable for any legal theory—and democratic theory, like legal positivism, comes in pragmatic and nonpragmatic versions. Furthermore, since the pragmatic judge disclaims being a mere mouthpiece for decisions made or values declared by the electorally responsible branches of government, pragmatic adjudication raises a question of democratic legitimacy.

The neglect of democracy is a particularly striking feature not only of previous discussions of pragmatic legal theory, including my own, but of legal theory in general. Legal professionals tend either to take democracy for granted or to regard it as something that gets in the way of law, since many of the most celebrated legal rights are rights against the democratic majority. The legal professionals' neglect of, even disdain for, democracy is abetted by the remarkable fact that there is at present no influential body of academic thought that makes the case for American democracy as it is actually practiced. Ian Shapiro remarks "democratic theory's apparently moribund condition."[2] The most influential bodies of contemporary academic reflection on democracy—deliberative democracy on the left and public choice on the right—are overwhelmingly critical of our actual democratic system. A major aim of this book is simply to make the case for contemporary American democracy. The making of that case will in turn assist in the construction of a theory of adjudication.

The democratic theory for which the book argues is pragmatic. We should not be afraid of pragmatism or confuse it with cynicism or with dis-

---

law, even if one excludes the distinguished dead, such as Oliver Wendell Holmes, Jr. and John Dewey. Notable recent contributions include Daniel A. Farber, "Legal Pragmatism and the Constitution," 72 *Minnesota Law Review* 1331 (1988); Brian Z. Tamanaha, *Realistic Socio-Legal Theory: Pragmatism and a Social Theory of Law* (1997); Thomas C. Grey, "Freestanding Legal Pragmatism," in *The Revival of Pragmatism: New Essays on Social Thought, Law, and Culture* 254 (Morris Dickstein ed. 1998); Robert Justin Lipkin, *Constitutional Revolutions: Pragmatism and the Role of Judicial Review in American Constitutionalism* (2000); Ward Farnsworth, "'To Do a Great Right, Do a Little Wrong': A User's Guide to Judicial Lawlessness," 86 *Minnesota Law Review* 227 (2001); David D. Meyer, "*Lochner* Redeemed: Family Privacy after *Troxel* and *Carhart*," 48 *UCLA Law Review* 1125, 1182–1190 (2001).

2. Ian Shapiro, *Democratic Justice* 4 (1999).

dain for legality or democracy. Its core is merely a disposition to base action on facts and consequences rather than on conceptualisms, generalities, pieties, and slogans. Among the pieties rejected is the idea of human perfectibility; the pragmatist's conception of human nature is unillusioned. Among the conceptualisms rejected are moral, legal, and political theory when offered to guide legal and other official decisionmaking.

Readers not captivated by pragmatism but interested in intellectual history may find some value in the unexpected links that I forge between John Dewey and Friedrich Hayek, between Hans Kelsen and Dewey (and other pragmatists), and between Joseph Schumpeter and—James Madison. Kelsen and Schumpeter, famous in their time as theorists of law and of democracy respectively, have been neglected in recent years.[3] One aim of this book is to remedy that neglect. Another is to encourage a different kind of scholarly research on issues of law and politics from the dominant mode today, which is discursive, normative, and abstract. Scholars in the fields touched on in this book tend to create theoretical models of adjudication and democracy and to judge specific institutions, decisions, policies, and proposals by their conformity to the model. It would be more constructive to focus on the practical consequences of such things, with theorization used only to illuminate the consequences—which is where economic theory and the empirical methods of economics come in. The theoretical uplands, where democratic and judicial ideals are debated, tend to be arid and overgrazed; the empirical lowlands are fertile but rarely cul-

---

3. Kelsen, once the leading figure in legal positivism, doesn't even rate an index entry in an excellent recent book on the subject, Anthony J. Sebok, *Legal Positivism in American Jurisprudence* (1998), or in Neil Duxbury's fine comprehensive work, *Patterns of American Jurisprudence* (1995). He receives passing mention in some of the essays in *The Autonomy of Law: Essays on Legal Positivism* (Robert P. George ed. 1996). And he retains a considerable following on the Continent. He was not an American but neither was H. L. A. Hart, who figures largely in both Sebok's and Duxbury's books, especially Sebok's; and unlike Hart, Kelsen lived and taught in the United States for many years. Schumpeter's *economic* theories, in particular his emphasis on innovation as the essential engine of economic progress, have a renewed following in economics. See, for example, Richard R. Nelson and Sidney G. Winter, "Evolutionary Theorizing in Economics," *Journal of Economic Perspectives*, Spring 2002, pp. 23, 33–34, 37; William J. Baumol, *The Free-Market Innovation Machine: Analyzing the Growth Miracle of Capitalism* (2002); Johannes M. Bauer, "Market Power, Innovation, and Efficiency in Telecommunications: Schumpeter Reconsidered," 31 *Journal of Economic Issues* 557 (1997). We shall see in Chapter 7 that Schumpeter's theories of democracy and of innovation overlap. A conspicuous exception to the neglect of Schumpeter's democratic theory by recent political theorists and political scientists is Bernard Manin's fine book *The Principles of Representative Government* (1997), which is Schumpeterian in spirit although Manin is critical of important aspects of Schumpeter's theory.

tivated. Granted, this book is not itself a work of empirical scholarship. The focus is on concepts (positivism, democracy, and so forth). But I try throughout to keep the discussion as concrete, practical, and straightforward as possible.

The first chapter examines the meanings of "pragmatism" and introduces the term "everyday pragmatism," which I distinguish from philosophical pragmatism and which plays a central role in the book. I argue that appeals to pragmatism to guide adjudication and other governmental action should largely be cut loose from philosophy. The cutting-loose thesis is not intended, however, to reject the many arresting propositions that the philosophical discourse on pragmatism has generated and that I set forth below. These are listed rather than defended; the book defends everyday rather than philosophical pragmatism. The two pragmatisms are related, however; the philosophical may create a receptive mood for the everyday and it does have some direct applications to law and policy.

The first and perhaps most fundamental thesis of philosophical pragmatism, at least of the brand of philosophical pragmatism that I find most congenial (an important qualification, given pragmatism's diversity), is that Darwin and his successors in evolutionary biology were correct that human beings are merely clever animals.[4] Mind is not something a benevolent deity added to the clay. Body is not a drag on mind, as Plato thought. (Inverting Plato is a generally reliable method of generating the main propositions of pragmatism.) Body and mind coevolved. Being thus adaptive to the ancestral human environment,[5] human intelligence is better at coping with practical problems, the only thing that preoccupied our ancestors 50,000 years ago, than at handling metaphysical entities and other abstractions. That is, our intelligence is primarily instrumental rather than contemplative. Theoretical reasoning is continuous with practical reasoning rather than a separate human faculty.

Since we are just clever animals, with intellectual capabilities oriented toward manipulating our local physical and social environment, we cannot be optimistic about our ability to discover metaphysical entities, if there

4. It would be more precise to say that pragmatic philosophers *believe* that Darwin and his successors were correct. Pragmatism makes no claims to ultimate truth or, specifically, to being able to arbitrate between scientific and religious worldviews.

5. The term that evolutionary biologists use to describe the environment in which human beings evolved to approximately their present biological state.

are any (which we cannot know),[6] whether through philosophy or any other mode of inquiry. We cannot hope to know the universe as it really is, the metaphysical universe, because to do so would require us to be able to step outside ourselves and compare the universe as it really is with our descriptions of it. Renouncing the quest for metaphysical knowledge need not be cause for disappointment, however, because it means "that appearances do not deceive, that the world is as it seems to be, and that there is no deep mystery at the heart of existence."[7] Or at least no deep mystery worth trying to dispel and thus worth troubling our minds about.

Not only is our knowledge local; it is also perspectival, being shaped by the historical and other conditions in which it is produced. Our minds race ahead of themselves, however, inclining us to universalize our local, limited insights. Influential writers on jurisprudence, such as H. L. A. Hart, Ronald Dworkin, and Jürgen Habermas, all purport to be describing law in the abstract, but Hart is really talking about the English legal system, Dworkin about the American, Habermas about the German.[8]

Not that racing ahead is a bad thing. Scientific theorizing is often far ahead of the facts; think only of non-Euclidean geometry, which was discovered in the nineteenth century yet had no empirical significance until Einstein—whose theory of relativity was itself developed before empirical testing of it became possible. And metaphysical theorizing, from Plato to Spinoza to Kant, while in one sense the product of mind on holiday, the clutch depressed and the engine revving up to a higher and higher pitch without turning any wheels, has insight and even charm, just as literature and art do. But unlike science, metaphysics lacks agreed-upon criteria for the evaluation of its theories. As a result, in an open, diverse, competitive culture, the kind a pragmatist, being a Darwinian, tends to prefer, metaphysical disputation is interminable. This does not mean that the pragmatist "rejects" metaphysics. He rejects the possibility of establishing the truth of metaphysical propositions a priori; and it is in the nature of metaphysics that its propositions cannot be established empirically. Metaphysical propositions may have value of a psychological or aesthetic character,

---

6. Concepts and numbers, as I'll note in the next chapter, are plausible candidates for real metaphysical entities. (That is, they are real but not physical.) But generally when I speak of "metaphysics" in this book I shall be referring to more ambitious forms of metaphysical realism than mathematical or other conceptual realism.

7. Alan Ryan, *John Dewey and the High Tide of American Liberalism* 344 (1995).

8. See *The Problematics of Moral and Legal Theory*, note 1 above, at 91–107.

however, in which event their lack of truth value is no better reason for rejecting them than the fictive character of most poetry is (as Plato thought) a good reason for rejecting poetry.

Neither logic nor any empirical protocol guarantees truth. So even scientific knowledge is tentative, revisable—in short, fallible. The significance of a proposition lies neither in its correspondence to an ultimate and hence unknowable reality, nor in its pedigree (that is, its derivation from accepted premises), but in its consequences. They are all that is within the grasp and interest of a normal human being. Pragmatists do not doubt that "true" and "false" are meaningfully ascribed to propositions, but, consistent with their emphasis on consequences, they like to say that a proposition is true ("true enough" might be more precise) if the consequences that it predicts or implies do indeed occur. "It is raining" is true, for example, if I get wet when I go outdoors without an umbrella or raincoat.[9]

The consequences that concern the pragmatist are actual consequences, not the hypothetical ones that figure prominently in Kant's moral theory. The pragmatist asks, for example, not whether it is true that man has free will but what the consequences would be, *for us*, of affirming or denying the proposition. (They could be political or psychological.) And this implies that pragmatists are forward-looking, antitraditionalist. The past is a repository of useful information, but it has no claims on us. The criterion for whether we should adhere to past practices is the consequences of doing so for now and the future. But this does not make pragmatism antihistoricist. On the contrary, the pragmatist's claim that knowledge is local inclines him to seek explanations for beliefs in their historical circumstances.

Emphasis on consequences makes pragmatism anti-essentialist. Consider, for example, authorship. A pragmatist doesn't ask whether authorship is the essence of writing any more than he would ask whether free will is the essence of responsibility or reason the essence of man. It is a fact that everything we treat as a writing has a writer or writers. But whether we choose to ascribe authorship to a writer is a social judgment, like the ascription of moral or legal responsibility. Authorship used often to be as-

9. The pragmatic conception of truth is misunderstood in Jed Rubenfeld, "A Reply to Posner," 54 *Stanford Law Review* 753, 764–765 (2002), who states: "Posner's 'pragmatist' thinks we should believe that dropped objects will fall toward the earth because it is useful to believe it . . . [He] will have a hard time explaining *why* it is so useful to believe that dropped objects will fall toward the earth." Not at all; if you fail to believe it, you may decide to skydive without a parachute.

cribed not to the writer but to some grandee whose association with the work gave it dignity; the psalms of David are an example. Modern counterparts include the copyright doctrine of "work for hire," which ascribes the authorship of a work done by an employee in the course of his employment to the employer rather than to the employee who wrote it; and the widespread practice of ghostwriting, where the ghost is not identified and instead authorship is ascribed to the politician, judge, or celebrity who commissioned the work. Ghostwriting and writing under a nom de plume continue what until relatively recent times was a common practice of anonymous authorship. But today ascription of authorship is more commonly used to identify to the public the actual writer. That identification may or may not provide valuable information to readers, censors, and others. What it clearly does is elevate the writer over other contributors to the published work, such as the compositor, translator, editor, patron, and bookbinder; and this may encourage certain kinds of writing, perhaps writing marked by strong originality. In short, the pragmatist wants to shift the investigation of authorship from asking whether authorship is inherent in the concept of writing to exploring the practical functions that ascriptions of authorship may serve in particular historical settings.[10]

Pragmatists are fallibilists, as I have said, but they are not skeptics or relativists. In fact, they are antiskeptics and antirelativists. They realize that nothing of any practical significance, in fact nothing of any conceivable significance except to a career in academic philosophy, turns on such assertions as that we are brains in a vat being fed deceptive impressions of an external world or that all factual or moral claims are merely individual opinions.[11] We know that such claims have no consequences for behavior because even radical skeptics and radical relativists decline to act on their skeptical or relativist beliefs. They are not skeptical about their skepticism, and they do not regard their relativism as a belief that is true only for themselves or for people who inhabit the same culture as they. No sane person is capable of actual doubt concerning such beliefs as that there is an external world, that other people have minds, and that in no human society is it true that the earth is the center of the universe. There may be no

10. See Michel Foucault, "What Is an Author?" in Foucault, *Language, Counter-Memory, Practice: Selected Essays and Interviews* 113 (Donald F. Bouchard and Sherry Simon eds. 1977). See also Richard A. Posner, *Law and Literature*, ch. 11 (revised and enlarged ed. 1998), *passim*, and references cited in id. at 381 n. 1.

11. "There is nothing either good or bad but thinking makes it so." *Hamlet*, act II, sc. 2, ll. 249–250.

certainties in any ultimate sense, but there are plenty of warranted certitudes.[12]

Pragmatists are skeptical or relativist in more limited senses of these words, however. They doubt that skepticism or relativism can be *proved* to be wrong. And being skeptical that metaphysical entities are knowable, they tend to turn relativist when asked to pass judgment on the mores of a different culture. They could make such a judgment confidently only if they thought there were universal moral principles against which to compare the moral principles of a specific society. When, for example, a person from a culture in which suicide is considered moral confronts a person from a culture in which it is considered immoral, and both agree on all the relevant facts (such as the motives for suicide and the emotional impact of a suicide on members of the suicide's family) but continue to disagree on the morality of the practice, to what can they appeal to resolve their dispute besides some concept fairly to be described as metaphysical because beyond the reach of science or of any other method of bringing about intercultural agreement? Or if though at one in their fundamental moral outlook they cannot come to an agreement about the relevant facts, then, though their disagreement will not be metaphysical, it still will be incapable of resolution by rational methods.

If the mores of a foreign culture rest on some demonstrable factual error, then one is entitled to regard the foreigners as merely deluded even if one cannot get them to agree about the facts. And in no case is the pragmatist *required* to withhold moral judgment on a foreign culture. Deprived of metaphysical backing, he may be less quick to pass judgment than he would be otherwise. But if he has studied the foreign culture carefully yet failed to discover any redeeming virtue in its mores, he is entitled to condemn them, provided he understands that he is basing the condemnation on the mores of his own society rather than on the universal moral law, for establishing the existence of such a law is, in the eyes of pragmatists, a hopeless undertaking.

---

12. "All I mean by truth is the path I have to travel." Letter of Oliver Wendell Holmes to Alice Stopford Green, Oct. 1, 1901, in *The Essential Holmes: Selections from the Letters, Speeches, Judicial Opinions, and Other Writings of Oliver Wendell Holmes, Jr.* 111–112 (Richard A. Posner ed. 1992). As an aside, the common criticism that skepticism and relativism are self-referential and therefore incoherent (the statement "there are no objective truths" applies to itself and thus denies its objectivity) is excessively literal-minded. When for example one says "all rules have exceptions," one means, obviously, that all rules *but this rule* have exceptions, a statement that may or may not be plausible but is not incoherent.

Because intelligence is environmentally adaptive rather than a means by which we can reason our way to ultimate truths, pragmatists believe that the *experimental* method of inquiry is best. That means trying one thing and then another in an effort to discover ways of better predicting and controlling our environment, both physical and social. The model is natural selection, a process essentially of trial and error, of experimentalism writ large. Natural selection has no teleology, and likewise experimentalism is not predestined to discover truth. If a believer in Biblical inerrancy claims that God seeded the earth with dinosaur bones upon its creation in 4004 B.C. in order to test our faith, there is no way to refute him. It is true that in the competition between the scientific and the religious worldview, the former has triumphed in the West and in much of the rest of the world as well. But it has triumphed not because it is true and the religious worldview false, a judgment impossible to make because these worldviews do not rest on common premises.[13] It has triumphed because it is more successful at giving human beings the control over the environment that the elites of the Western nations wanted.[14] It is possible for a pragmatist not to want these things, since pragmatism does not prescribe ends; and so a gloomy antimodernist like Heidegger can be an authentic pragmatist, and likewise William James despite his flirtation with spiritualism.

Experimentalism implies the desirability of a diversity of inquirers, just as natural selection depends on genetic diversity to bring about adaptive change (natural selection "chooses" which mutations shall survive and flourish). People of different background, experience, aptitudes, and temperament will be attuned to different facets of the environment and will have different ideas about how best to proceed in trying to predict and control it. Only by trying different things—not only different ideas but different ways of life—and comparing the consequences do we learn which approaches are best for achieving our goals, whatever they are (pragmatism doesn't say). This is the method by which moral principles evolve, though we can speak of their improving, as distinct from evolving—evolution has no teleology, it is from, not toward—only in relation to specified goals.

13. Compare Stanley Fish's analysis of the impossibility of deciding the ultimate truth of Holocaust denial. Fish, "Holocaust Denial and Academic Freedom," 35 *Valparaiso University Law Review* 499 (2001). He points out that someone who denies plain facts cannot be argued out of his position by the invocation of epistemological theories supposedly able to arbitrate between claims based on incompatible premises.

14. Richard Rorty, *Philosophy and the Mirror of Nature* 328–331 (1979).

Because no one has privileged access to the truth in any domain, the rule of philosophers sketched in Plato's *Republic*[15] cannot be thought superior to democratic government. Democratic government allows people to agree to disagree—that is, to acknowledge that there is no better method of resolving many disputes than by counting noses. This has a pacifying effect; conflicts over fundamental value, the kind that deeply upset and even enrage people, are bracketed. Which is not to say that democracy is always and everywhere the best form of government. History suggests that the preconditions of successful democracy are seldom satisfied. Between the end of Athenian democracy in the fourth century B.C. and the rise of New England town-meeting government in seventeenth-century America, a period of 2000 years, democracy was not a part of any serious political agenda.

The Darwinian notion of man as a clever animal joins with pragmatic skepticism about the cogency of moral argument to yield an unillusioned conception of human nature and potential, remote from the Socratic conception in which all people strive for the Good and commit Evil only through ignorance amenable, happily, to philosophical therapy.

By no means would all philosophers who consider themselves pragmatists agree with the foregoing summary of pragmatic tenets (especially the last one). And a number of other tenets are held by many pragmatic philosophers, though they are tenets that I find uncongenial, as will become apparent in subsequent chapters. They are that truth is what rational inquiry would yield if continued long enough, that political democracy is epistemically superior to other forms of government (or, the same point in different words, that pragmatism implies the desirability of *deliberative democracy* in a strong sense of that term), that there is no important difference between scientific and moral reasoning, that liberal policies are easier to justify pragmatically than conservative ones, and that pragmatism clears the ground for secular liberalism.

What follows for law, or politics and government more generally, from accepting or rejecting *any* of the propositions that I have listed? Not much, which is one reason why I have not tried to prove or disprove any of them. (Another reason is that I couldn't prove or disprove them if I tried, and a third is that, if one may judge by the interminability of philosophical de-

15. And not as a mere fantasy either, though Plato was aware of the practical obstacles. See Malcolm Schofield, "Approaching the *Republic*," in *The Cambridge History of Greek and Roman Political Thought* 190, 224–228 (Christopher Rowe and Malcolm Schofield eds. 2000).

bate, no one could.) I do suggest in Chapter 3 that Dewey's theory of democracy has two useful implications for law; and in Chapter 10 I discuss the implications of the pragmatic theory of truth for freedom of speech. There are some other applications of philosophical pragmatism in the book but not many—and I actually try to break the link that Dewey drew between his pragmatic philosophy and political democracy.

One reason for the disconnect between philosophical pragmatism and legal and political practice is that the propositions that define pragmatism are propositions of academic philosophy, a field that has essentially no audience among judges and lawyers—let alone among politicians—even when philosophy is taken up by law professors (some of whom have a Ph.D. in philosophy) who think it *should* influence law. This gap between theory and practice might be thought to imply that judges should be educated in philosophy—with emphasis on pragmatism! I doubt that that is a good idea, even if judges are considered, as politicians would not be, educable in philosophy. Philosophizing, for example about causation and free will, is relevant to a few of the legal issues that come before judges. But only a few. And we might expect the disconnect between law and *pragmatist* philosophy to be especially pronounced because *that* philosophy, being critical of theory rather than of practice, has little to say about specific practices, such as those involved in the administration of the law. Because pragmatists are not skeptics and thus don't deny that $2 + 2 = 4$ or that the conclusion of a syllogism is true if its premises are true, one can be a committed philosophical pragmatist but believe that the law is a closed logical system. One can think experimental procedures epistemically superior to a priori ones and science therefore more fruitful than theology yet think law committed to a priori reasoning. One might be persuaded by John Dewey that deliberative democracy (real deliberative democracy rather than "deliberative democracy" as a euphemism for limited democracy) is epistemically the most robust form of democracy, yet deny that Deweyan democracy is the theory of the U.S. Constitution.

If you are an *everyday* pragmatist, however, your pragmatism is likely to spill over into your practice as a judge or practicing lawyer. Certain characteristics of American society first noted in a systematic way by Tocqueville but already epitomized in the career and attitudes of Benjamin Franklin—primarily the commercial values that have, since almost the beginning, largely defined American society—discourage reflection and abstract thought, neither of which has a commercial payoff, and encourage the bracketing of deep issues because they tend to disrupt and even poison commercial relations among strangers. An everyday pragmatist in law, an everyday-pragmatist judge for example, wants to know what is at stake in a practical sense in deciding a case one way or another. This does not mean, as detractors of legal pragmatism such as Ronald Dworkin assert, that such a judge is concerned solely with immediate consequences and the short term. The pragmatic judge does not deny the standard rule-of-law virtues of generality, predictability, and impartiality, which generally favor a stand-pat approach to novel legal disputes. He just refuses to reify or sacralize those virtues. He dares to balance them against the adaptationist virtues of deciding the case at hand in a way that produces the best consequences for the parties and those similarly circumstanced. He is impatient with abstractions like "justice" and "fairness," with slogans like "self-government" and "democracy," and with the highfalutin rhetoric of absolutes—unless he is persuaded that such flag-waving has practical social value. For the everyday pragmatist, as for the sophists of ancient Greece whom he resembles (they are among his ancestors), moral, political, and legal theories have value only as rhetoric, not as philosophy.

The everyday pragmatist, if reflective, is likely to be drawn to philosophical pragmatism—although, strangely enough, the reverse is not true. Everyday pragmatists tend to be "dry," no-nonsense types. Philosophical pragmatists tend to be "wets," and to believe that somehow their philosophy really can clear the decks for liberal social policies, though this is largely an accident of the fact that John Dewey was a prominent liberal.

The characteristics that gave rise to everyday pragmatism in the United States eventually led reflective people to philosophize it. And so we got Emerson, and later Peirce, Oliver Wendell Holmes, Jr., William James, John Dewey, George Herbert Mead, and others. Their writings, even Peirce's (many of them anyway), are accessible to a lay audience, although rarely read outside the academy today. Holmes is an exception, since his opinions and to a lesser extent his other writings still have an audience among judges, lawyers, and law students. With the increasing academization of philosophy, the philosophical and the everyday pragmatist have drawn apart in language and tone. Many of the best-regarded modern philosophical pragmatists, such as Quine, Davidson (who resists the label of pragmatist, however), and Putnam, are readable only by other academics, and by few even of them outside philosophy. The eminently readable contemporary pragmatic philosopher Richard Rorty has written about law and public policy, and yet, as we shall see, his writings on this subject are not closely connected to his philosophy. The same is true of John Dewey's writings on law and policy. Almost by default, pragmatists at the operating level of law—judges and practitioners, as distinct from law professors—are an everyday sort untutored by philosophical pragmatism.

Drawing out the implications of everyday pragmatism for adjudication and political governance, and thus for legal positivism and for democracy, is the principal undertaking of the book. Chapter 1 elaborates on the difference between philosophical and everyday pragmatism but distinguishes en route between two types of philosophical pragmatism. One, which I call "orthodox" pragmatism and is mainly what I have been discussing thus far, is within the mainstream of academic philosophy. The other, which I call "recusant" pragmatism and associate primarily with Rorty among living philosophers, seeks a new role for philosophy, one that will enable philosophers to make a constructive contribution to the solution of practical social problems, including legal problems. I doubt the feasibility of this quest.

Building on Chapter 1, Chapter 2 tries to explain pragmatic adjudication more carefully than I have attempted in my previous books. The core of the concept is simple enough: the pragmatic judge aims at the decision that is most reasonable, all things considered, where "all things" include both case-specific and systemic consequences, in their broadest sense, and perhaps, as we shall see, even more. (One of the canards directed against legal pragmatism that I hope to refute is that the legal pragmatist cares only about the *immediate* consequences of a decision or policy. He does not even limit consideration to *consequences*.) I add detail to this description by proposing a number of principles of pragmatic adjudication, all drawn from everyday rather than philosophical pragmatism, and I discuss Chief Justice John Marshall as an exemplar of judicial pragmatism. The main aim of the chapter is to show that there is more structure to pragmatic adjudication than the existing literature suggests. A pragmatic judge is not a legal ignoramus, navigating by the seat of his pants.

Chapter 3 takes up the pragmatist philosopher who had the most to say about both law and democracy: John Dewey. I distinguish among the various senses in which Dewey used the word "democracy," accepting his concept of epistemic democracy but not his concept of political democracy, accepting much of what he had to say about law—in particular his belief, the core of pragmatic adjudication, that legal reasoning is continuous with ordinary practical reasoning[16]—and drawing out two further implications of epistemic democracy for law that he failed to discuss. One is the importance of a diverse judiciary. The other is the need for self-restraint by judges in the exercise of their power to invalidate in the name of the Constitution legislation and other products of the democratic branches of government.

The discussion of democracy is continued and elaborated in Chapters 4 through 6. Chapters 4 and 5 throw more cold water on Dewey's idea of political democracy. They do this in the course of expounding and comparing two concepts of democracy. One is deliberative democracy in the strong, Deweyan form that I call "Concept 1 democracy," though I do not limit the concept to the specifics of his thought. (Among other Concept 1 democrats whom I discuss are Rawls, Habermas, Bohman, Cohen, Gutmann and Thompson, Fishkin, and Sunstein.) The other concept of democracy—essentially an elaboration of Joseph Schumpeter's democratic theory, which is usually called elite democracy but sometimes procedural democracy, competitive democracy, or revisionist democracy—I call "Concept 2 democracy." I am not a big fan of neologisms, but to use the conventional terms "deliberative democracy" and "elite democracy" would be misleading. The former term equivocates between an ideal form of democracy (it is that that I dub "Concept 1") and the type envisaged by the hard-headed framers of the U.S. Constitution, while the latter term obscures the fact that, as we'll see, deliberative democracy is actually more elitist than so-called elite democracy.

Concept 1 presupposes an informed and public-spirited electorate, and so its promoters, heirs of Rousseau,[17] urge the nation's leaders and educators to try somehow to move the electorate in that direction. Concept 2 accepts people as they are, does not think it feasible or desirable to try to change them into public-spirited and well-informed citizens in the sense understood in Concept 1, and regards representative democracy as a pragmatic method of controlling, and providing for an orderly succession of, the officials who (not the people) are the rulers of the nation.

16. I mean "practical reasoning" in its everyday sinse: The reasoning employed by practical people. I do not limit it to its usual philosophical sense of reasoning that issues in a decision to act rather than in the formation of a belief. See, for example, *Practical Reasoning* (Joseph Raz ed. 1978).

17. See Patrick Riley, "Rousseau's General Will," in *The Cambridge Companion to Rousseau* 124, 144 (Patrick Riley ed. 2001).

Schumpeter's concept is a better description of our actual existing democracy than Concept 1 and is also normatively superior because it keeps politics within proper, narrow bounds. It is my candidate for the theoretical defense of democracy against the criticisms of Concept 1 democrats from the left and public-choice theorists from the right. That defense is the focus of Chapter 5, where I also note the tendency of the Schumpeterian concept to converge with the deliberative and also argue that the concept can be used to demonstrate the democratic legitimacy of pragmatic adjudication. The main task of that chapter, however, is to elaborate Schumpeter's description of Concept 2, left sketchy by him and not much elaborated by his followers, now much diminished in number. With the assistance particularly but not only of economics, I try to give Schumpeter's theory the structure and detail that it needs if it is to serve as the democratic leg of pragmatic liberalism.

"Democracy" is used in so many senses[18] and with so little effort at careful definition, at least in legal circles, that I am going to pause here and, in an attempt to orient the reader to the discussion of the term in subsequent chapters, review some of those senses.

The word is used in an *epistemological* sense, notably by Dewey, to denote a mode of inquiry, whether scientific, ethical, political, or everyday, that assumes that intellectual skills and information are distributed widely throughout the population rather than concentrated in a handful of experts, such as Plato's philosopher kings. (This of course is not intended to suggest that intellectual abilities are distributed *equally* among people or that untrained people can actually do science.)

It is used, notably by Tocqueville, in a *social* sense to denote the attitudes and character, strongly influenced by notions of political and moral equality and of equality of opportunity, that accompany, whether as cause or effect or both or neither, American-style political democracy.

It is used in a related, but utopian rather than realistic, social sense to denote the radical equality that some students of democracy believe would ensue from bringing nonpolitical institutions, such as business firms and universities (shades of 1960s radicalism), under democratic control. "Industrial democracy" is one version of this concept of democracy, which

---

18. See Raymond Geuss, *History and Illusion in Politics* 110–128 (2001), and Carlos Santiago Nino, *The Constitution of Deliberative Democracy*, ch. 4 (1996), for helpful discussions of the variety of meanings of "democracy."

might be called *ideological* democracy and is sometimes called *participatory* democracy,[19] though that term is used in other senses as well.

The other senses of democracy are different versions of *political* democracy, or, as it is often unreflectively termed in judicial opinions and law review articles, *majoritarianism*. At one end of the political-democracy spectrum we find *transformative* democracy, which is closely related, however, to what I have called ideological democracy. (*Participatory* democracy is sometimes used to denote both types.) Its most extreme proponents urge that democracy be wholly freed from the constraints of liberalism—such constraints as judicially enforceable constitutional rights and government by representatives who though elected cannot be recalled mid-term, or instructed how to vote on legislative proposals, by the electorate. Lifting those constraints, it is argued, would alter people's character so that they became radical egalitarians. The more tempered forms of transformative democracy are better termed *populist* democracy.

At the other end of the spectrum is *elite* democracy, Schumpeter's concept as slightly refined by economists and political scientists. Here democracy is conceived of as a method by which members of a self-interested political elite compete for the votes of a basically ignorant and apathetic, as well as determinedly self-interested, electorate. When an optimistic spin is imparted to Schumpeter's concept we have *liberal* democracy, which is just the sunny name for America's actual existing political regime. We shall see that a two-party system tends to be more Schumpeterian than a multiparty system, and since presidential systems tend to be two-party rather than multiparty systems (because a third-party candidate cannot hope to be elected president, and therefore a third party cannot attract the ablest politicians), presidential systems in general tend to be more Schumpeterian than parliamentary systems.

Schumpeter's concept invites attention to the *institutional* side of democracy (including informal institutions, such as political parties, which in a democracy are private rather than public institutions) and hence to the distinction between *direct* democracy (including plebiscitary democracy, a form of direct democracy that includes the initiative, referendum, and recall authorized in some U.S. states) and *representative* democracy. His concept emphasizes the wedge that representative democracy inevitably drives between rulers (the members of the political elite who compete

19. Patrick Neal, "Theory, Postwar Anglo-American," in *Political Philosophy: Theories, Thinkers, Concepts* 195, 200 (Seymour Martin Lipset ed. 2001).

for office, corresponding to sellers in an economic market) and ruled (the voters—the political "consumers" who determine which elite competitors shall prevail). A related concept, I'll argue in Chapter 5, is *pluralist* democracy, which, in the sense in which I shall be using it, emphasizes, over and against majoritarianism, competition among different agencies and branches of government as a means of giving minorities a voice in the political process.

In between transformative and elite democracy, though closer to and sometimes verging on the former, is *deliberative* democracy, which adapts Dewey's notion of epistemic democracy to the political realm. In the most idealistic version of deliberative democracy, voters and officials alike are politically informed and engaged, and also public-spirited. That is, they are both interested and disinterested. They vote (the voters do) and formulate and execute policy (the officials) on the basis of their beliefs about what is good for the society as a whole. And they engage in reasoned debate in an effort that the deliberative democrat thinks can often succeed to harmonize or compromise their differing conceptions of the public interest.

Deliberative democracy comes in both instrumental and intrinsic versions. That is, it can be valued as a means of improving government or as an end in itself—a noble activity that exercises man's highest moral and intellectual capacities. Its instrumentalism can be direct or indirect; it is indirect when deliberation is thought to improve the political character of the citizenry. This kind of indirect instrumentalism is common to other democratic concepts as well, notably the transformative.[20] The Schumpeterian concept of democracy, in contrast, is purely and directly instrumental.

In Bruce Ackerman's *dualist* conception, democracy oscillates between elite and deliberative democracy and the judges use their power of constitutional review to freeze into place the policies adopted in the deliberative phases so that those policies cannot be undone when politics returns to its normal condition of logrolling, interest-group pressures, an apathetic electorate, and the other characteristics of elite democracy.

The mind reels at all these distinctions. But this book endeavors to clarify them and I hope will persuade at least some of my readers that elite democracy is the best pragmatic understanding of what American democracy

---

20. For a helpful discussion, using somewhat different terminology, see Jon Elster, "The Market and the Forum: Three Varieties of Political Theory," in *Deliberative Democracy: Essays on Reason and Politics* 3, 19–26 (James Bohman and William Rehg eds. 1997).

should be and is. At the very least it should persuade them that academic lawyers have been too casual in their analysis of democracy, considering how fundamental an understanding of democracy is to deciding how much scope to give judges to invalidate laws and otherwise check, subvert, or delay measures taken in the name of the people by their elected officials.

Chapter 6 applies the analysis of Concept 1 and Concept 2 democracy to the impeachment of President Clinton, the litigation that arose out of and eventually resolved the deadlocked 2000 Presidential election, and other issues in the legal regulation of the electoral process. I try to solve the puzzle of why judges and most law professors evince little interest in the meaning of democracy, and I propose a Schumpeterian antitrust approach to the legal regulation of American democracy. Chapter 6 largely completes my case for Concept 2 democracy.

Joseph Schumpeter was an Austrian economist. Chapter 7, shifting the focus of the book back from democratic theory to legal theory, explores the relation of pragmatic adjudication to the legal theories of two other Austrians, Hans Kelsen and Friedrich Hayek, lawyer and economist respectively, and to the economic analysis of law, an important application of legal pragmatism. I argue counterintuitively that Kelsen, the legal positivist, the author of a "pure" theory of law, provides a more hospitable venue for pragmatic adjudication, with or without an economic inflection, than the economist Hayek does. Kelsen's positivism, which is also to be distinguished from the positivisms of H. L. A. Hart and my distinguished judicial colleague Frank Easterbrook, is jurisdictional rather than substantive in character. Law has no prescribed content; it is simply what people authorized to do law do until their authority is withdrawn from them by death, retirement, or forced removal from office by impeachment or other means. By thus treating law as the activity of judges within the bounds of their jurisdiction rather than as a body of principles or a methodology for extracting rules and outcomes from texts and principles, Kelsen's theory creates a space for bringing ideology and social science (some cynics consider social science largely ideology) into the practice of judging. Hayek, in contrast, thought formalist judging—an essentially mechanical process of applying antecedently given principles to new disputes, one that leaves little room for utilizing the insights of economics or any other body of thought external to law—indispensable to his concept of good government, even though that concept was pragmatic. Kelsen's concept of law, I argue further, has a deep affinity to Schumpeter's concept of democracy, pointing us toward the unified pragmatic theory of government that I am calling "pragmatic liberalism."

The words "formalism" and "formalist" recur throughout this book and let me pause here to explain them; this will also be a suitable juncture for explaining two other recurrent terms, "positivism" and "natural law." Legal formalism is to Platonism and the orthodox philosophical tradition roughly as legal pragmatism is to philosophical pragmatism. Legal formalism emphasizes logic, legal pragmatism experience. Formalism signifies the denial of the policy-political-ideological component of law; antiformalists equivocate between saying that formalism produces bad cases and saying that it is a fake, a disguise for political decisionmaking. Formalism responds to the legal profession's deeply felt need to represent judicial decisions as the product of an objective process of distinctively legal reasoning, a process that operates independently of the judge's personality and requires little knowledge of the social context of a case; legal pragmatism blurs the distinction between legal reasoning and other practical reasoning. Legal formalism and legal pragmatism are opposites, with the important qualification that a pragmatic judge might in some circumstances decide to adopt a formalist rhetoric for his judicial opinions—might even decide to embrace formalism as a pragmatic strategy rather than just as a pragmatic rhetoric.

Formalism in my description may seem little better than a straw man. It depicts law as a system of rules and judicial decisions as the result of deduction, with the applicable rule supplying the major, and the facts of the particular case the minor, premise of the syllogism. Surely, it will be argued, all responsible legal professionals outgrew that delusion a long time ago. Maybe not.[21] But no matter. Law is still formalistic when outcomes are thought to be determined by principles immanent within the law as well as by rules, even though the intellectual procedures used to connect principles to cases are more complex and less determinate than the syllogism. So Jerome Frank's definition of formalist adjudication remains valid: "the judge begins with some rules or principles of law as his premise, applies this premise to the facts, and thus arrives at his decision."[22]

21. See, for example, Antonin Scalia, "The Rule of Law as a Law of Rules," 56 *University of Chicago Law Review* 1175 (1989); Ernest J. Weinrib, *The Idea of Private Law* 146 (1995) ("formalism treats the law's concepts as pathways into an internal intelligibility").

22. Jerome Frank, *Law and the Modern Mind* 101 (1930), quoted in Lonny Sheinkopf Hoffman, "A Window into the Courts: Legal Process and the 2000 Presidential Election," 95 *Northwestern University Law Review* 1533, 1544 n. 29 (2001). For a superb discussion of for-

Legal formalism in either the rules sense or the principles sense is thus connected with the idea of law's autonomy (its "integrity," as Ronald Dworkin prefers to say), legal pragmatism with a sociological conception of law. This contrast points up an analogy, I hope not too esoteric, to two interpretations of modernist American painting. In abstract paintings of the 1950s and early 1960s by such artists as Louis, Noland, Stella, and Olitski, the notion that a painting is a depiction, even a depiction of abstract shapes, disappears. Painting ceases not only to be representational but also figurative (that is, the distinction between figure and ground is obliterated). Instead it becomes "about" such things as "a conflict between paint and the *support*"[23] or the relation between the painting itself and the framing edge (the borders of the canvas); painting becomes about painting itself. This could be a development, an evolution, purely within art, powered by artists seeking to purify painting of accidental elements, such as the illusion of depth or any other reference to a world outside of painting. That is the type of explanation artists themselves tend to give.[24] Or it could be a response to painting's loss of its traditional functions under the pressure of such external developments as the invention of photography and cinematography and the decline of religious iconography and artistic patronage.[25] In the same way we might try to account for Surrealist art by saying that it was responding to a change in consumer demand from one type of image that photography could not supply, namely the supernatural, to another, namely dream states.

The first class of explanations is Hegelian, the second Darwinian. The first is Whiggish—a field unfolds, develops, in accordance with its internal laws, its program, in much the same way that a human being develops from a fertilized ovum in accordance with its genetic program, though

---

malism, see Thomas C. Grey, "The New Formalism" (Stanford Law School, Sept. 6, 1999, unpublished).

23. Michael Fried, "Jules Olitski," in Fried, *Art and Objecthood: Essays and Reviews* 132, 145 (1998) (emphasis in original). The "support" is the canvas or other material to which the paint is applied plus the wooden frame or other object on which the canvas is mounted.

24. See Michael Fried, "Three American Painters: Kenneth Noland, Jules Olitski, Frank Stella," in id. at 213, 216–218. Cf. Fried, *Absorption and Theatricality: Painting and Beholder in the Age of Diderot* 4–5 (1980).

25. "By about 1905, almost every cinematic strategy since employed had been discovered, and it was just about then that painters and sculptors began asking, if only through their actions, the question of what could be left for *them* to do, now that the torch had, as it were, been taken up by other technologies." Arthur C. Danto, *The Philosophical Disenfranchisement of Art* 99–100 (1986).

outside influences (the condition of the womb, for example) play a role. The second class of explanations sees the field changing, not necessarily "developing," prospering, or even surviving, in response to external shocks.

For formalists, law is an autonomous discipline, isolated, to a degree at any rate, from its social environment, unfolding petal by petal in accordance with developing notions of justice, exfoliating principles implicit in the very idea of law; and legal theorists are the competent experts to explain the nature and direction of the change. For pragmatists, in contrast, law is a field of social conflict. Its "laws" of change are sociological or economic rather than jurisprudential. These "laws" might dictate a formalist phase for law, if the highest priority of a nation's legal system was the creation of clear and uniform rules—as was indeed the case, I have argued in defense of Savigny's formalist approach to the law of possession, of German law in the early nineteenth century.[26] But it would just be a phase, and as society's priorities changed, law might move into a pragmatic phase. It might even cease to resemble law as we have known it,[27] just as modernist painting seemed (except to cognoscenti) no longer to resemble painting as we had known it.

Legal formalism is often found conjoined with the idea of natural law. This is the idea that law has an ultimate source or criterion, such as God or the moral law, that is distinct from an official promulgator, such as a legislature or a court. In its most aggressive version, natural-law theory claims not only that positive laws that are inconsistent with natural law are invalid but also that natural law should be legally enforceable even if it is not embodied in positive law. Especially but not only when conceived of in religious terms, natural law is generally imagined as universal rather than as tied to a particular society at a particular time; a typical natural-law tenet is the injustice of slavery regardless of its status under positive law. Positive law, being the product of official promulgation and therefore of specific national and local governments (the "positive" in positive law means posited, that is, promulgated), is, with the exception of some international-law principles, national or subnational in scope.

Legal positivism at its most elementary is the idea that positive law is

26. Posner, *Frontiers of Legal Theory*, note 1 above, at 219–220.
27. A development that Holmes foresaw in his article "The Path of the Law," 10 *Harvard Law Review* 457 (1897), and that I label the "supersession thesis" and discuss sympathetically in *The Problematics of Moral and Legal Theory*, note 1 above, at 206–211.

valid irrespective of its correspondence to natural law. The legal positivist either disbelieves in natural law altogether or denies that it trumps positive law. The conditions for the validity of positive law do not include conformity to natural law, although natural-law notions might influence the content of the law by influencing the thinking of legislators and judges.

We shall see in Chapter 7 that Hayek's version of legal formalism is tied to natural law, but we shall also see, examining Frank Easterbrook's theory of law, that it is possible for a strict positivist to be a formalist as well. We shall also see that the pragmatist is not innately hostile to either legal positivism or natural law, although he rejects an essentialist concept of natural law because he rejects essentialism. This is an example of the overlap between everyday and philosophical pragmatism.

Chapter 8 examines judicial pragmatism in the context of specific cases and issues in which pragmatic concerns seem salient. *Clinton v. Jones*, the Supreme Court decision that by denying President Clinton the temporary immunity that he sought from having to defend against Paula Jones's sexual harassment suit set the stage for Clinton's eventual impeachment, is one of these cases. But the particular emphasis of the chapter is on what is likely to prove the next crux in debates over the proper role of pragmatism in law—the legal response to the terrorist threat to the United States—against the background of the legal responses, invariably pragmatic and strongly criticized by civil libertarians, to earlier national emergencies.

Chapter 9 continues the examination of judicial pragmatism, focusing on the 2000 Presidential election deadlock and ensuing litigation from a pragmatic rather than (as in Chapter 6) a democratic angle. It amplifies the argument that I have made elsewhere[28] for a pragmatic defense of the Supreme Court's controversial decision in *Bush v. Gore*. I argue that the danger that there would be a Presidential succession crisis if the Court failed to intervene was one of the pragmatic considerations that should have weighed (and perhaps did weigh) with the Supreme Court, but not the only one. I find myself increasingly critical of the Court's performance. The result was defensible—and that matters a great deal to a pragmatist! It was not the outrage to democracy and the rule of law that the critics of the decision have claimed it was, unless the Justices' motives were as malign as some of their critics have charged. But the Justices' choice of the ground of decision, and other strategic choices that various Justices

28. *Breaking the Deadlock: The 2000 Election, the Constitution, and the Courts*, note 1 above.

made in the course of the litigation, turned *Bush v. Gore* into a pragmatic donnybrook.

Because constitutional decisions often have great practical consequences, pragmatism has much to contribute to the formulation of sensible principles of constitutional law, as I have argued elsewhere with particular reference to free speech.[29] Chapter 10 of the present book replies to Professor Rubenfeld's attack on the pragmatic interpretation of the free-speech clause of the First Amendment.[30] I defend the pragmatic interpretation as superior to his own "purposivist" approach. I criticize the idea that First Amendment freedoms are "absolute" and explore the relation between pragmatic adjudication and the use by judges of cost-benefit analysis in "noneconomic" cases. There are echoes of Chapter 7, which also examines, though very briefly, the relation between pragmatism and economics, and also of the chapters on democratic theory, since the constitutional right of free speech at once supports and undermines political democracy, though the first effect predominates. There are echoes of Chapter 8 as well, where I point out the dangers of dogmatic adherence to current free-speech doctrine in the face of grave threats to public safety.

Throughout the book, despite the reliance I place on Continental theorists, the focus is very much on American institutions. This is a book about American democracy and the American legal system, and I leave to others to explore the possible applications of the analysis to other countries. Political and judicial systems, pragmatists insist, are relative to national cultures.

In arguing for Kelsen's positivism, Schumpeter's concept of democracy, and everyday pragmatism in adjudication and political governance, and against philosophical pragmatism and Hayek's liberalism as well as against pragmatism's usual opponents, left and right, I may have painted myself into a tiny, friendless corner. But some readers may be persuaded that the position the book describes and defends is both a fair approximation to our actual existing law and democracy and a reasonably attractive and, unlike most normative political theories, feasible guide for improvement. Others will at least carry away a clear sense of my position. And maybe a few academic readers persuaded that my approach has merit will set aside grand theorizing for a time and embrace and extend the everyday-pragmatic approach to government and the law.

29. See, for example, *Frontiers of Legal Theory*, note 1 above, ch. 2.
30. Jed Rubenfeld, "The First Amendment's Purpose," 53 *Stanford Law Review* 767 (2001).

CHAPTER ONE

Pragmatism: Philosophical versus Everyday

❦

A pragmatist turns his back resolutely and once for all upon a lot of inveterate habits dear to professional philosophers. He turns away from abstraction and insufficiency, from verbal solutions, from bad *a priori* reasons, from fixed principles, closed systems, and pretended absolutes and origins. He turns towards concreteness and adequacy, towards facts, towards action, and towards power. That means the empiricist temper regnant, and the rationalist temper sincerely given up. It means the open air and possibilities of nature, as against dogma, artificiality and the pretence of finality in truth.[1]

Pragmatism, notwithstanding William James's effort at definition, is a devil to define. That's because it's not one thing, one body of ideas, but at least three and maybe, as we shall see, five. The simplest place to begin, although I don't think it leads anywhere interesting, is with the "classical American pragmatists"—Charles Sanders Peirce, William James, and John Dewey. Along with Josiah Royce they were the first philosophers to call themselves pragmatists (although Peirce repudiated the term, popularized by James, because he disagreed with James's use of it).[2] And none of their successors seems "classical." Either they lack the stature of Peirce, James, and Dewey, or, as in the case of such renowned modern philosophers as

1. William James, *Pragmatism: A New Name for Some Old Ways of Thinking* 31 (1975 [1907]).

2. Other names could be added, such as F. E. Abbott, Chauncey Wright, Oliver Wendell Holmes, Jr., Horace Kallen, C. I. Lewis, and George Herbert Mead. On the early history of American pragmatism, see Louis Menand, *The Metaphysical Club: A Story of Ideas in America* (2001); H. S. Thayer, *Meaning and Action: A Critical History of Pragmatism*, pt. 2 (2d ed. 1981); Bruce Kuklick, *The Rise of American Philosophy: Cambridge, Massachusetts 1860–1930*, pts. 1–3 (1977); Kuklick, *A History of Philosophy in America, 1720–2000*, pt. 2 (2001); Herbert W. Schneider, *A History of American Philosophy*, pt. 8 (1946).

Quine, Sellars, Davidson, Putnam, and Rorty, one is not quite sure that "pragmatist" is the correct, or an informative, label—even for Rorty. He describes himself as a pragmatist, wrapping himself particularly in the mantle of Dewey. Yet he has been criticized as not really being in the pragmatic mainstream—as not even getting Dewey right.[3]

As it happens, Peirce, James, and Dewey each held very different views. Peirce in particular may well have had more in common with other philosophers not usually classified as pragmatists, such as Frege and Russell (the latter notoriously hostile to pragmatism, and especially to Dewey), than with Dewey or, especially, James. James's interest in psychology links him to Nietzsche. James's famous dictum that "the true" "is only the expedient in the way of our thinking"[4] is *echt* Nietzsche; and in the Introduction I cited the essay on authorship of Michel Foucault, a distinguished Nietzschean, as an exemplary work of pragmatic analysis. Dewey's conception of intelligence as coping rather than speculative reasoning links him to Heidegger and Wittgenstein as well as to the earlier "common sense" philosophers, such as Thomas Reid and later G. E. Moore. The pre-Socratics are proto-pragmatists, as we'll see shortly; likewise Hume, Bentham (I am thinking in particular of his criticisms of Blackstone and his views of language), and certainly Mill—not to mention Hegel. Habermas's notion of truth is derivative from Peirce's and makes him another honorary pragmatist (honorary if pragmatism is regarded as a distinctively American philosophy), though only if Peirce's notion that truth is simply the outcome of rational inquiry continued indefinitely is accepted; I said in the Introduction that it is one of the pragmatic propositions that I do not accept.

By means of linkages of this sort, which exploit a family resemblance of astonishing scope, a vast amount of philosophy becomes pragmatic. Utilitarianism does,[5] for example, and other consequentialist moral theories as well (though I shall emphasize in subsequent chapters the difference between pragmatism and consequentialism); even Kantian epistemology

3. See, for example, Robert B. Westbrook, "Pragmatism and Democracy: Reconstructing the Logic of John Dewey's Faith," in *The Revival of Pragmatism: New Essays on Social Thought, Law, and Culture* 128–129 (Morris Dickstein ed. 1998).

4. James, note 1 above, at 106.

5. "The virtue of utilitarianism [from John Dewey's pragmatic standpoint] was to place at the center of ethical theory a regard for consequences and a willingness to think about how to promote desirable consequences and escape undesired consequences." Alan Ryan, *John Dewey and the High Tide of American Liberalism* 90 (1995).

does. For Kant claimed that our knowledge of the external world is conditioned by mental concepts, such as causation, time, and space, that we cannot get around; so we cannot hope to obtain unmediated knowledge of the world.[6]

The basic problem is that pragmatism is more a tradition, attitude, and outlook than a body of doctrine; it has affinities rather than extension. So instead of starting with the classical American pragmatists and sweeping outward in concentric circles until much of the Western philosophical tradition has been brought under the sway of pragmatism, we may do better by recognizing that, as suggested in the quotation from James that forms the epigraph for this chapter, there is a pragmatic *mood*, that it is ancient, and that from its ancient roots it branched into a philosophy of pragmatism (which has itself ramified in recent years) and into an everyday practice of pragmatism.

The Pragmatic Mood and the
Rise of Philosophical Pragmatism

The pragmatic mood is already visible in the *Odyssey*.[7] The poem opens with Odysseus living on a remote island ruled by a nymph who offers him immortality if he will remain as her consort. A bit surprisingly to anyone steeped in the orthodox Western religio-philosophical-scientific tradition, he refuses, preferring mortality and a dangerous struggle to regain his position as the king of a small, rocky island and be reunited with his son, aging wife, and old father. He turns down what the orthodox tradition says we should desire above all else, the peace that comes from overcoming the transience and vicissitudes of mortality, whether that peace takes the form of personal immortality or of communing with eternal verities, moral or scientific—in either case ushering us to the still point of the turning world. Odysseus prefers going to arriving, struggle to rest, exploring to achiev-

6. "Kant was the first really to see that describing the world is not simply copying it." Hilary Putnam, *Pragmatism: An Open Question* 28 (1995). Charles Sanders Peirce greatly admired Kant—whom he called "a somewhat confused pragmatist." Quoted in Eric MacGilvray, *The Task before Us: Pragmatism and Political Liberalism*, ch. 5, p. 6 n. 7 (Social Science Collegiate Division, University of Chicago, Nov. 18, 2001, unpublished).

7. After writing this sentence, I discovered the distinguished philosopher Robert Brandom remarking that pragmatism's concept of reason "is the reason of Odysseus rather than of Plato." Robert B. Brandom, "When Philosophy Paints Its Blue on Gray: Irony and the Pragmatist Enlightenment," *Boundary 2* Summer 2002, pp. 1, 7.

ing—curiosity is one of his most marked traits—and risk to certainty.[8] The *Odyssey* situates Calypso's enchanted isle in the far west, the land of the setting sun, and describes the isle in images redolent of death. In contrast, Odysseus's arrival at his own island, far to the east, a land of the rising sun, is depicted in imagery suggestive of rebirth.

Another thing that is odd about the protagonist, and the implicit values, of the *Odyssey* from the orthodox standpoint is that Odysseus is not a *conventional* hero, the kind depicted in the *Iliad*. He is strong, brave, and skillful in fighting, but he is no Achilles (who had a divine mother) or even Ajax; and he relies on guile, trickery, and outright deception to a degree inconsistent with what we have come to think of as heroism or with its depiction in the *Iliad*. His dominant trait is skill in coping with his environment rather than ability to impose himself upon it by brute force. He is the most intelligent person in the *Odyssey* but his intelligence is thoroughly practical, adaptive. Unlike Achilles in the *Iliad*, who is given to reflection, notably about the heroic ethic itself, Odysseus is pragmatic. He is an instrumental reasoner rather than a speculative one.

He is also, it is true, distinctly pious, a trait that the *Odyssey* harps on and modern readers tend to overlook. But piety in Homeric religion is a coping mechanism. Homeric religion is proto-scientific; it is an attempt to understand and control the natural world. The gods personify nature and men manipulate it by "using" the gods in the proper way. One sacrifices to them in order to purchase their intervention in one's affairs—this is religion as magic, the ancestor of modern technology—and also to obtain clues to what is going to happen next; this is the predictive use of religion and corresponds to modern science. The gods' own rivalries, mirroring (in Homeric thought, personifying or causing) the violent clash of the forces of nature, prevent human beings from perfecting their control over the environment. By the same token, these rivalries underscore the dynamic and competitive character of human existence and the unrealism of supposing that peace and permanence, a safe and static life, are man's lot.

Odysseus's piety has nothing to do with loving God as creator or redeemer, or as the name, site, metaphysical underwriter, or repository of the eternal or the unchanging, or of absolutes (such as omniscience and omnipotence) and universals (numbers, words, concepts). Odysseus's piety

8. These character traits molt via Dante's censorious depiction of Ulysses in the *Inferno* into the extreme restlessness of Tennyson's Ulysses: "I cannot rest from travel: I will drink/ Life to the lees."

is pragmatic because his religion is naturalistic—is simply the most efficacious means known to his society for controlling the environment, just as science and technology are the most efficacious means by which modern people control their environment.

I called Odysseus an instrumental reasoner; and this invites the objection that instrumental (means-end) reasoning is not enough; means are relative to ends, and to choose an end must require a different kind of reasoning. But the choice of an end need not, perhaps cannot, be a product of reasoning. Odysseus's ends—home, family, vengeance on one's enemies—are ones that are natural to human beings. Culture too can produce ends, including ones that may be more edifying than those intrinsic to our animal nature. But Richard Rorty is correct that "moral progress is a matter of wider and wider sympathy. It is not a matter of rising above the sentimental to the rational. Nor is it a matter of appealing from lower, possibly corrupt, local courts to a higher court which administers an ahistorical, incorruptible, transcultural moral law."[9] For aid in developing these capacities Rorty looks to literature, to him a compendium of images and narratives designed to widen our sympathies by moving us.[10] Experiencing literature is often a reflective activity, but it is not a form of deliberation. Similarly, Achilles was reflective rather than deliberative.

The pragmatic mood began to assume a philosophical form with the pre-Socratic philosophers and a demotic one in the practice of Athenian democracy. The sophists—instructors in the rhetorical techniques employed in the legal and political tussles in the Athenian courts and Assembly—bridged the two forms. Heraclitus emphasized the character of experience as flux rather than fixity[11] and of concepts as attempts to impose order on the flux rather than to discern fixity within it. Protagoras said that man is the measure of all things, by which he meant that reality is what human beings make of the external world for their own purposes.[12] This pragmatic dictum sorted nicely with democratic practice, which was hu-

9. Richard Rorty, *Philosophy and Social Hope* 82–83 (1999).

10. Richard Rorty, *Contingency, Irony, and Solidarity* xvi (1989).

11. G. S. Kirk, J. E. Raven, and M. Schofield, *The Presocratic Philosophers* 194–195 (2d ed. 1983).

12. Id. at 411. Consistent with this view, Protagoras wrote that he was unable to determine whether the gods existed. Richard Winton, "Herodotus, Thucydides, and the Sophists," in *The Cambridge History of Greek and Roman Political Thought* 89, 95 (Christopher Rowe and Malcolm Schofield eds. 2000). Heraclitus's dictum that the way up is the way down, Kirk, Raven, and Schofield, note 11 above, at 188–189, is another example of a relativist or perspectivist approach to reality.

man-centered in the same sense. Citizens debated politics from the stand-point of their opinions and interests rather than from that of abstract prin-ciples of the public good or credible claims to possess ultimate truth.[13] The sophists, whose role like that of modern lawyers was to persuade citizens to take one side or the other of political and legal disputes, were not inter-ested in discovering truth; they were interested in crafting persuasive ap-peals to the imperfect understanding, the opinions and even the preju-dices, of particular audiences. To the extent that they tried to justify and not merely to practice their art, they were philosophers too—Protagoras being a notable example—though Plato was successful in obscuring this fact and pretending that philosophy had begun with Socrates.

With the defeat of Athens in the Peloponnesian War, a disaster that Thucydides blamed on the excesses of Athenian democracy,[14] and the en-suing period of political instability quickly followed by the condemnation of Socrates by the restored democracy, the time was ripe for a reaction to the pragmatic mood in philosophy and politics. The time was ripe, that is, for a Plato to inaugurate the orthodox tradition of Western thought. Plato turned Homer, the pre-Socratic philosophers, and the sophists upside down by celebrating stasis over flux, the permanent over the contingent, peace over struggle, knowing over doing, logic over coping, abstract divin-ity over naturalistic gods, universals over particulars, abstract reason over practical intelligence (and thus philosophy over rhetoric), truth over opin-ion, reality over appearance, principle over expedience, unity over diver-sity, objectivity over subjectivity, philosophy over poetry, and rule by phi-losophers over popular rule.

Plato set the agenda for philosophy for the next 2,000 years and more—indeed to the present day—by assigning to philosophy the task of discov-ering by speculative reasoning the truths that would provide secure foun-

13. Josiah Ober, "How to Criticize Democracy in Late Fifth- and Fourth-Century Ath-ens," in Ober, *The Athenian Revolution: Essays on Ancient Greek Democracy and Political Theory* 10–11, 141 (1996), notes the pragmatic character of Athenian democracy. And Protagoras was famously quoted by Plato as defending democracy on the ground that while most citizens lacked expert knowledge about the specific undertakings of government, such as the con-struction of warships, they could be expected to take the advice of experts about such matters, and that the most important character trait from the standpoint of political governance, namely a sense of political justice, was, unlike expertise, distributed among the population rather than being concentrated in a handful of specially trained persons. Winton, note 12 above, at 96–100. See also Peter Levine, *Living without Philosophy: On Narrative, Rhetoric, and Morality* 96 (1998).

14. See Simon Hornblower, *Thucydides* 160–176 (1987).

dations for scientific knowledge and moral, political, and aesthetic beliefs. His grip did not begin to loosen in a serious way until the late eighteenth and early nineteenth centuries, with Hume and Hegel (and to a degree, as I have suggested, with Kant) and in the United States with Emerson.

The simplest definition of pragmatism is that it is the rejection of Platonism root and branch.[15] But the accuracy of the definition depends on the precise meaning assigned to "Platonism." Pragmatists don't reject Plato's insight that mathematical concepts are "real" in a meaningful sense that does not depend on their being embodied. They are plausibly regarded as actually existing metaphysical entities. A point, or a line, in Euclidean geometry is real even if there are no one- or two-dimensional physical objects in the universe; and likewise the word "chair," which names an indefinite number of physical objects but is not itself physical. (So Heraclitus was mistaken to claim that you can't step into the same river twice.)[16] But these are "metaphysical" entities in the modest sense of things that while useful and discussable have no location in space and time, things in other words that are real (or real enough) though nonphysical, as distinct from those nonsensory and often supernatural entities that are believed to generate or undergird the physical and moral worlds. Those entities, being inaccessible to empirical inquiry, arouse the pragmatist's skepticism. Gods are that kind of metaphysical entity, likewise Kant's noumena and scientific realists' notion of the universe as it really is, as distinct from our descriptions of it. And likewise Plato's Forms—he believed that every number, every word, was the projection of a Form that existed in a supernatural Heaven of Forms. Pragmatists don't buy that but, more important, they reject Plato's confidence in a method of inquiry based on appeal to a rational faculty capable with the proper training and guidance of grasping deep truths about ethics, politics, and science, and his disdain for empiricism as an alternative, let alone, as pragmatists tend to believe, a superior method of inquiry.

15. Of Platonism, not of Plato—who was not himself a Platonist, at least in the sense in which the word is usually used. The point was made by arch anti-Platonist John Dewey: "I am unable to find in [Plato] that all-comprehensive and overriding system which later interpretation has, it seems to me, conferred upon him as a dubious boon . . . [His] highest flight of metaphysics always terminated with a social and practical turn." Dewey, "From Absolutism to Experimentalism," in *John Dewey: The Later Works, 1925–1953*, vol. 5: *1929–1930*, at 147, 154–155 (Jo Ann Boydston ed. 1984). Plato was a thoroughly engaged intellectual, not an academic or an author of scholarly treatises.

16. If that's what he actually said and meant, which is unclear. See Kirk, Raven, and Schofield, note 11 above, at 194–197.

The rise of commercial society may have been responsible for the loosening of Platonism's hold on the philosophical mind. People engaged in trade have little interest in ultimate truths. The idea of society's being ruled by philosophers strikes them as daft. Not only do philosophical, theological, and even scientific theories have little direct relevance to commercial life; they impede it, by drawing resources and attention away from the market and by stirring conflict and animosity. The last thing a merchant wants is a debate with a customer over fundamental issues, the kind of debate that upsets people by challenging their way of life. (That argument, debate, and discussion can be divisive as well as harmonizing is a point to which I return again and again in this book. It is one of the keys to the pragmatic theory of democracy and adjudication.) Markets are a means of enabling potentially antipathetic strangers to transact peaceably with one other; and a superficial relationship, in which all deep issues are bracketed, is the most productive basis on which to deal with strangers. The most efficient markets are those in which the transacting parties don't even know each other's identity, as in trading on a stock exchange. Philosophers do not do much trading, but they are part of society and absorb its attitudes. Pragmatic philosophy started out as everyday pragmatism academized.

After the rise of commerce, the next great blow to the orthodox philosophical tradition was struck by Darwin. If, as his theory implied, man had evolved from some ape-like creature by a process of natural selection oriented toward improved adaptation to the challenging environment of earliest man, human intelligence was presumably adapted to coping with the environment rather than to achieving metaphysical insights that could have had no adaptive value in the ancestral environment. When man achieved a measure of leisure, his large brain, no longer fully engaged in quotidian tasks, could be turned to metaphysical pursuits. But there was no warrant of success in such endeavors,[17] as there might be if human intelligence were the gift of a benevolent deity—in which event human beings,

17. "Pragmatists are committed to taking Darwin seriously. They grant that human beings are unique in the animal kingdom in having language, but they urge that language be understood as a tool rather than as a picture. A species' gradual development of language is as readily explicable in Darwinian terms as its gradual development of spears or pots, but it is harder to explain how a species could have acquired the ability to *represent* the universe—especially the universe as it really is (as opposed to how it is usefully described, relative to the particular needs of that species)." Richard Rorty, "Pragmatism," in *Routledge Encyclopedia of Philosophy*, vol. 7, pp. 633, 636 (Edward Craig ed. 1998) (emphasis in original).

since they would be, in Holmes's sarcastic phrase, "in on the ground floor with God,"[18] "the friend God needed in order to find out that he exists,"[19] might aspire to a quasi-angelic understanding.[20]

This is not to denigrate the role that speculative intelligence, imagination, and abstract thought have played in human progress, including scientific and technological progress. Another implication of Darwinism, however, places the theory side of intellectual activity in perspective: our most cogent intellectual procedures are likely to be experimental rather than aprioristic ones. Evolution is an experimental process, a process of trial and error. Mutations create heritable variations, and natural selection in effect picks the most adaptive. Pure trial and error operates too slowly to be a feasible research strategy, and this is where theorizing comes in. The theories pick out the most promising paths for experimental inquiry. But this means that theorizing is the beginning of inquiry, not its end. And given the finitude of human intelligence, it may make more sense, rather than to commit oneself at the outset to a single line of inquiry, to try different theoretical approaches and by a process of directed rather than random selection pick the best—which is to say the best adapted to human needs—by observing the results.

In Chapter 3 we shall see how John Dewey elaborated the experimentalist conception of inquiry; but Mill already had the idea.[21] *On Liberty* bases the case for freedom of expression on the fallibilist argument later emphasized by Charles Sanders Peirce that the validity of a hypothesis cannot be determined without making the hypothesis run the gauntlet of hostile challenge, and on the further argument that intellectual and social progress is impossible without experimentation, including, in the realm of conduct, "experiments in living,"[22] which presuppose diversity of taste and outlook.

18. Letter of Oliver Wendell Holmes to Harold Laski, Feb. 26, 1918, in *The Essential Holmes: Selections from the Letters, Speeches, Judicial Opinions, and Other Writings of Oliver Wendell Holmes, Jr.* 112 (Richard A. Posner ed. 1992).

19. Letter of Oliver Wendell Holmes to Alice Stopford Green, Nov. 9, 1913, in id. at 22, 23. "Not that I shouldn't like to have an angel about a span long light on the top of my inkstand here and say, 'God directs me to tell you that it's you and He, that He made the rest but you made yourself and He desires your friendship.'" Letter of Oliver Wendell Holmes to Harold Laski, in id. at 112.

20. "What piece of work is a man, how noble in reason, how infinite in faculties, in form and moving how express and admirable, in action how like an angel, in apprehension how like a god." *Hamlet*, act II, sc. 2, ll. 303–306.

21. Pragmatism's debt to Mill is acknowledged by William James's dedication of his book *Pragmatism*, note 1 above, to him.

22. John Stuart Mill, *On Liberty* 54 (David Spitz ed. 1975 [1859]).

Here is a homely illustration. Ask yourself: if you were a man wanting to marry, would it make more sense to formulate a concept of the ideal wife and then seek the closest approximation to it in the real world, or, without preconceptions, to try to meet a number of eligible (in terms of age and background) unmarried women and through this exploratory process learn what kind of woman you would be most likely to be happy being married to? My guess is that the latter, the pragmatic, search process would be the more sensible one today, as undoubtedly it was 30,000 years ago. This is true in many other problem-solving situations, including legal and political ones, as well. We may call this the priority of the empirical. Suppose you're a strong believer on theoretical grounds in free markets, but you also consider National Public Radio far superior to any commercial radio network. If your fandom causes you to qualify your free-market ideology, you are prioritizing experience, the empirical. But if your ideology causes you to decide that you must have a screw loose in preferring NPR to commercial radio, then you are prioritizing theory.

Giving the evolutionary narrative a social twist, Nietzsche depicted intelligence as an invention of the weak to achieve dominance over the strong. Intelligence on this construal is a manipulative rather than contemplative faculty. It has everything to do with power and nothing to do with the quest for certainty. Truth, in Nietzsche's account, is far down the list of the things that are important to man and society.[23] Thus he argued for a pragmatic conception of the writing of history against the conventional belief that a historian's duty is to tell the truth, come what may.[24]

Nietzsche was the greatest of the proto-pragmatists. Yet he acknowledged Emerson's influence on his thinking; and before Nietzsche's ideas were widely disseminated in the United States, pragmatism had emerged as America's first and perhaps only original contribution to philosophical thought. This was a natural development. The United States was at once the most democratic nation in the world, the one most imbued with commercial values, and the most diverse religiously and ethnically, and hence morally.[25] Diversity and commercial orientation pushed for a bracketing of

23. See Brian Leiter, *Nietzsche on Morality*, 42–43, 266–268 (2002). As Holmes, the American Nietzsche, put it, "A new untruth is better than an old truth." Letter of Oliver Wendell Holmes to Harold Laski, June 24, 1926, in Holmes, note 18 above, at 116.

24. See Friedrich Nietzsche, "On the Uses and Disadvantages of History for Life," in Nietzsche, *Untimely Meditations* 57 (R. J. Hollingdale trans. 1983); Richard A. Posner, *Frontiers of Legal Theory*, ch. 4 (2001).

25. Some other nations, notably Russia and Austria-Hungary, had immensely heterogeneous populations, but the minority groups were firmly subordinated, as only blacks were in America.

fundamental issues, while democracy imparted a pragmatic cast to politics, as it had in ancient Athens, because the average citizen has little interest in issues of principle. The pragmatic mood, clearly observed (though not named) by Tocqueville in the 1830s,[26] fostered a self-consciously pragmatic philosophy, and that philosophy spilled over into law in the influential jurisprudence of Holmes, John Chipman Gray, Benjamin Cardozo, and the legal realists of the 1920s and 1930s, as into other fields.[27]

America's religious and ethnic, and hence moral, diversity has additional significance for the rise of pragmatism. Confidence in the foundations of knowledge is hard to sustain in the face of widespread disagreement. We believe most of the things we do simply because no one has ever given us a reason to doubt them. We believe them by habit. An example is our date of birth, which we know only as the final link in a long chain of unverified hearsay. In a religiously uniform culture, it is natural for people to take for granted the truth of the prevailing religion and its associated metaphysical propositions. The more diverse and individualistic a culture is, the more permeable it is to outside influences; and the freer and more mobile the population, the fewer are the certitudes. In America people are constantly rubbing shoulders, figuratively speaking, with fellow Americans known to have emphatically different views on the big issues, such as evolution, sexual morality, the nature of God, the importance of money, the value of fetal life, the morality of euthanasia, the rights of animals, the scope of equality, the proper aims and methods of international relations, the structure of the family, and the significance of race. Pragmatism, with its lesson of tentativeness (the milder versions of skepticism and relativism, which I mentioned in the Introduction), flourishes in a climate of heterogeneous values.

A number of currents of twentieth-century philosophy swelled the pragmatic stream. The most important was logical positivism (logical empiricism, the Vienna Circle, the early Wittgenstein). The logical positivists

26. See, for example, Alexis de Tocqueville, *Democracy in America* 403–404, 434–437 (Harvey C. Mansfield and Delba Winthrop trans. 2000). "Tocqueville sketched, half a century before it emerged, the striking features of pragmatism." James H. Nichols, Jr., "Pragmatism," in *Political Philosophy: Theories, Thinkers, Concepts* 145, 146 (Seymour Martin Lipset ed. 2001).

27. See, for example, Cecil V. Crabb, Jr., *American Diplomacy and the Pragmatic Tradition*, ch. 1 (1989). The pragmatic vein in American literature is explored in two books by Richard Poirier: *The Renewal of Literature: Emersonian Reflections* (1987) and *Poetry and Pragmatism* (1992). I wish to leave open, however, the extent to which Holmes's jurisprudence was effect rather than cause of his embrace of philosophical pragmatism. See Chapter 2.

were, it is true, in quest of the conditions of knowledge, which was not a pragmatic quest and which led them to adopt verifiability as the criterion of "real" knowledge. What could not be verified was not knowledge. Logical relations were matters of definition and so mere tautologies—you got out what you had put in, nothing more—while moral and aesthetic propositions were merely emotive. Modern pragmatic philosophy, the revival of pragmatism by Quine, Putnam, and others, undertook to knock logical positivism off its perch,[28] and largely succeeded. But it was a family quarrel.[29] The logical positivists had argued in effect that only the experimental methods of scientists yielded knowledge worth the name. Logical positivists had rejected the aprioristic methods used to establish metaphysical propositions and thus banished to the outer darkness theology, moral philosophy, transcendental speculations, and political theory—in other words, much of the orthodox philosophical tradition. By doing these things they had set the stage for a renewal of pragmatism.

Orthodox versus Recusant Pragmatism

With its precision and rigor, logical positivism made the classical American pragmatists, especially James and Dewey, seem woolly and verbose. It put pragmatism under a cloud at the same time that it was unwittingly preparing the ground for its revival. That revival, which can be dated from works of Wittgenstein and Quine published in the early 1950s, quickly reached a fork in the road. One branch led to what I shall call "orthodox" or "academized" pragmatism, the other to what I shall call "recusant"[30] pragmatism. Both challenge the obsession of the philosophical tradition with establishing the conditions that make it possible (or impossible—for philosophical skepticism is part of the tradition) to affirm the certainty of "obvious" propositions, scientific, moral, and political. Illustrative propositions are that there is an external world, that the universe did not spring into existence last week, that other people have minds, that science can provide correct descriptions of reality, that $2 + 2 = 4$, that cats do not grow on trees, that no human being has ever eaten an adult hippopotamus

28. Rorty, note 17 above, at 637.

29. On the complementaries between pragmatism and logical positivism, see Daniel J. Wilson, "Fertile Ground: Pragmatism, Science, and Logical Positivism," in *Pragmatism: From Progressivism to Postmodernism* 122 (Robert Hollinger and David Depew eds. 1995).

30. The latter a term originally applied to English Roman Catholics who refused to attend Church of England services though required by statute to do so.

at one sitting, that the Nuremberg Tribunal was legal, and that torturing children is wrong.

Orthodox pragmatism disagrees with the way in which the central tradition handles these questions. It claims that many of the traditional problems of philosophy can be dissolved by being shown to be pseudo-problems, or even ignored completely, such as the problem of skepticism, which is fundamental to epistemology.[31] Thus Wittgenstein pointed out that the knowledge that one has a body is firmer than any method of proving it could be, since a proof can be doubted but no sane person doubts that he has a body.[32] To seek warrants for believing (the project of epistemology) what we cannot doubt, to seek foundations for beliefs more confidently held than the foundations could be, is pointless. Similarly, although the fact that no human being has ever eaten an adult hippopotamus at a sitting cannot be verified, it is more certain than most phenomena of which we have direct sensory perception. This further suggests the pointlessness of prescribing conditions, such as verifiability, for certifying empirical knowledge as true, or of prescribing a hierarchy of criteria of validity.

Philosophers used to think that "testimony" (that is, what other people tell us) was at the bottom of that hierarchy; above were perception, memory, and inference, in descending order of reliability. Yet for reasons that Wittgenstein demonstrated, the ladder is rotten.[33] Because of limitations of time and intellect, we perforce base most of our beliefs on testimony, such as the testimony of scientists concerning cosmological and microscopic phenomena. Many of these beliefs are more reliable than those based on perception, memory, or inference. This is true even though we judge the reliability of testimony largely on the basis of *other* testimony (I believe that my birth certificate has the date of my birth right in part because of what I have heard about governmental recording of vital statistics and in part because of what my parents told me)—that is, even though much of our knowledge is based on hearsay, much of it double or triple or even more remote hearsay. "That babies are born of women in a certain way is known to all of us and it is a fact of observation but very many of us

31. "Nobody would want 'human knowledge' (as opposed to some particular theory or report) justified unless he had been frightened by skepticism." Richard Rorty, *Philosophy and the Mirror of Nature* 229 (1979).

32. See, for example, Ludwig Wittgenstein, *On Certainty* ¶¶ 32, 111, 125 (1969).

33. Id., ¶¶ 144, 240, 282, 288, 604.

have not observed even one birth for ourselves."[34] We are often fooled by testimony; but we often misperceive, misremember, and use faulty inferential procedures or err in their application as well. Perception itself, Sellars, argued, is theory-laden rather than foundational: in Brandom's useful summary, "instead of coming to have a concept of something because we have noticed that sort of thing, to have the ability to notice requires already having the concept, and cannot account for it."[35]

Popper, Goodman, and others, following Hume, challenged induction, and with it verifiability. They argued that hypotheses can be falsified but never confirmed; however many confirming instances have been observed, the next one may be disconfirming. Even falsification is not an infallible criterion of invalidity, however; it is always possible, and in fact is common in scientific practice, to reject evidence that contradicts a hypothesis on the ground that the observations or experiments that yielded the evidence were unreliable, rather than to reject the hypothesis and possibly have to abandon a heretofore successful theory. Kuhn produced the ultimate pragmatic theory of science, in which scientific theories are adopted not because they are true, or better approximations to truth, but because they are better adapted to current needs and interests.

Quine knocked logic off its pedestal. Suppose that a swan is defined as a bird that has various characteristics including being white. Then one day someone sees a bird that has all the same characteristics except the color. We can either change the definition of "swan" to include this new bird, or we can stick with the old definition and call it something else. Neither response to the new observation is superior to the other. This means that logical ("necessary") truths are not immune from empirical refutation, as genuine tautologies would be. Also, and more important, it means that the decision whether to respond to a new experience by altering a logical or an empirical belief is an expedient one, in the same way that disconfirming evidence can be accommodated either by changing one's theory or by rejecting the evidence. "For Quine, a necessary truth is just a statement such that nobody has given us any interesting alternative which would lead us to question it."[36]

34. C. A. J. Coady, *Testimony: A Philosophical Study* 81 (1992).

35. Robert Brandom, "Study Guide," in Wilfrid Sellars, *Empiricism and the Philosophy of Mind* 119, 167 (1997).

36. Rorty, note 31 above, at 175. The example of the swan has an interesting theological counterpart. Cardinal Bellarmine, Galileo's antagonist, took the position that if a scientific

When the pragmatists are through, not much of the Platonic tradition is left intact. Yet the examples that I have been discussing suggest that orthodox pragmatism is continuous with the central tradition. Orthodox pragmatists accept its agenda. They just think they can do a better job with it. Orthodox pragmatism is antifoundationalist and in a loose sense antimetaphysical, but it is not a rupture with the philosophical tradition (hence my calling it "orthodox"). Indeed, it draws heavily on philosophers normally thought to fit squarely within the tradition, such as Hume, Mill, and the logical positivists. Often when pragmatists seem to be criticizing the traditional philosophical questions, they actually are trying to persuade others to adopt their answers to those questions; and they employ the traditional philosophical styles of analysis to achieve this end. Some of them consider pragmatism primarily or even exclusively a theory of meaning and justification and propose the following as canonical propositions of pragmatism so understood: that the meaning of a concept lies in the consequences that follow from acting upon it and that the validity of a belief lies in the fact that it leads to the expected consequences when acted upon.[37] This is subtle academic philosophy.

Whether it is sound is a separate question. To define meaning in terms of consequences has a certain oddness;[38] and to ground justification in predictive success will be contested by Popperians, who argue that hypotheses can be refuted but never confirmed, and will be treated as banal by other philosophers of science. But this back-and-forthing just underscores the

---

fact was firmly established, scripture would have to be reinterpreted to accommodate it, but until the fact was firmly established it would be rejected if it conflicted with scripture. His view was that Copernican theory was the second kind of fact—and it was on this point only that Galileo disagreed with him. Richard J. Blackwell, *Galileo, Bellarmine, and the Bible* 166–173 (1991). (So Bellarmine was an early Quine!) Eventually the Church did accept Copernicus's theory as proven fact and reinterpreted scripture to accord with it.

Brandom elucidates the pragmatic character of Quine's position in the following passage: "Quine objects to the notion of meaning-analytic claims (claims true in virtue solely of the meanings of their words) on the broadly pragmatist grounds that there is no practically discernible status corresponding to this supposed category. Claims taken to be analytic, such as 'All bachelors are unmarried males,' are not immune from revision, known a priori, or otherwise distinguished from statements of very general facts, such as 'There have been black dogs.'" Brandom, note 35 above, at 155 n. 13.

37. I am quoting here from an e-mail exchange with Eric MacGilvray. See also MacGilvray, note 6 above, ch. 4, p. 27. For a helpful exposition of what I am calling "orthodox pragmatism," see John P. Murphy, *Pragmatism: From Peirce to Davidson* (1990).

38. If belief in the existence of God is predicted to lead to a feeling of contentment, and the prediction is fulfilled, does it follow that God exists? Surely not. All that would follow would be the desirability of the belief.

orthodoxy of many philosophical pragmatists, those fighting on the same terrain and with the same weapons as the followers of opposing philosophies. Recusant pragmatists, in contrast, such as Dewey, the later Wittgenstein in some moods, Karl Marx, and Richard Rorty, don't think that the epistemological and ethical questions that have largely defined the classical tradition and that many pragmatists have tried to answer are worth asking because they don't think anything of consequence other than to a career in academic philosophy turns on the answers. The questions are merely distractions from the business of helping us to understand and improve the world, whether the physical or the social. Nothing is at stake, for example, in asking whether science provides us with true descriptions of reality. Science has dramatically increased our ability to control our environment, and nothing more is necessary to establish that it is a useful method of inquiry—and anyway no serious person is questioning its utility,[39] so what is there to defend? Whether science is successful because its theories accurately describe the universe is irrelevant to any practical human interest. We now think Euclidean geometry, Ptolemaic astronomy, and Newtonian physics are all erroneous theories, yet each of them was and remains useful in practical ventures. Sailors still navigate by the Ptolemaic map of the universe, builders base their blueprints on Euclidean geometry, and artillerists calculate trajectories using Newton's law of gravity.

Similarly, though less clearly, if asked to accept a utilitarian or a Kantian or a religious approach to moral questions, the recusant pragmatist will want to know what the likely consequences of the various approaches are for the things he is interested in. If he doesn't like the consequences of a particular approach, if in other words his moral intuitions clash with the teachings of a moral theory, he will go with his intuitions. He will not be impressed, for example, by the utilitarian arguments for infanticide or euthanasia, or the Kantian argument for never lying, or Catholic arguments that abortion violates natural law. He will want to know the consequences for him of believing any of these things before he abandons his current beliefs, however ungrounded in "reason" they are.

I called the impotence of moral theory less clear than that of epistemology because, while debates over the foundations of knowledge have no

39. Even creationists do not disparage science in general. Many of them, moreover, describe their position as "creation science," in effect acknowledging the epistemic authority of science. Nor do moral criticisms of particular scientific findings or lines of research question that authority.

power at all to change people's behavior (no one doubts that he has a body and can't swallow a hippo), debates over morality may have some power. People do sometimes act from a sense of duty or out of a fear induced by belief in a punitive deity. But moral *philosophy*, as opposed to religion and charismatic leadership, has little power to change people's attitudes and through such change to alter their behavior.[40] And because it has few consequences in the real world, as distinct from the theory world of the academic philosopher, the recusant pragmatist is inclined to think normative moral philosophy a waste of time.

While the orthodox pragmatist is, as I have said, firmly within the modern philosophical mainstream (none more securely so than Quine, Davidson, and Putnam),[41] battling over the traditional questions with the traditional rhetorical and dialectical weapons, only reaching different conclusions from the classics, the recusant pragmatist is hostile to the mainstream.[42] One is tempted therefore to describe his type of pragmatism as antiphilosophical. I have yielded to this temptation on occasion, but was mistaken to do so. It is one thing to ignore mainstream, or indeed all, philosophy, as most people do. It is another thing to attack it. That is a move within philosophy, however heterodox a one. Philosophy has no fixed boundaries; if someone spends his career writing against philosophy, what else might one usefully call him but a philosopher? If Rorty and the other recusant pragmatists are not philosophers, what are they? Rorty no longer teaches in a philosophy department because he disapproves of what academic philosophy has become. But he still considers himself a philosopher. He does not want to abandon philosophy; he wants to redirect it, to substitute "a less professionalized, more politically-oriented conception *of the philosopher's task* for the Platonic conception of the philosopher as 'spectator of time and eternity.'"[43]

It is true that Rorty has taken to describing himself as a "*post-philosophical* pragmatist,"[44] who hopes that philosophers will evolve into

40. See Richard A. Posner, *The Problematics of Moral and Legal Theory*, ch. 1 (1999).

41. Richard Rorty, the leading living recusant, describes Quine and Davidson as "systematic philosophers." Rorty, note 31 above, at 7.

42. For a good illustration of the contrast, see Donald Davidson, "A Coherence Theory of Truth and Knowledge: Afterthoughts," in Davidson, *Subjective, Intersubjective, Objective* 154, 157 (2001).

43. Rorty, note 17 above, at 634 (emphasis added).

44. Richard Rorty, "Pragmatism and Law: A Response to David Luban," in *The Revival of Pragmatism*, note 3 above, at 304, 311 n. 1 (emphasis added). See also James Ryerson, "The Quest for Uncertainty: Richard Rorty's Pragmatic Pilgrimage," *Lingua Franca*, Dec. 2000/ Jan. 2001, p. 42.

"all-purpose intellectuals"[45] from their present condition as specialists in the traditional problems and literature of philosophy. These all-purpose intellectuals, the equivalent of what are increasingly referred to as "public intellectuals," would comment on the urgent social and cultural issues of the day in a nontechnical vocabulary rather than pursue the abstract conceptual inquiries that are the philosopher's traditional stock in trade, inquiries into such questions as "What is truth?" and "Are there universal moral duties?" After the evolution is complete, we may no longer call such people philosophers. Meanwhile, however, the recusants' principal activity is not redeeming such promises for the future but combatting the current enemy, the academized philosopher.

The Influence of Philosophical Pragmatism on Law

It is time to ask what any of this philosophy or antiphilosophy might have to do with law. I mean law on the operational level—adjudication, legal practice, counseling, and such. Academic lawyers are obliged to take note of philosophical theories that might relate to theories of law; indeed, that is what I am doing in this chapter. Other lawyers are not.

What I am calling orthodox pragmatism has little to contribute to law at the operational level. It has become a part of technical philosophy, in which few judges or practicing lawyers take any interest. Or could readily take any interest: Wittgenstein, Quine, Davidson, Putnam, Habermas, and other postclassical philosophical pragmatists—except Rorty, but he is the least orthodox of them—are not easy reads.[46] Orthodox pragmatism is not completely unrelated to what judges do, because the philosophical issues it addresses occasionally crop up in litigation.[47] And for the few judges who have some acquaintance with philosophy, orthodox pragmatism might undermine whatever belief they may have picked up from their philosophical reading that law might have an autonomous logical structure that would enable the soundness of judicial decisions to be determined with certainty without any messing about with empirical issues. In other

45. Richard Rorty, *Consequences of Pragmatism (Essays: 1972–1980)*, at xxxix–xl (1982).

46. See, for example, Putnam, note 6 above; Robert B. Brandom, *Making It Explicit: Reasoning, Representing, and Discursive Commitment* (1994). Actually, Rorty is only a partial exception; *Philosophy and the Mirror of Nature* is a difficult book, as are some of his more recent essays as well.

47. See, for example, Richard A. Posner, *The Problems of Jurisprudence*, ch. 5 (1990), where I use philosophical pragmatism to illuminate issues of causation in tort cases and voluntariness in coerced-confession cases.

words, orthodox pragmatism might clear the judicial decks. But just for a handful of judges. And it would put nothing on those decks to replace what it had swept off them; it would not give the judges an alternative conception of the judicial role to replace the discredited logical one. "Legal pragmatism does not depend on and indeed can make no use of the pragmatist philosophers' critiques of metaphysics and epistemological foundationalism."[48]

Even recusant pragmatism has at most an atmospheric effect on thinking about law. Judges are no more familiar with Rorty, despite his superior readability, than with Kant; and in any event recusant pragmatism is mainly about refusing to take canonical philosophy seriously, which judges refuse to do anyway, if only out of ignorance. Yet many recusant pragmatists anticipate a practical payoff—they are pragmatists after all—from encouraging a mindset that will be more conducive than the traditional philosophical outlook to constructive engagement with the world's problems. It would be a mindset skeptical of abstraction and disdainful of certitude, of coming to rest—the dogmatic slumber. A mindset that regarded knowledge as a tool for coping rather than a glimpse of eternity, science as a process of inquiry rather than a pipeline to ultimate reality, and morality as a set of useful rules for getting along rather than an imperative duty either imposed upon us by God or immanent in our possession of the power of reason. Nonacademic people believe things when it is useful to believe them and therefore demand evidence of the likely consequences before according belief to a proposition.

All these points can be made just against the mainstream philosophers who reject them. But Dewey believed and Rorty believes that the style of thinking that their versions of pragmatism encourage can spill over into nonphilosophical fields, and even into the activity of judging, with good results. Dewey wrote, and in a law review no less, so he was trying to reach—and teach—the legal profession, that what law needed was "a logic

---

48. Thomas C. Grey, "Freestanding Legal Pragmatism," in *The Revival of Pragmatism*, note 3 above, at 254, 259. Cf. Stanley Fish, *The Trouble with Principle* 304 (1999): "nothing follows from [philosophical] pragmatism, not democracy, not a love of poetry, not a mode of doing history." Jules L. Coleman, a philosopher who teaches at the Yale Law School, would disagree. In his book *The Practice of Principle: In Defence of a Pragmatist Approach to Legal Theory* (2001), he uses orthodox philosophical pragmatism in its most forbidding technical sense (see id. at 6–9), a sense that refuses to have anything to do with the likes of Dewey, James, or Rorty (see id. at 6 n. 6), to expound legal positivism and a corrective-justice theory of tort law. Coleman's book is too abstract to speak to a legal professional; I at any rate am unable to discern its bearing on the issues discussed in this book.

relative to consequences rather than to antecedents." It would be a logic (he means a method) that would treat general rules and principles as "working hypotheses, needing to be constantly tested by the way in which they work out in application to concrete situations."[49] He concluded that "infiltration into law of a more experimental and flexible logic is a social as well as an intellectual need."[50] This conclusion, however, is not an *implication* of pragmatism. There is no intrinsic incompatibility between any version of philosophical pragmatism and a belief that a judge should *not* consider the consequences of what he's doing. That was the position of Friedrich Hayek, who defended it, in part anyway, on a ground congenial to a pragmatist—that judges would produce better results if they just enforced existing rules and understandings, come what may, leaving any improvements to legislation or the evolution of custom.[51] Nothing in philosophical pragmatism enables a choice between Dewey's and Hayek's approach to law; it is an issue in the design of political institutions.

To the practitioner or reformer, philosophy in any form is merely a distraction, taking time away from constructive engagement with America's problems, in the same way that we might think the life of a monk who spent all of every day in prayer and contemplation less constructive than that of a parish priest. Rorty, like Dewey, doesn't think the orthodox philosophical tradition merely a distraction, however. He thinks it creates a psychological barrier to the quest for social justice. With its claim to possess privileged access to ultimate truths, traditional philosophizing resembles theology in fostering an outlook that, being dogmatic, is unfriendly to compromise and tolerance and therefore to democracy. Rorty believes that "philosophical superficiality and light-mindedness helps . . . make the world's inhabitants more pragmatic, more tolerant, more liberal, more receptive to the appeal of instrumental rationality."[52] Social reform will be

49. John Dewey, "Logical Method and Law," 10 *Cornell Law Quarterly* 17, 26 (1924) (emphasis in original). On legal pragmatism generally, see Thomas F. Cotter, "Legal Pragmatism and the Law and Economics Movement," 84 *Georgetown Law Journal* 2071 (1996), as well as the references in the first footnote in the Introduction.

50. Dewey, note 49 above, at 27.

51. See, for example, F. A. Hayek, *Law, Legislation and Liberty: A New Statement of the Liberal Principles of Justice and Political Economy*, vol. 1: *Rules and Order* 87, 97, 119, 121 (1973), and Chapter 7 of this book, where I note a parallel between Hayek's and Dewey's conceptions of knowledge and inquiry. On formalism as a possible pragmatic strategy for interpreting statutes, see William D. Popkin, *Statutes in Court: The History and Theory of Statutory Interpretation* 222 (1999).

52. Richard Rorty, "The Priority of Democracy to Philosophy," in *Reading Rorty: Critical Responses to* Philosophy and the Mirror of Nature *(and Beyond)* 279, 293 (Alan R. Malachowski

delayed, moreover, if "judgment must remain suspended on the legitimacy of cultural novelties until we philosophers have pronounced them authentically rational."[53] And having to lay philosophical foundations for political programs discourages support for social experimentation, which, Rorty argues in the spirit of Mill, is essential to social progress. Rorty wants to help "free mankind from Nietzsche's 'longest lie,' the notion that outside the haphazard and perilous experiments we perform there lies something (God, Science, Knowledge, Rationality, or Truth) which will, if only we perform the correct rituals, step in to save us."[54]

There is something to these points; but the suggestion that the pragmatic outlook favors social democracy or legal liberalism is unconvincing. Pragmatism has no political valence. Brian Leiter has identified an influential current in pragmatism that he calls "classical realism" and associates with Thucydides, with Thrasymachus, Gorgias, and other sophists, and with Machiavelli, Freud, Marx, Nietzsche, Justice Holmes, and (I am flattered to note) me. Classical realism mixes "naturalism" and "quietism" with pragmatism.[55] Leiter could also have remarked the powerful vein of hard-hearted pragmatic thinking in German jurisprudence during the Weimar and Hitler eras. Carl Schmitt, one of the most influential German legal thinkers of that period, grounded his rejection of liberal legal theory in a belief that the real logic of the law was a logic of consequences rather than one of antecedent principles.[56] Structurally, his view of law was the same as Dewey's or Rorty's; as for law's content, pragmatism was and is silent.

In a chapter section alarmingly captioned "Pragmatism as a Fascist Ide-

---

ed. 1990). He has said elsewhere that he thinks that "a world of pragmatic atheists . . . would be a better, happier world than our present one." Richard Rorty, "Response to Frank Farrell," in *Rorty and Pragmatism: The Philosopher Responds to His Critics* 189, 195 (Herman J. Saatkamp, Jr. ed. 1995).

53. Richard Rorty, "Philosophy and the Future," in id. at 197, 201.

54. Rorty, note 45 above, at 208.

55. Brian Leiter, "Classical Realism," 11 *Philosophical Issues* 244 (2001). By "naturalism" he means "there exist (largely) incorrigible and generally unattractive facts about human beings and human nature," by "quietism" that "any normative theorizing which fails to respect the limits imposed by these facts about human nature is idle and pointless; it is better to 'keep quiet' about normative matters, than to theorize in ways that make no difference to practice," and by pragmatism that "only theories which make a difference in practice are worth the effort: the effect or 'practical pay-off' is the relevant measure of value in theoretical matters." Id. at 245.

56. See William E. Scheuerman, *Carl Schmitt: The End of Law*, ch. 1 (1999). Cf. Richard A. Posner, *Overcoming Law* 155–157 (1995).

ology of the Deed," Hans Joas points out that American pragmatism "was adopted as the ideology of a whole group of German intellectuals who sympathized with National Socialism," and that Mussolini credited William James as one of the sources of his ideas.[57] "As a philosophy of action, pragmatism became caught up in the enthusiasm for decisiveness, action, and power which characterized National Socialist intellectuals."[58] Heidegger was both a pragmatist[59] and, for a time anyway, a Nazi.

The Darwinian underpinnings of pragmatist philosophy, which are particularly marked in Dewey's version of pragmatism, fairly *invite* reactionary pragmatism, though Dewey of course declined the invitation. Darwin's picture of nature is bleak; it is dog eat dog in virtually a literal sense; the adaptionist process that produced us is genocidal. From social Darwinism in the nineteenth century to Nazism and sociobiology in the twentieth, Darwinism has inspired or nourished ideologies that have reactionary or (in the case of sociobiology) conservative implications. There is no reason why pragmatists steeped in Darwinism should *not* be reactionary or conservative, and so it is no surprise that some have been.

Dewey himself was famously "liberal" in the modern sense. Modern pragmatists, most of them liberal in the same sense, are reluctant to admit that Dewey's liberalism was unconnected, save possibly in a psychological sense, to his philosophy. The psychology comes from the parallelism between the Western philosophical tradition that begins with Plato, the Western religious tradition dominated by Christian doctrines that borrowed heavily from Platonic and other classical philosophical thought, and the Western legal tradition, which was greatly influenced by Christianity. The type of mind that is restive with regard to Platonism is quite likely to be restive with regard to these parallel structures as well, structures that have generally conservative political implications though they serve such different purposes that it is possible to abandon one or two and retain the third, or abandon one and retain the other two. There is no logical inconsistency between being a philosophical pragmatist and a devout Christian and a legal formalist, but there may be psychological tension. Yet even if knocking the props out from under Plato and his philosophical successors

---

57. Hans Joas, *Pragmatism and Social Theory* 107 (1993). See also id. at 108–111.

58. Id. at 111.

59. Id. at 105–107; Richard Rorty, "Introduction: Pragmatism and Post-Nietzschean Philosophy," in Rorty, *Philosophical Papers*, vol. 2: *Essays on Heidegger and Others* 1, 3–4, 10–11 (1991).

upends Christianity and law, the political consequences can be—anything. National socialism was philosophically pragmatic, atheistic, and disdainful of legality.

Pragmatism applied to law at most takes away from judges the claim to be engaged in a neutral scientific activity of matching facts to law rather than in a basically political activity of formulating and applying public policy called law. That is a claim made on behalf of left-wing as well as right-wing legal theories. Ronald Dworkin claims to be engaged in an objective quest for right answers to constitutional and other difficult legal questions, and despises the adherents of the critical legal studies movement and other "postmodernist" legal theories, and criticizes Rorty, for arguing that the quest is futile. So pragmatism undermines Dworkin, a left liberal—while it has no traction against the German judges who during the Nazi period rejected formalist decisionmaking as an impediment to bringing law into conformity with the spirit of the regime.[60] Rorty abhors Nazism and sees eye to eye politically with Dworkin. Yet Rortyan pragmatism, applied to law, challenges Dworkin's jurisprudence but not that of the Nazis.

Rorty advocates a "visionary" conception of constitutional adjudication. "A paradigm shift," he argues, may be "needed in order to break up 'bad coherence' . . . Such a shift can be initiated when visionary judges conspire to prevent . . . the 'complacent pragmatic judge' . . . from perpetuating such coherence."[61] Rorty calls paradigm shifts brought about by visionary judges "breakthroughs into romance" and examples of "the poetry of justice."[62] Yet he is well aware that the term "complacent pragmatic judge" is no oxymoron. He is alert to "the possibility that equally romantic and visionary, yet morally appalling, decisions may be made by pragmatist judges whose dreams are Eliotic or Heideggerian rather than Emersonian or Keatsian."[63]

The connection between the liberal-visionary and the pragmatic is purely historical and contingent. It happens that John Dewey and some other pragmatist philosophers were also left-leaning political visionaries. As a result, "in American intellectual life, 'pragmatism' has stood for more than just a set of controversial philosophical arguments about truth,

60. See Posner, note 56 above, at 155.
61. Richard Rorty, "The Banality of Pragmatism and the Poetry of Justice," 63 *Southern California Law Review* 1811, 1817–1818 (1990) (footnote omitted).
62. Id.
63. Id. at 1818.

knowledge, and theory. It has also stood for a visionary tradition to which, as it happened, a few philosophy professors once made particularly important contributions."[64] "As it happened" is key; that they were philosophy professors was adventitious. And "stood for" is an evasion; it's like saying that Charles Lindbergh has come to "stand for" the American First movement and meaning by this to insinuate that there is something in flying a plane well that makes a person an isolationist.

I did suggest in the Introduction that pragmatism undermines Plato's preference for rule by philosophers over democratic rule. But rule by philosophers is only one, and indeed one of the most infrequent, forms of nondemocratic government (it may be approximated by theocracy, however, as in Iran, and conceivably by Confucian China). Pragmatism does furnish arguments against censorship and for democracy and social experimentation, but it also undermines liberalism (including the rule of law) and democracy by questioning the possibility of basing these ideologies on anything firmer than expedience.

Pragmatism does not lead in a straight line to a philosophy of adjudication any more than it leads in a straight line to liberal democracy. It may encourage or fortify a mindset that is skeptical of any philosophy of adjudication that casts the judge in the role of a quester after certainty who employs to that end tools as close to formal logic as possible. And it may encourage the thought that judges should reconceive their mission as that of helping society to cope with its problems, and therefore that the rules that judges create as a byproduct of adjudication should be appraised by a "what works" criterion rather than by their correspondence to truth, natural law, or some other abstract validating principle. My guess, however, is that the pragmatic outlook precedes acquaintance with pragmatic philosophy rather than is shaped by it. In any event Rorty's advocacy of what appears to be a specific pragmatic philosophy of adjudication, namely a *visionary* mode of judicial decisionmaking, owes little that I can see to pragmatic philosophy; lacks texture, structure, and factual support; and will simply frighten judges, for whom "visionary" is not part of the job description.[65] If all Rorty wants to argue is that given the bankruptcy of formalism we must acknowledge that judges just *are* visionaries in the sense that all they have to guide their decisions are their own political visions, the only

64. Id.
65. For a good discussion of Rortyan jurisprudence, see Douglas E. Litowitz, *Postmodern Philosophy and Law* 145–155 (1997).

objection is that the word "visionary" is a little grand to describe a judge who has no alternative to drawing on his own political and personal values to decide indeterminate cases. If Rorty has something more ambitious in mind, something that would mark a real break in judicial thinking rather than merely a desire for the appointment of judges who share his values, then he ought to address the potential dangers of visionary adjudication—of an immodest judicial role—to democracy and political stability.

He should also consider the *rhetorical* stakes in the debate between formalism and antiformalism. They may be the most important. It is always possible to cast a judicial decision in the formalist mold, as the logical or algorithmic exercise of a strictly constrained judgment. Formalism is the more effective rhetoric when judges are trying to go against the political grain because it enables them to shift (or rather to pretend to shift) responsibility for unpopular actions from themselves to an impressive abstraction, "the law." (With its pretense of objectivity and certainty, formalism may also make a better fit with judicial psychology.[66] Judges like to think they know what they're doing!) That is Dworkin's tactic; and a Rortyan visionary would be wise to embrace it rather than declare himself a judicial Don Quixote. Antiformalism is the more effective rhetorical mode when judges are trying to go with the political grain and do not want to be held back by legal doctrines, which tend to lag behind social change; that was Carl Schmitt's advice. Some radicals think they need a powerfully grounded body of thought, something with metaphysical heft, to move public opinion in their favor. This is doubtful, but it is in any event to one side of the debate between legal formalism and legal antiformalism. Radicals are not looking for a legal doctrine to move the world with. They are looking for a political doctrine, a variant of or a successor to Marxism.

It is no accident that formalist rhetoric is a more pervasive feature of constitutional adjudication and constitutional theory than it is, say, of antitrust law and antitrust theory. Constitutional decisions are, prima facie at least, antidemocratic—they buck the actions of elected officials or of the elected officials' appointees. So they are unpopular, potentially and often actually, and because of this judges and their academic backers are at pains to show that the decisions are compelled by something more impressive than the judges' political preferences. Hence the outpouring of theories (such as originalism, textualism, intertextualism, dualism, translationism, representation reinforcement, purposivism, the moral reading of the Con-

66. As powerfully argued in Dan Simon, "A Psychological Model of Judicial Decision Making," 30 *Rutgers Law Journal* 1 (1998).

stitution, public-values expressivism, and neutral principles—the list could be extended) that seek in formalist fashion nonpolitical, impersonal, in short "objective" criteria by which to justify or condemn particular constitutional decisions. Viewed as rhetorics rather than theories, they are as available to the pragmatic judge who wishes to sugarcoat his decisions as they are to formalists. In contrast, the courts have thought nothing of conforming antitrust law to modern economic theory with nary a glance at the language of and the intentions behind the antitrust statutes, enacted in earlier eras in response to concerns remote from those of the modern economist. In nonconstitutional fields, at least the specialized ones, it is difficult even to interest practitioners, judges, and professors in interpretive theories.

Formalism can be a pragmatist's strategy rather than merely a rhetoric. As a strategy it resembles rule utilitarianism, which rests on a recognition that the means to an end need not have the same structure as the end. A rule against punishing a person known to be innocent, come what may, does not aggregate and compare pains and pleasures, yet it may be the best means of promoting that aggregation and comparison because of the danger of vesting any official with the power to decide when to punish the innocent. Similarly, one might think that the responsibility for considering and if necessary altering (through a change in law) the consequences of judicial action are best lodged elsewhere than in the judiciary, that judges should confine themselves to applying the law as previously laid down, come what may. That was Hayek's approach[67] and it is a far cry from deducing formalism from a philosophical system, such as utilitarianism or Catholic natural law or the political morality of Kant or Rawls.

But the suggestion that formalism might be a pragmatic rhetoric or strategy owes nothing to pragmatic *philosophy*, and so leads me to my next topic.

Everyday Pragmatism

I have found little in classical American pragmatism or in either the orthodox or the recusant versions of modern pragmatic philosophy that law can use. But the pragmatic *mood*, the pragmatic culture that Tocqueville described, has given rise to a different pragmatism—what I call "everyday pragmatism"—which has much to contribute to law. Everyday pragma-

67. Also Savigny's, as I mentioned in the Introduction. I think Savigny's approach was correct for his time and place, but (as we'll see in Chapter 7) that Hayek's is not.

tism is the mindset denoted by the popular usage of the word "pragmatic," meaning practical and business-like, "no-nonsense," disdainful of abstract theory and intellectual pretension, contemptuous of moralizers and utopian dreamers. It long has been and remains the untheorized cultural outlook of most Americans, one rooted in the usages and attitudes of a brash, fast-moving, competitive, forward-looking, commercial, materialistic, philistine society, with its emphasis on working hard and getting ahead.[68] It is the attitude that predisposes Americans to judge proposals by the criterion of what works, to demand, in William James's apt phrase, the "cash value" of particular beliefs, to judge issues on the basis of their concrete consequences for a person's happiness and prosperity. It is a mentality that finds immodest and self-indulgent Robert Nozick's statement of the philosopher's creed: "The philosopher's deepest urge . . . is to articulate and understand the ultimate basis and nature of things . . . What could be more worth thinking about? And what could be more ennobling than thinking about these things? It is, Aristotle said, the most godlike of human activities."[69] The pragmatist has trouble understanding what it might mean for "things" to have a "basis" or a "nature" or how ruminating about such will-o'-the-wisps could be "ennobling," let alone "godlike."

"Pragmatism" in the everyday sense that I am describing shades into "hard-nosed" and in some circles is viewed negatively as "policy without principle, goal-oriented but lacking a moral anchor . . . [the mentality of] cunning and pliable men with few consistent values or ideals."[70] Cecil Crabb points out the ambivalence of our usage:

> If a political leader is described as pragmatic, this might mean one or
> more of the following: (1) he lacks clear ideological goals; (2) his ac-

68. "He who has confined his heart solely to the search for the goods of this world is always in a hurry, for he has only a limited time to find them, take hold of them, and enjoy them. His remembrance of the brevity of life constantly spurs him." Tocqueville, note 26 above, at 512. The idea that Americans are natural pragmatists crops up in the oddest places, as when the art critic Clement Greenberg remarked that "[Winslow] Homer was a good American and like a good American, he loved *facts* above all other things." "Winslow Homer," in Greenberg, *Art and Culture: Critical Essays* 184, 188 (1961) (emphasis in original).

69. Robert Nozick, *Socratic Puzzles* 10–11 (1997).

70. Morris Dickstein, "Introduction: Pragmatism Then and Now," in *The Revival of Pragmatism*, note 3 above, at 1, 2. See also Nichols, note 26 above, at 148. Here are some examples of this usage: "The *Detroit News* did an about-face last week and threw out principle for P. C. pragmatism on the subject of racial preferences at public universities." *Weekly Standard*, Dec. 24, 2001, p. 2. "[California Governor] Davis'[s administration] is an administration of foolishness and panic, searching for bits of flotsam on the sea of pragmatism, rather than one of ideas and wisdom for the future." *Los Angeles Times* (home ed.), Jan. 7, 2002, pt. 2, p. 10. "The cries of school lobbyists alternated between piety (depriving deserving foreigners of

tions do not appear to be guided by adherence to clearly defined moral-ethical principles; (3) he is motivated by immediate, here-and-now considerations, as distinct from long-term goals and strategies; (4) he is "opportunistic" and seeks to achieve the maximum benefit or gain from opportunities available to him; (5) he is skilled in compromise and gaining agreement among divergent positions; (6) he is flexible, capable of learning from experience, and of adapting his position to changing realities; (7) he is prudent, judicious, tends to avoid extremist solutions and understands that politics is "the art of the possible."[71]

President Kennedy and his advisers were called "pragmatists" because they rejected moralism and ideology—as embodied in such liberal stalwarts as Adlai Stevenson and Chester Bowles, whom the Kennedy insiders derided as babblers and softies—in the conduct of governmental affairs both foreign and domestic.[72] Some observers consider the Vietnam War a legacy of this kind of thinking. Everyday pragmatism of the hard-nosed variety could be said to descend from Machiavelli, though he is better regarded not as an amoralist (the popular sense of "Machiavellian") but as someone who, being a realist about politics, understood that public morality, which is the kind required for the performance of political tasks, not only differs from private morality but should not be judged by its proximity to the latter.[73] Joseph Schumpeter's theory of democracy, we shall see in later chapters, is "pragmatic" in the unedifying sense of the word.[74]

The everyday sense of "pragmatic," stripped of the cynical overtones, is

---

valuable education and exposure to democracy) and pragmatism (the loss of revenue would be devastating)." *Insight on the News*, Jan. 7, 2002, p. 48.

71. Crabb, note 27 above, at 57.

72. Cf. J. F. O. McAllister, "'An Instinct for the Important': Sandy Berger Brings Carter-Era Ideals Tempered by Pragmatism to the New Foreign Policy Team," *Time*, Jan. 11, 1993, p. 20. For a generally favorable view of Kennedy's pragmatism, see Kenneth W. Thompson, "Kennedy's Foreign Policy: Activism versus Pragmatism," in *John F. Kennedy: The Promise Revisited* 25, 28–33 (Paul Harper and Joann P. Krieg eds. 1988). Woodrow Wilson and Jimmy Carter are the two U.S. Presidents most often derided as tilting the balance between idealism and pragmatism too far in favor of the former. In this polarity, pragmatism is associated with self-interest, expediency, selfishness, and *Realpolitik*. See, for example, Lincoln P. Bloomfield, "Idealism and Pragmatism in American Foreign Policy" (MIT Center for International Studies, Feb. 1974, unpublished).

73. The distinction, though imperfectly articulated, loomed large in the debates over the impeachment of President Clinton. See Richard A. Posner, *An Affair of State: The Investigation, Impeachment, and Conviction of President Clinton*, ch 4 (1999).

74. Cf. Ian Shapiro, *Democratic Justice* 4 (1999); Patrick Neal, "Theory, Postwar Anglo-American," in *Political Philosophy*, note 26 above, at 195, 198–199.

consistent with the philosophical sense although independent of it. The differences are largely institutional. The philosophical discourse of pragmatism is academic, subtle, complex, and carried on in a forbidding technical vocabulary. (It also tends to be contemplative rather than action-oriented. The everyday pragmatist uses common sense to resolve problems; the pragmatist philosopher explains why this is a sensible procedure.)[75] Remember the proposition that the meaning of a concept inheres in the consequences that would follow from acting on it? This doesn't work as a definition of "meaning." The meaning of the sentence "God is the prime mover" (as distinct from conceiving of God as not just getting things started but in addition responding to prayers or providing afterlife rewards and punishments) is clear enough, even though there are no consequences of acting on a belief that the sentence is true—there is nothing to act on. The value of the pragmatic approach to meaning lies not in definitional accuracy but rather in getting us to consider what is at stake in believing one thing rather than another. Nothing seems to follow from believing that "God is the prime mover" that would not follow from believing there is no God. If so, the everyday pragmatist will ask, why should I bother my head about the question of a prime mover?

Elizabeth Anderson offers the following description of pragmatic ethical inquiry:

> First, pragmatists avoid appeal to ethical principles that reside at too high a level of abstraction from the particulars of human experience. They do not attempt to articulate or justify ethical principles supposed to be true in all possible worlds or valid for all rational beings. Pragmatic ethical principles are contingent, reflecting the circumstances of culture, locality, and history. Second, pragmatists conduct their ethical inquiries hand-in-hand with empirical investigations into the particular features of the institutions, practices, and predicaments real agents participate in, construct, and confront. Third, pragmatists justify their recommendations contextually. They see the quest for livable ethical principles as arising from concrete practices and predicaments, situated in particular historical and cultural contexts. Justification . . . works by demonstrating the practical superiority of the

75. Though I note that pragmatism both questions and commends common sense. The questioning of it is part of pragmatism's general stance of resistance to habit; common sense is habitual thinking.

proposed solution to the finite, concrete alternatives imagined at the time.[76]

In this description couched in ordinary language without reference to technical concepts in philosophy we can recognize the method of inquiry used by ordinary people; and if we just substitute "legal" for "ethical" in the description we can recognize the method of inquiry used by ordinary judges. To those who are skeptical that philosophy, pragmatic or otherwise, has resources for inspiring or underwriting practical proposals for human betterment,[77] who doubt that philosophers have a future as lay preachers, and who realize that philosophy has no purchase on the judicial mind, the constructive side of pragmatic philosophy falls away, and, if the destructive is accepted, there is no longer anything *in philosophy* to help a judge decide cases. We are back in the sunlight.

But wait—in a nation as religious as the United States, a nation in which so much public rhetoric is couched in moralistic terms even in the amoral sphere of geopolitics,[78] a nation of emphatic patriotism expressed in reverence for the U.S. Constitution and the American flag as unifying symbols for a heterogeneous population, a nation that rejects Old World cynicism, a nation in which only a handful of intellectuals gives a positive or even neutral valence to the word "Machiavellian," how can "everyday pragmatism," hard-nosed or otherwise, with its insistence on subjecting every claim to a close examination of its concrete consequences, be thought the basic outlook of the American people?

The answer requires distinguishing behavior from rhetoric in its narrow sense of manner of expression, as opposed to the sophistic and Aristotelian concept of rhetoric as a method of reasoning about issues that cannot be resolved by logic, mathematical calculation, scientific experimentation, or other methods of exact reasoning. No one employs a consistently pragmatic vocabulary; yet it is possible that most behavior can be translated into such a vocabulary. As Professor Mearsheimer observes of U.S. foreign

76. Elizabeth Anderson, "Pragmatism, Science, and Moral Inquiry," in *In Face of the Facts: Moral Inquiry in American Scholarship* 17 (Richard Wightman Fox and Robert B. Westbrook eds. 1998).

77. See id. at 10, 11–14, where this position is succinctly and powerfully argued. See also Posner, note 40 above, ch. 1 (1999); Richard A. Posner, *Public Intellectuals: A Study of Decline*, ch. 9 (2001).

78. A considerable irritant to foreign-policy realists. See, for example, John J. Mearsheimer, *The Tragedy of Great Power Politics* 22–26 (2001).

policy, "It should be obvious to intelligent observers that the United States speaks one way and acts another."[79] Consider, too, the low turnout in our elections, the widespread cynicism about politics even on the part of those who do vote, and the readiness of most people to endorse criticisms of particular judicial decisions as "legalistic" in a bad sense because neglectful of "real world" consequences. These behaviors and attitudes coexist with the voicing by the same people of pietistic sentiments regarding the democratic and judicial processes.

If anything, Americans are at once more pietistic and more pragmatic than other peoples—a "contradiction" that we live without sensing it as such. Think of the amount of puffery in advertising.[80] Advertisers describe their product as the best there is and pretend to an altruistic concern with the consumer's welfare, yet there is a strong consilience between commercial and pragmatic values; so here, at the very heart of American culture, we find piety and pragmatism comfortably coexisting. The causes of advertisers' hyperbole are obscure. One may be that advertisers employ a rhetoric designed to bypass the consumer's rational faculties and exert a strong emotional appeal. Another may simply be that once one advertiser boasts about the quality of his product and about his altruism in order to gain a competitive edge, his competitors come under irresistible pressure to follow suit lest a negative inference be drawn about their products' quality and their altruism.[81] The hyperbolic spiral is limited, however, by the fact that there are costs to boastful advertising; in particular, if the advertised goods were bad, puffery would merely breed cynicism and invite ridicule. Similarly, if the United States did not have constitutionalism, legality,[82] democracy, religiosity, enormous wealth, a certain history, a special position in the world, and so forth, nationalistic slogans would fall flat. Because there is *some* truth to our hyperbolic, aspirational, self-congratulatory civic rhetoric, we would find total realism deflating and in a sense misleading.

79. Id. at 26. See also Jack Goldsmith and Eric A. Posner, "Moral and Legal Rhetoric in International Relations: A Rational Choice Perspective," 31 *Journal of Legal Studies* S115 (2002).

80. See Ivan L. Preston, *The Great American Blow-Up: Puffery in Advertising and Selling*, ch. 2 (1975).

81. See Eric A. Posner, "The Strategic Basis of Principled Behavior," 146 *University of Pennsylvania Law Review* 1185 (1998).

82. The U.S. answer to the communist-socialist holiday "May Day" was to declare May 1 "Law Day." This quickly became, as a practical matter, lawyers' self-congratulation day.

It is not terribly important to change how people talk, though I shall give examples later of how judges can get into trouble by taking goody-goody slogans, such as "no man is above the law" or "one person one vote," at face value. What is important is that judges and other policy-makers should think in terms of consequences without taking the rhetoric of legal formalism seriously and without bothering their heads about pragmatic philosophy either; that they should be, in short, everyday pragmatists. The choice of vocabularies is a secondary consideration, though a certain transparency is desirable in judicial opinions in order to make it easier for people to conform to the rules expressed or implied in them; and therefore I think that judicial opinions should be more candid than they typically are about the pragmatic factors that determine the outcome of the most difficult and the most important judicial decisions. I try in my own opinion writing, within the limits permitted by my judicial colleagues (the "opening night" audience for a judicial opinion consists of the other judges on the panel), to be candid about the role of such factors in the judicial process. But the choice of vocabulary is itself a pragmatic decision. It is not necessarily deceptive for judges to couch their opinions in terms that mesh with the moralistic, nonpragmatic vocabulary of ordinary folk. The vocabulary of everyday pragmatism that this book deploys would in a judicial opinion rather than an academic work give some people a misleading impression of cynicism. Everyday pragmatism sounds cynical, and, I admit, is sometimes touched with cynicism. But it is not cynical at its core; it is merely realistic. Similarly, the moralistic, pietistic vocabulary employed by advertisers and politicians gives a misleading impression of the extent to which commercial and political attitudes and behavior are determined by moralistic and pietistic considerations rather than pragmatic ones.

Emphasis on everyday pragmatism brings to the fore, however, the most common criticism of pragmatism as a guide to behavior: its lack of a moral compass. Even philosophical pragmatism, we saw, lacks any political valence and thus is equally compatible with reactionary and revolutionary social visions. Pragmatism seems to come down to "Just the facts, ma'am," thus bringing us right up to the fact-value gap.

I think it's quite true that pragmatism, whether of the philosophical or everyday variety, and if the former whether orthodox or recusant, has no moral compass. But I see this not as a criticism but as an essential step in refocusing legal and political theory. Pragmatism helps us see that the dream of using theory to guide and constrain political, including judicial, action is just that—a dream. If political action is to be constrained, it must be by psychological, career, and institutional factors rather than by conversation leading to a moral or political consensus. We must accept the irreducible plurality of goals and preferences within a morally heterogeneous society such as that of the United States, and proceed from there.

CHAPTER TWO

Legal Pragmatism

❦

If judges are pragmatic, as I think they largely are in our system, it can only be in the everyday sense of the term.[1] But immediately the counter-example of Holmes, a gifted and serious though not systematic philosophical thinker, comes to mind. His famous dictum "The life of the law has not been logic: it has been experience"[2] could be the slogan of legal pragmatism (reading "logic" as formalism and "experience" as empiricism). Holmes was a friend of Peirce, James, and other early pragmatists, and his philosophical outlook is strongly pragmatic.[3] I said in the Introduction that pragmatism is historicist. Holmes's *The Common Law* from which I just quoted sought the origins of law in social need. Holmes's historicism was an antidote to legal formalism, in which law forgets its origins and

1. That the *philosophy* of pragmatism is unlikely to alter the practice of judges is strongly argued in Stanley Fish, "Almost Pragmatism: Richard Posner's Jurisprudence," 57 *University of Chicago Law Review* 1447, 1465–1472 (1990). I now think Fish is largely correct on this point. See also Matthew H. Kramer, *In the Realm of Legal and Moral Philosophy: Critical Encounters*, ch. 5 (1999), and the quotation from Thomas Grey in the text at note 48 in Chapter 1.

2. Oliver Wendell Holmes, Jr., *The Common Law* 1 (1881).

3. See Thomas C. Grey, "Holmes and Legal Pragmatism," 41 *Stanford Law Review* 787 (1989); Catharine Wells Hantzis, "Legal Innovation within the Wider Intellectual Tradition: The Pragmatism of Oliver Wendell Holmes, Jr.," 82 *Northwestern University Law Review* 541 (1988). See also Richard A. Posner, "Introduction," in *The Essential Holmes: Selections from the Letters, Speeches, Judicial Opinions, and Other Writings of Oliver Wendell Holmes, Jr.* ix, xvi–xx (1992).

pretends to be an autotelic body of thought. In Holmes philosophical and everyday pragmatism unite in the person of an influential judge and legal thinker and one might expect that through him philosophical pragmatism would irradiate judicial practice. This has not happened. The distinctively philosophical touches in Holmes's judicial oeuvre, such as the "outrage" test for holding statutes unconstitutional (see Chapter 5), the prediction theory of law (Chapter 7), the option theory of contract law, and his emphasis on law as delegation (also discussed in Chapter 7), are not prominent in modern cases. (His competitive theory of free speech remains prominent, as we shall see in Chapter 10.)

Holmes's theory of contract is such a clear example of the pragmatic approach to law that I will pause to explain it. The traditional view was that when you sign a contract you assume a legally enforceable duty to perform your contractual undertaking. But "duty" is vague, abstract. Holmes pointed out that in a regime in which the sanction for breach of contract is merely an award of compensatory damages to the victim, the entire practical effect of signing a contract is that by doing so one obtains an option to break it. The damages one must pay for breaking the contract are simply the price if the option is exercised.[4] In this fashion Holmes defined or, better, dissolved the concept of contractual duty by reference to practical consequences.

He did this when pragmatism was still in its germinal stage, however; and whether his theory of contract owed something to philosophy or his embrace of philosophical pragmatism followed from its congeniality to an outlook that had already produced his theory of contract is a matter of conjecture. Mark DeWolfe Howe believed that Holmes and another lawyer member of the "Metaphysical Club" at which pragmatism was born "exposed their philosopher friends to the common-law lawyer's distrust of general principles and by the vigor of their challenge drove the philosophers towards pragmatism."[5] Howe went on to argue that the lawyers'

4. See Holmes, note 2 above, at 300–302; Holmes, "The Path of the Law," 10 *Harvard Law Review* 457, 462 (1897). The problem with the theory is that when damages are not an adequate remedy for a breach of contract, the victim of the breach can obtain an injunction forcing the promisor to perform and thus taking away the promisor's option to break the contract.

5. Mark DeWolfe Howe, *Justice Oliver Wendell Holmes: The Shaping Years, 1841–1870*, at 269 (1957). Howe gives 1870–1872 as the dates of the Metaphysical Club, id., but Menand says it was formed in 1872. Louis Menand, *The Metaphysical Club: A Story of Ideas in America* 200–201 (2001). I don't know which date is the correct one. Holmes's option theory of contracts was first presented in a lecture in 1872. Mark DeWolfe Howe, *Justice Oliver Wendell Holmes II: The Proving Years, 1870–1882*, at 77, 276–277 (1963).

invigorating distrust was rooted in British empiricism, from which pragmatism is in the line of descent.[6] Maybe so. But that is consistent with
Holmes's having been, to a considerable extent at least, an everyday rather
than a philosophical pragmatist so far as his leading ideas about law were
concerned. Thomas Grey is correct to regard the question of Holmes's in-
debtedness to philosophical pragmatism as an insoluble mystery.[7]

Some Principles of Pragmatic Adjudication

Holmes's theory of contract law points us to the core of pragmatic adjudication or, more broadly, of legal pragmatism: a heightened concern with
consequences or, as I have put it elsewhere, "a disposition to ground policy judgments on facts and consequences rather than on conceptualisms
and generalities."[8] But this formulation is incomplete and unspecific. Additional structure is needed, along with qualification, detail, and examples.[9] I try to respond to this need in subsequent chapters through an examination of specific cases and issues, but the following generalizations
may be useful:

1. Legal pragmatism is not just a fancy term for ad hoc adjudication; it
   involves consideration of systemic and not just case-specific consequences.
2. Only in exceptional circumstances, however, will the pragmatic
   judge give controlling weight to systemic consequences, as legal formalism does; that is, only rarely will legal formalism be a pragmatic
   strategy. And sometimes case-specific circumstances will completely
   dominate the decisional process.
3. The ultimate criterion of pragmatic adjudication is reasonableness.
4. And so, despite the emphasis on consequences, legal pragmatism is

---

6. Howe, *Justice Oliver Wendell Holmes: The Shaping Years*, note 5 above, at 269–270. See
also Grey, note 3 above, at 788–789.

7. Id. at 864–870.

8. Richard A. Posner, *The Problematics of Moral and Legal Theory* 227 (1999).

9. I supply some of these in id., ch. 4, and in my books *Overcoming Law* (1995) and *The
Problems of Jurisprudence* (1990). See also Matthew H. Baughman, "In Search of Common
Ground: One Pragmatist Perspective on the Debate over Contract Surrogacy," 10 *Columbia
Journal of Gender and Law* 263 (2001), esp. 308–309, an exemplary everyday-pragmatic analy-
sis of a current legal issue, the enforceability of contracts of surrogate motherhood; and Ward
Farnsworth, "'To Do a Great Right, Do a Little Wrong': A User's Guide to Judicial Lawless-
ness," 86 *Minnesota Law Review* 227, 240–263 (2001), a constructive effort to devise guidelines for pragmatic adjudication.

not a form of consequentialism, the set of philosophical doctrines (most prominently utilitarianism) that evaluates actions by the value of their consequences: the best action is the one with the best consequences.[10] There are bound to be formalist pockets in a pragmatic system of adjudication, notably decision by rules rather than by standards. Moreover, for both practical and jurisdictional reasons the judge is not required or even permitted to take account of *all* the possible consequences of his decisions.

5. Legal pragmatism is forward-looking, regarding adherence to past decisions as a (qualified) necessity rather than as an ethical duty.

6. The legal pragmatist believes that no general analytic procedure distinguishes legal reasoning from other practical reasoning.

7. Legal pragmatism is empiricist.

8. Therefore it is not hostile to all theory. Indeed, it is more hospitable to some forms of theory than legal formalism is, namely theories that guide empirical inquiry. Legal pragmatism is hostile to the idea of using abstract moral and political theory to guide judicial decisionmaking.

9. The pragmatic judge tends to favor narrow over broad grounds of decision in the early stages of the evolution of a legal doctrine.

10. Legal pragmatism is not a supplement to formalism, and is thus distinct from the positivism of H. L. A. Hart.

11. Legal pragmatism is sympathetic to the sophistic and Aristotelian conception of rhetoric as a mode of reasoning.

12. It is different from both legal realism and critical legal studies.

Each of these points requires amplification.

1. Pragmatic adjudication is not, as its ill-wishers charge, a synonym for ad hoc decisionmaking, that is, for always deciding a case in the way that will have the best immediate consequences without regard to possible future consequences. Such an approach would be unpragmatic in disregarding the adverse systemic consequences of ad hoc adjudication. Nothing in legal pragmatism requires, or for that matter permits, the dismissal of consequences on the ground that they are systemic rather than case-specific. "Shortsighted" is not part of the definition of "pragmatic."

The systemic consequences of ad hoc adjudication are summed up in

10. See David McNaughton, "Consequentialism," in *Routledge Encyclopedia of Philosophy*, vol. 2, p. 603 (Edward Craig ed. 1998).

the expression "the rule of law." To a pragmatist this does not signify legal formalism in the sense of blind conformity to preexisting norms—*ruat caelum ut fiat iustitia* (let the heavens fall so long as justice is done)—and thus a renunciation of all judicial flexibility, creativity, and adaptivity. It signifies a due regard (not exclusive, not precluding tradeoffs) for the political and social value of continuity, coherence, generality, impartiality, and predictability in the definition and administration of legal rights and duties. It recognizes the desirability not of extinguishing but of circumscribing judicial discretion.[11]

Most formulations of the rule of law specify as well the separation of the judicial from the legislative and executive functions.[12] The separation envisaged has two aspects, one almost too obvious to require mention, the other dubious. The obvious aspect is institutional and procedural, and is summarized in the term "independent judiciary." Judges must be able to make their decisions without interference by or retribution from other officials, and they must make their decisions in the style of judges rather than legislators, that is, as a byproduct of deciding specific cases and with due regard for the rule-of-law virtues. The dubious aspect of separation-of-powers thinking is the idea that judges are not to make law (that being the legislature's prerogative) but merely to apply it. The common law shows that this is not so. But in interpreting the Constitution and statutes as well, judges make up much of the law that they are purporting to be merely applying. Constitutional law is largely the creation of Supreme Court Justices as a byproduct of loose interpretation of the constitutional text. Antitrust law is another example of a statutory field decisively shaped by judicial decisions. There are enough other examples to show that while the judiciary is institutionally and procedurally distinct from the other branches of government, it shares lawmaking power with the legislative branch.

The significance of the slogan that judges are to find rather than make law is merely as a reminder that aggressive judicial lawmaking is likely to undermine important systemic values. It is difficult to plan one's activities if the judges are liable at any moment to veer in a new direction; and

11. See, for example, Ronald A. Cass, *The Rule of Law in America* (2001); Daniel H. Cole, "'An Unqualified Human Good': E. P. Thompson and the Rule of Law," 28 *Journal of Law and Society* 177, 185–186 (2001); Michel Rosenfeld, "The Rule of Law and the Legitimacy of Constitutional Democracy," 74 *Southern California Law Review* 1307 (2001).

12. One corollary is the subjection of government officials to judicial process, a point to which I return in Chapter 8.

judges who become too caught up in the essentially political role of making new policies are apt to lose their neutrality and become partisans. We might even note a tension between two of the components of the rule of law, impartiality and predictability. Partial judges may be all too predictable.[13] Impartial judges are predictable only if their discretion is circumscribed, either by precise and detailed rules laid down by a legislature or by a commitment to deciding cases in accordance with precedent, which is how the common law is stabilized.

A systemic value that requires particular emphasis is the importance of preserving language as an effective medium of communication. If judges did not generally interpret contracts and statutes in accordance with the ordinary meaning of the sentences appearing in those texts, certainty of legal obligation would be seriously undermined. For judges in run-of-the-mill contract and statutory cases to subordinate this consideration to a weighing of case-specific consequences would therefore be unpragmatic, although it would be equally unpragmatic to refuse to consider case-specific consequences altogether just because the language of the contract or statute in issue seemed clear on its face. Doctrines such as the extrinsic-ambiguity rule of contract law, which allows the introduction at a trial for breach of contract of evidence that the contract does not mean what a reader ignorant of the context illuminated by that evidence would think it means, or the principle that statutes will not be given a literal interpretation when the result of doing so would be absurd,[14] sensibly recognize that while language is an indispensable medium of communication, it can also be a deceptive one. The existence of these doctrines shows, by the way, that interpretation can be a good deal more complicated and uncertain than deduction, contrary to the view of those legal formalists who equate interpretation to deduction in an attempt to show that the language of a contract or a statute provides a sure guide to "objective" adjudication.

Despite these qualifications, most contract and statutory cases are decided quickly and easily on the basis of the "plain meaning" of the relevant texts. These are pragmatic decisions too and thus illustrate, what would be obvious were it not questioned, that there are easy pragmatic decisions as well as difficult, open-ended, "all relevant facts and circumstances" ones.

13. See F. Andrew Hanssen, "The Effect of Judicial Institutions on Uncertainty and the Rate of Litigation: The Election versus Appointment of State Judges," 28 *Journal of Legal Studies* 205 (1999).

14. For a helpful recent discussion, see Jonathan R. Siegel, "What Statutory Drafting Errors Teach Us about Statutory Interpretation," 69 *George Washington Law Review* 309, 326–335 (2001).

Not all pragmatic adjudications demand a canvass of the full range of possible consequences of alternative outcomes.[15] Uncertainty and interminability are pragmatic concerns, not pragmatic values.

At the other end of the spectrum from contract cases, so far as the relative weight of case-specific and systemic consequences is concerned, are cases in which the legal standard applied by the courts is "balancing," as in negligence, nuisance, and most other tort cases, and in many constitutional cases as well (we'll take a close look at several classes of such cases in Chapters 8 and 10). A balancing test *means* the weighing of case-specific consequences, for example weighing expected accident costs against the costs of accident avoidance in the typical negligence case.

The opposite of the fallacy that pragmatic adjudication requires too much of judges is the fallacy that it is too easy because it lacks the discipline of legal formalism—lacks in fact *any* structure or discipline. This is a particular concern of law professors. They fear that premature exposure to pragmatism's seductive charms will make law students cynical and lazy. That is a danger but a small one because, as every law teacher knows, the law-student subculture is strongly formalist; law students want to think they're being initiated into a deep mystery. In any event, it should be possible to make clear to the students that they cannot maneuver as lawyers without mastering the vocabulary and rhetoric of legal formalism and also that *responsible* pragmatic analysis requires careful, informed consideration of consequences. (Good "crit" law teachers make the first point but usually not the second.) Pragmatism may tend to dissolve law into policy analysis but there is no reason why it should dissolve law into careless, shortsighted, superficial policy analysis.

The medley of systemic judicial virtues that I have been describing implies a respectful attitude by judges not only toward constitutional and statutory text but also toward precedents. In fact, it requires judges ordinarily to treat text and precedents as the most important materials of judicial decision, for they are the materials on which the community necessarily places its principal reliance in trying to figure out what the "law" is, that is, what the judges will do with a legal dispute if it arises. A good pragmatic judge will try to weigh the good consequences of steady adherence to the rule-of-law virtues, which tug in favor of standing pat, against the bad con-

---

15. See Brian Z. Tamanaha, *Realistic Socio-Legal Theory: Pragmatism and a Social Theory of Law*, ch. 7 (1997), esp. pp. 214–215. For a recent effort to elaborate a pragmatic theory of statutory interpretation, see William D. Popkin, *Statutes in Court: The History and Theory of Statutory Interpretation*, ch. 7 (1999).

sequences of failing to innovate when faced with disputes that the canonical texts and precedents are not well adapted to resolve. This adaptationist perspective, which echoes Darwinian thinking, is emphasized in Dewey's essay on law, discussed in the next chapter.

2. If enough stress is laid on the systemic consequences of adjudication, legal pragmatism merges into legal formalism. Indeed, as I noted in the last chapter, legal formalism could be a sound pragmatic strategy by analogy to rule utilitarianism. Could be, but is unlikely to be in a complex, case-based rather than code-based legal system, above all in the most powerful court in our heavily case-based system, the United States Supreme Court. The immediate consequences of a decision by the Supreme Court can be momentous; and especially when the decision is premised on the Constitution, it may be impossibly difficult to undo. We shall see in Chapter 9, with reference to *Bush v. Gore*, that had the Court forborne to stop the Florida election recount, there was nothing to head off a crisis of Presidential succession. The situation demanded pragmatic adjudication. Pragmatism is further encouraged at the level of the Supreme Court by the fact that the Constitution offers little guidance to the solution of most modern legal problems and by the further fact that the Justices are not constrained to the formalist straight and narrow by the prospect of being reversed by a higher court.

3. There is no algorithm for striking the right balance between rule-of-law and case-specific consequences, continuity and creativity, long-term and short-term, systemic and particular, rule and standard. In fact, there isn't too much more to say to the would-be pragmatic judge than make the most reasonable decision you can, all things considered. (There is a little more to say; I am trying to say it.) "All things" include not only the decision's specific consequences, so far as they can be discerned, but also the standard legal materials and the desirability of preserving rule-of-law values. They include even more—they include psychological and prudential considerations so various that exhaustive enumeration is impossible. It's hard to improve on Holmes's description of what drives decision for the judge who in good pragmatic fashion places "experience" above "logic": "the felt necessities of the time, the prevalent moral and political theories, intuitions of public policy, avowed or unconscious, even the prejudices which judges share with their fellow-men."[16]

16. Holmes, note 2 above, at 1.

4. If a consequentialist is someone who believes that an act, such as a judicial decision, should be judged by whether it produces the best overall consequences, pragmatic adjudication is not consequentialist, at least not consistently so. That is why I prefer "reasonableness" to "best consequences" as the standard for evaluating judicial decisions pragmatically. I do not use the word in the all-encompassing sense that it bears in modern political theory, in works by Brian Barry, Timothy Scanlon, and others; I use it rather in the narrower sense in which it is used in law, as I explain later in this chapter.

The dominant brand of consequentialism is utilitarianism, which shares some features with pragmatism but is certainly distinct from it. It is one thing to care about consequences, including consequences for utility (welfare), and another to be committed to a strategy of maximizing some class of consequences, a commitment that, as the large critical literature on utilitarianism attests, can lead to just the kind of dogmatic absurdities that pragmatists are determined to avoid.

I do not know of any pragmatists who have considered themselves consequentialists, but two notable precursors, Bentham and John Stuart Mill, did, and there is no doubt that pragmatism is closer to consequentialism than it is to deontology (duty-based as distinct from consequence-based ethics). But there is a considerable difference. Partly it is a matter of scope. When deciding whether to cross a street against the light, one is in some sense, and I think a meaningful sense, balancing costs and benefits. One is not, however, taking a position on act versus rule utilitarianism, on whether average or total utility should be one's maximand, on whether the pain and pleasure of animals should be a part of the utilitarian calculus, on the relative roles of offer and demand prices (the price one would offer to obtain something versus the price one would demand to give it up if one already owns it) in a system of wealth maximization (a consequentialist ethics related to but distinct from utilitarianism), and on other philosophical issues of consequentialism. Judicial decisionmaking is likewise a truncated form of consequentialism.

Suppose someone challenged, as an unconstitutional deprivation of liberty, a law that forbade incest without an exception for adult incest when one or both members of the incestuous couple are sterile. It is difficult to see what good consequences the denial of such an exception (an exception found in some states to their prohibitions against marriage between first cousins) could have; the bad consequence would be forbidding a harmless intimate relationship that might be indispensable to the happiness of the participants. Yet the pragmatic judge would be most reluctant to invalidate such a statute as an arbitrary interference with liberty. Horror at incest is a brute fact about present-day American society that, were the statute invalidated, would, at least if the incestuous couple consisted of siblings rather than merely cousins, cause a degree of public upset disproportionate to the benefits of invalidation to the very occasional would-be participants in such a relationship.

Miscegenation once aroused the same horror as incest still does. Not until 1967 did the Supreme Court hold that a law forbidding marriage between whites and nonwhites was a denial of the equal protection of the laws.[17] By then those laws, once very common, had been repealed in all but the southern states. In 1883 the Court had in effect upheld such laws by ruling that Alabama had not violated the Constitution by punishing interracial adultery more heavily than other adultery.[18] And as recently as 1956 the Court had declined to consider the constitutionality of statutes forbidding miscegenation.[19] Was the Court wrong to uphold their constitutionality in 1883 and to duck the issue in 1956? Today we think those laws as ridiculous as they are offensive. But we must think our way into the past. In 1883 public opinion was too solidly in favor of such laws for judges seriously to consider invalidating them. In 1956, just two years after the decision in *Brown v. Board of Education* outlawing public school segregation had outraged the South—inciting charges that mixing black and white children in school would lead inevitably to miscegenation—a decision outlawing laws against miscegenation would have been one judicial bombshell too many.

I have spoken of emotion and public opinion as factors bearing on the pragmatic judge, but what of fairness and equality? Should they not be in the picture too, and if so does this not undermine the suggestion that it was all right for the Supreme Court to wait as long as it did before outlawing antimiscegenation laws and that it is all right for the courts to turn a blind eye to arguments against the validity of exceptionless adult-incest laws? The problem with words like "fairness" and "equality" is that they have no definite meaning. They are words to conjure with rather than to facilitate analysis or decisionmaking; in this they resemble a lot of other

17. Loving v. Virginia, 388 U.S. 1 (1967).
18. Pace v. Alabama, 106 U.S. 583 (1883).
19. See Naim v. Naim, 350 U.S. 891, 985 (1956) (per curiam).

pious words and phrases encountered in law talk, such as "no man is above the law," which I take to pieces in Chapter 8 in discussing *Clinton v. Jones.* When the words "fairness" and "equality" as used by lawyers and judges are analyzed carefully, they dissolve into considerations of consequence. A procedure is "fair" if it reasonably balances the risk of error against the cost of reducing error. And treatment is "unequal" in an invidious sense if the overall consequences of such treatment are bad. Like legal formalism, justice talk at the judicial level is mainly rhetoric, usually disguising pragmatic judgments. Where powerful moral intuitions or overwhelming public opinion point, notions of fairness, equality, liberty, justice, and so forth, being infinitely malleable, and conclusional rather than analytic, follow. Judges are not a moral vanguard, and the highfalutin words they use tend to be labels for convictions based on hunch and emotion. Rhetorical inflation, like sheer loquacity and impenetrable jargon, is one of the occupational hazards of adjudication, as of law generally.

A complication is that almost every nonconsequentialist consideration can be recharacterized in consequentialist terms. The judges can be said to have refrained from striking down laws forbidding miscegenation because of the adverse consequences for judicial power or for the happiness of the popular majority that supports such statutes. But it would be more accurate to say that the judges simply regarded the project of invalidating them as having been removed from the judicial agenda by the force of public opinion.

Certainly the vast number of judicial decisions that are genuinely interpretive are not consequentialist in a useful sense of the word. When it is plain what the draftsmen of a contract or a statute were driving at, or when there is no factual difference between the case at hand and a well-established body of earlier case law, the judges will decide the case as if "bound" by the contractual or statutory language or by the precedents and not worry about whether the decision will produce the best consequences.

Judicial interpretation generally proceeds in two steps. The first is to infer a purpose from the language and context of the contractual or statutory text in issue, or from a body of pertinent judicial decisions that have established a rule. The second step is to decide what outcome in the case at hand would serve that purpose best. Consider the Wagner Act (the National Labor Relations Act). A salient purpose, evident from the Act's language, structure, and background, was to make it easier for unions to organize workers. That purpose provides the essential guidance to applying the Act to specific cases. Yet many lawyers and economists believe that the overall effects of unionization are bad, that it reduces productivity and actually harms the poorest workers by placing a floor under wages, thus rendering the least productive workers unemployable, and that there are no offsetting social gains. Yet none of the unionization skeptics believes that a proper judicial office is to disregard the Act's purpose in deciding a case under it. It is not part of the judge's role to second-guess the legislative policy judgments that motivate and animate a constitutional statute. The Act's purpose delimits the consequences that it is proper for the judges to consider, though, as always, room should be left for the extreme case where going with the statutory purpose would produce results so outlandish that the orthodox mode of decision becomes unreasonable.

Such cases are exceptional. Unexceptional are cases in which a consequence-delimiting contractual, statutory, constitutional, or common law purpose cannot be discerned. Common law principles, moreover, are open to revision by pragmatic judges on the basis of a judgment about the consequences of adhering to existing law even if the law's purpose is clear; the purpose is given by the judges and can be altered by them. Absence of guiding purpose is a pervasive feature of constitutional adjudication because of the antiquity and vagueness of so many constitutional provisions and because of ineradicable uncertainty about how far original intentions should guide constitutional interpretation. It is especially in constitutional cases, moreover, that the case-specific consequences of a decision often are so great that they override the sensed purpose of the constitutional provision being applied. The upshot is that federal constitutional law is functionally a body of common law, that is, of judge-made law. And common law, as I have just noted, provides even more scope for consequence-driven adjudication than statutory law does.

The issue of consequentialist adjudication is sharply posed by the distinction, fundamental to the legal process, between a standard and a rule. A driver could be punished for driving carelessly, or for driving in excess of the posted speed limit. Eligibility to become President might be limited to mature adults, or (as it is) to persons who have reached their thirty-fifth birthday. A deliberate wrongdoer might be liable to pay punitive damages in an amount determined by a jury, or might be ordered to pay three times the compensatory damages determined by the jury. Standards invite trade-offs and conduce to producing the decision that yields the best consequences for the case at hand, while rules truncate inquiry and, specifically, curtail judicial consideration of consequences. Rule application is formalistic, even syllogistic, with the rule providing the major premise for decision, the facts of the case the minor premise, and the decision itself the conclusion. Subsumption or classification (for example, of the defendant as someone who exceeded the speed limit) substitutes for tradeoffs. Is decision according to rule therefore unpragmatic? No, because the loss from ignoring consequences in the particular case must be balanced against the gain from simplifying inquiry, minimizing judicial discretion, increasing the transparency of law, and making legal obligation more definite. The choice of a rule over a standard to govern a particular area of behavior may therefore be thoroughly pragmatic even though as a result some cases will be decided in a way that fails to produce the best consequences in that case. It is no answer that the case will be decided that way because the rule-of-law consequences outweigh the case-specific consequences in that particular case. The judge will not be estimating either set of consequences or comparing them. He will simply be interpreting the legal rule.

I am oversimplifying. A litigant is free to invoke case-specific consequences in support of an argument that an exception to the rule should be recognized. Pragmatic judges, being more sensitive to case-specific consequences than formalist judges are—the latter being powerfully attracted to syllogistic decisionmaking—*may* be quicker to recognize exceptions to rules, though tugging the other way is the fact that pragmatic judges are apt to be more sensitive than formalists to the *practical* benefits of decision according to rules that allow only limited, narrow exceptions. In any event, rule-plus-exception decisionmaking is not the same thing as all-relevant-consequences decisionmaking under a standard.[20] Unless the exception swallows the rule, there will be cases in which applying the rule produces untoward consequences in the case at hand that applying a standard would avoid; and yet on balance adherence to the rule might be the better course. That is a pragmatic judgment as well, though not necessarily a consequentialist one.

Another respect in which consequentialism cannot be a synonym for legal pragmatism is jurisdictional in character and returns us to the separation of powers, here viewed not as a curtailment of power but merely as a

20. See Hilary Putnam, "Taking Rules Seriously," in Putnam, *Realism with a Human Face* 193 (James Conant ed. 1990). I shall point out an exception in Chapter 8: the likely legal response to the threat of international terrorism.

rational division of labor. Different kinds of consequence are weighed at different levels in the governmental system. Judicial decisions applying statutes are constrained to be purely interpretive when the balance of consequences has been struck by the legislature in enacting the statute. More generally, the constitutional and legislative demarcation of the judicial role curtails judicial discretion to weigh consequences; the judge is not to assume jurisdiction over a matter just because he thinks the consequences of his doing so would be on balance good. There is nothing unpragmatic about the division of labor, or about thinking that it would be both infeasible and undemocratic to set judges wholly at large to prescribe the rules of conduct that people are to follow. Where the pragmatist is likely to differ from a more conventional legal thinker in this regard is in believing that there should probably be *some* escape hatch from virtually any rule curtailing judicial discretion, as we'll see in Chapters 8 and 9.

If the reason for limiting the judge's consideration of consequences is that it will conduce to a more accurate weighing of the total consequences of his decisions, the judge is still a consequentialist, albeit an indirect rather than a direct one. But the constitutional and legislative determinations that limit the judicial role need not be consequentialist in motivation or effect, and then the judge, when deciding cases within the limits formed by those determinations, is an impure rather than an indirect consequentialist.

Here is an analogy. The decision of how best for me to get to work—drive, take the train, take the bus, take a cab—is made on consequentialist grounds. But my consideration of options and hence of consequences is limited by my inability to burrow underground or transport myself via the Internet as a packet of data. It doesn't matter where these limitations come from; they truncate my consideration of consequences but do not alter the fundamentally consequentialist character of my decision. As always, the analysis can be recast in consequentialist terms: the costs of my burrowing underground or transporting myself over the Internet are infinite. But this flourish adds nothing to the analysis.

Another way to make the point is that as a guide to judicial decision-making, unconstrained consequentialism is immodest. It denies the benefits of the division of labor and the political counterpart of that division, the separation of powers. It is immodest in a second sense as well, one of particular resonance to a pragmatist. It implies something close to omniscience. To be able to determine what judicial decision would have the best consequences globally as it were would require just the kind of godlike reasoning powers that pragmatists deride as the illusion of Platonists.

I have said nothing about how the judge is to decide which consequences of the class of consequences that he is authorized and competent to consider are good and which bad, let alone how much weight to place on each consequence. No doubt goodness and badness are to be determined by reference to human needs and interests, but how are these to be determined? And if they are not determinable (nothing in consequentialism or pragmatism helps to determine them), then isn't a directive to judges to consider consequences empty? No. It just means that different judges, each with his own idea of the community's needs and interests, will weigh consequences differently. That is an argument for a diverse judiciary, discussed in the next chapter.

May the judge challenge the legislative valuation of consequences? Suppose a legislature has made certain crimes capital and the Supreme Court has held that the legislation is constitutional. A lower-court judge is opposed to capital punishment. Should he out of obedience to the legislature and his judicial superiors consider himself absolutely precluded from factoring his opposition to capital punishment into the decision of a capital case? Or should he consider such obedience merely another systemic, rule-of-law type of concern, to be considered along with the case-specific consequences of a decision for or against the imposition of capital punishment in the particular case? My answer is that only in the extreme case would the judge be justified in disregarding the legislative judgment. For judges to conduct guerrilla warfare against legislatures and higher courts is destabilizing, and in general a bad thing, but it is not *always* worse than the alternative.

5. Legal pragmatism is forward-looking. Formalism is backward-looking, grounding the legitimacy of a judicial decision in its being deducible from an antecedently established rule or principle. In other words, to satisfy the formalist, the decision must have a pedigree. That approach gives the past power over the present. The pragmatist values continuity with past enactments and decisions, but because such continuity is indeed a social value, not because he feels a sense of duty to the past. He is emancipated from such a duty not only by the character of pragmatic analysis, with its insistence that conceptualizations be shown to have a practical payoff in the here and now, but also by skepticism about the methods by which lawyers build bridges from the past to the present. The logical and

analogical methods that lawyers use to go from decided cases, statutory text, and the other conventional materials of legal reasoning to the case at hand are notoriously inadequate to resolve genuinely novel legal issues and thus to decide the cases that push law forward, the cases whose residue *is* law. Legal pragmatists are historicist, but in the distinct sense of recognizing the extent to which particular legal doctrines may be historical vestiges rather than timeless truths; theirs is a *critical* use of history.[21]

The kind of interpretive truth that historians try to extract from the record of the past, or judges or law professors when playing historian, is elusive. Originalists, mistakenly thought of as historicist, know this. Their method is to decide cases by reference to the historical meanings of specific words, to which they then apply rules of interpretation (the "canons of construction") to derive the meaning of the constitutional or statutory provision in contention.[22] They seek to cabin judicial discretion by rejecting speculative history. The project is quixotic. It may be unsound even in principle. As Professors Grundfest and Pritchard explain,[23] if courts adopted a truly objective, utterly predictable method of disambiguating statutory ambiguities, statutes would no longer *be* ambiguous; for it would be apparent how a statutory ambiguity would be dispelled. But ambiguity is essential to the legislative process because the supporters of a bill often cannot muster a majority unless certain issues are left unresolved for the courts to straighten out later.

Originalists also seek, of course, to upend the liberal precedents created in the Earl Warren, and to a lesser extent the Warren Burger, eras of the Supreme Court. Originalism is formalist, but the past to which it commands obeisance is not the past that consists of judicial decisions; it is an earlier past, the past to which many of those decisions were, in the originalists' view, unfaithful.

This discussion opens me to the charge that I am counseling disobedience to the oath that Article VI of the Constitution requires of all officials, including judges, "to support this Constitution."[24] This would be so if the oath were interpreted to require obeisance to specific text or precedents;

21. See Richard A. Posner, *Frontiers of Legal Theory* 206 (2001).
22. See id. at 167–169.
23. See Joseph A. Grundfest and A. C. Pritchard, "Statutes with Multiple Personality Disorders: The Value of Ambiguity in Statutory Design and Interpretation," 54 *Stanford Law Review* 627, 629 (2002).
24. The charge is made in Jed Rubenfeld, "A Reply to Posner," 54 *Stanford Law Review* 753, 767 (2002).

but that would be ridiculous, since precedents are overruled and the text of the Constitution has frequently been rewritten by the Supreme Court in the guise of interpretation. The oath is a loyalty oath rather than a directive concerning judicial discretion. The loyalty demanded is to the United States, its form of government, and its accepted official practices, which include loose judicial interpretation of the constitutional text and occasional overruling of decisions interpreting that text.

6. Nebulous and banal, modest and perhaps even timorous—or maybe oscillating unpredictably between timorous and bold—the pragmatic approach to adjudication that is beginning to take shape in this chapter (the judge "should try to make the decision that is reasonable in the circumstances, all things considered") will horrify many legal professionals. It will strike them as a belittlement of legal reasoning and hence an insult to their mystery. But law could do with some demystification. If the everyday-pragmatic approach to law is right, there is no special analytical procedure that distinguishes legal reasoning from other practical reasoning. Judges know some things that lay persons do not know; they deploy a special vocabulary; they have certain heightened sensitivities, for example to rule-of-law values. Legal education is not a scam, though it could be shortened. And the practice of law is also a process of socialization into a distinct professional culture. But there is no intrinsic or fundamental difference between how a judge approaches a legal problem and how a businessman approaches a problem of production or marketing. We shall see in Chapter 9 that the list of considerations proper for judges to take into account in making decisions is not completely open-ended; but the same is true for businessmen.

The same is true, for that matter, for politicians in a liberal society—and does this mean that, to a pragmatist, law is just "politics"? That depends on what is meant by politics. If what is meant is the operation of the system that guides and controls the actions of government, then what judges do is politics. But when deep legal skeptics—adherents of the almost-vanished critical legal studies movement, for example—say that law is just politics, they don't mean merely that legal reasoning is continuous with other practical reasoning, so that no wide gulf separates judges from other decisionmakers, public and private. They mean that judges decide cases in exactly the same way that legislators and other politicians decide what policies to advocate or oppose. And that is inaccurate. Judges, even when they are elected rather than (as in the case of federal judges) appointed for life, are not responsive to the same range of influences as politicians. Their training, outlook, background, selection, self-image, incentives, constraints, and legal powers all differ from those of the people we call politicians, so that to equate law to politics, or adjudication to legislation, is misleading and uninformative. What is true, however, is that the gulf between judges and politicians is narrower than the official picture of the judiciary would have it, in which judges are seen as engaged in a deductive or algorithmic process rather than in policymaking.

The Supreme Court took a step toward the merger of legal into practical reasoning in its influential decision in the *Chevron* case,[25] holding that when there is a gap in a regulatory statute, the gap is to be filled by the regulatory agency rather than the reviewing court, even though filling gaps in a statute is an exercise in statutory interpretation, normally viewed as presenting a pure issue of law, which is an issue for appellate judges, not administrative agencies, to resolve. But when there is a gap in a statute, filling it requires a policy judgment and the agency is the policy expert. And so "when a challenge to an agency construction of a statutory provision, fairly conceptualized, really centers on the wisdom of the agency's policy, rather than whether it is a reasonable choice within a gap left open by Congress, the challenge must fail."[26] In saying this, the Court was acknowledging the actual character of statutory interpretation in cases of genuine ambiguity: interpretation as the making of policy judgments rather than as a distinctively *legal* form of reasoning.

My use of the word "reasonable" to describe the goal of the pragmatic adjudicator is intended in part to narrow the perceived gulf between decisions on issues of law and other sorts of decision. The word is ubiquitous in law. Notice its appearance in the passage just quoted from the *Chevron* opinion. The "reasonable person" standard of tort law is fundamental. A judge's discretionary rulings are reviewed for "abuse of discretion," which means that they are reversed only if found by the reviewing court to be "unreasonable." The doctrine of promissory estoppel makes a promise that was relied on enforceable—provided the promisee's reliance was "reasonable." In all these cases, as generally when "reasonable" or its cognates are incorporated into a legal doctrine, the word is used to guide a factual or discretionary determination or the application of a legal rule to the facts, rather than to guide a ruling on pure issues of law. To argue as I do

25. Chevron U.S.A., Inc. v. National Resources Defense Council, Inc., 467 U.S. 837 (1984).
26. Id. at 866.

that those rulings too should be guided by a standard of reasonableness rather than anything more grand is to argue for narrowing the gap between the bottom and the top of the legal dispute resolution process—the bottom where judges and jurors engage in practical reasoning about concrete issues of fact and case management, and the top, the supposed empyrean of legal reasoning where pure issues of law are resolved. The legal thinker who has broken out of the shell of formalist thinking will consider, in deciding how a particular issue of law should be resolved, the consequences that would occur to an ordinary person thinking about the issue— just as a judge or jury appraising as a *factual* matter the reasonableness of particular conduct in the particular case would do.

7. Thus legal pragmatism is empirical in its orientation, just like ordinary practical reasoning. This does not mean that every case is to turn on its unique facts; the systemic consequences of adjudication are also matters of fact. Nor does an empirical orientation imply a rejection of legal principles. The question is the right level of abstraction. Principles that organize empirical inquiry must be distinguished from principles designed to supplant it, such as "justice," "fairness," "liberty," "autonomy," the "sanctity of life," and other high-level normative abstractions. A legal principle such as negligence—the principle that a failure to exercise reasonable care gives rise to legal liability if an injury results from that failure—directs the judge or jury to the facts (What precautions were available to the defendant? How effective would they have been? How great a burden would have they imposed on the defendant? How likely was the accident to occur? Could the victim have avoided it and if so at what cost?), and to the relation among the facts, that determine the outcome of the particular case. This is the usual character of common law principles. Holmes liked to say that general principles do not decide particular cases. That is because, as I have said, *useful* general principles, the sort one finds in common law fields (and not in them alone), direct rather than supplant factual inquiry; that inquiry is necessary to decide the case.

It may be objected that the adjudicative process, at least in the adversarial format used in our courts, is not particularly good at determining facts accurately and, a more far-reaching objection, that at best it can determine only a subset of the facts that are necessary for a sensible decision. A trial determines the who-did-what-where-when-to-whom kind of fact but not equally (and often more) important background facts, such as the purposes behind a statute or regulation, how particular markets work, the incentives that particular transactions create, the characteristic behaviors of police and other public employees and officials, and the deterrent effects of different punishments. The distinction is (in legal lingo) between "adjudicative" and "legislative" facts, the former being not only specific to the case but provable only by sworn testimony or other trial-type methods, the latter constituting the background or context of the dispute giving rise to the case.

Judges often know few facts of the second kind and therefore fall back on hunch, intuition, and personal experiences that may be misleading. How to make judges better informed is a great challenge to the American judiciary. But one thing that is clear is that this deficit of judicial knowledge cannot be cured or elided, but only concealed, by formalist adjudication. To try, for example, to answer the question whether there should be a right to physician-assisted suicide by conceptualizing it as a conflict between the principle of autonomy and the principle of the sanctity of life, or as a matter of interpreting the word "liberty" in the due process clauses of the Fifth and Fourteenth Amendments to the Constitution, is just an evasion. The important thing is to get a sense of the factual consequences of physician-induced suicide, for example by study of the effects of the practice in the Netherlands, the only country in which it is fully legal. Knowledge of those consequences will affect the judgments of those judges who do not have unshakable priors—priors inevitably based not on philosophy or deliberation but on religious belief (or lack thereof), ideology, temperament, and one's general bent in constitutional adjudication.

I do not in this book make or evaluate proposals for increasing the empirical competence of judges. The possibilities are many and include changes in legal education, changes in the criteria for judicial appointment, changes in the rules of evidence relating to testimony by expert witnesses, and the substitution of specialized courts for courts of general jurisdiction. First must come a change in attitude, then concerted attention to remedies.

8. Related to the fallacy that legal pragmatism implies ad hoc adjudication is the fallacy that a good legal pragmatist is hostile to all theory. I have been called a *faux* pragmatist for arguing that economic theory is useful to law; that is said to make me a dogmatist, and a dogmatist can't be a pragmatist.[27] But dogma isn't a synonym for theory; and since pragmatism,

27. Carl T. Bogus, *Why Lawsuits Are Good for America: Disciplined Democracy, Big Business, and the Common Law* 57–59 (2001). Cf. James T. Kloppenberg, "Pragmatism: An Old Name for Some Old Ways of Thinking?" in *The Revival of Pragmatism: New Essays on Social Thought,*

even legal pragmatism interpreted merely as a directive to conform law to everyday pragmatism, is a theory, a pragmatist can't be against *all* theory. Moreover, while pragmatist philosophers do not think that scientific theories can be shown to embody final truths about the structure of the universe, they do not doubt the utility of such theories. It is no more unpragmatic for judges to use economics to help them reach a decision than it is for them to use chemistry, the findings of cognitive psychology, or actuarial computations.[28] In Chapter 6 of this book I use a theory of democracy to analyze some issues of election law; that is not a betrayal of pragmatism, especially since the theory in question is a pragmatic theory of democracy.

If anything, the pragmatist, being unconcerned with maintaining law's conceptual autonomy and formalist pretensions, is more open to invasions of law from other provinces of thought than a more conventional legal thinker would be. Borrowing from Brian Leiter's analysis of legal realism, we may say that legal pragmatists advocate "a naturalized jurisprudence, that is, a jurisprudence that eschews armchair conceptual analysis in favor of continuity with a posteriori inquiry in the empirical sciences."[29] Pragmatic reasoning is empiricist, and so theories that seek to guide empirical inquiry are welcomed in pragmatic adjudication.

This discussion should help to refine the sense in which pragmatism is suspicious of abstractions. All of science depends on abstraction. Scientific theories are abstract. The causal laws that are the glory of science, such as Newton's universal law of gravitation, are abstract; they abstract from the welter of particulars whose behavior they seek to explain and predict. But abstraction as a tool of empirical science is very different from abstraction as a stopping point, which is the kind of abstraction one encounters in most moral, philosophical, and legal theory. The economist who uses a highly stylized, descriptively unrealistic model of "rational man" to predict the response of, say, the demand for cigarettes to a rise in the cigarette tax is employing abstraction to guide empirical inquiry. What would be un-

---

Law, and Culture 83, 109 (Morris Dickstein ed. 1998): "Posner embraces pragmatism as a fig leaf to conceal economic dogmas concerning market efficiency."

28. The compatibility of pragmatism with rational-choice theory, which is largely synonymous with economic theory, is argued in Jack Knight and James Johnson, "Inquiry into Democracy: What Might a Pragmatist Make of Rational Choice Theories?" 43 *American Journal of Political Science* 566 (1999). The use of economics as a tool of pragmatic analysis of law is illustrated by Michael J. Whincop and Mary Keyes, *Policy and Pragmatism in the Conflict of Laws* 3–7 (2001).

29. Brian Leiter, "Legal Realism and Legal Positivism Reconsidered," 111 *Ethics* 278, 283 (2001).

pragmatic in an economist would be indifference to the result of the inquiry, ignoring his theory's refutation by data. Or an attempt to deduce from utilitarianism, or Thomism or Ayn Rand's objectivism, or the political philosophies of Locke or Kant, or some other comprehensive normative theory a duty of judges and legislators to make law conform to the teachings of economics or some other social science. It has been many years since I flirted with such an approach.[30]

The significance of economics for law is that economists are engaged in mapping many of the consequences that are central to pragmatic legal analysis, such as the economic effects ("economic" in a broad or a narrow sense) of unions, cartels, divorce, disability, discrimination, punitive damages, regulations of safety and health, prison sentences, and so on without end. My argument for judges' trying to decide common law cases in a way that will promote efficiency is simply that it's a useful thing that judges can do, whereas they lack effective tools for correcting maldistributions of wealth.[31] It has been said that this last point "grates on pragmatist sensibilities (or at least on the sensibilities of those pragmatists who value some form of distributional equity!)."[32] The phrase introduced by "or at least" is key; "pragmatist sensibilities" are not the same thing as the sensibilities of pragmatists who happen to be liberals. The association of pragmatism with liberalism is fortuitous. Ask Carl Schmitt.

It may be objected that pragmatic receptivity to economic analysis disarms criticism of that most criticized of Supreme Court decisions, *Lochner v. New York*.[33] The Court invalidated a state law limiting hours of work on the ground that it interfered unreasonably with freedom of contract, a form of liberty protected, the Court held, by the due process clause of the Fourteenth Amendment. The decision drew a scornful dissent from Justice Holmes, which contains the famous line: "The Fourteenth Amendment does not enact Mr. Herbert Spencer's Social Statics."[34] Most economists, however, believe that limiting hours of work by law is inefficient. If workers are willing to work long hours, presumably for more pay than

30. See Richard A. Posner, "Utilitarianism, Economics, and Legal Theory," 8 *Journal of Legal Studies* 103 (1979).

31. See, for example, *The Problems of Jurisprudence*, note 9 above, at 387–389; Richard A. Posner, "Wealth Maximization and Tort Law: A Philosophical Inquiry," in *Philosophical Foundations of Tort Law* 99 (David G. Owen ed. 1995).

32. Thomas F. Cotter, "Legal Pragmatism and the Law and Economics Movement," 84 *Georgetown Law Journal* 2071, 2107 (1996).

33. 198 U.S. 45 (1905).

34. Id. at 75.

if they insisted on shorter hours, then that is the efficient employment contract and refusing to enforce it can only impair the efficiency of the labor market and make the workers themselves worse off. (This incidentally is an example of the economist's concern with long-term consequences, which I have said pragmatic judges should be concerned with too.) This is a pragmatic argument for the result in *Lochner*, and a now extensive literature demonstrates that the decision was not "lawless" in the conventional sense; it was a plausible though certainly not inevitable application of settled principles.[35]

Yet there is a pragmatic argument against the result in *Lochner*. The case was decided in 1905, when social legislation of the kind at issue in the case was in its infancy. No one could be *confident* at so early a date that a maximum-hours law was inefficient. The effect of the Court's decision was thus to stifle, for a time, potentially worthwhile social experimentation. So pragmatic concerns were on both sides of the case—disfavoring the law on strictly economic pragmatic grounds but also disfavoring, on broader pragmatic grounds, the use of the Constitution to strike down such a law without insisting on a more convincing demonstration of its inefficiency. All that is certain is that *Lochner* was no more willful than aggressive modern decisions such as *Roe v. Wade*. Both *Lochner* and *Roe* can be described as activist pragmatic decisions. But while as we shall see in the next chapter *Roe* has for a quarter of a century now seriously impeded experimentation in the regulation of abortion and seems bound to continue doing so indefinitely, *Lochner* had no lasting effect on social welfare legislation.

The kinds of theory that legal pragmatists dislike are not limited to abstract philosophical theory. They include the lower-level but still abstract theorizing of which professors of constitutional law are enamored, in which decisions are evaluated by reference to abstractions common in law talk such as fairness, justice, autonomy, and equality. Pragmatists think that if the constitutional issue is, say, whether the children of nonnaturalized immigrants should be entitled to a free public education, or whether per-pupil expenditures on public school education should be equalized across school districts, or whether prayer should be allowed in public schools, the constitutional lawyer should study education, immigration, public finance, and religion rather than inhale the intoxicating vapors of

35. See Barry Friedman, "The History of the Countermajoritarian Difficulty, Part Three: The Lesson of *Lochner*," 76 *New York University Law Review* 1383 (2001), and references cited there.

constitutional theory the better to manipulate empty slogans (such as "the wall of separation [between church and state]") and question-begging vacuities (such as "equality" and "fundamental rights"). What sensible person would be guided in such difficult, contentious, and fact-laden matters by a philosopher or his law-professor knock-off? In short, the pragmatist's objection is not to theory, but to bad theory, useless theory, and the bestowal of the honorific title of "theory" on formalist rhetoric.

9. The pragmatic judge tends to favor narrow over broad grounds of decision in the early stages in the development of a legal doctrine. That is the route of prudence and also of empiricism; it is not skepticism about theory. What the judge has before him is the facts of the particular case, not the facts of future cases. He can try to imagine what those cases will be like, but the likelihood of error in such an imaginative projection is great. Working outward, in stages, from the facts before him to future cases with new facts that may suggest the desirability of altering the contours of the applicable rules, the judge avoids premature generalization, the kind of thing that gave us a full-blown doctrine of the constitutional limitations on defamation suits in the first case on the matter that the Supreme Court heard, *New York Times Co. v. Sullivan*.[36] A newspaper was challenging a blatant misuse of defamation law to intimidate press critics of southern segregation practices. "The case marked a major battle between the entrenched racist Southern power structure and the civil rights movement. The purpose of the litigation was to chill press efforts to cover the civil rights movement, and Sullivan's initial victory in the Alabama courts was a significant step in that direction."[37] The case could have been resolved in favor of the press without creating in the name of the First Amendment a general privilege to defame public figures.

10. Legal pragmatism is not a mere supplement to legal formalism. Belief that it is comes in part from confusing legal pragmatism with H. L. A. Hart's superficially similar concept of legal positivism. To the legal positivist "law" is what is promulgated as law, normally by a legislature.[38] But what if the meaning of a statute cannot be discerned? Cases that turn on that meaning must still be decided. Hart argues that in such a case, one

36. 376 U.S. 254 (1964).
37. William P. Marshall, "The Supreme Court, *Bush v. Gore*, and Rough Justice," 29 *Florida State University Law Review* 787, 792 (2001) (footnote omitted).
38. On legal positivism, see Anthony J. Sebok, *Legal Positivism in American Jurisprudence* (1998). In Chapter 7 I argue that the pragmatic approach to law is consistent with Hans Kelsen's version of legal positivism though not with Hart's.

in which the conventional materials of decision give out, the judges have to "legislate."[39] Judicial legislating is obviously at the pragmatic end of the pragmatism-formalism spectrum. But Hart goes only half the distance to pragmatism. He limits the judge's pragmatic, legislative discretion to filling gaps in "the law." The Hartian judge employs, to borrow John Dewey's terminology, a logic relative to antecedents until he encounters a gap, whereupon he switches to a logic relative to consequences.

The wholehearted pragmatist eliminates Hart's boundary between the closed and open areas, "the law" and "legislating." In doing so he tracks the actual psychology of judges, for whom the duty to decide is primary and erases any sharp line between applying and creating law. A judge doesn't say to himself, "I've run out of law to apply, so now it's time for me to put on my legislator's hat and make up some new law." Law has no gaps, because it is not a thing; it is the activity of judges and of certain other officials. Well, but neither (except on rare occasions) does a judge say that he is engaged in economic analysis, or even that he is a pragmatist; so we may seem to have a standoff between Hart and the pragmatic theory of adjudication as far as accuracy in describing the self-understanding of judges is concerned. But the issue is not the vocabulary employed by judges; it is the best conceptualization of judges' activity by the theorist. Aristotle's theory of corrective justice, set forth in the *Nicomachean Ethics*, appears to be the generalization into philosophical terminology of the practices (or at least aspirations) of the Athenian legal system of his time. The relation of the economic theory of law, and more broadly the pragmatic theory of adjudication, to the practices of the modern American legal system is similar. The economic or the pragmatic approach to law is external only in a purely linguistic sense; it is consilient with the legal way of thinking, as Hart's theory is not. The important point is not that judges don't talk like economists or philosophers, but that they do not think or act as if they were engaged in two different activities, "adjudication" and "legislation."[40]

Hart held the belief, one that strikes an American lawyer as peculiar but came naturally to Hart because of the cut-and-dried character of the English legal system of his time, that the only important source of legal uncer-

39. See, for example, H. L. A. Hart, *The Concept of Law* 252, 272–273 (2d ed. 1994).

40. Mention of Aristotle brings out the oddness of Ernest Weinrib's effort, in his book *The Idea of Private Law* (1995) and elsewhere, to ground legal formalism in Aristotle's theory of corrective justice. Aristotle thought law a part of ethics, which in turn was and is closely related to politics. He was not a formalist.

tainty is unclear statutory language. From this it seemed to him to follow that if a statute's language *was* clear, there was no occasion to go beyond it; so most of the time the judge was just a reader, and reading is very different from making policy. Hart was wrong, at least from an American perspective, about the nature and sources of legal uncertainty.[41] Not only are there many other sources of such uncertainty besides semantic ambiguity, but the clarity of statutory or constitutional language, legislative history, contracts, and other textual sources of legal meaning can be deceptive. The principle mentioned earlier that statutes are not to be read literally when doing so would produce absurd consequences implies that there are few if any cases in which consequential considerations could not possibly be decisive. Yet it would be misleading to infer that in most cases judges are "legislators" (a term anyway to be resisted because of its incongruity with judges' self-understanding and because of the many practical differences between real legislators and judges). In most cases it makes sense for the judge to stop with the language of the contract or statute in issue, or with a precedent. In most, but not all. The pragmatic approach permits the judge to pry open the closed area, though cautiously, upon a careful sifting of the consequences of doing so, of somewhat unsettling the law in order to achieve some immediate practical goal.

In short, pragmatism is not merely a supplement, a tie-breaker for cases in which the conventional materials of adjudication—constitutional and statutory text, the text of a contract, case law, and so forth—run out, perhaps cases in which truly exigent circumstances, a national emergency for example, exert unbearable pressure on formalist methodology. The emergency cases, of which I shall give examples in Chapter 8, are the most dramatic examples of the need for pragmatic adjudication, but they are not typical of such adjudication.[42] The conventional materials of adjudication have no absolute priority over other sources of information concerning the likely consequences of deciding a case one way or another. When the consequences are not catastrophic or absurd, it usually is sensible to go with the plain meaning of a statute or contract in order to protect expectations and preserve ordinary language as an effective medium of legal communication. But, as I have been at pains to emphasize, the root of the decision is still pragmatic.

41. Leiter, note 29 above, at 295–297.
42. For examples of other types of pragmatic adjudication, see Posner, note 8 above, at 243–252, 258.

11. Legal pragmatists are more sympathetic to rhetoric (though not to formalist rhetoric) than conventional legal theorists are. Plato, whose philosophy is continuous with the rationalist assumptions of conventional legal theory, considered rhetoric the very antithesis of reason—a collection of low tricks for persuading ignorant, emotional people, such as Athenian jurors, rather than a method of discovering truth. Aristotle took a kindlier view. He thought that when pruned of its most disreputable techniques rhetoric was a reasonable and indeed an inescapable method of persuasion in areas that exact reasoning could not reach. Pragmatists, whether of the philosophical or the everyday variety, are of the same mind as Aristotle. Difficult legal questions tend not to have "right" answers in a sense that Plato would recognize. Instead they have better or worse answers—and often it is unclear which are which. These uncertainties reach their apogee at law's turning points, where the judges face the unknown across an abyss that they lack the materials to bridge. At such turning points, in the presence of such discontinuities, a penetrating insight, aphoristically expressed, though reflecting a merely partial truth—though maybe just a shot in the dark—may rightly play an influential role in the development of law. It may be the best that can be expected.

Early in our constitutional history the Supreme Court ruled in a famous opinion by John Marshall that the Constitution forbids states to tax federal instrumentalities (specifically, the Bank of the United States, a largely private company that Congress had established in order to place the nation's finances on a sound basis) with the quip that "the power to tax involves the power to destroy."[43] Marshall was expressing a partial truth. But he was expressing it in a way that dramatized the central issue in the case—the degree to which the states would be permitted to limit federal power. The nation faced a choice between states' rights and a strong national government. The quip focused this choice by interpreting states' rights as a claim to be entitled to "destroy" the national government. Put in those terms, the choice was an easy one. Plato would have been appalled by such sleight-of-hand. Yet there was no way so early in our constitutional history that Marshall could have proved the rightness of his decision; there may still be no way. Rhetorical assertion was the only arrow in his quiver. It did the job.

A disproportionate number of our most celebrated judges have been

---

43. McCulloch v. Maryland, 17 U.S. (4 Wheat.) 316, 431 (1819).

distinguished rhetoricians and are celebrated in significant part for their rhetorical prowess. Marshall is one; others include Holmes, Cardozo, Jackson, and Hand. Many would add to this list Brandeis and Black. It is notable that all but Black would also be regarded as pragmatic judges. That is not an accident.[44]

12. Legal pragmatism is not merely warmed-over legal realism or critical legal studies. (Neither is it postmodern legal theory—the successor to critical legal studies—in any useful sense of that word,[45] though there are affinities.)[46] Both legal realism and critical legal studies were (are, if there are any crits left) skeptical of legal formalism; and their adherents made a number of good points. Both movements, however, were intensely political, though legal realism less so than critical legal studies, and faded when the political concerns that animated them faded. Legal realism was closely identified with the New Deal, and critical legal studies with the radicalism of the late 1960s and early 1970s in American universities. More important, both movements were weak on policy analysis. This gave them a negative cast—they had little but their politics to replace legal formalism with. Legal realism's crowning achievement, the Uniform Commercial Code, orchestrated by Karl Llewellyn, was a successful effort to ground commercial law in actual trade usages, but there were not enough such constructive projects to keep the movement alive after its political impetus faded.

Legal pragmatism in the form defended in this book lacks the political commitments of the realists and the crits. It has no inherent political valence at all. It relies on advances in economics, game theory, political science, and other social-scientific disciplines, rather than on unexamined political preferences and aversions, to take the place of legal formalism. These social sciences have both liberal and conservative practitioners, a fact that should go some distance toward allaying concerns that the social sciences in general and economics in particular are merely the masks of politics.

In brutally brief summary, legal pragmatism is not concerned just with

44. See, for example, Richard A. Posner, *Cardozo: A Study in Reputation* 136–137 (1990).

45. See Posner, note 8 above, at 265–280.

46. Though critical of legal pragmatism, Allan C. Hutchinson's postmodernist approach in his book *It's All in the Game: A Nonfoundationalist Account of Law and Adjudication* (2000) is pretty close to my position, as are many of the writings of such crit-postmodernists as Jack M. Balkin and Sanford Levinson. See, for example, Balkin and Levinson, "Legal Historicism and Legal Academics: The Roles of Law Professors in the Wake of *Bush v. Gore*," 90 *Georgetown Law Journal* 173 (2001). But to attempt a fuller comparison in the present book would carry me too far afield.

immediate consequences, is not a form of consequentialism, is not hostile
to social science, is not Hartian positivism, is not legal realism, is not critical legal studies, is not unprincipled, and does not reject the rule of law. It
is resolutely antiformalist, it denies that legal reasoning differs importantly
from ordinary practical reasoning, it favors narrow over broad grounds of
decision at the outset of the development of an area of law, it is friendly to
rhetoric and unfriendly to moral theory, it is empirical, it is historicist but
recognizes no "duty" to the past, it distrusts exception-less legal rules, and
it doubts that judges can do better in difficult cases than to reach reasonable (as distinct from demonstrably correct) results.

These generalizations are intended to supplement what at the outset I
described as the core of pragmatic adjudication—"a disposition to ground
policy judgments on facts and consequences rather than on conceptualisms and generalities"—rather than to supplant it. To make sure that we
don't lose sight of the core, let me give another example (the original one
was Holmes's theory of contract law). Judicial opinions are replete with the
language of "free will"—judges are constantly describing criminal defendants, for example, as acting deliberately, as having chosen a life of crime,
as having violated the law intentionally, as failing to exercise self-control,
and so forth—and numerous opinions state or imply that the criminal law
rests on a belief in free will and rejects determinism. Does this mean that
the judges are taking sides in the age-old philosophical controversy over
whether people have free will? It does not. When ordinary people use
terms like "free will," they refer to situations in which a normal person's
behavior is responsive to incentives and constraints, such as the threat of
punishment. As long as punishment enters the causal chain that leads to
committing or refraining from committing a crime, that is, as long as punishment has good consequences, punishing has social value; and so the
philosophical issues are elided.[47]

John Marshall as Pragmatist

Nothing that I have said so far *proves* that most American judges, being
Americans, are pragmatists, although I have thrown out some hints and
will give some evidence in subsequent chapters. Actually I don't think *most*
judges are pragmatists, if one just counts noses. It is the most influential

47. See Posner, *The Problems of Jurisprudence*, note 9 above at 167–179; W. V. Quine,
"Things and Their Place in Theories," in Quine, *Theories and Things* 1, 11 (1981).

judges who are pragmatists. To be an influential judge is to change the law or to make new law where there was none before, and legal formalism has no resources for bringing about change or for innovation. As method rather than merely as rhetoric, formalism is about applying and defending existing principles.

I have mentioned several American judges generally acknowledged to be outstanding (influential in a good sense—no one will deny that William Brennan was an influential judge, but there is disagreement about whether his influence was a healthy one) who were pragmatists. Others could be mentioned, such as Charles Evans Hughes and Henry Friendly. And this is to speak only of the dead. I do not attempt a study of pragmatic judges in this book.[48] But I do want to elaborate on the pragmatism of John Marshall, a somewhat neglected theme in the voluminous literature about him. I will use him to bolster my claim that influential judges tend to be pragmatic judges.

Marshall was innocent of philosophy, and of course pragmatic philosophy had not yet been invented. Indeed, although he was pretty well read and was the author of a massive biography of George Washington, he was not really an intellectual—he was not *widely* read and did not have a speculative mind or intellectual interests; the contrast with Jefferson, his bitterest foe, is striking. Before becoming Chief Justice, Marshall was a highly successful trial and appellate lawyer with a knack for cutting through legalisms to the practical considerations favoring his clients' causes. He also had extensive military and political experience. Moderate in his political opinions (a close ally of John Adams, who was considered a traitor by the extreme Federalists, the ones itching for war with revolutionary France), easygoing and likable ("clubbable," the English would have called him), an avid and successful land speculator, politically astute in a turbulent political era in which the role of the Supreme Court and the shape of American constitutional law were as yet undetermined, and above all a clever and resourceful legal practitioner, he didn't bring to the office of Chief Justice a philosophy. He brought a determination to make the federal judiciary an effective check on what he thought the fissiparous and radicalizing tendencies of Jefferson's Democratic-Republican Party. He pursued this aim with extreme shrewdness and without any of the hang-ups that might have been engendered by a commitment to particular political or jurisprudential the-

48. My book on Cardozo, cited in note 44 above, is a case study of a pragmatic judge.

ories. Indeed his antipathy to Jefferson came in part from the fact that "Marshall moved comfortably in the experiential, nontheoretical gradualist world of incremental change. Jefferson was an Enlightenment thinker who believed that philosophic speculation was the key to civic redemption."[49] Jefferson was a philosophical radical, Marshall "a pragmatic conservative."[50] "Theory and philosophy he left to others."[51]

Holmes, with a touch of envy, acknowledged "that there fell to Marshall perhaps the greatest place that ever was filled by a judge."[52] Holmes could not "separate John Marshall from the fortunate circumstance that the appointment of Chief Justice fell to John Adams, instead of to Jefferson a month later, and so gave it to a Federalist and loose constructionist to start the working of the Constitution."[53] In other words, Marshall and we were lucky. For Holmes was unwilling to say that "Marshall's work proved more than a strong intellect, a good style, personal ascendancy in his court, courage, justice and the convictions of his party," so that "if I were to think of John Marshall simply by number and measure in the abstract, I might hesitate in my superlatives."[54] I think that what Holmes, a man of erudition and culture, a man touched by genius—and a man congenitally ungenerous in his assessment of others—was saying—with considerable insight, however—is that Marshall was not a very *interesting* person. He was basically just a very good lawyer with considerable political savvy and experience (and with something else, something he shared with Holmes—rhetorical flair). But that was what America needed in the period of Marshall's chief justiceship, 1801 to 1835. To a great extent, subject to the needs of judicial diversity discussed in the next chapter, it is what we need today, although the meaning of "very good lawyer" may be changing as society becomes increasingly complex. It remains a good job description of the pragmatic judge.

A stronger criticism of Marshall, and implicitly of legal pragmatism, may be found in David Currie's magisterial survey *The Constitution in the Supreme Court.* Currie declares Marshall markedly deficient in the qualities

49. R. Kent Newmyer, *John Marshall and the Heroic Age of the Supreme Court* 149 (2001). This, Marshall's latest biography, contains much evidence of the pragmatic character of Marshall's judicial performance and general outlook.

50. Id. at 393.

51. Id. at 55.

52. Oliver Wendell Holmes, "John Marshall," in *The Essential Holmes*, note 3 above, at 206, 208.

53. Id. at 207.

54. Id. at 208, 207.

of a good judge, even of a good law student. Of Marshall's most important opinion, *Marbury v. Madison*,[55] which established the authority of the Supreme Court to invalidate acts of Congress, Currie writes that it exhibits

> great rhetorical power, invocation of the constitutional text less as the basis of decision than as a peg on which to hang a result evidently reached on other grounds, a marked disdain for reliance on precedent, extensive borrowing of the ideas of others without attribution, an inclination to reach out for constitutional issues that did not have to be decided, a tendency to resolve difficult questions by aggressive assertion of one side of the case, and an absolute certainty in the correctness of his conclusions.[56]

"*Marbury* illustrates," Currie continues, Marshall's "tendency to conclude that the Constitution means what he would like it to mean."[57] Currie grants, though, that the decision showed Marshall to be a "master tactician."[58] And summarizing the constitutional decisions rendered by the Supreme Court under Marshall's leadership, he acknowledges that Marshall "impressed thirty-four years of constitutional decision with his own personality as no one else has ever come close to doing."[59] We can hear an echo of Cardozo's famous (and accurate) summary of Marshall's achievement: "He gave to the constitution of the United States the impress of his own mind, and the form of our constitutional law is what it is, because he moulded it while it was still plastic and malleable in the fire of his own intense convictions."[60]

In fact, continues Currie, "this utter domination [of the constitutional decisionmaking process] is perhaps the greatest tribute to the force of John Marshall."[61] Greatest because the opinions themselves are, Currie believes, no great shakes. *Marbury* is all too typical. Marshall's

---

55. 5 U.S. (1 Cranch) 137 (1803).

56. David P. Currie, *The Constitution in the Supreme Court: The First Hundred Years: 1789–1888*, at 74 (1985).

57. Id. at 90.

58. Id. at 74.

59. Id. at 196. Michael J. Klarman, "How Great Were the 'Great' Marshall Court Decisions?" 87 *Virginia Law Review* 1111 (2001), though skeptical about the actual influence of Marshall's famous decisions, acknowledges that his "brilliant political gamesmanship" contributed significantly to the Supreme Court's stature and hence power. Id. at 1158.

60. Benjamin N. Cardozo, *The Nature of the Judicial Process* 169–170 (1921).

61. Currie, note 56 above, at 196.

disdain for precedent in general was extraordinary . . . He seldom missed the opportunity to rest a decision on two or three grounds when one would have sufficed . . . Sometimes Marshall was highly literal in his reliance on the constitutional text . . . ; at other times, . . . he reduced the applicable text to an afterthought . . . ; time and again he seems to have been writing a brief for a conclusion reached independently of the Constitution . . . In short, though Marshall has been generally admired, it is difficult to find a single Marshall opinion that puts together the relevant legal arguments in a convincing way.[62]

Currie's critique of Marshall raises a number of questions: How could Marshall have been such a successful Chief Justice if he failed to write a single first-rate judicial opinion and was not intellectually outstanding, though intelligent (the "strong intellect" that Holmes spoke of)? Might it not be that the conventional criteria of legal excellence, to the extent that Marshall failed to satisfy them, are unsound? If Marshall was a bad judge, doesn't this imply that we need more bad judges? Do some law professors perhaps have a crabbed view of what it takes to be a great judge and what makes a judicial opinion first-rate?[63] And should greatness be assessed sub specie aeternitatis, as the truth of scientific propositions might be assessed, or instead with reference to a person's historical circumstances?

Before becoming Chief Justice in his mid-forties, Marshall had more than two decades of successful law practice behind him. It is a characteristic of good lawyers, especially good litigators, like Marshall, that they are result-oriented. The desired result is given them by the client and they use all the rhetorical and tactical tricks of the lawyer's trade to achieve that result. Litigators are sophists, as Plato tells us in *Gorgias*. Marshall had the "*wily* intellect of a superb lawyer,"[64] to the later disdain of Holmes and exasperation of Currie. He wanted the Supreme Court to be a fully coequal branch of the federal government and he wanted the Constitution to be interpreted as having ordained a powerful national government that would promote commercial values and check democratic excess. He pursued those goals unremittingly and at times disingenuously and even, it may seem to a modern reader, unscrupulously. A number of the cases that were

---

62. Id. at 196–197.

63. Currie says that he is analyzing the cases "from a lawyer's standpoint," employing the "methodology" of "the rule of law." Id. at xi, xiii.

64. Newmyer, note 49 above, at 81 (emphasis added).

his vehicles for achieving his goals were feigned or collusive and so should have been dismissed out of hand; many could have been decided on narrower grounds; he treated the text of the Constitution as putty for judges to knead into constitutional law; he sat in cases in which members of his family had a direct and he often an indirect financial interest; he spent a lot of time cajoling other Justices in order to maintain an appearance, at times an illusion, of unanimity; he engaged in all sorts of tactical feints and thrusts that disguised his true intentions; he was an unabashed promoter of property and contract rights and an uncompromising foe of populist state legislatures; and he even did what he could to improve the electoral prospects of Federalists by careful timing of decisions in relation to election day.

Professor Newmyer, Marshall's most recent biographer, loves Marshall but even he is struck by "how much interpretive latitude [Marshall] carved out for himself,"[65] by his "habit of glossing over complex factual problems,"[66] and by his insistence that "doctrinal purity was not as important as practical result."[67] Marshall's attitude toward constitutional law was goal-oriented, manipulative, ideological, and at times politically partisan; it was not craftsmanlike, logically rigorous, or self-restrained.

Some people even today think the Supreme Court took a wrong turn in Marshall's day, that he made the Court too powerful in relation to the other, more democratic branches of the federal government, that he made the federal government too powerful in relation to the states, and that he succeeded too well "in identifying the Court with the Constitution."[68] Yet the danger that the new nation might dissolve back into the loose confederation established by the Articles of Confederation, or even into independent nations, was substantial in the first quarter of the nineteenth century and Marshall's Court did much to check these tendencies. For this most of us are profoundly grateful. Had it not been for Marshall's aggressiveness as Chief Justice, the United States might not be a nation today.

Pragmatists doubt that Marshall could have achieved this momentous success by being a "good judge" in Currie's sense—scrupulous about the facts, respectful of precedent, insistent on deciding a case on the narrowest

65. Id. at 244. This is the loose constructionism of which Holmes wrote in his essay on Marshall.

66. Id. at 312.

67. Id. at 315.

68. Id.

possible grounds. Those are, at best, precepts to guide judges in a mature legal system. The creator of the system must be a buccaneer, like other in-novators. Rather than crossing on a sturdy bridge from the existing law to the new case, he brings about a "paradigm shift" that enables his succes-sors to practice "normal science." That is a pretty fair description of the relation between Marshall and his avatars. It is the reason that the most in-fluential judges, like Marshall, have tended to be pragmatists. True formal-ists are incapable of innovation. Either they are committed to applying ex-isting law rather than creating new law, or, if they think that logic and the other tools of the formalist can actually create new law, they are fooling themselves.

Robert Lipkin makes a similar point in a recent book that I had not seen when I wrote this chapter. He notes the criticisms that legal scholars have made of *Marbury v. Madison* and concludes correctly "that there was no compelling basis for Marshall's decision. Instead, Marshall assumed the power of judicial review."[69] "Essentially, Marshall created judicial review as a pragmatic response to the inevitable crisis over the role of the judiciary in the constitutional scheme. Judicial review is conducive to creating a na-tional republic, and *that* is what Marshall sought."[70]

With (like me) a bow to Thomas Kuhn, Lipkin divides constitutional cases into revolutionary and normal.[71] The latter are the cases that are de-cided more or less formalistically. The former cannot be. Legal formal-ism is standpattism. Had formalists dominated the Supreme Court in the 1950s, *Brown v. Board of Education* would have been decided in favor of continuing to allow "separate but equal" public school education.[72] The Court would have noted the vagueness of the equal protection clause of the Fourteenth Amendment and the uncertainty as to whether it was in-tended to grant blacks more than political equality with whites, would have cited *Plessy v. Ferguson* as precedent for rejecting challenges to "sepa-rate but equal," would have explained that the South had built its institu-tions in reliance on that decision, would have derided the inconclusive social-scientific evidence presented by the plaintiffs to show the damaging effects of segregated education on black schoolchildren, and would have

69. Robert Justin Lipkin, *Constitutional Revolutions: Pragmatism and the Role of Judicial Re-view in American Constitutionalism* 164 (2000).

70. Id. at 168 (footnotes omitted).

71. See also Jack M. Balkin and Sanford Levinson, "Understanding the Constitutional Revolution," 87 *Virginia Law Review* 1045, 1092 (2001).

72. See Lipkin, note 69 above, at 135–142.

refused, as beyond its competence, to recognize the place of public school segregation in a mosaic of public institutions designed to keep black people in a subordinate, stigmatized social status. (That recognition was undoubtedly the motive for the *Brown* decision, though out of *politesse* it was not acknowledged.) The bulk of the legal academy would have applauded such a decision.

Pragmatists, whose orientation is historicist rather than timeless, will reject Currie's implicit view that the qualities of a good judge are historically constant. It was the extraordinary fit between Marshall's suite of qualities and the volatile historical setting in which he worked that mainly explains his success and his greatness. One of these qualities was his rhetorical skill (remarked by Currie only in passing), of which "the power to tax involves the power to destroy" is only one illustration. Rhetorical assertion is to judicial innovation what paradigm-shifting insight is to revolutionary science: the recognition of discontinuity, the announcement of a new beginning. Here is another example, this one from *Marbury:*

> It is emphatically the province and duty of the judicial department to say what the law is. Those who apply the rule to particular cases must of necessity expound and interpret that rule. If two laws conflict with each other, the courts must decide on the operation of each. So if a law be in opposition to the constitution, if both the law and the constitution apply to a particular case so that the court must either decide that case conformably to the law disregarding the constitution or conformably to the constitution disregarding the law, the court must determine which of these conflicting rules governs the case. This is of the very essence of judicial duty. If then the courts are to regard the constitution, and the constitution is superior to any ordinary act of the legislature, the constitution and not such ordinary act must govern the case to which they both apply. Those then who controvert the principle that the constitution is to be considered in court as a paramount law are reduced to the necessity of maintaining that courts must close their eyes on the constitution and see only the law.[73]

The paramountcy of the courts in the interpretation of the Constitution was not an established principle when Marshall wrote. It was arguable, and

---

73. 5 U.S. (1 Cranch) at 177–178. I have modernized the punctuation.

argued, that each branch of the national government had the ultimate power to determine the constitutionality of its actions. That would not have required the courts to "close their eyes on the constitution and see only the law," since they would still have had power to invalidate state laws and other state actions. In any event the statement that the courts would (if they had to defer to congressional or presidential interpretations of the constitutionality of congressional or presidential action) be "clos[ing] their eyes on the constitution and see[ing] only the law" is not a reason but a conclusion. Marshall does go on, after the passage I quoted, to give reasons why the Constitution implicitly authorizes the courts to invalidate acts of Congress. They are good reasons, not makeweights. But it was the emphatic character of the opening sentence that I quoted, and the endeavor to make it seem unnatural for the courts to "see only the law," that carried the real punch.

Finally, here are the ringing words in which Marshall announced the policy of loose construction of the Constitution, one of his greatest and most enduring legacies: "In considering this question [whether Congress had the power to create the Bank of the United States as a measure 'necessary and proper' to the carrying out of Congress's express legislative powers], then, we must never forget that it is a *constitution* we are expounding."[74] Pure assertion, but an assertion that in the manner of great rhetoric carried its own warrant of authority, if not of "truth." The test of a great judicial opinion is not its conformity to the tenets of legal formalism. It is how good a fit it makes with its social context. Often that fit is cemented by a rhetorical flourish.

The Objections to Legal Pragmatism Recapitulated

A recapitulation of the major objections to legal pragmatism may help the reader follow the arguments of the subsequent chapters.

The basic objection is that while pragmatism undoubtedly explains much of the form and content of legislation and of governmental action generally, pragmatic adjudication is formless; the principles that I have outlined place some bounds on it but they leave a very large, as it were blank, space in which the judge is at large. Pragmatism, it is argued, counsels and ratifies lawlessness, accepting and embracing the inevitability that

74. McCulloch v. Maryland, note 43 above, 17 U.S. (4 Wheat.) at 407 (emphasis in original). I have again modernized Marshall's punctuation.

like cases will not be treated alike, since different judges weigh consequences differently, depending on each judge's background, temperament, training, experience, and ideology.

Legal pragmatism provides no dike against either revolutionary or reactionary changes in law. Pragmatic judges who decide to embrace a new ideology will override precedent, "plain meaning," settled doctrine, and other formalist obstacles to legal change, just as German judges did in the Hitler era.

A related point is that pragmatism has no soul; it has no roots in concepts of justice or natural law; it has nothing to set against public opinion.

Legal pragmatism, it is feared, breeds cynicism about law, which in turn induces intellectual laziness in students, law professors, lawyers, and, most ominously, judges. The legal pragmatist may be unwilling to invest significant time and effort in learning the rules of law and the methods of legal reasoning. He may regard these things as obstacles to getting to the point, the point being a weighing of consequences or some other method of practical rather than professional reasoning.

All these points have some merit—indeed, enough merit to establish, to my satisfaction anyway, that legal pragmatism is not always and everywhere the best approach to law. Whether one says that in some circumstances formalism is the best pragmatic strategy, or, cutting out the middleman as it were, says simply that in some circumstances formalism is a better approach to law than pragmatism is, the important point is that a pragmatic mindset is not always the best thing for the legal profession to cultivate.

But in twenty-first-century America there is no alternative to legal pragmatism. The nation contains such a diversity of moral and political thinking that the judiciary, if it is to retain its effectiveness, its legitimacy, *has* to be heterogeneous; and the members of a heterogeneous judicial community are not going to subscribe to a common set of moral and political dogmas that would make their decisionmaking determinate. Our judicially enforceable Constitution, our common law heritage, and our undisciplined legislatures compound with the heterogeneity of the judges to create an immense irreducible domain of discretionary lawmaking; and formalism has no resources to guide the exercise of judicial discretion, the making of new law as distinct from the ascertainment of the old. The formalist attributes encompassed by the concept of the rule of law have great social value, but in present circumstances only as elements of an overall approach to law that is pragmatic.

Moreover, pragmatism does *not* leave judges at large. The pragmatic judge is less constrained by doctrine, by theory, than the formalist judge thinks himself to be. But the material, psychological, and institutional constraints on pragmatic as on other judges are considerable and limit the discretion even of the perfectly self-aware pragmatic judge.

The pragmatic judge is, moreover, constrained to an extent by legal doctrine, though the constraint is indirect. Doctrine creates expectations in the people subject to law, and the social value of protecting those expectations, in facilitating commerce for example, is something a pragmatic judge must take into account in deciding when and whether and how much to depart from existing principles. European judges are more formalistic than American judges are; but they too are so because of material and institutional constraints, not because they are inherently more docile or more rationalistic than Americans. The European legal systems, and their systems of government more broadly, have been constructed along lines designed to limit judicial discretion. Of particular importance is the bureaucratic organization of European judiciaries. The judiciary is a career. You start at the bottom and get assigned and promoted at the pleasure of your superiors. Such a career attracts the type of person who is comfortable in a bureaucracy, and it breeds habits of obedience to directives and to authoritative texts; bureaucratic administration is government by written rules. Europe doesn't have the common law and until recently did not have judicial review of the constitutionality of statutes. European governments tend, moreover, to be highly centralized. Separation of powers is limited. Government is by parliaments that are both functionally unicameral and, relative to American legislatures at least, highly disciplined and professionalized. More European law is codified, and the codes generally are clearer and more detailed than ours. The typical European legal system is simpler and more streamlined than ours, enabling administration by rule-following bureaucratic judges who are less independent than American judges. Most European courts are specialized (labor courts, criminal courts, etc.), and specialists tend to share the premises of analysis and decision, enabling them to derive conclusions by logical processes.

If we had structures and institutions similar to Europe's, we too would have a formalist judiciary. Because we don't have such institutions, for us formalism just is not in the cards. And yet there is evidence (noted in Chapter 7) that our courts, despite or maybe even because of their pragmatic character, protect property rights, a cornerstone of freedom and prosperity, better than European courts do. One reason is that career judges, having less worldly experience than our lateral-entry judges, are less comfortable with commercial and other economic issues. The career structure of the European judiciaries is fundamental to the formalist cast of their adjudication. It may be a good thing that we do not have that structure and so do not have a formalist judiciary, but a pragmatic one.

Might it not be even better, though, for our judges to be closet pragmatists, indeed unconscious pragmatists? Might it not be better in two respects—reassuring the public that judges are really doing law as the public understands law, that is, applying preexisting norms in an "objective" fashion; and keeping the judges from becoming drunk with a sense of power? Maybe so, but there are offsets. Against the first point must be weighed, first, the desirability in a democracy of making government transparent to the people and, second, the fact that people have a more realistic understanding of the judiciary than the point assumes. They care passionately about results and so through their representatives blocked Robert Bork from appointment to the Supreme Court even though he was a foremost advocate of judicial formalism. As for whether judges who wake up to their pragmatic nature are likely to become intoxicated with a sense of their power, people usually do better if they know what they're doing than if they're in a trance. Judges are less rather than more likely to be power-mad if they know they are exercising discretion than if they think they're just a transmission belt for decisions made elsewhere. If the judge who issued a death sentence had to pull the switch or inject the poison, there would be (for better or worse) fewer death sentences.

John Dewey on
Democracy and Law

❧

Of the leading pragmatic philosophers, John Dewey did the most to try to apply philosophy to law and other domains of public policy. This was consistent with his view that philosophers should play an active, constructive role in society rather than a merely academic one. Richard Rorty, Dewey's most prominent contemporary avatar, has also written extensively about policy issues, including some legal ones. But Rorty's discussion of those issues owes little to his philosophy—or at least is not closely integrated with it. As we know, he rejects much that passes for philosophy, including the sorts of moral and political philosophy that might be thought to inform commentary on public issues. In contrast, Dewey's discussion of policy, and especially of law, owes much to his philosophy—or at least appears to.

We must not exaggerate either Dewey's significance for law or the unity of his thought. We have seen that legal pragmatism stands free of philosophical pragmatism; Holmes, the most influential expositor of legal pragmatism, preceded Dewey; and while Dewey is heavily cited by academic lawyers,[1] it is less for his specific statements about law than for his general

---

1. He has been cited in more than 600 articles published in law reviews in the Lexis database in the last decade.

philosophical stance[2]—pragmatism or, his preferred term, "experimental-ism"—and for his views on democracy and education.[3]

As for the unity of his thought, most of his commentaries on public affairs have no organic relation to his philosophy. Consider his support for making war illegal,[4] his criticism of the New Deal as too timid and his advocacy of public control of the economy, and his isolationism before Pearl Harbor. In retrospect most of us think poorly of people who thought we could just sit out World War II; and many New Deal programs are now believed to have been excessively rather than insufficiently *dirigiste*, especially those based on a belief—fostered, naturally, by businessmen—that the Depression had been caused by excessive competition. We think that Roosevelt had a better grasp of the nation's problems both domestically and internationally than Dewey did.[5] And whether right or wrong, most of Dewey's commentaries on public affairs are hopelessly dated.

But the important point is that these commentaries are to one side of his philosophy; they belong rather to his career as a public intellectual.[6] As so often with academics, that career was a mixed bag, though on the plus side must be reckoned Dewey's steadfast anti-communism after the briefest of flirtations with the Soviet Union following a visit there in 1928. He has been praised as a model public intellectual—"one of the last of what seems to be a dying breed," "represent[ing] what social philosophy can hope to

2. On which see the excellent anthology *The Philosophy of John Dewey* (John J. McDermott ed. 1981).

3. For a notable example of heavy citation of Dewey by a law professor, see Cass R. Sunstein, *Democracy and the Problem of Free Speech* (1993), described as "remarkably Deweyite" in J. M. Balkin, "Book Review: Populism and Progressivism as Constitutional Categories," 104 *Yale Law Journal* 1935, 1957 (1995). Articles in recent years devoted to Dewey's legal thought have been rare. For an example, see Walter J. Kendall III, "Law, China and John Dewey," 46 *Syracuse Law Review* 103 (1995).

4. John Dewey, "Apostles of World Unity: XVII—Salmon O. Levinson," in John Dewey, *The Later Works, 1925–1953*, vol. 5: *1929–1930*, at 349 (Jo Ann Boydston ed. 1984).

5. Dewey strongly opposed the election of Franklin Delano Roosevelt in 1932. See "Prospects for a Third Party," in id., vol. 6: *1931–1932*, at 246; "After the Election—What?" in id. at 253. He stated during the campaign, "Governor Roosevelt holds the same position as predatory wealth . . . Governor Roosevelt is speaking for the class he trains with." "Roosevelt Scored on Relief Policy," in id. at 395. Dewey supported the socialist candidate for President, Norman Thomas.

6. Well illustrated by the *New Republic* essays collected in John Dewey, *Individualism, Old and New* (1930). But those essays are merely illustrative. The thirty-seven volumes of Dewey's complete works, edited by Boydston, note 4 above, contain a staggering number of usually very brief essays on current events and controversies. For a comprehensive and sympathetic but not uncritical examination of Dewey's career, emphasizing his public-intellectual work, see Alan Ryan, *John Dewey and the High Tide of American Liberalism* (1995). That work is also described in considerable detail in William R. Caspary, *Dewey on Democracy* (2000).

become," his "sustained philosophical engagement with the social and political issues of his day stand[ing] as an attractive beacon."[7] But he can
equally well be viewed as a cautionary example, one of many (Russell,
Heidegger, and Sartre come immediately to mind),[8] of the dangers of trying to lever philosophy into commentary on current affairs. Philosophy is
not the master key to knowledge. Dewey wrote on too many subjects remote from his discipline; his reach exceeded his grasp.[9] And he was handi-
capped in addressing concrete issues of policy by lacking either a consistent or a realistic understanding of human motivation. He was too much
the preacher.[10]

Deweyan Democracy: From Epistemic to Deliberative

The master concept that unites Dewey's philosophy with the policy realm
is that of "democracy." "Democracy" is a word of many meanings, as
we know, but two are especially pertinent to Dewey's take on law and policy. They are *epistemic* democracy, the idea that the best forms of inquiry
and of decisionmaking in general, not just political inquiry and decisionmaking, are democratic in character;[11] and *political* democracy, a system of
political governance the defining feature of which in modern times is that
all legislators, as well as the head of the executive branch of the govern-

7. Debra Morris and Ian Shapiro, "Editors' Introduction," in John Dewey, *The Political Writings* ix, xi (1993)

8. See, for example, Mark Lilla, *The Reckless Mind: Intellectuals in Politics* (2001); Richard A. Posner, *Public Intellectuals: A Study of Decline*, chs. 8, 9 (2001).

9. See, for example, his essay on agricultural policy during the Depression, "What Keeps Funds Away from Purchasers," in John Dewey, *The Later Works, 1925–1953*, vol. 5: *1929–1930*, at 81 (Jo Ann Boydston ed. 1986). For a similar criticism of the public-intellectual forays of Richard Rorty, see Bruck Kuklick, *A History of Philosophy in America, 1720–2000*, at 280–281 (2001).

10. "He was always happy to use a religious idiom in talking about politics and social re-
form." Ryan, note 6 above, at 20. Of Dewey's book *Reconstruction in Philosophy*, Ryan says: "It is all rather reminiscent of a certain preaching style in which the preacher, not wishing to prescribe too minutely for his flock, reminds them to bear in mind the distinction between the sheep and the goats and sends them out of church with no more than the thought that one becomes a sheep or a goat action by action and instance by instance." Id. at 232.

11. This vein in Dewey's philosophy has been explored extensively by Hilary Putnam. See, for example, Putnam, "A Reconsideration of Deweyan Democracy," 63 *Southern California Law Review* 1671 (1990). See also Caspary, note 6 above; Robert B. Westbrook, "Pragmatism and Democracy: Reconstructing the Logic of John Dewey's Faith," in *The Revival of Pragmatism: New Essays on Social Thought, Law, and Culture* 128 (Morris Dickstein ed. 1996). On Dewey's views of political democracy, see, for example, James Campbell, *Understanding John Dewey: Nature and Cooperative Intelligence* 177–184, 200–223 (1995).

ment (even if he is not a legislator, as he will normally be in a parliamentary democracy), are popularly elected for limited terms. Dewey's attempt
to join these two conceptions is one of the distinctive features of his version of pragmatism. But I do not mean by attaching the label "democracy"
to both to suggest that he succeeded.

Epistemic democracy challenges the tenacious and, when Dewey wrote,
the orthodox conception of scientific and other inquiry as essentially an individual search for truth using logic either to reveal truth directly, as in
mathematics and some versions of moral reasoning, or, in the case of the
natural and some of the social sciences, to derive, from precise and formal
theories, hypotheses verifiable or refutable by experimental or other exact
data. In the case of moral or political reasoning, hypotheses were to be
tested if at all by intuition, but the emphasis was not on hypothesis testing
at all; instead it was on deduction from accepted premises, just as in mathematical reasoning. The search in any case was for the antecedently real—
that which exists independently of human cognition. The universe, including mathematical and even moral and political entities or concepts, was regarded as a passive object waiting to be discovered by human beings using
the methods of exact reasoning. The quest for its secrets was seen as both
lofty and lonely, conducted by trained experts, or by persons of great insight, operating as individuals or in small teams.

Dewey, following in the footsteps of Peirce and James, questioned the
emphasis the approach placed both on truth and on the individual. Scientific and other inquiry, he argued, is actually oriented toward the *cooperative* acquisition of *useful* knowledge by whatever tools lie to hand, including imagination, common sense, know-how, and intuition. Knowledge
thus includes tacit ("how to") knowledge as well as the articulate knowledge acquired by formal reasoning and systematic empirical methods.
Dewey deemphasized the pursuit of truth not only by emphasizing the
nontheoretical side of knowledge but also by rejecting the possibility of
completely objective inquiry; there is no way of knowing when one has
found the truth because one cannot step outside the universe and observe
the correspondence between it and one's descriptions. All that people are
capable of and, fortunately, all that they are really interested in is getting
better control over their environment, enlarging their horizons, and en-
riching and improving their lives. The knowledge required for these endeavors is collective. It is acquired by the cooperative efforts of diverse inquirers—intelligence being distributed throughout the community rather

than concentrated in a handful of experts—and validated by the community's judgment of its utility. As a practical matter, truth is consensus.

Dewey's skepticism about the truth claims of conventional epistemology is more precisely described as "fallibilism." Fallibilists reject the idea that the repeatedly demonstrated ability of scientists to produce useful knowledge is due to a specific methodology (the "scientific method") that if followed rigorously leads to ultimate truth. Rather it is due to the ethics of scientific inquiry, with its insistence on willingness to test belief against evidence and thus to accept—what people not schooled in the scientific ethic find so difficult to do—the possibility that many of one's beliefs are false. A scientist may discover by the end of his career that his entire life's work has been superseded. Its significance was in keeping the game going rather than in winning it. It is never won.

The choice of subjects to study (for example, rocks rather than souls) is of course another factor in the success of science. But the choice is itself guided by the ethics of scientific inquiry, which requires that hypotheses be testable because if they are not testable they cannot be falsified and what cannot be falsified cannot be confirmed either.

The pragmatic philosophers also criticized the conventional philosophy of science for overlooking the importance of doubt as the essential stimulus of challenges to existing beliefs (a point emphasized by Peirce), of habit as reluctance to give up existing beliefs and therefore as an obstacle to progress (a Deweyan emphasis), and of diversity and competition as conditions that favor, as in Darwin's theory of natural selection, the creation of new theories by an unplanned process akin to trial and error. Dewey's theory of science, and of inquiry more broadly, is thus Darwinian. Darwinian also was his belief that reasoning is a method of coping with the environment rather than of establishing a pipeline to truth. We are just clever animals and, as in the case of the other animals, our brains are designed for controlling our environment rather than for producing metaphysical insights.

The value of diversity in inquiry is connected to the incapacity of the scientific method to generate the theories that it tests and explores. Scientific methodology provides no guidance at the most fundamental level of science; methodology is for testing theories, not for creating them. Peirce called the process of theory creation "abduction" to emphasize that it was neither deduction nor induction. Abduction belongs to the domain of the imagination rather than to that of formulaic procedures. Because there is

no algorithm for creating new theories, a diversity of approaches is necessary if there is to be a good chance of hitting on one that works. Progress is
a social rather than an individual undertaking and achievement because
people see things differently. Think of the contributions of female primatologists to a field formerly dominated by men. Male primatologists un-
consciously modeled nonhuman primate family structures on those of human beings. This led them to underestimate the number and social role of
female primates, to misunderstand the sexual and parental behavior of
those females, and to ignore the matriarchal structure of the family life of
the bonobo, a close cousin of the chimpanzee.[12]

Although this is not a Deweyan example, its egalitarian implications
would have appealed to him, and they suggest a third, a social rather than
an epistemological or political, concept of democracy. This is the democratic temperament emphasized by Tocqueville and by advocates of transformative democracy. Egalitarianism is not a necessary implication of
epistemic democracy, however. Hayek's influential idea that socially valuable knowledge is widely distributed throughout the community in tiny
packets rather than concentrated in a handful of experts (see Chapter 7)
resembles Dewey's notion of distributed intelligence. Yet he and Hayek
drew opposite implications for policy. Hayek argued that markets were the
most efficient method of pooling individuals' knowledge; because prices
encapsulate all the relevant knowledge of the demanders and suppliers
of the goods and services that make up the economy, government
should keep its hands off markets. Though Dewey distrusted experts for
epistemic reasons similar to Hayek's,[13] he believed in central planning,
Hayek's bête noire.

Remember that Dewey's preferred term for his epistemic approach,
what I am here calling "distributed intelligence" (as in "distributed processing" of data by computers),[14] was not pragmatism but "experimental-

12. See, for example, Carol Jahme, *Beauty and the Beasts: Woman, Ape and Evolution* (2000);
Londa Schiebinger, *Has Feminism Changed Science?* 126–136 (1999); Linda Marie Fedigan,
"The Paradox of Feminist Primatology: The Goddess's Discipline?" in *Feminism in Twentieth-Century Science, Technology, and Medicine* 46 (Angela N. H. Creager, Elizabeth A. Lunbeck,
and Londa Schiebinger eds. 2001).

13. Dewey's argument for political democracy "is epistemological rather than economic:
the principal threat of oligarchy is conceived not so much in terms of the innate acquisitive-
ness of the governing classes' motivations as in the distortion imposed by their position as an
elite on their capacity to discern the public's needs and interests." Matthew Festenstein, *Pragmatism and Political Theory: From Dewey to Rorty* 97 (1997).

14. "True distributed processing has separate computers perform different tasks in such a

ism." The word aptly conveys the tenor of his thought. He was constantly commending the temper that, impatient with convention and the accustomed ways of doing things—the sediment of habit—insists on trying now this, now that, in a creatively restless search for better means. The search yields, as a byproduct, better ends as well. One might take up ballet to improve one's posture and discover that one loved the ballet for its beauty; a means would have become an end. (Such examples refute the charge that pragmatism is philistine.)

Dewey's epistemic approach is "democratic" in the loose sense of emphasizing the community (the many) over the handful of exceptional individuals (the few). Knowledge is not produced mechanically by the repeated application of algorithmic procedures by expert investigators all trained the same way. It is produced by the tug of communal demands, the struggle between doubt and habit, the strivings of individuals of diverse background, aptitude, training, and experience, and the application of methods of inquiry, such as imagination and intuition, that owe little to expert training. No elite has a monopoly of truth. In fact, truth is always just out of reach, is at most a regulatory, an orienting, ideal. If this is the case with scientific truth, it is all the more likely to be the case with moral and political truths as well. To Dewey, the proposal in Plato's *Republic* of rule by an elite of individuals who are to have "a comprehensive rational understanding of eternal reality and truth, to be nurtured by a rigorous and extended higher education in all the mathematical sciences from arithmetic to astronomy,"[15] was quixotic. "For Plato and Aristotle," says one critic of contemporary pragmatism, "philosophy begins in wonder and ends in the rapt, silent, yet active contemplation of truths—regardless of whether they pay."[16] To which the Deweyan responds: "What truths?"

Conceiving of science as a branch of practical reason, that is, as oriented toward helping us cope rather than toward revealing the external world as it really is, Dewey was led to argue that scientific reasoning is not fundamentally different from the reasoning used to solve such "practical" problems as how to govern a society or organize its economy. Science is better than our more common modes of inquiry only because scientists have an

---

way that their combined work can contribute to a larger goal." Microsoft Press, *Computer Dictionary* 154 (3d ed. 1997).

15. Malcolm Schofield, "Approaching the *Republic*," in *The Cambridge History of Greek and Roman Political Thought* 190, 224 (Christopher Rowe and Malcolm Schofield eds. 2000).

16. David Luban, *Legal Modernism* 126 (1994).

attitude toward inquiry—one emphasizing open-mindedness, intellectual flexibility, a practical orientation, and a readiness to be disproved—that is more likely to achieve useful solutions than the slapdash approximations to scientific inquiry that politicians and other "men of affairs" use. If the scientific approach thus is not fundamentally different from the epistemic procedures used by the ordinary person, maybe the general public can someday learn to approach moral and political issues in a scientific spirit.[17] Then political democracy would be unproblematic. But even short of that day, epistemic democracy has implications for political governance. If rule by experts is out, out with it go theocratic or "scientific" (for example, Marxist) justifications for authoritarian rule, any basis for the censorship of moral and political ideas on the ground that they are false, and any legitimating ground for a fixed and durable political hierarchy. Dewey's philosophical project of overturning Platonic epistemology provides support for making democracy the default rule of political governance[18] in the same way that Platonic epistemology provides support for the authoritarian political system described in the *Republic*.

In short, Dewey turned Plato on his head by accepting the linkage between knowledge and politics but arguing that knowledge is democratic[19] and so should politics be:

Democracy for Dewey is a good form of political organisation because it is the appropriate political modelling of a more general form of human interaction which has both epistemological and valuative

17. See Eric A. MacGilvray, "Experience as Experiment: Some Consequences of Pragmatism for Democratic Theory," 43 *American Journal of Political Science* 542, 551, 562 (1999); Jack Knight and James Johnson, "Inquiry into Democracy: What Might a Pragmatist Make of Rational Choice Theories?" 43 *American Journal of Political Science* 566 (1999). Harvey C. Mansfield and Delba Winthrop, quoting Tocqueville, contrast "democratic eagerness to get practical applications of science to the 'ardent, haughty, and disinterested love of the true' characteristic of a few." Mansfield and Winthrop, "Editors' Introduction," in Alexis de Tocqueville, *Democracy in America* xvii, xxxii (Mansfield and Winthrop trans. 2000). Cf. David Zaret, *Origins of Democratic Culture: Printing, Petitions, and the Public Sphere in Early-Modern England* 272–273 (2000), arguing that the successes of experimental science promoted faith in the power of reason to resolve public issues. The continuity of ordinary and scientific reasoning is a staple of pragmatic thought. See, for example, Wilfrid Sellars, *Empiricism and the Philosophy of Mind* ¶¶ 40–41 (1997 [1956]).

18. See, for example, John Dewey, "Philosophy and Democracy," in Dewey, note 7 above, at 38, 45–46.

19. Dewey "stresses the communicative and collective aspects of science whereas [Karl] Popper displays a more individualist concern with the inventiveness, boldness, and determination of the person who launches the hypothesis into the world." Ryan, note 6 above, at 101.

advantages, and which finds its best realisation in a free scientific community devoted to experimental research. Just as such a research community is trying to invent theories that will allow us to deal with our environment in a satisfactory way, so a good human society would be one that was a kind of experimental community devoted to trying to discover worthwhile and satisfying ways of living.[20]

This is not, however, a compelling argument for political democracy. It is an argument by analogy—a procedure full of pitfalls. At best, the democratic character of knowledge creates merely a rebuttable presumption in favor of political democracy; no reason is given to suppose that the democratic character of knowledge is the only precondition of successful political democracy. As we shall see in the coming chapters, it may not even be a necessary condition.

Hans Kelsen found in the Gospel according to St. John a clue to another way in which pragmatism might be argued to underwrite political democracy. When Pilate asked Jesus Christ "What is truth?" he was responding to Jesus' statement that it was indeed true that he (Jesus) was the King of the Jews. After getting no answer to his rhetorical question Pilate asked the Jews whether they wanted him to free Jesus or the thief, Barabbas, and they chose Barabbas. Kelsen's interpretation is that because Pilate's question evinced skepticism that he had privileged access to truth, he could imagine no better way of answering the question of Jesus' fate than by allowing the answer to be given democratically.[21] Very few pragmatists believe in this kind of "popular justice." Yet, doubting that anyone has a handle on the really big truths, especially those of a moral, religious, or political cast, pragmatists are inclined to throw up their hands and say,

---

20. Raymond Geuss, *History and Illusion in Politics* 124–125 (2001).

21. Hans Kelsen, "On the Essence and Value of Democracy," in *Weimar: A Jurisprudence of Crisis* 84, 109 (Arthur J. Jacobson and Bernhard Schlink eds. 2000). This anecdote also appears in Hans Kelsen, "State-Form and World-Outlook," in Kelsen, *Essays in Legal and Moral Philosophy* 95, 112–113 (Ota Weinberger ed. 1973). It reflects a generally relativistic view of morality and justice well brought out in another essay of Kelsen's in the Weinberger volume: "Absolute justice is an irrational ideal. From the point of view of rational knowledge, there are only human interests, and thus conflicts of interest. To solve them, there are only two methods available: either to satisfy one interest at the expense of the other, or to engineer a compromise between the two. It is not possible to prove that one solution alone, and not the other, is just." Kelsen, "What Is Justice?" in id. at 1, 22. Kelsen's relativism is debated in Jes Bjarup, "Kelsen's Theory of Law and Philosophy of Justice," in *Essays on Kelsen* 273 (Richard Tur and William Twining eds. 1986), and Philip Pettit, "Kelsen on Justice: A Charitable Reading," in id. at 305.

let the people decide such matters because there are no trustworthy experts on them.[22]

Kelsen's argument for democracy is the fruit of the purely negative project of refuting Platonism. But unlike Kelsen and that early anti-Platonist Protagoras,[23] Dewey was not content to defend political democracy on negative grounds. He thought political democracy a good thing and not just the only thing. He was right to doubt that rejecting Plato was a sufficient basis for democratic theory. Rejecting Plato may dish rule by philosophers, but it leaves room for a variety of nondemocratic alternatives, since rule by philosophers and rule by the *demos* are not the only political regimes on offer. Maybe today there is no alternative to democracy for any but the poorest or most disordered nations, but if so there is no need to justify democracy.

Dewey sought a tighter connection between epistemic democracy and political democracy than would be possible just by using the former to upset Plato's case for authoritarian rule. A name for that connection is "deliberative democracy," not Dewey's term but a good description of his approach.[24] Deliberative democracy is political democracy conceived of *not* as a clash of wills and interests, or as an aggregating of preferences (the Benthamite conception of democracy), or as merely a check on the officials, elected and otherwise, who are the real rulers (Schumpeter's conception of democracy).[25] None of these conceptions would be epistemically robust. None of them even has epistemic pretensions—they are about power and interests rather than truth. Deliberative democracy, in contrast, is political democracy conceived of as the pooling of different

22. Of course, some of these issues may be withdrawn from the democratic process by liberal principles (freedom of religion, for example); but that is not inconsistent with pragmatism.

23. See Chapter 1. Protagoras "believes that moral and political questions have no correct answers that can be deduced by means of a specialized intellectual process, such as Socrates' dialectic. To practice medicine or to navigate a ship requires study of the relevant Promethean disciplines; but the truth about moral questions can only be ascertained as a result of an inclusive dialogue. The right answer *just* is the one that seems best to everyone, so everyone must be able to participate in political discourse." Peter Levine, *Living without Philosophy: On Narrative, Rhetoric, and Morality* 96 (1998) (emphasis in original). It would give a better sense of Protagoras's position to put "truth" in quotation marks.

24. See Westbrook, note 11 above, at 138; and references to essays by Hilary Putnam and Joshua Cohen in id. at 139–140. Cf. Cass Sunstein, *Republic.com* 37–39 (2001); Sunstein, "Interest Groups in American Public Law," 38 *Stanford Law Review* 29, 81–86 (1985).

25. I discuss Schumpeter's concept of democracy at length in the next three chapters, but it figures in this one as well as a pretty accurate description of our actual existing democracy and as a better approximation to a pragmatic theory of political democracy than Dewey's own theory.

ideas and approaches and the selection of the best through debate and discussion.[26]

The problem with the suggested linkage between epistemic and political democracy, the problem that gave rise to Dewey's pessimism about our
actual existing democracy, is that deliberative democracy, at least as conceived of by Dewey, is as purely aspirational and unrealistic as rule by Platonic guardians. With half the population having an IQ below 100 (not a
point that Dewey himself, a liberal, a "wet," would have been comfortable
making, however), with the issues confronting modern government highly
complex, with ordinary people having as little interest in complex policy
issues as they have aptitude for them, and with the officials whom the people elect buffeted by interest groups and the pressures of competitive elections, it would be unrealistic to expect good ideas and sensible policies to
emerge from the intellectual disorder that is democratic politics by a process aptly termed deliberative. Part of what lay behind Dewey's interest in
the reform of education was his belief that political democracy would not
work well unless people learned to think about political questions the way
scientists think about scientific ones—disinterestedly, intelligently, empirically. He thought that ordinary people *could* learn to think this way but he
was not optimistic that they would. And since he also thought that until
the public had acquired the scientific ethic democracy would remain an
unsatisfactory, perhaps even a vulnerable, system of government,[27] he was
pessimistic about the future of American democracy.

His concern was with the quality rather than the quantity of education.
So he would not have been reassured by the vast expansion since his time
in the number of college graduates. There is no indication that people
think more scientifically about politics than they did before our era of mass
higher education; yet the tasks of government are more various and more
complicated. But his pessimism was misplaced. He had succumbed to the

26. The concept of deliberative democracy has captivated political scientists and political
theorists, producing an immense literature well illustrated by John S. Dryzek, *Deliberative
Democracy and Beyond: Liberals, Critics, Contestations* (2000); *Deliberative Democracy: Essays on
Reason and Politics* (James Bohman and William Rehg eds. 1997); and Amy Gutmann and
Dennis Thompson, *Democracy and Disagreement* (1996). We shall see in the next chapter
that deliberative democracy comes in a number of different flavors, not just John Dewey's.
See also David M. Estlund, "Who's Afraid of Deliberative Democracy? On the Strategic/De-
liberative Dichotomy in Recent Constitutional Jurisprudence," 71 *Texas Law Review* 1437
(1993).

27. See, for example, John Dewey, *The Public and Its Problems*, ch. 4 and pp. 166–167
(1927); John Dewey, "Science and Free Culture," in Dewey, note 7 above, at 48, 56–57; Margaret Jane Radin, "A Deweyan Perspective on the Economic Theory of Democracy," 11 *Constitutional Commentary* 539, 543–544 (1994–1995).

intellectual's typical mistake of exaggerating the importance of intellect and of associated virtues such as commitment to disinterested inquiry. Some minimum educational level may be required for democracy to be viable in a complex society (though India, with its 50 percent illiteracy rate, is a counterexample). The system does require, after all, that the citizenry make occasional political decisions. But if we may judge from the U.S. experience, the minimum required may be slight enough to be supplied by television rather than by formal education, which anyway seems less inclined to provide it. It is true that people who have more formal education tend to be more involved and interested in politics than other people and more understanding of democratic values, such as tolerance for minority views.[28] But the direction of causation is unclear—it could be that people who are predisposed to take an intelligent interest in politics are also more likely than other people to value education.

Democracy does have decisive advantages, at least for wealthy, secure societies, over alternative forms of government. But they are not advantages that depend on deliberation, on analogies to scientific inquiry, on a lively and informed public interest in public issues, or on civic-mindedness. Democracy's only epistemic advantage is one that Dewey did not emphasize and that is unrelated to deliberation or high-mindedness: it enables public opinion to be reliably determined, which provides indispensable feedback for the policy initiatives of political leaders and other officials. Nondemocratic regimes find it difficult to gauge public opinion and as a result sometimes adopt, as it were inadvertently, policies so radically unpopular as to doom the regime. And we must not overlook the epistemic *dis*advantages of the purest forms of democracy, such as Athenian direct democracy, disadvantages due in part to the intellectual and moral limitations of the citizenry. Those disadvantages are decisive for the shape that modern democracy has assumed—that of *representative* democracy. The classical tradition regarded representative democracy as "aristocratic" in the Aristotelian sense,[29] rule by "the best" *(hoi aristoi)*.[30] The

28. See, for example, Norman H. Nie, Jane Junn, and Kenneth Stehlik-Barry, *Education and Democratic Citizenship in America* (1996); Henry E. Brady, Sidney Verba, and Kay Lehman Schlozman, "Beyond SES: A Resource Model of Political Participation," 89 *American Political Science Review* 271 (1995).

29. See Bernard Manin, *The Principles of Representative Government* (1997); Aristotle, *Politics* (B. Jowett trans.), in *The Complete Works of Aristotle*, vol. 2, pp. 1986, 2064 (Jonathan Barnes ed. 1984) (1300b4–5).

30. This sense of aristocracy is to be distinguished from hereditary aristocracy, which is rule by a privileged class determined by genealogy and (usually) ownership of land, as distinguished from rule by elected representatives of the people at large.

characterization grates but is apt. In representative democracy the people do not rule, though they decide who shall rule. The rulers are officials selected in an electoral competition among contestants who are by no means ordinary men and women but instead belong to an elite of intelligence, cunning, connections, charisma, and other attributes that enable them to present themselves to the public plausibly as "the best." They in turn appoint subordinate officials who are even more remote in values and outlook from the general public.

The resulting division of labor in political governance, with the people only intermittently and remotely engaged and actual governance delegated to specialists in politics and government, is a sensible bow to the claims of expertise and the principle of division of labor. But it is not democratic in Dewey's demanding sense when one considers the role of parties and interest groups, the variety and complexity of the issues that confront modern government, the political apathy and ignorance of the great mass of the people most of the time, and how much of the real power of government resides in unelected officials, many of them judges and civil servants with secure tenure. People's interests, preferences, and opinions influence government, certainly, through the electoral process and otherwise.[31] But not in the way that views expressed in a faculty meeting influence faculty decisions, through debate and pooling of ideas. The role of the people at large in the governance of a large democratic nation is a mere shadow of its role in the concept of deliberative democracy. People know when things are going well or going badly whether for themselves personally or for the nation as a whole (their own welfare is of course bound up with the nation's) and will vote accordingly. But that is about it. The political parties know this and so their campaigns appeal mainly to interests, rather than to the Good, and do so largely in simplistic slogans.

That the United States is a democracy, and that the dominant theme of our political history is the growth of democracy, are shibboleths. It could not be otherwise because politicians outdo each other in flattering the voters by hailing them as the nation's real rulers (government not only of and

31. Cf. George Orwell, "The English People," in *The Collected Essays, Journalism, and Letters of George Orwell*, vol. 3: *As I Please 1943–1945*, at 1, 16–17 (Sonia Orwell and Ian Angus eds. 1968): "If democracy means either popular rule or social equality, it is clear that Britain is not democratic. It is, however, democratic in the secondary sense which has attached itself to that word since the rise of Hitler. To begin with, minorities have some power of making themselves heard. But more than this, public opinion cannot be disregarded when it chooses to express itself. It may have to work in indirect ways, by strikes, demonstrations and letters to the newspapers, but it can and visibly does affect government policy. A British government may be unjust, but it cannot be quite arbitrary."

for but *by* the people). It would be more realistic to return to an older vocabulary and describe the United States as a mixed republic and to recognize that despite the expansion of the suffrage the democratic proportion of the mixture may be smaller today than it was in the early nineteenth century (after the election of Andrew Jackson in 1828) outside the slaveholding region. Much more of the business of government was done then by the states, and state governments are more democratic than the federal government. Terms of office are shorter; judges' tenures are less secure; more nonlegislative officials, including judges in most states, are elected rather than appointed (the only elected federal officials other than the members of Congress are the President and Vice President and even they are elected indirectly, via the Electoral College); state constitutions are easier to amend than the federal constitution; the issues with which state government deals are less incomprehensible to the electorate; there is less delegation of governance to administrative agencies headed and staffed by nonelected officials; and the people influence state government by "exit" as well as by "voice," that is, by the threat to move out of the state as well as by voting. Yet from a pragmatic standpoint it is hard to argue that the shift in power from the states to the federal government has been on balance a bad thing; pragmatism and political democracy are not synonyms.

The real political spillover from a pragmatic theory of knowledge, such as Dewey's theory of epistemic democracy, is, as John Stuart Mill implies in *On Liberty*, not a boost for democracy but a boost for liberty. The first chapter of *On Liberty* explains the dependence of sound government on freedom of inquiry and expression. Liberty is at once a precondition of and a limitation on democracy—a precondition because without liberty the people lack the independence and competence to perform their role in democratic governance, that of controlling the officials. But liberty is not democracy. The right to just compensation for taking private property for public use, the right of free speech, religious freedom, the procedural rights of criminal suspects—all these are rights primarily against popular majorities. They are legally protected rights because of fear that the people would sometimes want to infringe them. There is a related fear that democracy without rights against the democratic majority is unstable— that a temporary majority will entrench itself by intimidating the temporary minority that opposes it. In other words, the people cannot be fully trusted in the bestowal of authority and must be protected against themselves by having their power curtailed.

In *Considerations on Representative Government*, Mill's stress falls on democracy rather than on liberty. Mill was unquestionably a democrat. Indeed, he was one of the founders of deliberative democracy. But his version of deliberative democracy, like Dewey's but more so, was shot through with mistrust. He wanted to constrain the democratic process—by outlawing the secret ballot, giving bonus votes to the ablest voters, and excluding illiterates from the franchise—in order to prevent the people from running amok. The combination of deliberative and liberty constraints yields a truncated form of democracy—not that that is a bad thing. It is a version of what I am calling pragmatic liberalism.

Dewey's Concept of Political Democracy Evaluated

I am skeptical about Dewey's belief that political democracy requires adoption by the public at large of the scientific ethic. In the 1930s, the decade of many of his most emphatic warnings about the shortcomings of American democracy, Dewey had plenty of company in sensing a crisis of democracy—and today popular interest in the political process is even less. Election turnout is lower;[32] education in civics and political history has dwindled; the funding of political campaigns has blossomed into quasi-bribery; and we may be observing a long-term decline in the strength of the democratic principle in American politics because of the growth of the federal government relative to state government. Yet the sky has not fallen.[33] Dewey underestimated the robustness of democracy because he exaggerated the importance of knowledge, interest, impartiality, and intelligence in public matters. Remember what I said about Franklin Roose-

32. Dewey's "time" was so long that careful qualification is necessary. Turnout for a Presidential election peaked at 81.8 percent in 1876. It remained in the 70s for the rest of the century, then began dipping, reaching a low of 48.9 percent in 1924. It rebounded sharply, and did not fall below the 2000 figure (50 percent) until 1996, when it was only 49 percent. The sources for these data are U.S. Department of Commerce, Bureau of the Census, *Historical Statistics of the United States: Colonial Times to 1970*, pt. 2, pp. 1071–1072 (Bicentennial ed. 1975) (ser. Y27) (through 1928); U.S. Department of Commerce, Bureau of the Census, *Statistical Abstract of the United States*, vol. 120, p. 291 (2000) (tab. 479) (1932–1996); Federal Elections Commission Website, http://www.fec.gov/pubrec/fe2000/prespop.htm. See also Ruy A. Teixeira, *The Disappearing American Voter* 8–9 (1992). For the complete statistics, see the chart in Chapter 4.

33. "Nonvoting [low turnout] not only makes little difference to election outcomes, it also makes relatively little difference to policy outcomes as well." Id. at 104. "Between turnout size and government excellence exists zero correlation." Arthur T. Hadley, *The Empty Polling Booth* 114 (1987).

velt, a man far less learned, intelligent, or disinterested than Dewey, a man, indeed, who was intellectually lazy, manipulative, and not a little cynical—yet a man more perceptive about the great issues of the day than Dewey. Which is what Dewey himself should have expected: as a consummate politician, Roosevelt was much better plugged into the distributed intelligence of American society than Professor Dewey.

Utopian thinking, which tends to breed pessimism, is easy, especially for intellectuals, whose minds move easily from the actual to the imaginable. There is an "if only" quality about Dewey. If only *hoi polloi* were like us, and if only the educational system realized that and educated kids accordingly . . . But besides practical constraints on educational reform, and the persisting lack of a good educational theory 2,400 years after Plato first wrote about it, there is the sad fact that Socrates was wrong to think that people are selfish and nasty only because they are ignorant. No one familiar with universities would make Socrates' mistake. Education is a fine thing but it does not improve character.

Like Socrates, Dewey was insufficiently tuned to the fact that conflict is an inescapable feature of political life. To say as he did that the problem of democracy "is primarily and essentially an intellectual problem"[34] is to miss the point. The problem of democracy, as of government generally, is to manage conflict among persons who, often arguing from incompatible premises, cannot overcome their differences by discussion.[35] If we are realistic about human nature and hence about the edifying as distinct from the vocational effects of education, and realistic too about the limitations of reason, we shall be left with no grounds for supposing that we could have improved the operation of our democratic system by taking Dewey's advice.

We might well have done worse. A strong interest in politics, especially in a heterogeneous society, foments painful, divisive, time- and energy-consuming conflicts of worldviews and fundamental values, conflicts better left latent and inarticulate.[36] When dragged into the open such conflicts both embitter social relations and distract people from private pursuits, including business, science, art, and the professions, that contribute

34. Dewey, *The Public and Its Problems*, note 27 above, at 126, 327.
35. See Eric MacGilvray, *The Task before Us: Pragmatism and Political Liberalism*, ch. 5, pp. 17–28 (Social Science Collegiate Division, University of Chicago, Nov. 18, 2001, unpublished).
36. See James Johnson, "Arguing for Deliberation: Some Skeptical Considerations," in *Deliberative Democracy* 161, 165–170 (Jon Elster ed. 1998).

vitally to social welfare, in part by building prosperity, which is an emollient of political and social tensions. It is rather a strength than a weakness of representative democracy that in contrast to direct democracy, especially in its town-meeting form, which demands a substantial investment of time by private citizens, it allows most of the people to tune out politics most of the time. We don't have to spend all our time fending off crazy political initiatives. One shudders at Bonnie Honig's desire to restore "politics as a disruptive practice that resists the consolidations and closures of administrative and juridical settlement for the sake of the perpetuity of political contest."[37]

Another reason for not wanting to raise the political consciousness of the U.S. population is that even well-educated and well-informed people find it difficult to reason accurately about matters remote from their immediate concerns. People who vote on the basis of their self-interest are at least voting about something they know at firsthand, their own needs and preferences. Beware the high-minded voter.

Dewey's Theory of Law

If I am right so far, Dewey's idea of "distributed intelligence," the idea that is at the core of his political philosophy as well as of his theory of knowledge, is not well connected to the realistic conditions of modern democratic political governance. It is therefore unlikely to bear helpfully on the legal aspects of that governance. The bridge he tried to build between epistemic and political democracy is too flimsy to carry heavy traffic. But this is merely a hypothesis, which I shall try to test by examining Dewey's most extended foray into law, the essay "Logical Method and Law."[38]

First, though, a glance at his other major essay on law, "The Historic Background of Corporate Legal Personality."[39] It takes on the theory (primarily Germanic) that corporations have "real personality"—that is, that they are not merely legal constructs, which when Dewey wrote was, as it is now for that matter, the prevailing view of Anglo-American lawyers. The essay makes a nice pragmatic point—that the entire meaning of corporate "personality" resides in the legal consequences annexed to the corporate form. Instead of asking whether a corporation has enough "personality"

---

37. Bonnie Honig, *Political Theory and the Displacement of Politics* 4, 124 (1993).
38. John Dewey, "Logical Method and Law," 10 *Cornell Law Quarterly* 17 (1924).
39. 35 *Yale Law Journal* 655 (1926).

to be a "person" within the meaning of the Fourteenth Amendment or to shoulder sole liability for "its" debts rather than just be a conduit to the shareholders, as under partnership law, we need ask only whether the courts have given corporations the status of persons for Fourteenth Amendment purposes and whether they have limited the liability of the corporation's shareholders to their investment in the corporation so that the corporation's creditors cannot sue the shareholders personally for its debts. All we care about is the answers to these practical legal questions. We can leave to philosophy the ontological question whether and in what sense a corporation "exists" apart from the individuals who have rights and duties recognized by corporate law.

This is fine as far as it goes but leaves unexplained where the courts should go for answers to practical legal questions about the corporation.[40] Dewey is of no help with that question. He is right that whatever the right starting point for thinking about corporate law may be, it is not the metaphysics of personality. That was a fresh and useful point when he made it. The article owes nothing to Dewey's concept of democracy, however, and neither does an interesting short piece, "My Philosophy of Law," that he wrote some years later. It repeats and generalizes the pragmatic point in his corporate-law piece—"the standard [for evaluating law] is found in consequences, in the *function* of what goes on socially." But it adds the arresting thought that

> from any practical standpoint, recognition of the relatively slow rate of change on the part of certain constituents of social action is capable of accomplishing every useful, every *practically* needed, office that has led in the past and in other cultural climes to setting up external sources such as the Will or Reason of God, the Law of Nature . . . and the Practical Reason of Kant.[41]

Habit and custom, which shape law, change so slowly as to create the *illusion* of permanence, leading us to reify our habits and customs as tenets of natural law and thus elevate our quotidian concerns to eternal principles.

40. See David Luban, "What's Pragmatic about Legal Pragmatism?" in *The Revival of Pragmatism*, note 11 above, at 275, 298.

41. John Dewey, "My Philosophy of Law," in *My Philosophy of Law: Credos of Sixteen American Scholars* 73, 81, 84 (1941) (emphases in original).

We shall discover a closely related idea in "Logical Method and Law," to which I now turn.

That article begins by distinguishing between two types of human action: the instinctive or intuitive, which is swift and inarticulable yet not necessarily unreliable; and the deliberative. Actions of the first type are often reasonable; actions of the second type are reasoned but may or may not be reasonable. "Logical theory" is Dewey's term not for logic in the orthodox sense best illustrated by the syllogism but for the procedures followed in reaching decisions of the second type. These procedures are common to lawyers, engineers, doctors, and businessmen and approximate those employed by scientists,[42] for remember that Dewey believed that science is the model for *all* sound reasoning. Logic in Dewey's sense "is ultimately an empirical and concrete discipline."[43] When lawyers such as Holmes describe law as existing in the tension between "logic and good sense," Dewey explains, they mean by "logic" not what he means but "formal consistency, consistency of concepts with one another irrespective of the consequences of their application to concrete matters-of-fact,"[44] or, in short, the syllogism. Law exaggerates the importance of logic in this narrow sense because "concepts once developed have a kind of intrinsic inertia on their own account; once developed the law of habit applies to them" and makes it difficult for judges to adapt legal doctrines in a timely fashion to changing circumstances.[45] To do that requires "another kind of logic[,] which shall reduce the influence of habit, and shall facilitate the use of good sense regarding matters of social consequence."[46] Recall that Dewey had pointed out in "My Philosophy of Law" that the inertial force of habit is augmented by reifying the familiar, the customary or habitual, as a permanent, unchangeable Truth.

The essential problem is that syllogistic reasoning, the core of legal formalism, requires "that for every possible case which may arise, there is a fixed antecedent rule already at hand," whereas sound "general principles emerge as statements of generic ways in which it has been found helpful to treat concrete cases";[47] in short, they are generalizations from experience.

42. Dewey, note 38 above, at 17–18.
43. Id. at 19.
44. Id. at 20.
45. Id.
46. Id. at 21.
47. Id. at 22.

"We generally begin with some vague anticipation of a conclusion (or at least of alternative conclusions), and then we look around for principles and data which will substantiate it or which will enable us to choose intelligently between rival conclusions."[48] The distinction is thus between a method of inquiry and one of exposition. Law needs the former as well as the latter—the former to reach the legal conclusion, the latter to set it forth in an articulate, coherent ("logical") form that will provide both a public justification and a guide for the future.

Regarding the justificatory role of the judicial opinion, Dewey speculates that "it is highly probable that the need of justifying to others conclusions reached and decisions made has been the chief cause of the origin and development of logical operations in the precise sense; of abstraction, generalization, regard for consistency of implications."[49] But the power of the "logical" opinion to make law predictable is limited by the gap between *theoretical* certainty and practical certainty." The former is based on "the absurd because impossible proposition that every decision should flow with formal logical necessity from antecedently known premises."[50] Certainty is highly desirable but can be achieved to only a limited degree—that is the "practical" aspect—when social and economic conditions are rapidly changing, for then law itself must change if its rules are not to become obsolete. The social interest in the law's continuity or constancy, which is important to enable people to plan their affairs, must be traded off against the social interest in the law's adaptability to change, which is important to the making of sound legal rules and of decisions responsive to the particular circumstances of the individual case. The difference is between short-run and long-run legal certainty. Just as fixed currency exchange rates promote short-term financial certainty at the expense of long, because in a system of fixed exchange rates changes in the relative value of currencies explode from time to time in dramatic devaluations and revaluations, so legal formalism promotes short-term certainty at the expense of long-term certainty by preventing continuous small adjustments to a changing social environment. Such adjustments might obviate the need for convulsive changes when law and social conditions drift too far apart.

48. Id. at 23.

49. Id. at 24. This is a clue to Dewey's rejection of traditional epistemology in favor of what Rorty calls "epistemological behaviorism": "we understand knowledge when we understand the social justification of belief." Richard Rorty, *Philosophy and the Mirror of Nature* 170, 174 (1979).

50. Dewey, note 38 above, at 25 (emphasis in original).

Moreover, when "circumstances are really novel and not covered by old rules, it is a gamble which old rule will be declared regulative of a particular case."[51] And old rules breed a "virtual alliance between the judiciary and entrenched interests that correspond most closely to the conditions under which the rules of law were previously laid down," and so "the slogans of liberalism of one period often become the bulwarks of reaction in a subsequent era."[52] Those slogans include "liberty in use of property, and freedom of contract,"[53] slogans that when Dewey wrote were being used to invalidate state social-welfare legislation (remember *Lochner?*) and later would be used to invalidate federal New Deal legislation. He hoped the old slogans would give way to newer rules based on "social justice." But he warned against the hardening of such rules in their turn "into absolute and fixed antecedent premises,"[54] which would just be modern versions of Platonic absolutes or of natural law. In fact, just such hardening has occurred in those precincts of legal thought in which the liberal decisions of the Supreme Court during the chief justiceship of Earl Warren are treated as holy writ.

What is needed, Dewey's article advises, is "a logic *relative to consequences rather than to antecedents,*" a logic that is forward-looking rather than, as is the natural bent of lawyers and judges, backward-looking, a logic that treats general rules and principles as "working hypotheses, needing to be constantly tested by the way in which they work out in application to concrete situations . . . Infiltration into law of a more experimental and flexible logic is a social as well as an intellectual need."[55] What is also needed, in only apparent tension with the presentist character of pragmatic law, is the historical sense, and specifically the realization that the existing body of legal doctrine is not as the rocks are, unchanged since time immemorial, but instead recent, contingent, and mutable.

Dewey's essay is a clear statement of the pragmatic theory of adjudication. His essential point, which as far as I know had not been made previously though it is implicit in much of what Holmes (heavily quoted in Dewey's essay) wrote, was that legal reasoning is *au fond* just like other practical reasoning. This is because all practical reasoning is a closer or

51. Id. at 26.
52. Id.
53. Id. at 27.
54. Id.
55. Id. at 26–27 (emphasis in original).

more distant approximation to scientific reasoning. Since the law's concerns are practical, law cannot be "logical" in the strict sense; nothing practical can be.

The shortcoming of the essay, as of so much of Dewey's policy-oriented writing, is its paradoxical lack of engagement with concrete problems and real institutions. The essay is *about* practical reasoning rather than being an example of it. (Its brevity—it is only ten pages long—is suggestive.) It is top-down reasoning, not the bottom-up reasoning that he recommended. The same is true of his thinking about democracy and explains his pessimism. Instead of comparing our system with the political systems of other countries, he compares it with a democratic ideal of his own concoction and so naturally is disappointed. Dewey was very good at reasoning about practical reasoning but not very good at doing it. Similarly, while he commended scientific reasoning as the model of reasoned inquiry, the scientific spirit is not conspicuous in his own writings.

The intellectual kinship between Dewey and Holmes that is displayed in Dewey's essay is worth remarking. It undermines two canards about pragmatism: that pragmatism has no form or character (in which event we would not recognize any greater kinship between Dewey and Holmes than between two writers on law who were picked at random) and that pragmatism has a definite political cast (Dewey was a liberal in the modern sense, Holmes a conservative in that sense).

The Theory Extended

One of the peculiarities of "Logical Method and Law," as of the other two essays of Dewey's on law that I have discussed, is that it owes little to any concepts of democracy that engaged his attention. Democracy is the bridge on which he hoped to cross from philosophy to public issues, and yet his most successful forays into those issues, his essays on law, make little use of it. The notion of a logic of consequences is pragmatic but it is not distinctively Deweyan. The emphasis on habit as reifying merely expedient legal notions, and the notion of legal reasoning as adaptive to a changing social environment, are distinctively Deweyan but are not central to the essays.

The concept of distributed intelligence, though central to Dewey's epistemology, contributes little to his theory of law, a theory most parsimoniously understood as an application of everyday, not philosophical, pragmatism. But his epistemology does have two implications for law that he might have drawn had he engaged more closely with law. The first is the desirability of a diverse judiciary.[56] When lawyers, judges, and law professors talk about the qualities of a good judge, implicitly they assume that there is some optimum recipe of qualities; and since it *is* the optimum, the best, it is what every judge should have. So in an ideal world all judges would be alike. But Dewey's theory of distributed intelligence and its Darwinian underpinnings or analogy imply, once a Platonic conception of legal reasoning is rejected, that it would be good to have judges of diverse origins, experience, attitudes, values, and cast of mind. This is especially true at the appellate level. The deliberations of a panel of appellate judges will be improved, Dewey's entire philosophy implies, if the judges have (within limits) diverse qualities.[57] There is no single "ideal" judge. We want judges who are intelligent and learned, judges who are practical and down-to-earth, judges of austere intellectual independence and judges skilled at compromise, judges who have led worldly and those who have led sheltered lives, judges who are realistic and judges who are idealistic, judges who are passionate about liberty and judges who are passionate about order and civility. Each type of judge brings something different to the table.

We can sense in Ronald Dworkin's heuristic of Judge "Hercules," the judge who optimally combines all the moral and intellectual qualities requisite in a judge—and therefore deliberates alone—the remoteness of Dworkin's legal philosophy from Dewey's; and we are helped to understand Dworkin's disdain for pragmatism.[58] The disdain is unmerited. Hercules is a chimera. As Professor (now Judge) Noonan once cruelly but aptly observed, "It is strange to talk of Hercules when your starting point is Harry Blackmun."[59] No sensible person would want a court of Harry Blackmuns even if he thought that Blackmun had brought to the deliberative process a distinctive point of view that was worthwhile.

But we must no more exaggerate the deliberative potential of judges than that of voters. Not all disagreements among judges can be dissolved

56. See Richard A. Posner, *The Problems of Jurisprudence* 447–448, 458–459 (1990).

57. This is something even judges occasionally recognize, as shown in Jonathan M. Cohen, *Inside Appellate Courts: The Impact of Court Organization on Judicial Decision Making in the United States Courts of Appeals* 50–51 (2002).

58. See Ronald Dworkin, "Pragmatism, Right Answers, and True Banality," in *Pragmatism in Law and Society* 359, 360 (Michael Brint and William Weaver eds. 1991).

59. John T. Noonan, Jr., *Persons and Masks of the Law* 174 (1976).

by reason. Indeed, the more diverse the judges, the less likely that is to happen. If all judicial disagreements could be dissolved by deliberation, we would not see such startling correlations as that Roman Catholic judges are 11 percent more likely to rule against gay rights than Protestant judges and 25 percent more likely to do so than Jewish judges, while black and Hispanic judges are 20 percent more likely than whites to rule in favor of gay rights, and women (of whatever race or ethnicity) are 12 percent more likely to do so.[60] Values based on personal, including ethnic and religious, background influence judicial decisions not because judges are especially willful but because many cases cannot be decided by reasoning from shared premises of fact and value. This does not lessen—rather it increases—the value of a diverse judiciary. Such a judiciary is more representative,[61] and its decisions will therefore command greater acceptance in a diverse society than would the decisions of a mandarin court.

One argument for political democracy is that majority rule is a civilized method of accommodating unbridgeable differences of opinion, compared either to physical force or to interminable debate. The more homogeneous a society, the fewer such differences there will be and so the more feasible will be the substitution of rule by experts for majority rule. When because of cultural heterogeneity judicial decisions depend more on who is making them than on an objective decisionmaking procedure, it is better to make the judiciary representative than to seek a spurious neutrality by homogenizing it. If all U.S. judges were orthodox Roman Catholics, the issue of abortion rights would be resolved "objectively" against such rights because the judges would be reasoning from common premises about the sacredness of fetal life. But their decisions would lack credibility because a majority of the members of the political community would be unrepresented.

What this means, we must acknowledge if we are clear-eyed, is that the goal of uniform justice is unattainable in the United States. At every level

60. Daniel R. Pinello, *Gay Rights and American Law* 203 (City University of New York, John Jay College of Criminal Justice, Jan. 22, 2002, unpublished). Cf. Tracey E. George, "Court Fixing," 43 *Arizona Law Review* 9, 18–26 (2001).

61. The idea of a judiciary that is representative in the sense that the judges mirror to the extent possible the diversity of the population must be distinguished from efforts to democratize the judiciary, for example by making judicial appointment elective rather than appointive or by expanding the power of juries relative to that of judges. There are many practical objections to such measures. For an excellent discussion of the problems with parallel efforts to democratize administrative agencies, see Richard B. Stewart, "The Reformation of American Administrative Law," 88 *Harvard Law Review* 1669 (1975).

of the judiciary, judges exercise discretionary power, which means that two different judges faced with the same issue may reach different results without either judge being reversed. Trial judges exercise expansive discretionary powers with respect to factfinding, the admission and exclusion of evidence, the application of law to facts, and case management that often determine the outcome of a case without realistic prospects for correction on appeal; while intermediate appellate judges, whose discretionary authority extends to issues of law not yet resolved by the supreme court of their jurisdiction, often sit in panels much smaller than their court as a whole, and often there is little realistic prospect for correction either by the entire court or by a higher court—especially since supreme courts usually disclaim the function of correcting errors, even errors of law. The U.S. Supreme Court decides only a minute fraction of the cases appealed to it; if the Court decided all the cases appealed to it, it probably would reverse thousands of cases every year rather than fifty or so.

So a litigant's fate may be determined by the happenstance of which judge or judges happen to hear the successive stages of his case as it wends its way through the judicial system. This is regrettable and even frightening. But the only imaginable solutions—a homogeneous judiciary, in which judges, being alike, would tend to exercise discretion the same way, or a body of legal doctrine so detailed and rigid that judges would have no discretion—are as undesirable as they are unattainable. And even if it were feasible, as it is not, to have a single national supreme court sitting en banc to review every ruling by a lower-court judge, state or federal, it would be undesirable because it would centralize judicial power unduly, crushing healthy diversity and experimentation. There does not appear to be a happy medium. It seems inescapable that the American people will continue to be guinea pigs in a national experiment run by the courts.

The second implication for law of Dewey's epistemology is that courts should either have no power to invalidate legislation or exercise it only in extreme circumstances, when faced by a law patently unconstitutional or utterly appalling. By invalidating legislation, courts prevent political experimentation. Holmes had already described the states as "laboratories" in which social experiments could be carried out without endangering the nation as a whole.[62] He had done this in the context of protesting against

---

62. See, for example, Truax v. Corrigan, 257 U.S. 312, 344 (1921) (dissenting opinion). Compare Holmes's defense, in his dissenting opinion in Abrams v. United States, 250 U.S. 616, 630 (1919), of the First Amendment as an "experiment." See Chapter 10.

his fellow Justices' readiness to forbid such experimentation in the name of the Constitution. This emphatically pragmatic attitude toward judicial review of the constitutionality of statutes led Holmes to propose a very narrow test for invalidating a statute as a deprivation of liberty without due process of law. The test was "that a rational and fair man necessarily would admit that the statute . . . would infringe fundamental principles as they have been understood by the traditions of our people and our law."[63] A statute would be unlikely to flunk this test unless it outraged the judge.[64]

This was a Deweyan approach, and one might have expected Dewey to embrace it in his essay on law, given his familiarity with Holmes's work. In Dewey's intellectual universe, invalidating a statute is not just checking a political preference. It is profoundly rather than merely superficially undemocratic (superficially because the Constitution itself was a product of democracy, or at least what passed for democracy in the eighteenth century).[65] It places expert opinion over the distributed intelligence of the mass of the people and prevents the emergence of the best policies through intellectual natural selection.

This point is missed by many of Dewey's current avatars in the legal academy. They not only applaud the Supreme Court's snuffing out of democratic experimentation in areas such as abortion, school prayer, term limits, and criminal rights; many of them would like to see the Court do more to override democratic sentiment—would like to see it, for example, abolish capital punishment (which the vast majority of the population supports), require public funding of abortions, establish constitutional entitlements to minimum public protective and social services, such as police and

---

63. Lochner v. New York, 198 U.S. 45, 76 (1905) (Holmes, J., dissenting).

64. See Richard A. Posner, *The Problematics of Moral and Legal Theory* 147–149 (1999).

65. The Constitution is commonly said to have been ratified by "the people" rather than by the states, but this is imprecise. It is true (well, almost true—see Chapter 7) that the Constitution was ratified by popularly elected conventions in each of the states; and we recall from Chapter 2 that the Constitution's democratic pedigree was one of John Marshall's arguments for judicial supremacy. Yet the disfranchisement of women, of virtually all blacks, and of all white males who did not meet the property qualifications set by the states meant that only a minority of adults were actually eligible to vote for delegates to the conventions; and much like today, many who were eligible didn't bother to vote. It seems that at most only 25 percent of adult white males voted for delegates to the conventions, Robert J. Dinkin, *Voting in Revolutionary America: A Study of Elections in the Original Thirteen States, 1776–1789*, at 129 (1982), which would be less than 10 percent of the adult population, even if Indians are excluded. But why should they be? In 1788 there were between 200,000 and 250,000 Indians in the United States as then constituted (estimated from Douglas H. Ubelaker, "North American Indian Population Size, A.D. 1500 to 1985," 77 *American Journal of Physical Anthropology* 289, 292 [1988] [tab. 2]).

welfare, eliminate disparities among school districts in expenditures per pupil, require interdistrict busing to eradicate all actual or conjectured traces of school segregation, require that states guarantee a minimum income for their citizens, outlaw voucher systems, and bless homosexual marriage by invalidating the Defense of Marriage Act, passed by Congress with near unanimity and signed into law by President Clinton. Such judicial measures could not plausibly be considered democracy-promoting, as might, in contrast, decisions invalidating unreasonable impediments to voting in political elections or limitations on freedom of political speech. Contemporary Deweyans who advocate judicial adoption of the current left-liberal political agenda, bypassing legislatures, can have little respect for distributed intelligence, democratic diversity, or social experimentation. At some level they must believe that Supreme Court Justices guided by the best thinkers in the academy *can* build a pipeline to moral, political, and juristic truth. They fail to recognize, as Dworkin, at least, recognizes, the incompatibility of so Platonic a conception of the judicial role in constitutional adjudication with Deweyan pragmatism. Dworkin is right to see pragmatism as a challenge to his jurisprudential stance.

I mentioned outlawing voucher systems; the Supreme Court's recent decision refusing to do so[66] is a model of pragmatic decisionmaking. The idea behind such systems is to enlarge parental school choice and place increased competitive pressure on the public schools by giving parents public money that they can use to pay for tuition at a private school. Because most private schools are parochial schools (and the vast majority of parochial schools are Roman Catholic), the effect of such vouchers is to give a boost to religions education and expose more children to religious indoctrination. On this basis voucher systems were challenged as a violation of the establishment clause of the First Amendment ("Congress shall make no law respecting an establishment of religion"), a clause that the Supreme Court has held is applicable to state government as well by virtue of the provision of the Fourteenth Amendment that forbids states to deprive people of life, liberty, or property without due process of law. Whether funneling money to religious schools in the way that a voucher system does should be regarded as establishing religion, when property tax exemptions and federal tuition assistance for students who attend religious colleges and universities are not so regarded, is one of those all too com-

---

66. Zelman v. Simmons-Harris, 122 S. Ct. 2460 (2002).

mon constitutional questions that the constitutional text and the case law built on it do not answer. The practical considerations bearing on the case had to do with such things as the perceived crisis in public education, the inaccessiblity of private schools to persons of moderate means, and, over against these considerations favoring vouchers, the potential for social conflict arising from religious indoctrination of students, balkanization of the student population, and divisive government entanglements in religious issues.

No one could make a responsible predictive judgment as to how these considerations were likely to balance out and whether therefore a voucher system would be a good or a bad thing. The relevant considerations are too numerous, mixed, and imponderable. Fortunately, no predictive judgment was necessary. For here was the perfect opportunity for conducting a social experiment in the isolated laboratories of the states and cities. At issue was not a nationwide program of school vouchers but merely an option for states and cities that most would not take up. Those that did would provide invaluable information not obtainable in any other way. Should it turn out on the basis of the experiment that voucher systems are on balance highly undesirable, it would be time enough for the courts to step in and forbid them. It would have been profoundly unpragmatic for the Supreme Court to have stifled experimentation by invoking legal conceptualisms.

Consider *Roe v. Wade*.[67] Whatever its merits as a constitutional decision, they are not democratic merits. The Supreme Court was not implementing a democratic decision made when the original Constitution was ratified, or the Fourteenth Amendment in 1868. The seven Justices who made up the Court's majority in *Roe v. Wade* simply set a lower value on fetal life than on women's interest in the control of their reproductive activity.[68] This was a legislative judgment, owing nothing to democratic theory or preference. The democracy-reinforcing argument sometimes heard that women burdened with unwanted children would be in effect expelled from the public sphere and prevented from participating in political activity effectively, whether as voters or candidates, is unconvincing, as is another

67. 410 U.S. 113 (1973).
68. As Justice White, dissenting in the companion case of Doe v. Bolton, 410 U.S. 179, 222 (1973), put it bluntly: "The Court apparently values the convenience of the pregnant mother more than the continued existence and development of the life or potential life that she carries."

"democratic" argument for the decision—that women are underrepresented in the political process; they are not.

Had the Court upheld the constitutionality of the Texas abortion statute challenged in *Roe v. Wade* despite the fact that it permitted abortion only when the mother's life was in danger, some states would have retained their equally strict prohibitions—but these are the states in which legal abortions are still difficult to obtain because of hostility to and intimidation of abortion doctors, abortion clinics, and hospitals that perform abortions. In such states the principal effect of restoring the legal prohibition of abortions might just be to make girls and women somewhat more careful about sexual activity than if they still had access to abortion on demand as a backup to contraception—"somewhat" because access to abortion in such states is already limited as a practical matter.

I have said that American judges tend to be pragmatists; and we might think even *Roe v. Wade* a pragmatic decision. It may well have been based on a weighing of the consequences of the alternative outcomes, there being nothing in the text of the Constitution or in the case law to compel the Court's decision. But the Court ignored an important consequence—the stifling effect on democratic experimentation of establishing a constitutional right to abortion. Other possible consequences that were ignored, such as effects on the birth rate and on sexual practices, not to mention the theological and other moral consequences of feticide, were perhaps too speculative to be considered. But not the effect on experimentation. And so the Court's pragmatism was one-sided. We must be careful about using "pragmatic" as a compliment. There are bad pragmatic decisions as well as good ones.

There are also experiments clearly not worth trying. And others not worth continuing. One can imagine the Court's upholding the Texas abortion statute in *Roe v. Wade* but then revisiting the abortion issue after another decade of state experimentation with abortion laws. Maybe by then some approximation to consensus would have emerged that could have been used to justify invalidating the abortion laws of the remaining, outlier states. There would be an analogy to the way in which the Court abolished official racial segregation. It waited until such segregation was largely limited to the former confederate states and "separate but equal" was a proven failure before ruling that segregation was unconstitutional. It waited, in short, until the consequences of segregation were clear. And it waited until only two states forbade the sale of contraceptives before striking down those anachronistic laws.[69] Remember, too, how long it waited before invalidating the laws forbidding miscegenation.

It may have waited too long in the case of segregation or contraception; and likewise with respect to *Roe v. Wade* we cannot be certain that the benefits of delay in invalidating state abortion laws would have exceeded the costs to women denied legal abortions during the interim. We cannot even measure the benefits and costs. Pragmatic decisionmaking will inevitably be based to a disquieting extent on hunches and subjective preferences rather than on hard evidence.

Still another pragmatic option open to the Court in the abortion cases would have been to strike down the Texas statute but uphold the Georgia law challenged in the companion case to *Roe* of *Doe v. Bolton*.[70] Georgia's statute had been liberalized just five years previously as part of the wave of abortion-law reform that was gathering steam when *Roe* and *Doe* were decided and that was derailed by them. The Georgia statute authorized abortion not only when the mother's life was in danger but also when there was the threat of a serious and permanent injury to her, or the fetus was gravely defective, or the pregnancy was the result of rape (interpreted to include incest even if not forcible), though in any of these cases she had to get the permission of a physicians' committee. To uphold the Georgia statute while striking down the Texas one might have been a sensible compromise, less likely to incite an anti-abortion movement or straitjacket statutory reform and more respectful of experimentation and democracy.

This suggestion provides a way of distinguishing pragmatic from formalist adjudication. Traditional legal thinkers are not indifferent to consequences; only they tend to truncate their consideration of them more than a pragmatic legal thinker would be inclined to do. A formalist would be horrified by the idea of deciding a case even in part on the ground that it would lower the temperature of a passionate national debate, conduce to compromise, or simply remove a hot potato from the judicial plate for a few years. These are not considerations articulated in any legal doctrine; they are nakedly pragmatic. The pragmatist denies that there is a closed list of considerations that judges can properly take account of. Some considerations are out of bounds but the rest are fair game.

I don't mean to be beating up just on decisions, such as *Roe v. Wade*

---

69. Richard A. Posner, *Sex and Reason* 326 (1992). The cases are Griswold v. Connecticut, 381 U.S. 479 (1965), and Eisenstadt v. Baird, 405 U.S. 438 (1972).

70. See note 68 above.

and its companion *Doe v. Bolton*, that are popular on the left (left and center, in those cases). There is a complementary right-wing agenda, equally dubious from a pragmatic standpoint, that involves constitutionalizing laissez-faire economics, deeming the fetus a "person" whose life the due process clause of the Fourteenth Amendment requires the states to protect against abortionists, invalidating gun-control laws under the Second Amendment, and outlawing all affirmative action by public entities. The right-wing school of judicial activism is profoundly (but unapologetically) anti-Deweyan.

But wait—statutes, and not just constitutional decisions invalidating statutes, can themselves stifle experimentation. If homosexual marriage is considered, as surely it should be, a Millian "experiment in living," the Defense of Marriage Act is unpragmatic and a decision invalidating it on constitutional grounds would be pragmatic. The recent spate of Supreme Court decisions curtailing the power of the federal government relative to that of the states could be defended as creating additional space for social experimentation in those isolated laboratories. Pragmatism, then, could be thought to license its own form of judicial activism. But that is doubtful. If the agenda of the constitutional maximalists, whether of the left or the right (or, as I have just suggested, some hypothetical pragmatic or Millian middle), were adopted, the federal judiciary, advised by academic lawyers and by advocacy groups, would become the national legislature. Electoral politics would largely be reduced to choosing the officials to implement the judiciary's policies and to fill judicial vacancies. The President and the Senate would become, in effect, the electors of the national legislature through their exercise of the powers respectively to nominate and to confirm federal judges.

Conceivably Dewey might have been persuaded that in the circumstances of our actual existing democracy, which he thought so deficient, even popular laws could not be considered fully authentic democratic products. In that event there might be scope for rule by judicial experts after all. Dewey could not see this because when he wrote "Logical Method and Law" the Supreme Court was using its power of judicial review to invalidate legislation that he approved of, such as legislation forbidding child labor, fixing minimum wages, and fixing maximum hours of work. He may even have thought such measures products of epistemic democracy. Skeptical about political democracy in what he imagined to be an era of propaganda and a debased political culture, however, Dewey could not consistently have denied the possibility that public policy might be improved by intermittent substitution of the rule of judicial experts for popular rule. He hoped that education would give the average person something approaching the intelligence of the elite—eventually; but in the meantime there was a nation to govern. The Supreme Court's interference in the name of the Constitution with political experimentation is not as untoward as it would be if the United States and the individual states were Deweyan polities. Yet Dewey might have resisted this conclusion—he who said that

> in the absence of an articulate voice on the part of the masses, the best do not and cannot remain the best, the wise cease to be wise. It is impossible for high brows to secure a monopoly of such knowledge as must be used for the regulation of common affairs. In the degree in which they become a specialized class, they are shut off from knowledge of the needs which they are supposed to serve.[71]

He would also have resisted the following effort at a Deweyan justification of judicial power to invalidate government action in the name of the Constitution: democracy is deliberation; judges deliberate; therefore judicial review is democratic.[72] The Soviet Politburo, in the era of collective leadership that followed Stalin's death, deliberated; this did not make it a democratic organ or the Soviet Union a democracy. A Supreme Court of nine judges is not a large enough slice of the electorate to be a statistically significant sample of, and hence an adequate stand-in for, the electorate. It would not be a fully representative sample of the electorate no matter how assiduously the appointing authorities strove to make it demographically and ideologically representative. Most lawyers, whatever their background, have a narrow, professionally inflected perspective on governance; and anyway nine is too small a number for the Justices to represent all the important fractions (subcultures, interests, points of view, and so on) of the population of so vast and heterogeneous a society as that of the United States.

It is merely a detail that judges, including Supreme Court Justices, do not deliberate a great deal, especially in the most controversial cases. That was implicit in my suggestion that unbridgeable conflicts argue for a di-

71. Dewey, *The Public and Its Problems*, note 27 above, at 206.
72. See Christopher J. Peters, "Adjudication as Representation," 97 *Columbia Law Review* 312 (1997).

verse judiciary. Cases are controversial when they touch on deep value issues, the sort of thing people do not like to argue about with colleagues (friends, customers, and so on) because such arguments touch raw nerves and create animosities. An appellate judge is like a spouse in a culture of arranged marriage with no divorce. "Married" irrevocably to dissimilar personalities—even, in our morally diverse society, to colleagues who inhabit different moral universes—judges learn to avoid face-to-face debate, as distinguished from the more impersonal debate conducted in the judicial opinions themselves, on fundamental issues.

Particularly ironic from a Deweyan perspective is the heavy hand the Supreme Court has laid on legislative experimentation with democratic procedures. I mentioned term limits in passing. Consider now *California Democratic Party v. Jones.*[73] The Supreme Court in that case invalidated a state law requiring political parties to select their candidates in "blanket" primaries, that is, primaries in which any eligible voter can vote whether or not he is a member of the party conducting the primary. The law had been enacted not in the usual way, but by an initiative (like a referendum)[74] supported by 60 percent of the voters—direct democracy in action. The idea behind the blanket primary was to increase turnout by giving voters more options and to make intraparty debate more vigorous. The idea may well have been flawed; by blurring party differences and encouraging strategic crossover voting (for example, Republicans voting in the Democratic primary in an effort to swing the Democratic nomination to the weakest candidate), the blanket primary might make the parties even more alike, and voters even more turned off, than at present. We shall never know. The Court snuffed out the experiment before the first blanket primary could be held. (Where is the law's delay—one of Hamlet's examples of things that might incline one to consider suicide—when we need it?) It did so on the unconvincing ground that requiring a party to select its candidates by means of a blanket primary impairs the freedom of association of the party's members because freedom of association implies freedom to exclude. This is true but irrelevant; political parties do not turn away applicants for membership on the ground that the applicant is unsympathetic to the party's aims.

73. 530 U.S. 567 (2000).

74. Technically, a referendum is a vote on whether to ratify a legislative measure. An initiative is a proposal for legislative action that the people are asked to vote on.

CHAPTER FOUR

Two Concepts of Democracy

❧

"Democracy," as we know by now, is a word of many meanings. But as far as political democracy is concerned, two predominate in theoretical analysis; both were introduced in the last chapter. The first, which I call "Concept 1 democracy"—a term intended to denote the loftier versions of "deliberative democracy"—and focus on in this chapter, can be described variously as idealistic, theoretical, and top-down. The second, "Concept 2 democracy"—an approximation to Joseph Schumpeter's theory of "elite democracy"—is realistic, cynical, and bottom-up; my preferred term for Concept 2 is, of course, pragmatic. Concept 2 models the democratic process as a competitive power struggle among members of a political elite (not to be confused with a moral or intellectual elite) for the electoral support of the masses. The members of neither group are regarded as actuated to any great extent by motives other than self-interest in a narrow sense, and the masses are regarded as poorly informed about, and except in times of crisis little interested in, political matters. Concept 2 takes center stage in the next chapter, where I argue that it not only is the more accurate description of American democracy than Concept 1, as most proponents of Concept 1 would acknowledge, but also is normatively superior. In Chapter 6, I apply my analysis of the two concepts to the two most recent "crises" of American democracy—the impeachment and trial of President Clinton, and the 2000 election deadlock and the breaking of it by the

Supreme Court—and to more general questions concerning the U.S. law of democracy. I argue for a reformulation of that law to make it conform to Concept 2. I also remark in that chapter the oddity that judges and constitutional-law professors have failed to articulate a coherent conception of democracy even though the relation between law and democracy is fundamental to the proper role of judges in a democratic society.

Concept 1 Democracy: Idealistic, Deliberative, Deweyan

Concept 1 is premised on the idea that every adult who is not profoundly retarded has a moral right to participate on terms of equality in the governance of the society. With that moral right come the moral duties (1) to take sufficient interest in public affairs to be able to participate in governance intelligently, (2) to discuss political issues in an open-minded fashion with other citizens, and (3) to base one's political opinions and actions (such as voting) on one's honest opinion, formed after due deliberation, of what is best for society as a whole rather than on narrow self-interest. Concept 1 thus is civic-minded, oriented to the public interest rather than to selfish private interests. It insists that voters be both informed and disinterested and that voting be based on the ideas and opinions that emerge from deliberation among these informed and disinterested citizens. We recall that in John Dewey's democratic theory citizens are expected to address public questions with an approximation to the rigor, disinterest, and open-mindedness with which natural scientists address scientific questions. Political democracy is conceived of as a species of epistemic democracy and is expected both to yield the best results and to enforce the moral right of equal participation in governance. Democracy as thus conceived is remote from mere aggregation, through majority vote, of existing, unreflective, presumably selfish preferences.

Moral duty (3) posited by Concept 1 (the duty to vote in the public interest) makes moral duties (1) and (2) (the duties to take a serious interest in politics and to discuss political issues with one's fellow citizens in an open-minded way) more strenuous than they would otherwise be. It is far more difficult to form an informed opinion about what is good for society as a whole than it is to determine where one's self-interest lies. Not that one cannot be deceived on the latter score as well; but reasoning about the most effective means to a given end—instrumental reasoning, the type involved in self-interested action—is a good deal more straightforward than reasoning about ends, the type of reasoning required for determining what is best for society as a whole. In Chapter 1, I questioned the very possibility of such reasoning. That position may seem extreme. But what is undeniable is that because there is no consensus on what the goal of American society should be or even on whether the attainment of a goal or goals is the right way to think about the social good, Concept 1 democracy is deliberative in the strongest sense of the word, the sense that makes deliberation a cousin of philosophical debate, for example between Benthamite and Kantian concepts of the social optimum. Joshua Cohen claims that

> in a well-ordered democracy, political debate is organized around alternative conceptions of the public good. So an ideal pluralist scheme, in which democratic politics consists of fair bargaining among groups each of which pursues its particular or sectional interest, is unsuited to a just society ... When properly conducted, then, democratic politics involves *public deliberation focused on the common good.*[1]

Or in other words, deliberative democracy "gives moral argument a prominent place in the political process."[2] It requires that "1. Individual citizens must be willing to modify their conceptions of the public good; 2. These modifications must be responsive to reasons offered by others; and 3. Citizens must openly commit themselves to acting on this modified view of the public good."[3]

Granted, moral argument is not a synonym for philosophical argument. One can argue that slavery is wrong without engaging with the sort of arguments that a Kant or a Mill would make against it. But the quotations in the preceding paragraph indicate the tendency of Concept 1 theorists to envision moral argument on political questions as taking place on a philosophical plane. They doubt that "the public good" or the "just society" can be defined without engagement in philosophical reflection. The tendency

1. Joshua Cohen, "Deliberation and Democratic Legitimacy," in *The Good Polity: Normative Analysis of the State* 17, 18–19 (Alan Hamlin and Philip Pettit eds. 1989) (emphasis in original). Cohen's essay is an admirable summary of the concept of deliberative democracy, as is James Bohman, "The Coming of Age of Deliberative Democracy," 6 *Journal of Political Philosophy* 400 (1998).

2. Amy Gutmann and Dennis Thompson, *Democracy and Disagreement* 346 (1996). "When citizens or their representatives disagree morally, they should continue to reason together to reach mutually acceptable decisions." Id. at 1.

3. Henry S. Richardson, "Democratic Intentions," in *Deliberative Democracy: Essays on Reason and Politics* 349, 376 (James Bohman and William Rehg eds. 1997).

of Concept 1—itself an invention of political theory—is thus to make democratic politics a branch of political theory.

Immediately the objection arises that debates over moral and political philosophy are notoriously inconclusive—I would go further and call them indeterminate and interminable[4]—and in any event far above the head of the average, or for that matter the above-average, voter. Few citizens have the formidable intellectual and moral capacities (let alone the time) required for the role that Concept 1 assigns to the citizenry, although defenders of the concept believe that participation in democratic political activity strengthens these capacities, enabling a virtuous cycle. This is a theme common both to Tocqueville and to Mill. Even if it is correct, it leaves unanswered how the citizen is to be induced to participate in the first place.

Any effort, my own included, to define or describe "deliberative democracy" risks lumpiness because conceptions of deliberative democracy differ along a number of dimensions.[5] Abstractness—how closely a theorist models political deliberation on his own, academic mode of discussion—is only one. Cohen and Richardson, for example, are more abstract than Gutmann and Thompson. The difference is partly one of practical-mindedness, on how interested the theorist is in concrete policy issues, though it is possible to discuss even such issues in chillingly abstract terms.

Another dimension along which deliberative democrats differ is the stringency of the conditions believed necessary for deliberation to be effective. Some deliberative democrats think a substantial redistribution of wealth necessary in order to create enough political equality among citizens for deliberation to be genuinely democratic (poor people, they fear, may be too ignorant or dependent to contribute meaningfully to the deliberative democratic process), while others are content with milder legal and educational reforms.

A third area of difference is the level of the political structure at which deliberation is considered productive—among citizens, legislators, bureaucrats, or judges—and hence the optimal balance between popular and expert governance. Concept 1 democrats who are skeptical of the delibera-

---

4. See Richard A. Posner, *The Problematics of Moral and Legal Theory*, ch. 1 (1999).

5. "That deliberative democracy comes in many shapes is an understatement." Michael Saward, "Direct and Deliberative Democracy," 2 (Open University of the United Kingdom, n.d.) (paper presented at a conference on Deliberating about Deliberative Democracy held at the University of Texas, Feb. 4–6, 2000).

tive capacity of the people, who envisage deliberation as primarily an elite activity, may want an institutional structure that sharply limits popular democracy.[6] Such democrats, James Madison for example, may verge (as we shall see) on being Concept 2 democrats.

Fourth, while for some theorists democratic deliberation is instrumental to social welfare, for others it has intrinsic value. Learned Hand said that he would not like to be "ruled by a bevy of Platonic Guardians" because he would "miss the stimulus of living in a society where I have, at least theoretically, some part in the direction of public affairs."[7] Even if Platonic Guardians would govern better than a democratic government would, even if the citizen's participation in the direction of public affairs in a democracy is more theoretical than real (a proposition for which I shall offer some evidence shortly), and so even if Hand would have been better off in a practical, utilitarian sense to be governed in the manner thought best by Plato—even if, indeed, democratic self-government is completely illusory—he would consider himself deprived to live under such a regime. He would be deprived of participation in the high calling of political deliberation.

Hannah Arendt, echoing the ancient Greeks, took Hand a step further and argued that only in politics is the entire community engaged in deliberation over what matters to every member of the community, as distinct from the mundane, limited, and selfish concerns of private life. The kind of impartial high-level deliberation that she and other Concept 1 democrats envisage as the heart of the political process plays indeed only a slight role in people's vocational, recreational, and familial activities.

When politics is conceived of in Arendt's terms, Concept 1 democracy slides over into "transformative democracy."[8] This is the idea (hinted at in my quotation from Bonnie Honig in Chapter 3) that if only all institu-

---

6. Cass R. Sunstein, "Interest Groups in American Public Law," 38 *Stanford Law Review* 29, 45–49 (1985), comes close to defining deliberative democracy as an activity not of the people but of officials: "the federalists did not believe that representatives would or should respond mechanically to private pressure. Instead, the national representatives were to be above the fray of private interests. Above all, their task was deliberative." Id. at 46. The deliberative incapacity of the people, as compared to legislators, is asserted, among other places, in Julian N. Eule, "Judicial Review of Direct Democracy," 99 *Yale Law Journal* 1503, 1526–1527 (1990).

7. Learned Hand, *The Bill of Rights* 74 (1958).

8. Indeed, Jon Elster regards as central to what I am calling Concept 1 democracy "the transformation rather than simply the aggregation of preferences." Elster, "Introduction," in *Deliberative Democracy* 1 (Jon Elster ed. 1998).

tions, not just political ones, were subject to democratic control by the people affected by them, so that factories were controlled by workers, consumers, and suppliers as well as by mangers and owners, and universities by students and staff as well as by faculty and trustees, society would be fundamentally transformed, presumably in the direction of utopian socialism.[9] This illiberal concept of democracy—premised as it is on the elimination, in my two examples, of property rights and of academic freedom as normally understood, respectively—is in tension with the milder versions of Concept 1 democracy. Besides wanting to leave an extensive space for the traditional liberties and a private life, sober proponents of Concept 1 democracy realize that deliberation is not effective in bridging fundamental disagreements.[10] A Pentecostal and an atheist, a pro-lifer and a pro-choicer, a pacifist and a foreign-policy "realist," a hunter and a vegan, do not reach a modus vivendi through discussion; discussion exacerbates their differences by bringing them into open contention.

A faculty workshop is a productive forum for deliberation because the participants share the essential premises of their disagreements; they are on common ground. Modeling democracy on a faculty workshop, the tendency of Concept 1 theorists (though resisted by some), implies, therefore, limiting debate over fundamentals, a conspicuous feature of Rawls's concept of "public reason."[11] It also implies that political influence will flow to people who are "learned and practiced in making arguments that would be recognized by others as reasonable ones—no matter how worthy or true their presentations actually are."[12] "It is hard to avoid the suspicion that

9. See John Medearis, *Joseph Schumpeter's Two Theories of Democracy* (2001), arguing that Schumpeter's theory of democracy (essentially my Concept 2) was a reaction to transformative democracy, which was much in the air in Schumpeter's Austria in the immediate aftermath of World War I.

10. See, for example, Cass R. Sunstein, *Designing Democracy: What Constitutions Do* 8 (2001) ("in many cases, however, all the deliberation in the world will not dissolve disagreement"); Sunstein, *Legal Reasoning and Political Conflict*, ch. 2 (1996); Sunstein, *One Case at a Time: Judicial Minimalism on the Supreme Court* 14, 25 (1999). The limits to achieving consensus in political matters are well discussed in Raymond Geuss, *Public Goods, Private Goods* 96–104 (2001).

11. John Rawls, *Political Liberalism* 241–254 (1993). He modified his position in the introduction to the paperback edition of *Political Liberalism*, the relevant portion of which is reprinted as John Rawls, "Postscript," in *Deliberative Democracy*, note 3 above, at 131, 134–138—yet also says there that "public reason sees the office of citizen with its duty of civility as analogous to that of judgeship with its duty of deciding cases," id. at 137, though only with regard to issues "of constitutional essentials and matters of basic justice." Rawls, *Political Liberalism*, above, at 241.

12. Lynn M. Sanders, "Against Deliberation," 25 *Political Theory* 347, 349 (1997). For

deliberative democracy is the 'democracy' of elite intellectuals."[13] Its intellectual elitism disgusts radicals and populists.[14]

Philosophical pragmatists may reject deliberative democracy as an echo of Socrates' fallacious claim that the unexamined life is not worth living. Socrates thought that each of us has within him, though often deeply hidden, the essential truths of morality, including political morality. Through debate and education and introspection we can bring these truths to the surface. And since they are truths they must be the same for everybody, so that once they are brought to the surface disagreement ceases. Pragmatists consider this nonsense.

No doubt, if pressed, most Concept 1 democrats—though, being academics, they themselves deliberate in an academic fashion—would not insist that officials and ordinary citizens deliberate in the identical fashion as they. Nothing in the definition of deliberative democracy requires its adherents to adopt so austerely intellectualist a catalog of public virtues as I have ascribed to them. They might agree with Protagoras that the insights essential to political governance do not require specialized intellectual abilities at all. But they have said too little about the form that subacademic deliberation by the public as a whole might take to enable its feasibility to be assessed.[15] When they do envisage nonacademic deliberation it

these and other reasons, "deliberation has at least a few suspicious antidemocratic associations." Id. See also Elizabeth Anderson, "Pragmatism, Science, and Moral Inquiry," in *In Face of the Facts: Moral Inquiry in American Scholarship* 10, 36 (Richard Wightman Fox and Robert B. Westbrook eds. 1998).

13. Russell Hardin, "Deliberation: Method, Not Theory," in *Deliberative Politics: Essays on Democracy and Disagreement* 103, 112 (Stephen Macedo ed. 1999).

14. See, for a powerful statement, J. M. Balkin, "Populism and Progressivism as Constitutional Categories," 104 *Yale Law Journal* 1935, 1957, 1988–1999 (1995); see also John R. Wallach, *The Platonic Political Art: A Study of Critical Reason and Democracy* 401–410 (2001); Jeremy Waldron, *Law and Disagreement* (1999); Margaret Jane Radin, "A Deweyan Perspective on the Economic Theory of Democracy," 11 *Constitutional Commentary* 539 (1994–1995); Timothy V. Kaufman-Osborn, "Pragmatism, Policy Science, and the State," 29 *American Journal of Political Science* 827 (1985).

15. A much-discussed exception is James Fishkin's "deliberative poll" experiments. See James S. Fishkin, *The Voice of the People: Public Opinion and Democracy* 161–176 (1995). "The idea is simple. Take a national random sample of the electorate and transport those people from all over the country to a single place. Immerse the sample in the issues, with carefully balanced briefing materials, with intensive discussions in small groups, and with the chance to question competing experts and politicians. At the end of several days of working through the issues face to face, poll the participants in detail. The resulting survey offers a representation of the considered judgments of the public." Id. at 162. See also James S. Fishkin, *Democracy and Deliberation: New Directions for Democratic Reform* (1991). The BBC conducted such a poll in 1994, and, sure enough, it changed some of the political views of the participants. A similar poll was conducted in the United States in 1996. Although that is the only national-

is usually by judges and other highly educated experts engaged in a form of discourse similar to academic debate. Since so many Americans (but virtually none of the leading theorists of Concept 1 democracy) are religious, and religious belief is a showstopper so far as public debate in our society is concerned, it is doubtful that deliberation over fundamental political goals and values is feasible outside our leading universities, the ethos of which is secular.

Concept 2 democrats are not so cynical, or so irrationalist, as to deny that there are values in discussion. That would be absurd,[16] even for those who don't accept (as I do) Dewey's concept of epistemic democracy, which ascribes great benefits to sharing ideas and comparing perspectives. People respond to facts even if they don't respond to arguments, and deliberation can be a means of exchanging facts, pointing the way to new solutions even to long-festering disputes.[17] Deliberation even by ordinary citizens may be meaningful and productive in dealing with local political conflicts, which are more likely to involve practical issues having concrete, readily determinable stakes than disputes over fundamental values and ultimate goals. If they are homeowners, their wealth may be significantly affected by how local issues (public schools, zoning, police and fire protection, real estate taxes, and so forth) are resolved, even if they are not directly affected. For example, they might not have any children of school age, but the quality of the local public school and the size of the school tax will affect the value of all residential properties in the school district. Widespread home owner-

---

level U.S. poll, there have been several local such polls and several in foreign countries as well. Fishkin, who heads the Center for Deliberative Polling at the University of Texas, has been involved in all of these; and all have produced at least short-term changes in the opinions of the participants, although the long-term effects on them and on the larger public are unknown. See Center for Deliberative Polling, "Deliberative Polling Blue Book," May 2001, http://www.la.utexas.edu/research/delpol/bluebook/summary.html. Despite the lack of information about these effects, Fishkin and Bruce Ackerman have proposed that a new national holiday be created, "Deliberation Day," in the week before national elections. On that day all registered voters would meet in small groups in their neighborhoods to discuss the central issues of the political campaign. Each participant would receive $150, provided that he voted in the election. Bruce Ackerman and James Fishkin, "Deliberation Day," http://www.la.utexas.edu/conf2000/papers (paper delivered at a conference on Deliberating about Deliberative Democracy held at the University of Texas, Feb. 4–6, 2000).

16. See James D. Fearon, "Deliberation as Discussion," in *Deliberative Democracy*, note 8 above, at 44.

17. See William R. Caspary, *Dewey on Democracy* 148–149 (2000). For suggestions for enhancing deliberative politics at the local level, see Archon Fung, "Creating Deliberative Publics: Governance after Devolution and Democratic Centralism," *The Good Society*, no. 1, 2002, p. 66.

ship may do more for democracy than any measure advocated by delibera-tive democrats could do.

Only intellectuals believe either that discussion can resolve deep politi-cal or ideological conflicts, conflicts based not on easily resolved disputes over mere facts but rather on differences in deep-rooted values, life experi-ence, temperament, religious conviction, or upbringing, or that the demo-cratic political process at the national or state level as distinct from the lo-cal level much resembles a discussion. Carl Schmitt may have been guilty of overstatement in asserting that the natural state of man is enmity and therefore that the essence of politics is war.[18] But in a morally heteroge-neous nation like the United States, many issues can be resolved only by the force surrogate that is majority vote. It is a surrogate for force not only because it does not resolve issues on the basis of anything that resembles scientific reasoning or other forms of informed rational inquiry, but also because, as theorists of social choice have taught us, voting is not even a reliable method of aggregating preferences.[19] What voting has mainly go-ing for it is economy and a kind of equality, rather than anything to do with deliberation. A kind of equality because a person cannot be divested of his vote by reason of his not being able to mount an articulate defense of his political preferences.

Concerning the limits of deliberation, I can speak from more than twenty years of personal experience as an appellate judge. Appellate judges sit in panels rather than alone and after hearing the lawyers' arguments confer about how to decide the case. It has often been claimed that if only judges were more patient, or had more time for deliberation, they would

18. See Carl Schmitt, *The Concept of the Political* 35 (George Schwab trans. 1996). "A world without war would be a world without politics; a world without politics would be a world without enmity; and a world without enmity would be a world without human beings." Mark Lilla, *The Reckless Mind: Intellectuals in Politics* 58 (2001) (summarizing Schmitt's position). Hence, according to Schmitt, "there is 'absolutely no liberal politics, only a liberal critique of politics.'" Id. at 59. Conflicts between friends and enemies, which to Schmitt are the essential conflicts of politics, "can neither be decided by a previously determined general norm nor by the judgment of a disinterested and therefore neutral third party." Schmitt, above, at 27. Cf. Heraclitus: "It is necessary to know that war is common and [that] right [or justice, *diké*] is strife [*eris*] and that all things happen by strife and necessity." G. S. Kirk, J. E. Raven, and M. Schofield, *The Presocratic Philosophers: A Critical History with a Selection of Texts* 193 (2d ed. 1983). See also Friedrich Nietzsche, *The Pre-Platonic Philosophers* 64 (Greg Whitlock trans. 1995).

19. See, for example, William H. Riker, *Liberalism against Populism: A Confrontation be-tween the Theory of Democracy and the Theory of Social Choice* (1982).

iron out their differences; at least their decisions would be better.[20] But it is not impatience or the pressures of time that are responsible for the fact, noted in the last chapter, that judges discuss *least* the most sensitive cases, or the most sensitive issues in a case, the ones that stir judges most deeply. In such a case the judge will of course announce his position to his colleagues at the postargument conference at which the judges vote on how to decide the case, but he is unlikely to argue for it (and he will make himself obnoxious if he does), because argument over fundamentals creates anger and is more likely to deepen and congeal disagreement than to overcome it. What is true of the deliberations of judges is true also of the deliberations of legislators and of the citizenry at large. "Deliberation can bring differences to the surface, widening the political divisions rather than narrowing them. This is what Marxists hoped would result from 'consciousness-raising.'"[21]

Deliberation can, it is true, serve a political function even when it does not serve an epistemic one. Between transformative democracy and the most intellectualist versions of deliberative democracy we find the idea, which combines a Millian with a safety-valve or feedback-fostering concept of free speech, that debate over fundamentals can be valuable in allowing people to blow off steam, in enabling the authorities to monitor public opinion and emotion, and in shaking people out of their dogmatic slumbers without necessarily changing their minds on the spot. (The last point is Mill's, and was elaborated by Peirce.) None of these are points emphasized by deliberative democrats. None has much to do with deliberation as a means of bringing about consensus through calm reasoning. And none is incompatible with Concept 2, which does not seek to stifle debate over fundamentals but just doesn't want to make it the heart of politics.

It is important to note that Concept 1 is not a theory of direct democracy. Its proponents recognize that only in the tiniest polities is it feasible for the citizenry to determine policy or administer government directly. Even the town-meeting governments of colonial New England, which constituted the townspeople themselves (or at least those who showed up

20. For a classic statement, see Henry M. Hart, Jr., "The Supreme Court, 1958 Term—Foreword: The Time Chart of the Justices," 73 *Harvard Law Review* 84 (1959).

21. Ian Shapiro, "Enough about Deliberation: Politics Is about Interests and Power," in *Deliberative Politics*, note 13 above, at 28, 31. See also Daniel A. Bell, "Democratic Deliberation: The Problem of Implementation," in id. at 70.

for meetings) as the town's legislators, delegated management responsibilities to officials. The town meeting corresponded to the Assembly of ancient Athens, but the managers were elected, rather than, as in Athens, chosen by lot. In a modern polity, direct democracy of the Athenian or the New England town-meeting variety gives way to representative democracy, though sometimes with pockets of direct democracy, such as the Swiss and California referendums or, for that matter, those New England towns in which the town meeting is still the local legislature. Representative democracy is consistent with Concept 1 provided that the elected representatives are not imperfect agents, with their own interests, let alone oligarchs or aristocrats, nor mere conduits of the views of their constituents either. Provided, in other words, that they engage in the same kind of intelligent, civic-minded political deliberation in which their constituents are supposed to engage but with the advantage of the added skills and information that they possess by virtue of devoting their full time to public matters. Many Concept 1 democrats actually distrust direct democracy because it asks too much of the ordinary citizen in the way of acquiring and processing information about policy.[22] But representative democracy understood in Concept 1 terms asks too much of the representatives, in particular in asking them to set aside career imperatives and other tugs of self-interest.

The democratic ideal that I am describing approximates, except for its substitution of representative for direct democracy, what Benjamin Constant famously called the "liberty of the ancients." That was the Greek and Roman concept of liberty—more broadly, personal fulfillment—as political participation.[23] The liberty of the moderns is freedom from coercion by government, including democratic government. Free speech, freedom from arbitrary arrest and imprisonment, the right of just compensation for property taken for public use, the prohibition against retroactive criminal punishment, and the other familiar modern liberties are, in a democratic polity, restrictions on democratic preference, on the tyranny of the majority. Not on that alone, to be sure. To the extent that officials are imperfect agents of the people, the people need rights against them even if the majority of the population has no desire to tyrannize over anyone.

If Concept 1 democracy could be realized in practice, so that all government action was the product of intelligent and scrupulously civic-minded

22. See, for example, Eule, note 6 above. I return to this point in Chapter 7.
23. An excellent recent discussion is Geuss, note 10 above, ch. 1.

deliberation, there would be little room for the modern liberties, which operate largely either as constraints on democratic preference or as non-democratic features of the governance structure. The non- and sometimes antidemocratic cast of the modern liberties is why some adherents to Concept 1, "strong democrats" we might call them, regard the enforcement of constitutional rights by the unelected, life-tenured Justices of the Supreme Court as rather an embarrassment for democratic theory, or at least as requiring strenuous efforts at justification.

These strong democrats tend also to be egalitarian liberals, however, as the genealogy of Concept 1 democracy (Rousseau, Mill, Dewey, Habermas) reveals. Not all. The ancestry, after all, is mixed; consider Madison and Tocqueville, neither an egalitarian; and many social conservatives today would like to see moral deliberation play a larger role in politics. But partly just reflecting the current political coloration of American universities, most Concept 1 theorists are egalitarians—and many of them are egalitarians first and democrats second. Because equality of results, a leveling of incomes, a generous social safety net, and the other goals of the modern welfare state cannot be achieved without strong government, welfare statists—the modern egalitarians—want to believe in the goodness of government. They embrace Concept 1 democracy as the very model of governance in the public interest.

These democratic theorists are also engaged, however, in a complex negotiation between their warm and hopeful regard for democracy and their enthusiasm for the characteristic outcomes of constitutional adjudication by our oligarchic judiciary. They feel acutely the tension between the liberty of the ancients, the original Concept 1 democracy, and the liberty of the moderns, which constrains democracy and is exemplified by the interpretation of constitutional rights, overriding democratic preference, by the U.S. Supreme Court.[24] (Notice how the word "liberty" equivocates between democracy and antidemocracy.) If they are lawyers they may try to resolve the tension by emphasizing the deliberative and hence in a sense "democratic" character of appellate decisionmaking;[25] the democracy-reinforcing character of some constitutional rights; public-minded civil ser-

---

24. "Judicial review [that is, the judicial power to invalidate legislative and other governmental action on constitutional grounds] is a deviant institution in the American democracy." Alexander M. Bickel, *The Least Dangerous Branch: The Supreme Court at the Bar of Politics* 17–18 (1962).

25. For an extreme version of this position, see Christopher J. Peters, "Adjudication as Representation," 97 *Columbia Law Review* 312 (1997).

vants as "virtual representatives" of the electors who did not elect them, doing what the electors would want done had they the requisite expert knowledge; the Ur-democratic character of the constitutional provisions that the federal courts enforce; and the superior democratic legitimacy of policies or provisions, constitutional or otherwise, adopted in periods of exalted democratic passion. These gambits are defensive and unconvincing. They leech the blood out of the concept of democracy by making democracy a synonym for good government in the sense of enlightened rule by competent, well-meaning judges and bureaucrats.

Jed Rubenfeld, for example, is eloquent on the tension between deliberative democracy and judicial review.[26] His effort to dissolve it and so justify his liberal activist stance involves redefining democracy as adherence to the commitments implicit in our written Constitution.[27] Among these is a commitment that Rubenfeld calls "anti-totalitarianism" and interprets to forbid prohibiting abortion and discriminating against homosexuals, a prohibition and a discrimination that he considers designed to force women to bear children and homosexuals to be heterosexuals, respectively.[28] But that is not all that such laws do, and few readers of his ingenious book will be persuaded that his position on these questions (a position I personally agree with) reflects rather than constrains democracy.

The strains in the thinking of strong democrats may reflect the class gulf between theoreticians and the public as a whole.[29] The very wealthy and the very poor have in our society more in common with the average person than the political theorist does. The latter belongs to the intellectual class, which tends to be alienated from everyday American life and thought. "American intellectuals . . . are overwhelmingly adversarial toward the American system . . . Modern intellectuals pride themselves on their anti-Americanism."[30] Many intellectuals think they know what is true and what is right. They consider themselves wiser and more disinterested than politicians, business people, workers, and the public at large. Because like other people they tend to clump, associating mainly with one another

26. Jed Rubenfeld, *Freedom and Time: A Theory of Constitutional Self-Government*, ch. 3 (2001).

27. See id., pt. 3.

28. Id., ch. 12.

29. For an excellent discussion that has not dated, see Seymour Martin Lipset, *Political Man: The Social Bases of Politics*, ch. 10 (1960).

30. Robert Lerner, Althea K. Nagai, and Stanley Rothman, *American Elites* 138 (1996). The passage I have quoted is from the authors' conclusion to their exhaustive empirical study.

to the virtual exclusion of the rest of the population, their alienation is intensified by the constant reinforcement of their own views by exchange with like-minded others. The skepticism of a Learned Hand, the skepticism (detachment would be the better word) of a Holmes, who liked to say that if the people wanted to go to hell it was his job as a judge to help them find the path, is unusual. The typical theorist is unashamed to find himself at the extreme left or extreme right of the political spectrum, the places where in fact most political theorists can be found today. He is proud not to think like the average man. He stands fast, and calls on the mainstream to shift toward him. So we have left liberals claiming that there are no real liberals on the Supreme Court—not one—and rightists claiming that the Court has sold out to the secular liberalism of the left. The political theorist looks in the mirror and sees a philosopher king. Plato was at least consistent in believing that if there are objective truths of political morality accessible to the wise but not to the ordinary person, the wise should rule. He sounded a theme that continues to reverberate among intellectuals.

Most Concept 1 democrats are liberals, indeed left liberals; but most liberals, including left liberals, are not Concept 1 democrats. There is no reason why someone who favors liberal public policies should model democracy on a faculty workshop—no reason, therefore, why someone who identifies with the Democratic Party, as many prominent left-liberal academics do today, should be Concept 1 democrats. I will argue in Chapter 6 that a Concept 1 democrat who opposed Clinton's impeachment but also opposed *Bush v. Gore* was inconsistent; but a left liberal or a Democratic Party zealot who took these positions was not, unless he was a Concept 1 democrat.

Concept 2 Democracy: Elite, Pragmatic, Schumpeterian

When Concept 1 democrats endorse representative as distinct from direct democracy or accept the need for constitutional restrictions on majority rule, they bow in the direction of Concept 2, the democracy of the pragmatists, more precisely of the everyday pragmatists (to distinguish them from Dewey in particular). These pragmatists do not begin with moral or political theory but with the actual practice of democracy in its various instantiations from Athens in the fifth and fourth centuries B.C. to the United States in the twenty-first century A.D. From this history and their observations of human nature and social institutions these pragmatists infer that Concept 1 democracy is unworkable. It hopelessly exaggerates the moral and intellectual capacities, both actual and potential, not only of the average person but also of the average official (including judge) and even of the political theorists who seek to tutor the people and the officials. Concept 2 democrats reject "dewy-eyed idealization of 'endless conversation'"[31] along with the public-interest conception of the state. They see politics as a competition among self-interested politicians, constituting a ruling class, for the support of the people, also assumed to be self-interested, and to be none too interested in or well informed about politics. Democracy as pictured by Concept 2 democrats is not self-rule. It is rule by officials who are, however, chosen by the people and who if they don't perform to expectations are fired by the people at the end of a short fixed or limited term of office.[32]

They don't, these dyspeptic Concept 2 democrats, even accept all the aspirations of the Concept 1 democrat, noble as those aspirations sound in the abstract. Rather than considering public concerns worthier than private ones, they tend to consider politics ancillary rather than ultimate. They don't think jawing in the *agora* is the most productive way for people to spend their time. They don't believe that politics has intrinsic value or that political activity is ennobling. They thus stand at the furthest possible distance from Hannah Arendt and the ancient Greeks. Nor do they regard democracy as a creation of political theory and so as an apt candidate for improvement by it. The Athenians did not get the idea of democracy from a book.[33] And the renewed stirrings of democracy in the postmedieval West after a hiatus of two millennia following the fall of Athenian democracy owed less to political theory than to material factors, such as the in-

31. Stephen Holmes, *The Anatomy of Antiliberalism* 58 (1993). The pun is apt, though I assume unintended.

32. In the United States the terms of elected officials are almost always a fixed number of years, whereas in parliamentary systems they are limited—a maximum interval between elections is specified but elections can be held earlier if the government loses the support of a majority of the parliament and as a result parliament is dissolved.

33. See M. I. Finley, *Democracy Ancient and Modern* 49 (rev. ed. 1985). Josiah Ober, "How to Criticize Democracy in Late Fifth- and Fourth-Century Athens," in Ober, *The Athenian Revolution: Essays on Greek Democracy and Political Theory* 140 (1996), argues that the pragmatic character of Athenian democracy (on which see id. at 10–11, 141) provoked the efforts by Plato, Aristotle, and other philosophers to create philosophically rigorous political theory. (For a fuller exposition of Ober's view, see Josiah Ober, *Political Dissent in Democratic Athens: Intellectual Critics of Popular Rule* [1998].) In any event, political philosophy followed rather than preceded Athenian democracy, which was well established by 450 B.C. See R. K. Sinclair, *Democracy and Participation in Athens*, ch. 1 (1988).

vention of the printing press, which enabled a much larger slice of the public to become informed on public matters than had been possible previously, resulting in the emergence of public opinion formidable enough to compel rulers' attention.[34]

Concept 2 thus is unillusioned about democracy, which it regards as an accident, often but not always a fortunate one, of historical circumstances. Athens was a genuine democracy, though a limited one; only about 20 percent of the adult population were citizens, and only two-thirds of those 20 percent had full rights of citizenship, in particular the right to hold public office.[35] But Athens faltered, not only in the conduct of the Peloponnesian War (Thucydides ascribed Athens' defeat to democratic envy of Alcibiades, and to other deformities of democracy)[36] but also in the condemnation of Socrates[37] and, related to that, a failure to provide institutional safeguards for personal liberties. The Roman Republic mingled democratic with oligarchic and dictatorial elements. The last seventy-five years or so of the Republic, however, were a downward spiral toward anarchy. The empire created by Octavius Caesar in 27 B.C. ended the spiral. While not at all democratic, the Roman Empire, until it started to come apart in the middle of the third century and despite the egregious behavior of some of the emperors, may well have been the greatest political accomplishment in human history.

34. This is the thesis of David Zaret, *Origins of Democratic Culture: Printing, Petitions, and the Public Sphere in Early-Modern England* 272–273 (2000). See id., ch. 1, pp. 6–8, for a summary.

35. Mogens Herman Hansen, *The Athenian Democracy in the Age of Demosthenes: Structure, Principles and Ideology* 89, 93–94 (1991).

36. See Richard Winton, "Herodotus, Thucydides, and the Sophists," in *The Cambridge History of Greek and Roman Political Thought* 89, 117, 119–120 (Christopher Rowe and Malcolm Schofield eds. 2000); Ober, *Political Dissent in Democratic Athens*, note 33 above, at 104–121 (noting that Thucydides argued "the instability of error-prone democracy when it is reenvisioned as government by competing speeches," id. at 118); Simon Hornblower, *Thucydides* 160–176 (1987). Thucydides may have been wrong. Modern historians tend to ascribe Athens' defeat to Persia's aid to Sparta, or to the Athenian provocations that brought about the war in the first place. Id. at 174; Finley, note 33 above, ch. 2. Still, his criticism of the democratic decisionmaking that produced the disastrous expedition to Sicily, usually considered the turning point of the war, was cogent. See Ober, *Political Dissent in Democratic Athens*, above, at 104–120.

37. See David Cohen, *Law, Sexuality, and Society: The Enforcement of Morals in Classical Athens* 214–217 (1991), arguing that the prosecution of Socrates was not aberrational. Yet in fairness it should be noted that the death of Socrates was followed by three-quarters of a century that some historians consider the high point of Athenian democracy. See Hansen, note 35 above, at 300–320. Cf. Ober, "How to Criticize Democracy in Late Fifth- and Fourth-Century Athens," note 33 above, at 148–150.

Democracy was dropped from the world's political agenda for two millennia; there may be a lesson here. Even in the twentieth century, democracy was not always the best form of government. The Weimar Republic was a democracy of sorts, but Germany and the world might have been better off had Germany remained a monarchy after World War I. Spain might have been spared civil war and Franco had it not been a republic. Democracy let the French down in the decade that led up to World War II. Indeed, almost all the democracies faltered badly in the period between the world wars and were ill prepared to meet the aggression of Germany and Japan.

If Tocqueville was right, even American democracy is the accidental product of circumstances (largely though not entirely material)[38] rather than a creation of political theorists.[39] America lacked a hereditary aristocracy. Distance and estrangement from Britain had fostered self-government, especially in the New England towns, whose democratic systems of governance (which preceded Locke) became models for the nation as a whole.[40] And there was much greater equality of wealth, education, and class in colonial America than in Europe with its pattern of a few very rich and many very poor and few in the middle. With monarchy, dictatorship, theocracy, and aristocracy not in the running, democratic republicanism emerged as the default solution to the problem of how America would be governed after the break with Britain.

Tocqueville himself was, along with Mill, an ancestor of the "virtuous cycle" version of Concept 1 democracy, which in turn abuts or even overlaps the transformative version. He ascribed the productive energy of Americans to democracy, with emphasis on the New England town meeting, a classic venue of deliberative democracy, and thought that nondemocratic regimes had an enervating effect on the energy and ambition of the

38. See Alexis de Tocqueville, *Democracy in America* 265–267 (Harvey C. Mansfield and Delba Winthrop trans. 2000). In Tocqueville's view, "American democracy was compatible with political stability because of non-transferable factors such as cheap land and the open frontier (outlets for lower-class unrest), the remoteness of military threats, the lack of a single center such as Paris, the lack of a parasitic aristocracy needing to be uprooted, and the absence of a tradition of hostility between republicanism and religion." Stephen Holmes, "Both Sides Now," *New Republic*, Mar. 4 and 11, 2002, pp. 31, 37.

39. Pragmatists are therefore inclined to agree with Pocock that Machiavelli, a republican but not a democrat, had more influence (albeit indirect) on the formation of American political values and thought than Locke or Montesquieu did, J. G. A. Pocock, *The Machiavellian Moment: Florentine Political Thought and the Atlantic Republican Tradition* 545 (1975), because Machiavelli showed how republican government could be made to work.

40. Tocqueville, note 38 above, at 40, 42.

common man. He was wrong about the virtuous cycle and the effects of deliberative democracy. (Toward the end of *Democracy in America*, moreover, he, like his Concept 1 descendants, turned pessimistic, worrying that American democracy would make Americans infantile and complacent.) The distinctive American character, the character that is more commercial, egalitarian, individualistic, and inventive than the predemocratic European, was a cause rather than a consequence of American democracy. Consider: whatever may have been the case, or may have been thought by Tocqueville to have been the case, in the early days of the nation, Concept 2 democracy best describes the American political system today; is remote from the dreams of deliberative democrats; yet provides as nourishing a framework for America's distinctive economic and social culture as the American democracy described by Tocqueville did. His description of America's hard-working, upbeat, hands-on, endlessly inventive, philistine culture remains startlingly apt. The American character has changed less than American democracy has. How likely is it, therefore, that Americans would be much different from what they are if America were more democratic than it is, especially since an increase in democracy would probably have to be purchased with a reduction in liberty, the importance of which to a commercial culture can hardly be overestimated? Without secure protection of property rights, commercial enterprise is terribly risky; this is a major reason why the American political system was created to be and remains a mixed system rather than a pure democracy.

And even if Tocqueville was right about the *origins* of the culture that he observed, there is nothing to suggest that today's quite similar culture is delicately balanced on the precise configuration that American democracy has assumed. Whatever jump start the town meeting or other eighteenth-century democratic or proto-democratic institutions gave to the development of the distinctive culture of the United States, that culture is up and running and probably impervious to incremental adjustments in the system of political governance.

Another reason to reject Tocqueville's causal analysis is that, when he wrote, American democracy, especially at the federal level, was of a distinctly limited kind. If a version of Concept 1 democracy at all, it was an elite version, and this reinforces one's doubts that Americans' democratic attitudes and capacities depend on a commitment to Concept 1 democracy. Not only was suffrage far from universal, with women, slaves (and most free blacks as well), and the propertyless excluded, but among federal officials only members of the House of Representatives were elected directly. All other federal officials, including the President and Vice President, all other executive officials, all Senators, and all federal judges, either were elected indirectly or were appointed by the President or by subordinate executive officials. Among the rights conferred by the Constitution, the right to vote was conspicuous by its absence. The word "democracy" also does not appear. The reference to "We the People" in the preamble is a claim of popular sovereignty[41]—an assertion that the Constitution was adopted by democratic choice, not that it establishes a democracy. A dictatorship created by a plebiscite is still a dictatorship.

Mistrust of democracy was also reflected in the provisions of the Constitution splitting and overlapping governmental powers among different branches of government and enabling judicially enforceable rights against government, as well as in the emphasis that the founding generation placed on republican virtue—less grandly, civic-mindedness.[42] Civic-mindedness (never mind that by the time Tocqueville wrote, it had pretty much been obliterated by the Jacksonian revolution—and it had been eroding from the start) may seem the quintessence of Concept 1 democracy. That depends, however, on whether it is thought to be distributed throughout the population, as Protagoras and other radical democrats have believed, or to be the property of an elite. The latter is closer to the conception held by most of the framers. They ordained indirect election of the President, Vice President, and Senators in the hope that the electors (the members of the Electoral College in the case of the President and Vice President, and the state legislators, in the case of the Senators), a select rather than random group, would be better able than the public at large to pick the best people for public office. If indirect election bespoke distrust of the public, separation of powers and adoption of a judicially enforceable Bill of Rights bespoke distrust of officials despite the framers' hopes for a civic-minded officialdom that were lodged in indirect election. And though state governments were (and are) more democratic than the federal government, as I noted in the preceding chapter, a number of provisions of the Constitution, for example the prohibitions against states'

41. See Jeremy Waldron, "Judicial Power and Popular Sovereignty" (Columbia Law School, n.d., unpublished).

42. See, for example, Carl J. Richard, *The Founders and the Classics: Greece, Rome, and the American Enlightenment* (1994); Cass R. Sunstein, "Beyond the Republican Revival," 97 *Yale Law Journal* 1539, 1564–1565 (1988).

passing ex post facto laws or impairing the obligation of contracts, are designed to protect the people against oppression and exploitation by those governments. In sum, "The original Constitution reflected a particularly elite conception of democratic politics."[43] Since the enactment of the Fourteenth Amendment in 1868, moreover, the vast majority of legislative and executive actions invalidated by the federal courts have been actions by state and local government rather than by the federal government. Democracy continues to be distrusted.

Although the framers of the Constitution of 1787 envisaged what can fairly be termed an elite democracy, it would be anachronistic to call them elitists. Compared to English and other European statesmen of the time, they were radicals. But it would be a mistake to infer from this that if they were living today they would be radicals, or at least left liberals, and to conclude therefore that the Constitution should be interpreted as a charter of Concept 1 democracy. If the framers were living today they would be different people, people who knew a great many things that nobody in 1787 could have known, and it is impossible to say whether this additional knowledge would have made them more or less radical than the actual framers. The fact that a person is radical in a specific historical milieu doesn't mean he'll remain so when his milieu becomes more radical. He may remain constant in his opinions, in which event, as the mainstream moves to his left, he will, though standing still, be perceived as moving to the right. What the framers bequeathed to us was a governmental system

43. Samuel Issacharoff, Pamela S. Karlan, and Richard H. Pildes, *The Law of Democracy: Legal Structure of the Political Process* 17 (2001). To similar effect, see Robert A. Dahl, "On Removing Certain Impediments to Democracy in the United States," 92 *Political Science Quarterly* 1, 4–7 (1977). "The constitution's creators differed little in their expectation that gentlemen would continue to rule throughout the land, as they made clear through such mechanisms as the indirect election of senators and the president. The lower orders would continue to give deference to 'the elevated classes of the community.'" Ronald P. Formisano, "State Development in the Early Republic: Substance and Structure, 1780–1840," in *Contesting Democracy: Substance and Structure in American Political History, 1775–2000*, at 7, 11 (Byron E. Shafer and Anthony J. Badger eds. 2001). George P. Fletcher notes "the élitist republican scheme envisioned at the founding." Fletcher, *Our Secret Constitution: How Lincoln Redefined American Democracy* 54 (2001). Larry Kramer quotes a striking statement by Benjamin Rush, one of the founding fathers, that would have warmed Schumpeter's heart: The people "possess it [political power] only on the days of their elections. After this, it is the property of their rulers, nor can they exercise it or resume it, unless it is abused." Larry D. Kramer, "The Supreme Court, 2000 Term—Foreword: We the Court," 115 *Harvard Law Review* 4, 93 (2001). Kramer considers the original Constitution populist but argues that the Federalist position, at least with reference to the desirability of judicial checks on the whims and caprices of the people, eventually prevailed despite the collapse of the Federalist Party. The victory owed much to John Marshall, as I noted in Chapter 2.

that despite all subsequent changes remains closer to elite than to deliberative democracy.

American Democracy Today

In embracing the framers, notably Madison, the proponents of deliberative democracy overlook the biggest mistake the framers made. The mistake was excessive fear of democracy. It was not that the framers under-
rated the knowledge or character of ordinary people, but that they didn't
realize how robust American democracy would prove to be to mediocrity,
and worse, in both the elite and the masses. It was an understandable mistake. The prevailing view in the eighteenth century was that democracy
was workable only in small states, such as ancient Athens. Democracy on
the American scale was a gamble. It was natural to suppose that it wouldn't
work without a considerable dose of high-mindedness. But by the end of
George Washington's Presidency, high-mindedness was little in evidence;
vicious party politics was already the order of the day; and ever since,
the average quality, both intellectual and moral, of elected and unelected
officials alike has been unimpressive. On the state and local level it has frequently been appalling. But the nation has survived—indeed, has thrived,
reaching unimagined levels of freedom, wealth, and power. Common
sense on the part of the electorate, and political ability (which seems not to
be highly correlated with either intellect or character) on the part of the
senior officials, especially the elected ones, and ordinary competence on
the part of the junior officials seem to be all that a democratic political system requires to operate effectively.

Despite many legal and institutional changes since 1787, the American
political system still is better described as elite democracy than as either
deliberative or populist democracy. True, the progressive enlargement of
the franchise (to the unpropertied, to blacks, to women, to illiterates, to
eighteen-year-olds, to residents of the District of Columbia), the spread of
the primary system for selecting candidates, and the movement to popular
election of Presidential electors and U.S. Senators have made the federal
government more democratic than it was in 1789. But American government as a whole has not become notably more democratic. State government remains more democratic than the federal government[44] but has

44. In fact it has become *more* democratic because of the Supreme Court's insistence that
state senates be apportioned by population, just like the lower houses of the states and the

steadily lost power to it, and not only to its judicial branch. Voter turnout—as shown in the accompanying chart[45]—is near its all-time low and is far lower than it was throughout the latter half of the nineteenth century. With the growth of government and the acceleration in the rate of social change, the number and complexity of political issues have grown faster than the public's ability to understand them,[46] while interest in such issues has declined. Low turnout is a clue here—and even people who bother to vote often lack much interest in or knowledge of issues and candidates. "The classic texts of democratic theory (such as J. S. Mill and Rousseau [inventors of Concept 1 democracy]) assume that for a democracy to function properly the average citizen should be interested in, pay attention to, discuss, and actively participate in politics . . . Five decades of behavioral research in political science have left no doubt, however, that only a tiny minority of the citizens in any democracy actually live up to these ideals. Interest in politics is generally weak, discussion is rare, political knowledge on the average is pitifully low, and few people actively participate in politics beyond voting."[47]

Political power has shifted from elected officials to appointed officials and career civil servants, both groups with their own agendas and an "I know best" attitude. Federal courts, which are manned by appointed judges with life tenure, have become hyperactive in curbing democratic discretion through the enforcement of ever more broadly interpreted constitutional provisions as mushrooming case law buries the original instrument. Global competition has shifted power over the economy from voters to markets and international treaties and organizations. And the emergence of a huge voting bloc of elderly, together with the continuing disfranchisement of children, has created a perverse and undemocratic

U.S. House of Representatives. See Lucas v. Forty-Fourth General Assembly, 377 U.S. 713 (1964). The casualness with which the Supreme Court swept away a cornerstone of representative government is noted with incredulity in Issacharoff, Karlan, and Pildes, note 43 above, at 3.

45. Based on the same data sources as the turnout data in the preceding chapter. A recent study indicates, contrary to these data, that there has been no dip in turnout since 1972. But despite its title the study does not question the overall trend or the end point. Michael P. McDonald and Samuel L. Popkin, "The Myth of the Vanishing Voter," 95 *American Political Science Review* 963 (2001).

46. Cf. Russell Hardin, "Street-Level Epistemology and Democratic Participation," 10 *Journal of Political Philosophy* 212 (2002).

47. Richard R. Lau and David P. Redlawsk, "Voting Correctly," 91 *American Political Science Review* 585 (1997).

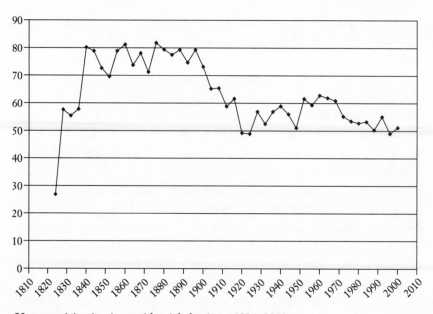

Voter participation in presidential elections, 1824–2000

power imbalance between these two groups, which compete for government largesse. It is evidence of the divided political selves of Concept 1 democrats that so many of these democrats support the undemocratic tendencies that I have just described.

There is still more to feed the pessimism of a Concept 1 democrat confronting our actual existing democracy. Voters hide behind the secret ballot, which though essential to prevent intimidation and fraud is a recipe for irresponsibility, as deliberative democrats such as John Stuart Mill argued. (Mill took deliberative democracy so seriously that he recommended that educated people be given bonus votes.)[48] With so little at stake for the individual voter, who cannot expect actually to swing the election by his vote or even to be blamed for voting the wrong way (for his vote is secret), he is prey to all those cognitive quirks that psychologists are busy documenting in their experimental subjects. There is not enough at stake for him to make the effort required to resist taking the path of least resistance, the path of lazy thought.

The dominance of the two-party system induces the parties to compete in the general election for the median voter, pushing the parties together

48. John Stuart Mill, *Considerations on Representative Government* 174–186 (1870).

(at the same time making them ideologically incoherent) and making it difficult for voters indifferent to the signature issues with which the parties inflame their respective constituent bases to choose between them. It is true that, being more extreme than the average voter, the bases tend to push the parties apart at the same time that duopolistic competition in the general election pushes them together. But radicalizing tendencies are checked by strategic voting in primaries: a voter will be reluctant to vote for the candidate whose views are closest to his own if he thinks that that candidate would lose in the general election. And to the extent that a party does yield to radicalizing tendencies in the primaries and the nominating convention only to abandon them in the general election, the party's ideological identity will be further blurred.

The prevalence of districted as distinct from at-large elections enables voter minorities to control legislatures,[49] while interest-group pressures make elected officials frequently unresponsive to the interests of ordinary, unorganized people. Because representatives have no legal duty to represent all their constituents fairly (the duty that labor law imposes on collective bargaining representatives), electoral minorities in safe districts may have no voice whatsoever in the legislature. In effectively one-party states they may have no voice even in Presidential elections—the situation of Republicans in Massachusetts and Democrats in Wyoming.

The increasingly sophisticated techniques employed in public-opinion polling and political advertising have made political campaigning manipulative and largely content-free. Fear of giving offense to voters causes politicians to shy away from acknowledging hard facts. More, it causes them to flatter the people and exaggerate the degree to which the people actually rule. Political rhetoric is deeply hypocritical.

The multiple dimensions of public office make it exceedingly difficult for voters to use the vote to influence public policy. A Presidential candidate might win election because a majority of the people thought him the stronger leader while preferring his opponent's policies; he would have no duty to adopt those policies. A legislator might be elected because of his

49. If a legislature has 100 members, each elected from a separate district, a party that receives at least 51 percent of the votes in at least 51 of the districts will have a majority of the legislature, though it may have as little as 26 percent (51 percent of 51 percent) of the votes cast in the election for the legislature. The broader point is that there is a well-nigh infinite variety of possible voting rules, few of which yield "majority rule" in some simple sense. See Gordon Tullock, *On Voting: A Public Choice Approach* (1998).

outstanding constituent service, or because 60 percent of his policies were popular, though the rest were not.

Even before it is distorted and circumscribed in the ways indicated, representative "democracy" is something of an oxymoron. As I noted in the last chapter, it is actually a form of aristocracy in Aristotle's sense of the word—rule by "the best."[50] Successful candidates are not random draws from the public at large. They are smarter, better educated, more ambitious, and wealthier than the average person. This fact alone, plus the difficulty of monitoring officials, makes the people's "representatives" at best highly imperfect agents of their nominal principals.[51] That is why the Athenians considered the selection of officials by lot an essential feature of democracy.[52] Elected officials, even if loyal agents (and why should they be expected to be?—they are self-interested like everybody else), are imperfect ones because, like political theorists, they are drawn from a different class from their constituents. The members of the U.S. Senate, regardless of party, have more in common with each other than with the majority of their constituents. We shall see that the framers of the Constitution, consistent with their suspicions of democracy, *wanted* to attenuate the principal-agent relation between the people and their elected officials. Anyway, it is hard to keep the rich and the brainy from rising; even in ancient Athens they held a disproportionate share of the principal offices of state.[53]

Concept 1 democrats are thus in a bind. Realism requires them to prefer representative to direct democracy. But realism teaches that elected representatives cannot be depended on to deliberate in the public interest. Realism is Concept 2 democracy.

50. It is also, however, as we'll see in the next chapter, Aristotle's conception of the best form of democracy.

51. See Pocock, note 39 above, at 517–520. "There was a distinction between the exercise of power in government, and the power of designating representatives to exercise it; and it could be argued both that all government was the people's and that the people had withdrawn from government altogether, leaving its exercise to a diversity of representatives who, situated as they were where the art of ruling might be learned from experience, took on the characteristics of the old natural aristocracy or specialized Few." Id. at 517.

52. See, for example, Neil Duxbury, *Random Justice: On Lotteries and Legal Decision-Making* 28–29 (1999); John V. A. Fine, *The Ancient Greeks: A Critical History* 404–405 (1985); Finley, note 33 above, at 19–20. Duxbury, above, at 23–41, discusses other examples of selection of public officials by lot as well as the Athenian. Benjamin R. Barber, *Strong Democracy: Participatory Politics for a New Age* 290–293 (1984), proposes such selection for some local officials. Finley, note 33 above, at 12–31, is a lucid description of the Athenian political system and culture.

53. See Sinclair, note 33 above, at 193–195.

Democracy and Condescension

The position in the democratic spectrum that has almost no support among political theorists is populist democracy.[54] This is the view that the people should rule, period: that is, without reeducation or elite tutelage to enable them to deliberate in an informed and responsible way. Populist democracy takes people as it finds them, warts and all, and argues that since democracy means rule by the people, the people are entitled to rule. Pragmatists are not impressed. Like populists, they take people as they find them; anything else would be unrealistic. But they do not see how entitlement enters the picture or how we would be better off without the limitations that the institutions of representative democracy, or for that matter the machinations of interest groups, impose on popular rule. Everyday pragmatists are liberals rather than democrats *tout court*. But what is more interesting is that most political theorists are not impressed by populist democracy either, even though they are not everyday pragmatists. They are drawn from a different class from the average voter and cannot stomach the idea of being ruled by people so different from themselves. One is reminded of Machiavelli's superficially very odd equation of democracy and tyranny. Like Nietzsche, he thought that in a democracy the many crush the few (the rich, the elite), whom they fear and envy, and in a tyranny the tyrant does the same thing—crush the few—because he fears them as potential rivals in a struggle for supremacy and wants to enlist the many against them.[55]

The alienation of the intelligentsia is an old story, but a true one, at least so far as the nonscientific departments of the modern American university are concerned. From the perspective of many (of course not all) of the faculty of those departments, the average voter is ignorant, philistine, provincial, selfish, excessively materialistic, puritanical (or libertine—depending on which end of the political spectrum the faculty member making the judgment occupies), superficial, vulgar, insensitive, unimaginative, complacent, chauvinistic, superstitious, uneducable, benighted politically,

54. Jeremy Waldron, *Law and Disagreement* (1999), and J. M. Balkin, "Populism and Progressivism as Constitutional Categories," 104 *Yale Law Journal* 1935 (1995), are notable exceptions. One of the most emphatic is Richard D. Parker, *"Here, the People Rule": A Constitutional Populist Manifesto* (1994). See also Parker, "Taking Politics Personally," 12 *Cardozo Studies in Law and Literature* 103, 114–117 (2000).

55. See Harvey C. Mansfield, *Machiavelli's New Modes and Orders: A Study of the Discourses on Livy* 37, 80–82 (1979).

prone to hysteria, and overweight. I am exaggerating, of course. Still, the gulf between the middle class and the academic elite is sufficiently wide that the members of the latter class, despite their own intense political and moral disagreements, are at one in their hostility to populism.

No American political or legal thinker who wants to be taken seriously, however, can openly oppose democracy or even deny that "here the people rule" in some meaningful sense. No matter; in contemporary American political discourse "democracy" is an all-purpose term of approbation, virtually empty of meaning. Cass Sunstein considers "majority rule" "a caricature of the democratic aspiration."[56] And Joshua Cohen describes not merely as unjust but as undemocratic an electoral majority's effort to suppress the religious observances of a minority.[57] The Concept 2 democrat regards majoritarianism as an incomplete theory of democracy, as we shall see in the next chapter, but he does not regard it as undemocratic.

Consider Bruce Ackerman's dualist theory of democracy, an ingenious yoking of Concept 1 and Concept 2 democracy.[58] Ackerman contrasts periods of heightened civic consciousness, such as Reconstruction and the New Deal, in which people think and debate and vote as citizens (as Concept 1 democrats, in other words), with the everyday politics of horse trades and interest groups (Concept 2 democracy). He argues that the popular will that is expressed, whether or not in valid legislation, during periods of Concept 1 democracy should be treated by the Supreme Court as amending the Constitution and so placed beyond the power of legislation to change. On this view, not the voters or elected officials, but the Supreme Court, is the oracle of democracy; the same is true, we recall, in Jed Rubenfeld's democratic theory.

In these examples and others that could be given, condescension toward ordinary people becomes the leitmotif of constitutional theorizing. "The conventional discourse of constitutional law breathes in the warm air of the academy, rises over the heads of many to whom it is supposedly addressed, and then sends down a subtle message of inadequacy to everyone

56. Cass R. Sunstein, *Designing Democracy: What Constitutions Do* 7 (2001). Peter Berkowitz, "The Demagoguery of Democratic Theory" (forthcoming in *Critical Review*, Winter–Spring 2003), aptly remarks the "conflation of democracy and justice" in the discourse of deliberative democracy.

57. Joshua Cohen, "Procedure and Substance in Deliberative Democracy," in *Deliberative Democracy*, note 3 above, at 407, 417–419.

58. See Bruce Ackerman, *We the People*, vol. 1: *Foundations* (1991); Frank I. Michelman, "Why Voting?" 34 *Loyola of Los Angeles Law Review* 985, 991–993 (2001); Richard A. Posner, *Overcoming Law*, ch. 7 (1995).

who is not 'in the know.'"[59] In *Planned Parenthood v. Casey* three Supreme Court Justices declared that Americans' "very belief in themselves" as "people who aspire to live according to the rule of law" is "not readily separable from their understanding of the Court."[60] And so we have the culminating paradox that in practice and tendency, deliberative democracy often turns antidemocratic. The theorist of deliberative democracy prescribes conditions of knowledge, attention, and public-spiritedness that the people cannot or will not satisfy in their political life. And so he is tempted to give up on the people and embrace rule by experts, judicial or bureaucratic, whom he deems capable of deliberation—experts much like himself.

59. Parker, *"Here, the People Rule,"* note 54 above, at 73.
60. 505 U.S. 833, 868 (1992) (concurring opinion).

CHAPTER FIVE

Democracy Defended

꿍꿍

> What a comfort to live in a world where one can delegate everything tiresome, from governing to making sausages, to somebody else.[1]

The Two Concepts Evaluated

Concept 1 democracy is aspirational and Concept 2 realistic. This has the curious consequence that many defenders of Concept 1, while they believe in deliberation and consider themselves true democrats, are in practice drawn to nondemocratic methods of governance. (This is especially true of lawyers because of their familiarity and comfort with the unelected federal judiciary.) For when they examine the actual operation of American democracy, they see, as I pointed out in the last chapter, that the conditions for deliberation in the electorate and in the elected officialdom are not satisfied.[2] As a result, the outcomes of democracy lack legitimacy in their eyes. They see it buffeted by ignorant public opinion. Believers in the power of deliberation to yield moral and political truths and not merely opinion, they cannot help feeling that they have a better grip on these truths than *hoi polloi* do. They turn instinctively to the unelected federal judiciary and the expert civil servants of the regulatory agencies to effectuate the policies that they despair of emerging from democratic deliberation in the real world—such policies as (depending on the political preferences of the particular theorist) the abolition of capital punishment, the prohibition

1. Aldous Huxley, *Point Counter Point* 270 (1928).
2. Cass R. Sunstein, "Deliberative Trouble? Why Groups Go to Extremes," 110 *Yale Law Journal* 71, 107 (2000), offers the following nonexclusive list of preconditions for deliberative democracy: "political equality, an absence of strategic behavior, full information, and the goal of 'reaching understanding.'" Intellectuals' dissatisfaction with American democracy is of course nothing new. Think only of Henry Adams's scathing fictional critique—*Democracy: An American Novel* (1880).

of abortion, interdistrict busing as a remedy for past public school segregation, homosexual marriage, animal rights, and rational environmental and safety and health policies. They may be said to desert democracy in the pinch.

Consider the example of capital punishment. "In most of the United States, popular support for capital punishment translated quickly into government policy. Many other countries, by contrast, abolished capital punishment *despite* considerable popular support for it . . . The difference between the United States and other wealthy democracies with respect to capital punishment may simply be that the United States is more democratic, in the sense that elected officials find it more necessary to implement policies supported by a majority of the voters."[3] Between 1977 and 1998, 66 to 76 percent of Americans supported capital punishment for murder, according to public opinion polls, and in no region or ethnic group was a majority opposed; yet Britain had abolished capital punishment when a majority of the population supported it and refused to reinstitute it in the 1970s when 80 percent of the population supported it.[4] If so strong a popular preference cannot get translated into government action, this suggests that democracy is not working; and so it is ironic that many deliberative democrats would like the Supreme Court to declare capital punishment unconstitutional, even though there is no solid basis in the Constitution for such a declaration.

We should not judge the power that deliberative democrats assign to unelected officials by the existing scope of policymaking by such officials. The bureaucrats, and especially the judges, are more timid than many deliberative democrats would like them to be. The Supreme Court has not abolished capital punishment, decreed homosexual marriage, and so forth. If it went as far as many deliberative democrats want it to go, the power of the elected branches of government would be significantly diminished.

Not all deliberative democrats are drawn to nondemocratic modes of governance. Jürgen Habermas, a German who well remembers the Hitler era (he was a member of the *Hitler Jügend* and was a month short of his sixteenth birthday when World War II ended), is not as critical of actual ex-

---

3. Stuart Banner, *The Death Penalty: An American History* 301 (2002). Banner is referring to the fact that after the Supreme Court invalidated the existing capital-punishment statutes in 1972, Congress and the states quickly enacted new statutes designed to meet the Court's objections.

4. Id. at 275–276, 301.

isting democracy as his American counterparts, who have never experienced anything else. He denies that the people are "'cultural dopes' who are manipulated by the [television] programs offered them."[5] He is skeptical of casting the Supreme Court in the role of "a pedagogical guardian or regent" of an incompetent "sovereign."[6] He points out that because political parties are coalitions, it is difficult for a politician to appeal for votes in terms limited to the narrowest self-interest of particular members of his coalition. The politician has to broaden his appeal, which he does by invoking broader concepts of welfare; and this in turn may encourage the voters to think beyond their own immediate interests.[7] Similarly, Jeremy Waldron, a law professor born in New Zealand, educated there and in England, and thus habituated to think of legislatures as supreme, rejects the idea that courts are essential checks on legislatures. Lacking the American law professor's inborn faith in government by the judiciary, he believes that democracy can be made to work without paternalistic guidance by courts.[8]

But even Habermas believes that rational politics has stringent conditions, such as that debate not be distorted by inequality of financial resources. Like Dewey, he equates political with epistemic democracy.[9] This equation marks a shift from conceiving of democracy as the actual democratic process to conceiving of it as the outcome of a hypothetical ideal process; it encourages the substitution of hypothetical for actual deliberation. (There is an analogy to the distinction in antitrust economics between competition as rivalry and competition as the allocation of resources that would occur under conditions of optimal competition; and to the role of hypothetical consent in social-contract theory.) This construal, which might be thought to turn democracy into very nearly its opposite,[10] invites judges to interpret the Constitution as commanding the results they think

5. Jürgen Habermas, *Between Facts and Norms: Contributions to a Discourse Theory of Law and Democracy* 377 (1996).

6. Id. at 278.

7. Id. at 340. The same point is made in Cass R. Sunstein, *Democracy and the Problem of Free Speech* 243–244 (1993), yet his emphasis falls on constitutional adjudication, on legislative interventions, and on deliberation by legislators rather than by citizens. See id. at 242, 247–252.

8. See Jeremy Waldron, *Law and Disagreement* (1999); Richard A. Posner, *Frontiers of Legal Theory* 19–20, 23–24 (2001).

9. See Richard A. Posner, *The Problematics of Moral and Legal Theory* 102 (1999).

10. In the words of one critic, to deliberative democrats "the real meaning of democracy consists in what people really and truly desire or prefer, that is, what people would say and do and will if their hearts and minds had not been twisted and degraded by oppressive social hierarchies, unjust economic arrangements, or false and contingent ideas masquerading as uni-

the people would choose if democracy functioned in accordance with Concept 1. The tension between democracy and judicial review is erased by a sleight of hand.

Remember Joshua Cohen's claim that a majority's effort to suppress the religious observances of a minority would be not merely unjust but undemocratic (see Chapter 4)? He likewise claims that a limitation on abortion that was adopted by "a considerable majority" on the basis of a religious view of when life begins would be undemocratic.[11] Ronald Dworkin says that "the American conception of democracy is whatever form of government the Constitution, according to the best interpretation of that document, establishes,"[12] when by "the best interpretation" he means his own interpretation—"the moral reading of the Constitution,"[13] a reading that imposes tight constraints on majority rule. But Dworkin, despite protestations,[14] may not be a *deliberative* democrat. He distinguishes policy from principle, regarding the former as the domain of legislatures and the latter as the domain of courts. Policies are utilitarian, and so if deliberative at all are so in a much more limited sense than his concept of deliberation, which entails nonutilitarian moral and political philosophizing.

The reciprocal relation between concepts of democracy and the optimal length of the judicial leash requires emphasis, as it indicates the neglected need for judges to make a choice among those concepts. The more demanding the criteria for effective democracy that the theorist imposes, the less democratic he will think our political system and so the more willing he will be to countenance frequent and drastic judicial interventions. It is an example of the best being the enemy of the good. The more one asks of democracy, the less satisfactory the answer and so the stronger the temptation to make the system even less democratic by handing more power to an elite of unelected, life-tenured judges.[15]

Other antidemocratic implications besides intrusive judicial review, rule

versal and commanding truths." Peter Berkowitz, "The Demagoguery of Democratic Theory" (forthcoming in *Critical Review*, Winter–Spring (2003).

11. Joshua Cohen, "Institutional Argument Is Diminished by the Limited Examination of the Issue of Principle," 53 *Journal of Politics* 221, 223 (1991). But see Robert A. Dahl, "A Rejoinder," 53 *Journal of Politics* 226, 229–231 (1991).

12. Ronald Dworkin, *Freedom's Law: The Moral Reading of the Constitution* 75 (1996).

13. See id.

14. See Ronald Dworkin, *Sovereign Virtue: The Theory and Practice of Equality* 364–365 (2000).

15. This is a temptation for the Right as much as for the Left, as argued in Philip P. Frickey and Steven S. Smith, "Judicial Review, the Congressional Process, and the Federalism Cases: An Interdisciplinary Critique," 111 *Yale Law Journal* 1707 (2002).

by experts, and undue influence of intellectuals lurk in deliberative democracy. A realist about the limited capacity of deliberation to forge consensus may be inclined to agree with Carl Schmitt that the *demos* must be homogeneous for deliberative democracy to work.[16] Thoughts of this kind inspire proposals to limit immigration to the United States from countries that lack democratic political values, to limit the franchise, and through public education and other means to inculcate sound political values in children. Desire to redress imbalances in "autonomous preferences, command of cultural resources, and cognitive capacities," all of which bear on deliberative capacity and opportunity, inspires proposals for establishing "political equality," deemed a precondition for deliberative democracy, by means of measures that "might entail constraints on the use of material resources in nonpolitical realms" and "in the public sphere . . . might entail the acceptance of inequalities in the treatment of citizens by the state."[17] Joshua Cohen goes so far as to argue that "a commitment to socialism follows naturally from a commitment to [deliberative] democracy."[18]

The discrepancies between the ideals of Concept 1 democracy and our actual democracy do not faze the Concept 2 democrat. Having no preconceived, idealized model of democracy to which to compare the practice of American or any other existing democracy, the Concept 2 democrat is inclined to take for granted the features of democratic practice lamented by Concept 1 democrats. They are simply what American democracy *is*. The Concept 2 democrat actually takes heart from the departures of our democracy from the Concept 1 ideal by noting that they refute any implication in Tocqueville that the productive energies and other wholesome features of the American people are dependent on our democracy's becoming deliberative.

Of course to the extent that Concept 1 is a normative rather than a positive theory, the fact that Concept 2 describes our system better need not

16. See Chantal Mouffe, "Carl Schmitt and the Paradox of Liberal Democracy," in *Law as Politics: Carl Schmitt's Critique of Liberalism* 159 (David Dyzenhaus ed. 1998).

17. Jack Knight and James Johnson, "What Sort of Political Equality Does Deliberative Democracy Require?" in *Deliberative Democracy: Essays on Reason and Politics* 279, 299, 304 (James Bohman and William Rehg eds. 1997). See also Cass R. Sunstein, "Democracy and Shifting Preferences," in *The Idea of Democracy* 196, 223 (David Copp, Jean Hampton, and John E. Roemer eds. 1993), arguing that "it would be a grave mistake to characterize liberal democracy as a system that requires existing preferences to be taken as the basis for governmental decisions."

18. Joshua Cohen, "The Economic Basis of Deliberative Democracy," 6 *Social Philosophy and Policy* 25, 26 (1989).

be a reproach to Concept 1 or an encomium for Concept 2. Concept 2's description, however, may identify circumstances that render Concept 1's normative vision unattainable, a pipe dream hardly worth the attention of a serious person. What is more, although positive and normative analysis are conceptually distinct, there is a tendency to convergence at the practical level. If what we have in fact is Concept 2 democracy and transforming it into Concept 1 democracy simply is not in the cards, we might as well orient reform toward improvements in Concept 2. Because the only means that Odysseus had of leaving Calypso's island was to build a raft, any improvement in transportation had to take the form of building a better raft rather than, say, of growing a pair of wings.

Advocates of Concept 1 are not unconcerned with issues of feasibility.[19] But most of them think that a reasonable approximation to Concept 1 democracy is attainable through reforms in the electoral or educational systems without need for wholesale redistributions of wealth designed to bring about real political equality among citizens. John Dewey exemplified this faith.[20] Concept 2 democrats reply that it is grounded in misconceptions about human nature and American society. No feasible reform is likely to increase significantly the interest of Americans in political deliberation. Better public schools? More attention to civics in the high school curriculum?[21] Fishkin's deliberative polls or his and Ackerman's Deliberation Day (see Chapter 4)? Limiting spending on political campaigns, which might shift the balance of dissemination of political information from advertisers to journalists? Moving election day from a workday to the weekend (or making election day a holiday), to encourage higher turnout in the hope that the new voters will become interested in and informed about political issues? Increasing government subsidies for noncommercial radio and television? Requiring broadcast licensees to devote more time to political reporting and debate? Adopting proportional representation in order to encourage the formation of ideologically coherent parties?

19. See, for example, David Estlund, "Democratic Authority: Toward a Philosophical Framework," pt. 4 ("Is Epistemic Democracy Incredible"?) (Brown University, Dept. of Philosophy, Jan. 17, 2000, unpublished).

20. See also Amy Gutmann and Dennis Thompson, *Democracy and Disagreement* 359 (1996): "In any effort to make democracy more deliberative, the single most important institution outside government is the educational system. To prepare their students for citizenship, schools must go beyond teaching literacy and numeracy." Although the authors think that *the* most important institution for making democracy more deliberative is government, they do not explain how government can do this.

21. See, for example, Amy Gutmann, *Democratic Education* 105–107 (rev. ed. 1999).

Some of these proposals are politically infeasible, even quixotic (no surprise, considering how many of the proposals are academic constructs); some raise serious concerns about the expansion of government power and the politicization of education;[22] others are of doubtful efficacy. The proponents pay little attention to costs and tradeoffs. If the civics component in high school education is expanded, for example, what other component is to be contracted to make room for it?

Even if all the proposals were adopted, one is skeptical that the result would be a different political culture. The United States is a tenaciously philistine society. Its citizens have little appetite for abstractions and little time and less inclination to devote substantial time to training themselves to become informed and public-spirited voters. It is also a society that disvalues government service, making it unlikely that the governing class, and in particular elected officials, can be made over into Concept 1 deliberators.

Concept 1 is, in short, utopian. Its essential utopianism is its conception of democracy as self-government, so that its implicit model is Athenian democracy, which is utterly unworkable under modern conditions. Concept 2 rejects the idea that democracy is self-government. Democracy is government subject to electoral checks.

Utopian thinking can have value in opening the mind to possibilities that, though unrealizable in the short term, may be the seeds of future reform. The utopianism of Concept 1 democrats is unpromising in this regard, however, and like other utopian thinking, breeds disillusionment and a resulting attraction to dystopic practices. By defining democracy in such exalted terms that the word no longer describes our system either as it exists or as it realistically might be reformed, the Concept 1 democrat opens the door to alternative methods of governance, namely rule by judges and bureaucrats under the tutelage of political theorists.

If utopianism and disillusionment go hand in hand, realism and complacency go hand in hand as well. So we must consider whether Concept 2 democracy is a complacent faith. There is an initial question whether it is a "faith" at all, in the sense of a body of beliefs that can be used to guide action, rather than merely being a repetition of Pangloss's claim that what-

---

22. Alan Wolfe, "Schooling and Religious Pluralism," in *Making Good Citizens: Education and Civil Society* 279, 286–294 (Diane Ravitch and Joseph P. Viteritti eds. 2001), warns against "guided pluralism," in which, as in Gutmann, note 21 above, at (for example) 33, 40, 307–308, illiberal (mainly religious) views are banished from school curricula.

ever is, is best. The only thing that Joseph Schumpeter, the inventor of the concept, thought Concept 2 democracy good for was to retard what he incorrectly believed to be an inexorable world-historical movement toward socialism. We need not follow him in this. The concept he invented can be separated from his personal political views, even if he incorrectly believed that those views were implications of the concept. For example, Carole Pateman's criticism of what I am calling Concept 2 democracy is based on Schumpeter's having attached little significance to the extent of the suffrage,[23] though in fact Concept 2 implies universal suffrage (or something quite close to it) in order to assure adequate representation of all interests.

Schumpeter should have perceived this implication. He drew from World War I and its aftermath the important lesson that autocracies (the German Empire, the Austro-Hungarian Empire, the Russian Empire, the Ottoman Empire) could not hold back the tide of socialism because they incubated revolution, which broke out in the wake of military defeat. Extension of the franchise operates to "buy off" workers or other potential revolutionaries by giving them political power that they can use to assure continuing redistributions of wealth to themselves. The extension is a commitment device, which makes such buyoffs credible and generous. A legislative program of wealth redistribution can be rescinded at any time (as we have seen recently with the curtailment of welfare benefits), whereas giving the vote to the potential beneficiaries of such programs provides, if they are numerous enough, a guaranty of continuation.[24]

By saying that Concept 2 "implies universal suffrage," I am recasting it as a normative rather than a merely positive concept (something Schumpeter did not do), that is, as a concept that can provide a critical perspective on our existing practices. The essence of Concept 2 democracy understood in normative terms is that the interests (preferences, values, opinions) of the population, whatever they may happen to be, be represented in government. Concept 1 is the democracy of ideas, in fact of elite ideas; Concept 2 is the democracy of interests and so of responsiveness to public opinion, to what people want as distinct from what political theorists think they should want or under different (better?) social or political conditions would want. Concept 2 is thus more respectful of people

23. See Carole Pateman, *Participation and Democratic Theory* (1970), esp. chs. 1–2.
24. See Daron Acemoglu and James A. Robinson, "Why Did the West Extend the Franchise? Democracy, Inequality, and Growth in Historical Perspective," 115 *Quarterly Journal of Economics* 1167 (2000).

as they actually are. And whereas Concept 1 democracy seems likely to increase ideological conflict, Concept 2 democracy encourages compromise, the buying off of clamorous interest groups, the maintenance of social peace by bracketing ideological differences—encourages, that is, the sort of thing that democratic politicians are good at. Interests, unlike ideas, can be compromised. This is done all the time in markets, and Concept 2 depicts democracy as a kind of market. Concept 2 democracy tends to align the behavior of politicians and officials with the people's interests as the people perceive them. It is not government by the people, but it is government of and more or less for the people.

"Liberals," Stephen Holmes remarks, "generally sort conflict into three types: conflicts of interest, conflicts of ideas, and conflicts of ultimate values. Conflicts of interests, they assume, are resolvable by compromise and negotiation, conflicts of ideas by rational discussion, and conflicts of ultimate values by the privatization of religion."[25] In fact, conflicts of ideas often cannot be resolved by rational discussion, especially (but not only) those conflicts rooted in religiously grounded disagreements over ultimate values—and people cannot be prevented from deriving their political views from their religious beliefs. It doesn't follow that rationally unresolvable conflicts cannot be compromised. On the contrary, those are the conflicts that can be resolved *only* by either compromise or the outright victory of one side. Think of abortion rights. The present scope of those rights represents a compromise (a de facto rather than a negotiated one— that is, a standoff) between the contending factions that favors the pro-choice side while satisfying neither. The pro-choice side wants public financing of abortions, the removal of all restrictions on abortion rights, and more vigorous protection of abortion clinics and doctors from harassment by pro-lifers. The pro-life side wants all abortions forbidden except those few in which the woman's life is at risk. Still, the compromise is effective in more or less keeping the peace, which a "principled" resolution in favor of either side would not do even if there were analytical tools that would enable such a resolution, which there are not.

The role of the politician tends to elude the understanding of the political theorist. The qualities requisite in a statesman or other leader are closer to those of a broker, salesman, actor, or entrepreneur than to those of an academic. They have little to do with logic or intellectuality. Book-

25. Stephen Holmes, *The Anatomy of Antiliberalism* 40 (1993).

ish, highbrow—these are not the qualities of an effective politician. They are instead strategic and interpersonal—manipulative, coercive, psychological, even thespian. They are quintessentially *social*. They form the morality, misunderstood as cynicism, expounded by Machiavelli, the morality that Max Weber (who with Aristotle and Machiavelli—and Madison—belongs among the ancestors of Concept 2 democracy) contrasted with an "ethic of ultimate ends,"[26] the sort of thing one finds in the Sermon on the Mount. The ethics of political responsibility require a willingness to compromise, to dirty one's hands, to flatter, cajole, pander, bluff, and lie, to make unprincipled package deals, and thus to forgo the prideful self-satisfaction that comes from self-conscious purity and devotion to principle.[27] These are qualities of all politicians but particularly of democratic ones. Democratic politicians are answerable to an electorate, and the relative weakness that such subservience implies compels them to be even wilier than their counterparts in nondemocratic regimes.

Representation is central to Concept 2 democracy in a way that it is not to Concept 1 democracy. In Concept 1, representative democracy is a second-best solution to the problem of governance, the first-best solution, infeasible in a complex polity, being direct democracy. Those Concept 1 theorists who have given up on citizen deliberation and placed their hopes instead on deliberation by elected representatives or other officials consider representation indispensable, but in a *faute de mieux* sense. Similarly, in public-choice theory (of which more shortly) it is a detail whether interest groups, the motive force of policy in most public-choice analysis, operate directly on voters or indirectly through puppet politicians. Concept 2 democracy, in contrast, presupposes the existence of two distinct classes, the "representatives"—the elected officials, who along with the officials whom they appoint are the rulers in a democracy—and the voters. Concept 2 is a theory of representative democracy and of nothing else. And although the representatives (a misnomer) are no more agents of the voters than actors are the agents of their audience, the electoral process does tend to align the representatives' interest with those of the voters—to keep the representatives on a tether, though a long one.

We must push on and consider why representation should be at the center of democratic theory. One reason, which I mentioned in connec-

26. Max Weber, "Politics as a Vocation," in *From Max Weber: Essays in Sociology* 77, 120 (H. H. Gerth and C. Wright Mills trans. 1946).
27. See id. at 118–128.

tion with the aftermath of World War I, is that when government is not broadly representative, political stability is endangered. Lacking a political voice, the unrepresented may turn disruptive. Not just because they *feel* ignored, but also because the government, lacking electoral pressure from them and even a clear sense of their desires and circumstances, is likely to be unresponsive to their grievances. Eventually there may be an explosion. More commonly, lack of representation gives rise to alienation (disaffection) that may cause the unrepresented to contribute less to society than they would do if their interests were represented in the political process— to work less hard, cooperate less with other people, and cease obeying laws unless the sanctions for disobedience are harsh enough to coerce obedience. People don't want to be lectured to by their intellectual superiors about needing to become informed about esoteric political issues, to participate actively in political and ideological deliberation, to subordinate their interests to some abstract public interest, and to allocate precious time to the political arena. But they do want to be heard concerning their interests by those who have power to do anything to protect or advance those interests. Concept 2 democracy caters to this desire.

Officials' lack of information concerning the people's desires and circumstances, one of the consequences of an absence of democracy, has an independent significance. The people as a whole may not be knowledgeable about specific policy issues and may have little deliberative interest or capacity, but by the same token they are free from the deformations of attitude and thought that are the corollaries of specialization and expertise. The people are the repository of common sense, which, dull though it is, is a barrier to the mad schemes, whether of social engineering or foreign adventures, hatched by specialists and intellectuals. When tempered by liberal institutions (an essential qualification), democracy is paradoxically a conservative system compared to governance by an elite (whether military, technical, or ideological) that is unconstrained by electoral competition.

Concept 2 may seem to presuppose not only that people know their own interests but also—what is less likely—that they know how those interests are affected by electoral outcomes. The distinction is important. People have a pretty good idea of their own interests, or at least a better idea than officials do. But often they have a poor idea of how those interests will be affected by the forthcoming election. That was my own situation in regard to the 2000 election, and I am better informed about political matters than the average American. I did not have a clear sense of which candidate was on balance likely to deliver more of the things that I seek from the federal government, and so I didn't bother to vote. (It would have been a bit more bother than usual because I was going to be out of the country on election day and would therefore have had to obtain, complete, and mail back an absentee ballot.) But this is just to say that often, in political as in economic markets, not much turns on which brand one buys—or even on whether one decides to buy at all. The decision not to vote is much like any other decision not to participate in a particular market—a point that casts doubt on the validity of the claim that "one likely consequence of this class bias in turnout [that is, the fact that the propensity to vote is positively correlated with income] is that government policies are less representative of general public preferences *and, thus, our governments are less democratic than they otherwise would be.*"[28] It is one thing to remove artificial barriers to voting; but once they are removed, the choice not to vote is as legitimate an exercise of democratic rights as voting.

Elections are important at historical turning points, such as 1860, 1932, 1934, 1964, and 1980, when big gaps yawn open between the parties and people feel strongly about which electoral outcome will best serve their interests. It is at such turning points that democracy comes into its own—and it is Concept 2 democracy. To put this differently, it is having rather than casting a vote that makes one a meaningful participant in the political community. Later in this chapter I shall present some evidence that voters are not *so* ignorant that they cannot play the role that Concept 2 assigns them.

Representation must not be equated to majoritarianism. Majoritarianism denies representation to electoral minorities unable to form coalitions with other electoral minorities. That is why inflexible adherence to the principle of "one person one vote" in redistricting a legislative body is questionable, though to the naive it is one of the bedrock principles of democracy. Imagine a state in which urban and rural dwellers have sharply and durably different interests, and the former, the urbanites, have a strong electoral majority; then the rural minority will not be represented effectively in the legislature. But now suppose that the upper house of the legislature, like the U.S. Senate, is apportioned on the basis not of population but of "arbitrary" geographical units, with the rural units (counties,

28. Kim Quaile Lee and Jan E. Leighley, "Political Parties and Class Mobilization in Contemporary United States Elections," 40 *American Journal of Political Science* 787 (1996) (emphasis added).

say) being less populous than the urban. Then rural interests will have disproportionate weight in one branch of the legislature, and this will enable them to wrest some concessions from the majority.

This analysis casts doubt on the soundness of the Supreme Court's insistence in the *Lucas* decision (see Chapter 4) that state senate districts be of equal population, just like house districts. The decision is not only questionable but paradoxical, given the solicitude for minorities that is reflected in the Court's equal protection decisions. Are courts to be the only institution of government permitted to protect minorities from being overwhelmed by majorities?

Concept 2 democrats worry (or should worry—they may not actually worry because many of them are political conservatives first and democrats second) about imbalances in representation, such as the skewing of voting power in favor of the elderly and against the interests of children, and about efforts by the two major parties to forestall the formation and stifle the growth of third parties. They should worry about such efforts not because Concept 2 values a multiplicity of parties (quite the opposite—the more parties there are, the more divisive ideological conflict there is likely to be), but because a meaningful threat of entry by third parties may be necessary to the preservation of competition under conditions of political duopoly (the two-party system).

Concept 2 democrats do not, however, judge suggestions for reform according to conformity with an ideal of democracy remote from our historical and current system. So, for example, if urged to embrace campaign-finance "reform," the Concept 2 democrat asks what the consequences of the reform, good and bad, are likely to be if it is adopted, and whether the good will predominate. One bad or at least questionable consequence would be to magnify the influence of journalists, celebrities, and media moguls because there would be less offset from political advertising. Political competition would be reduced if, as widely believed, the media exhibit a liberal bias in their coverage of political controversies and electoral campaigns.[29] And limiting political spending by corporations may increase political extremism. Individual donors tend to be more ideological than corporate ones,[30] since the latter desire access to and influence over politicians not to advance an ideological agenda but to protect their financial interests. And because the major parties between them control the political sys-

---

29. Bradley A. Smith, *Unfree Speech: The Folly of Campaign Finance Reform* 79–83 (2001).
30. See id. at 45–48.

tem, any campaign-finance law acceptable to both is likely to be tilted against third parties. On the other side of the ledger, if campaign-finance reform freed up politicians' time from fund-raising, they would have more time to think about public policy and abler individuals might be attracted to a career in politics.

As this discussion suggests, Concept 2 democrats often find redeeming value in features of American democracy that Concept 1 democrats deplore. Another example: while recognizing the distortions to which interest-group politics give rise, Concept 2 democrats point out that interest groups generate information essential to the formation of public policy. They are a partial corrective to one of the serious limitations of voting as a method of preference aggregation—that votes in political elections, as contrasted with elections by a corporation's shareholders, are not weighted by intensity or stake. (This is another example of the tension between representation and majoritarianism.) Interest groups "amplify voices; they articulate demands; they promote issues; they identify common interests. Their stock in trade is information—political intelligence—not pressure."[31] And they can soften political conflict by creating overlapping interests among ideological enemies. Most important, interest groups operate as a flywheel, braking the potentially terrifying momentum of simple majoritarianism. The smaller an interest group is relative to the society as a whole, the less the per capita burden that a policy favoring it will impose on the rest of the society; so lack of voting strength, *the* critical deficit in a system of simple majoritarianism, becomes a strength.[32] Interest groups are minorities, though not always the fashionable ones; it is a professional deformation of lawyers to suppose that courts are the only institution of government that protects minorities. In any event, the social costs imposed by interest groups are not a cost of democracy; they are a cost of government—for, looking around the world, one does not have a sense

31. John Mark Hansen, *Gaining Access: Congress and the Farm Lobby, 1919–1981*, at 229–231 (1991). See also id. at 227–229. Hansen concludes his very interesting study by stating: "On the one hand, we sympathize with interest groups because they *represent* popular demands, in many cases more effectively than parties or unassisted public officials . . . On the other hand, we distrust interest groups because they represent only *some* demands, and by no means the most popular . . . Interest groups are both democratic and elitist institutions." Id. at 230. My only quarrel is with the term "elitist." Interest groups do play a large role in Schumpeter's concept of democracy, and that concept is often and not inaccurately termed "elite democracy," but it is not elitist, as it emphasizes the representation of all interests.

32. Gary S. Becker, "Pressure Groups and Political Behavior," in *Capitalism and Democracy: Schumpeter Revisited* 120, 137 (Richard D. Coe and Charles K. Wilber eds. 1985).

that the distortions produced by interest-group politics are greater in democracies than in other types of regime.

Not being simple majoritarians, Concept 2 democrats also don't lose sleep over the possibility that an election might be won by a candidate who got fewer votes than his competitor, provided the margin is small. They worry more about deadlocked elections that produce delay or make Presidential succession uncertain. One of the just boasts of democratic government is that it solves better than any other system of government the problem of choosing competent new officials to succeed incumbents who have died, retired, or performed their official duties ineptly or dishonestly. Monarchy establishes a clear line of succession, in principle, but the practice depends on the vagaries of reproduction and longevity; and even when a king has an adult child to succeed him, the child may be ruinously less competent than his father. The father, for that matter, even if competent may long outstay his welcome. In dictatorships the method of succession is ad hoc and frequently violent, and again there is the problem of removing the incumbent when old age, poor health, or the corruption of power destroys his effectiveness. Succession becomes uncertain in a democratic regime only when an election is so close that a recount is necessary to figure out who really won. But if the election is *that* close, there is no discernibly worse matching of officials to public opinion if the candidate who got slightly fewer votes ends up being declared the winner.

Concept 2 democrats regard the marginalizing of politics in the American practice of democracy, which Hannah Arendt and others have so deplored,[33] as a social gain, for much the same reason that many students of history consider Protestantism a social gain over the medieval Catholicism that it challenged. Protestantism demanded faith, but not works or the elaborate institutional structure of Catholicism that went with them. This change in emphasis enlarged the space for commercial and other private activities, spurring Europe's emergence into modernity. Representative democracy is to participatory democracy as Protestantism was to medieval Catholicism. It is a system of delegated governance. The participation required of the people is minimal. They are left free to spend their time on other, more productive activities, undistracted by the animosities, the polarization, and the endless inconclusive debates of an active political life. In

33. See, for example, Benjamin R. Barber, *Strong Democracy: Participatory Politics for a New Age* (1984); Sheldon S. Wolin, *Tocqueville between Two Worlds: The Making of a Political and Theoretical Life* 569–572 (2001).

our system "for most people politics is not the center of their daily lives, but one might wonder why it should be."[34] "Modern citizens treasure representation for a modern reason: it provides an institutional framework for satisfying their desire not to participate continuously and exclusively in politics."[35] The point can be put even more strongly: "Despite the origins of the word and the way it is typically used in popular and academic discourse, either democracy cannot entail massive citizen participation or it is irrelevant to actual practice in modern politics."[36]

The religious analogy is imperfect. In one sense Protestantism is more participatory and deliberative than Catholicism. Protestants are encouraged to read and ponder the Bible for themselves—to think for themselves, to deliberate as it were upon religious questions—and Catholics are told to defer to their specialized "representatives," as one might loosely term the priests, intermediaries between man and God in somewhat the way that legislators are intermediaries between citizen and state. Encouraging people to think for themselves may well have promoted economic progress at the same time that resources were being shifted from the religious to the commercial sector. But it is doubtful whether political deliberation would today have fruitful spillovers to private or commercial life, and, if not, the reallocation of time from private and commercial activities to the political realm could reduce social welfare.

Commercial activity and private life are not only more productive of wealth and happiness than the political life; they are also more peaceable, which in turn reinforces their positive effect on wealth and happiness. Competition for wealth and other private goods is intense. But it is less tense, less emotional, and less dangerous than the struggle for power, which is to say for the means of physical coercion. As Samuel Johnson said, men are rarely so innocently engaged as when they are trying to make money. Commercial rivalry is, in a sense, deliciously superficial, lacking the threat of "psychic annihilation"[37] that is latent in political conflict even when it does not lead to violence, because political beliefs are often deeply

34. Robert A. Dahl, "The Problem of Civic Competence," 3 *Journal of Democracy* 45, 48 (1992).

35. Stephen Holmes, *Benjamin Constant and the Making of Modern Liberalism* 73 (1984).

36. Russell Hardin, *Liberalism, Constitutionalism, and Democracy* 169 (1999).

37. James Johnson, "Arguing for Deliberation: Some Skeptical Considerations," in *Deliberative Democracy* 161, 165 (Jon Elster ed. 1998), quoting Karl Mannheim. Gutmann and Thompson, note 20 above, at 347, acknowledge that "moral argument in politics can be socially divisive, politically extremist, and morally inconclusive."

rooted in people's sense of identity. Political competition, like war, which it resembles (Clausewitz's dictum can be run backwards—politics is the continuation of war by other means),[38] is often a zero-sum or even a negative-sum game. Economic competition is more likely to be a positive-sum game. Though there is a Darwinian aspect to it, commerce mostly brings people closer together. Deliberation, paradoxically, often drives them apart. Deliberation within a like-minded group tends to induce agreement with the most extreme views of the members because it is they who tend to have the most definite views.[39] The result is to push ideologically defined groups further apart from each other, polarizing public opinion.

Concept 2 democrats are thus not disturbed to be told that our democratic politics is not "an organic expression of any preexistent 'popular will'" but instead is shaped by a "specific institutional framework" that has made our politics "unimaginative, frozen, devoid of genuine significance, and personality-rather-than-issue driven."[40] They *like* the fact that "the American political order was deliberately tilted to resist, so to speak, the upward gravitational pull of politics toward the grand, dramatic, character-ennobling but society-wracking opinions about justice and virtue."[41] That is one reason proportional representation, a staple proposal of Concept 1 democrats,[42] is anathema to the Concept 2 democrat. It fosters the emergence of ideologically uniform parties by enabling minority parties, parties that do not blunt their message by bundling issues in order to appeal to the median voter, to obtain legislative representation and, provided no party has a majority, to achieve significant power by joining in a coalition with other minority parties. The necessity of forging a governing coalition may prevent ideologically uniform government in a system of pro-

38. In fact, Carl Schmitt argues, "the politician is better schooled for the battle than the soldier, because the politician fights his whole life whereas the soldier does so in exceptional circumstances only." Carl Schmitt, *The Concept of the Political* 34 (George Schwab trans. 1996).

39. See Posner, note 8 above, at 362–363, and references cited there; Sunstein, note 2 above; Sunstein, "The Law of Group Polarization" (University of Chicago Law School, Dec. 7, 1999, unpublished). "The mechanisms that underlie group polarization raise serious questions about any general enthusiasm for deliberative processes." Id. at 30. This from one of our leading deliberative democrats!

40. Samuel Issacharoff and Richard H. Pildes, "Politics as Markets: Partisan Lockups of the Democratic Process," 50 *Stanford Law Review* 643, 644 (1998).

41. Martin Diamond, "Ethics and Politics: The American Way," *in The Moral Foundations of the American Republic* 75, 92 (Robert H. Horwitz ed. 1977).

42. See, for example, Sunstein, note 17 above, at 223—and, most famously, John Stuart Mill, *Considerations on Representative Government* 153–167 (1870).

portional representation, but the character of the parties brings ideological conflict to the fore. A winner-take-all system blunts it. Even though ideological parties in a multiparty system may reappear as factions within parties in a two-party system, their strength will be diluted because a faction in one party cannot credibly threaten to form a governing coalition with a faction of another party. Each party must select a platform and candidates that appeal to the swing voters, and thus must curb its ideological extremes.

Multiparty democracy can still be Schumpeterian, in the sense that the politicians constitute a distinct governing class characterized by a competitive jockeying for power while the electorate is poorly informed and largely apathetic, though it may be somewhat better informed and somewhat less apathetic than in a two-party system. What is lost is the benefit of Schumpeterian democracy in reducing the amount and intensity of citizen involvement in politics, freeing up time for other, potentially more rewarding and socially beneficial activities and reducing the temperature of political debate and so the level of social conflict, thus promoting political stability. Granted, there can be too much political stability—as a pragmatist, with his understanding of the importance of competition and diversity to the advance of knowledge, his Darwinian take on social progress, and his preference for Homer and Heraclitus over Plato (see Chapter 1), should be the first to realize. Urgent social problems that happen not to trouble the median voter are less likely to be addressed in a two-party Schumpeterian democracy than in a democracy in which ideologically defined parties have political clout. The failure of the United States to abolish slavery before the Civil War, its failure to protect the rights and interests of the freed slaves after the Civil War, and its post–World War I isolationism are examples of the tendency of a Schumpeterian democracy to defer consideration of serious problems until they become so grave that they finally arouse the swing voters.

But is the "disproportionate" weight of swing voters really such a bad thing? They are, after all, the moderates, the neutrals; who better to hold the balance of power? It is not as if the extremes have no weight at all in American politics. Both parties have to worry about the potential defection of their extremists to third parties. Such defections have occurred— think of the Dixiecrats in 1948 or the Naderites in 2000—and they would be more common if the parties did not conciliate their extremists with various concessions, notably judicial and other appointments. Not all major-party candidates, even for the Presidency, have been centrists, moreover; think only of Goldwater, McGovern, and Reagan.

It is important, moreover, not to take "swing voters" as a fixed quantity. A two-party system increases their number. In forging a coalition of voters that will have a good chance of commanding a majority of votes, each party has to emphasize the things that the members of its coalition have in common, so that the coalition is not destroyed by internal disagreements. "A common political denominator must be found," and the candidate who finds it "has made a great contribution toward reconciling all the groups in a country—rich and poor, Christians and Jews, people of all types of national descent—with each other,"[43] whereas with proportional representation we might have a Christian party, a Jewish party, an Italian-American party, and so on. A two-party system tends to make people more moderate, more centrist. This is the positive side of the tendency of Concept 2 democracy to lower the temperature of political debate. It cools but it does not freeze.

That phrase I quoted earlier from one of the critics of Concept 2 democracy, describing, regretfully, what that concept is not—"an organic expression of any preexistent 'popular will'"—should cause a shudder. For it is a reminder of the historically seductive democratic pretensions of dictatorship, a Schmittian theme.[44] By insisting on the inherent difference in outlook and character between representatives and voters, that is, between the leaders and the followers, Concept 2 resists the argument that dictatorship is a way, maybe the only way, of fusing the leaders (or rather the leader) with the followers. The argument is clearest in the case of plebiscitary dictatorships, such as those of Napoleon and Hitler, in which the dictator, until failure overcomes him, can make a plausible claim to be the embodiment of the popular will. That such unity of purpose is unattainable in a system of representative democracy is a strength rather than a weakness. This is an insight denied to the Concept 1 democrat. He regrets the division between leaders and followers in a system of representative democracy because he wants government policy to grow out of consensus forged in deliberation rather than merely to reflect the balance of political power. The Concept 2 democrat regards the fusion of officials with voters

43. F. A. Hermens, "Democracy and Proportional Representation," 7 (University of Chicago Press Public Policy Pamphlet No. 31, Harry D. Gideonse ed. 1940).

44. See the helpful discussion in Andrew Arato, "Good-bye to Dictatorships?" 67 *Social Research* 925, 941–943 (2000).

as undesirable, indeed as retrograde, primitive, like erasing the distinct categories of sellers and buyers by regressing to a state in which the division of labor is unknown and people make what they consume rather than obtaining what they consume in exchange for what they make.

This, by the way, is another reason the Concept 2 democrat rejects proportional representation. Concept 2 democracy is about picking leaders rather than about picking policies. Carried to the limit, proportional representation would create a legislature that mirrored the policy preferences of the electorate exactly. That would be an approximation of direct democracy. "If acceptance of leadership is the true function of the electorate's vote, the case for proportional representation collapses because its premises are no longer binding. The principle of democracy then merely means that the reins of government should be handed to those who command more support than do any of the competing individuals or teams."[45]

We should consider the position of the Concept 2 democrat with respect to judicial review (that is, judicial enforcement of constitutional rights). Jed Rubenfeld, one of the few constitutional theorists to advert to Schumpeterian democracy—for which he is to be commended—senses a tension between it and judicial review. Schumpeterian democracy "is to be understood as a system of governance accountable to present voter preferences,"[46] whereas constitutional adjudication gives great weight either to past political settlements or to judges', not voters', current policy preferences. I disagree with the implied antithesis. Being skeptical about the deliberative incentives and capacities of voters and of elected officials alike, the Concept 2 democrat can issue no blanket condemnation of placing constitutional limits, enforced by judges, on democratic choice. Whether the consequences are good or bad is an empirical question. The answer depends on such things as the methods of selecting and constraining judges and the historical record of judicial review. The Concept 2 democrat is skeptical about constitutional rulings that confuse majority rule with representation, such as adoption of the "one person one vote" standard across the board; he would oppose representation-reducing judicial decisions; and he would want a diverse judiciary, one reasonably representative of the American people. But he senses no general tension between electoral democracy and a judge-enforced constitution that places

45. Joseph A. Schumpeter, *Capitalism, Socialism, and Democracy* 273 (1942).
46. Jed Rubenfeld, *Freedom and Time: A Theory of Constitutional Self-Government* 55 (2001).

limits on that democracy. He is a pragmatic liberal rather than a radical democrat.

But Is the Well Poisoned?

The genealogy of Concept 2 democracy may seem to tell against it. Concept 2 democracy is, of course, essentially Joseph Schumpeter's concept,[47] presented in 1942 in his book *Capitalism, Socialism, and Democracy*. In it members of an elite (the political class, the political "aristocracy") compete for office and power, with the voting public functioning, most of the time at any rate, as little more than an audience whose applause (votes) determines which elite contestants prevail.[48] "The democratic method is that institutional arrangement for arriving at political decisions in which individuals acquire the power to decide by means of a competitive struggle for the people's vote."[49] "Democracy is a method, rather than an ideal of political culture, in which certain individuals, rather than the public at large, acquire the power to decide on questions of public policy. Its principal mode of operation, therefore, is a competitive struggle for the people's vote and not discussion and decision among the people themselves."[50]

Schumpeter did not *invent* Concept 2 democracy. He was generalizing from the mixture of democratic and aristocratic elements in the government of Great Britain, which he greatly admired. He could as well have drawn inspiration from the U.S. Constitution of 1787, as we saw in the last chapter. Even the conceptualization was not wholly novel, for we can find something quite like Schumpeter's concept of democracy in Aristotle's "least bad" version of democracy, summarized by Josiah Ober as follows:

> The primarily agricultural demos is content to govern itself under established laws and only foregathers in Assembly when absolutely necessary. Indeed, the farmer-citizens actually *prefer* their economically remunerative work on the land to actively engaging in politics

47. See Schumpeter, note 45 above, chs. 22–23, reprinted as chapter 9 of *Political Philosophy* (Anthony Quinton ed. 1967). The essential theory is presented in less than five pages. See Schumpeter, note 45 above, at 269–273.

48. For an excellent summary, see John Medearis, *Joseph Schumpeter's Two Theories of Democracy* (2001); see also Peter Bachrach, *The Theory of Democratic Elitism: A Critique* (1967). On the analogy of voters to an audience, see Alexander A. Schuessler, *A Logic of Expressive Choice* 46 (2000).

49. Schumpeter, note 45 above, at 269.

50. Albert Weale, *Democracy* 98 (1999).

. . . Most of the citizens prefer not to participate very actively and willingly leave most aspects of political business to the minority of wealthy men who can afford the time to serve as leaders . . . A well-to-do minority—or better yet, the few who are especially capable—make up the office-holders and actually manage public affairs. The people, who come occasionally to Assembly, retain formal authority; they fulfill whatever public instinct they may have (qua political animals) by choosing (through voting) among a select group of those who are rich and/or competent as officials, and by subsequently conducting audits of their elected officials.[51]

All that is missing is emphasis on the competition *within* the elite class for office.

Even Tocqueville, despite his affection for deliberative democracy, can be placed among the "non-visionary students of politics" who "define democracy not as the unachievable 'rule of the people,' but as a system in which parties lose elections."[52] "A non-heroic politics tainted by the profit motive could nevertheless win Tocqueville's partial admiration."[53]

Derided by Robert Westbrook as a conception that "narrows democracy to little more than an ex post facto check on the power of elites, an act of occasional political consumption affording a choice among a limited range of well-packaged aspirants to office,"[54] and by Benjamin Barber as "the wan residualism of liberal democratic pluralism, which depicts politics as nothing more than the chambermaid of private interests,"[55] Schumpeter's concept of democracy stands at the farthest possible distance from transformative democracy. For Schumpeter, "democracy is simply synonymous with the existence of familiar electoral and legislative institutions."[56] "The transformative concept of democracy highlighted the radicalizing, dynamic effects of movements that attempt to realize democratic values and act on democratic ideologies, while . . . [Schumpeter's] elite model de-

51. Josiah Ober, *Political Dissent in Democratic Athens: Intellectual Critics of Popular Rule* 334 (1998) (emphasis in original). Among other notable antecedents of Schumpeter's theory, see Henry Sumner Maine, *Popular Government: Four Essays* (1886), esp. essay 2.

52. Stephen Holmes, "Both Sides Now," *New Republic*, Mar. 4 and 11, 2002, pp. 31, 37.

53. Id. at 34.

54. Robert B. Westbrook, *John Dewey and American Democracy* xv (1991). For criticism of Schumpeter's conception as basically authoritarian as well as excessively pessimistic, see William Scheuerman, *Carl Schmitt: The End of Law* 194–206 (1999).

55. Barber, note 33 above, at 118.

56. Medearis, note 48 above, at 2.

picted democracy in static terms and as institutionally stable, . . . simply an arrangement of *political* institutions."[57]

John Medearis, whom I am quoting, presents evidence that Schumpeter was a reactionary, a monarchist, and eventually (while living in the United States!) a Nazi sympathizer, who disliked democracy in any form but hoped that elite democracy might delay the triumph of democratic socialism.[58] Most early proponents of elite democracy were also reactionaries, such as Mosca, Maistre, Pareto, and Schmitt.[59] But motives or character do not discredit analysis. To reject a good idea because of its provenance is to cut off one's nose to spite one's face. And the qualification "early" is important—Schumpeter's theory of democracy influenced thinkers whose political views were the opposite of his.[60] Consider liberal political scientist Robert Dahl's concept of American democracy:

> I have shown both that elections are a crucial device for controlling leaders and that they are quite ineffective as indicators of majority preference. These statements are not really in contradiction . . . We expect elections to reveal the "will" or the preferences of a majority on a set of issues. This is one thing elections rarely do, except in an almost trivial fashion. Despite this limitation the election process is one of two fundamental methods of social control which, operating together, make government leaders so responsive to non-leaders that the distinction between democracy and dictatorship still makes sense. The other method of social control is continuous political competition among individuals, parties, or both . . . The making of governmental decisions is not a majestic march of great majorities united upon certain matters of basic policy. It is the steady appeasement of relatively small groups . . . [Democracy] appears to be a relatively efficient system for reinforcing agreement, encouraging moderation, and maintaining social peace in a restless and immoderate people

57. Id. at 4 (emphasis in original).

58. See id., esp. ch. 2. Schumpeter admired the ability of the English aristocracy to control (at least until World War I) the increasingly democratic English political system.

59. See, for example, Carl Schmitt, *The Crisis of Parliamentary Democracy* (Ellen Kennedy trans. 1986); Holmes, note 25 above, at 48, 271 n. 36.

60. See Medearis, note 48 above, at 10; David M. Ricci, "Democracy Attenuated: Schumpeter, the Process Theory, and American Democratic Thought," 32 *Journal of Politics* 239 (1970).

operating a gigantic, powerful, diversified, and incredibly complex society.[61]

Another liberal who accepted Schumpeter's concept of democracy was his fellow Austrian (a Jewish refugee from Hitler), Hans Kelsen.[62] Kelsen emphasized the discrepancy between the rhetoric and the actuality of modern democracy.[63] We say that to live under democracy is freedom, but democracy enables electoral majorities to beat up on minorities and thus to curtail their freedom. The solution to this problem we call "liberal democracy"—an oxymoron because democracy is illiberal and liberalism nondemocratic. (I would prefer to call liberalism the fusion of democracy with legally protected liberty.) We speak of "self-rule," but modern democracy is not self-rule; it is the means by which the electorate decides which officials shall rule. Anarchism, not representative democracy, is the political theory of self-rule.

I said that Schumpeter's theory of democracy "influenced" political thought, not that it "has influenced" or "influences" it. The Dahl and Kelsen works that I cited date from the 1950s; later I shall cite Schumpeterian writing by economists, but most of it dates from the fifties too. In the half-century since, democratic theory has forked, with most conservatives taking the road that emphasizes the paradoxes of social choice and the failures of government regulation and most liberals taking the deliberative-democracy route. Schumpeter has been largely forgotten.[64] A revival of his theory is overdue, if only because without it there are

61. Robert A. Dahl, *A Preface to Democratic Theory* 131–132, 146, 151 (1956). See Edward A. Purcell, *The Crisis of Democratic Theory: Scientific Naturalism and the Problem of Value* 258–261 (1973), placing Dahl's book at the center of a realist school of democracy (my Concept 2). Dahl moved closer to deliberative democracy in later years, see, for example, Robert A. Dahl, *Democracy and Its Critics* 121–122 (1989), though not close enough to satisfy all Concept 1 democrats. See Cohen, note 11 above.

62. See Hans Kelsen, "Foundations of Democracy," 66 *Ethics* 1 (1955); see also Kelsen, "On the Essence and Value of Democracy," in *Weimar: A Jurisprudence of Crisis* 84 (Arthur J. Jacobson and Bernhard Schlink eds. 2000), an essay I cited in Chapter 3. Elsewhere Kelsen associates democracy with a world outlook that is relativistic in character, that is hostile to absolutism and to the deification of the state, and that tends toward pacifism. Hans Kelsen, "State-Form and World-Outlook," in Kelsen, *Essays in Legal and Moral Philosophy* 95, 112 (Ota Weinberger ed. 1973).

63. Kelsen, *Weimar,* note 62 above, at 88–94.

64. Not completely, however. Russell Hardin's recent book has a Schumpeterian flavor and includes favorable citations to *Capitalism, Socialism, and Democracy.* See Hardin, note 36 above, ch. 4 (on democratic theory) and p. 374 (index references to Schumpeter). I give

no wholehearted academic defenders of the most successful political system since the Roman Empire! Not that either conservatives or liberals are *wholly* negative about our system. Each camp defends various institutions of American democracy, and sometimes they are the same institutions, such as freedom of speech and the right to vote. But both camps think that the system needs radical reform in order to function well, and that is a conclusion that Schumpeterians reject.

The essentials of our pragmatically successful democracy, which we have ridden, as it were, to unprecedented prosperity and power, are discernible even in Westbrook's and Barber's dyspeptic summaries of Schumpeter's concept. American democracy enables the adult population, at very little cost in time, money, or distraction from private pursuits commercial and otherwise, to punish at least the flagrant mistakes and misfeasances of officialdom, to assure an orderly succession of at least minimally competent officials, to generate feedback to the officials concerning the consequences of their policies, to prevent officials from (or punish them for) entirely ignoring the interests of the governed, and to prevent serious misalignments between government action and public opinion. All this is accomplished, thanks to the manifold limitations of the democratic principle, without placing electoral minorities at substantial risk of having their property rights or other liberties curtailed by the democratic majority. With the modern rights-based liberties in place, democracy operates to diffuse rather than to concentrate (as direct democracy does) political power.

An *authoritarian* liberal state is not a contradiction in terms, however, and we should consider the possibility that it would be an improvement over Concept 2 democracy. Schumpeter would have thought so had he not feared that it could not prevent a slide to democratic socialism. A dictator might adopt liberal institutions, such as freedom of speech and secure property rights, to strengthen his control by conciliating the population, encouraging investment, and generating useful feedback. The joinder of authoritarianism with the rule of law is what Voltaire hoped Frederick the Great was trying to bring about.[65] But it is an unstable combination be-

---

examples later of current economic writing on politics that draws on or has affinities to Schumpeter.

65. See, for example, Peter Gay, *Voltaire's Politics: The Poet as Realist*, ch. 3 (1988); David Williams, "Introduction," in Voltaire, *Political Writings* xiii, xv (David Williams trans. 1994).

cause in a pinch the ruler is likely to override the rights he has granted his subjects (for they are subjects still, and not citizens). And so the grant of rights will lack credibility. Furthermore, authoritarian liberalism leaves the problem of succession unresolved.

With authoritarianism rejected, Schumpeter's approach becomes the case for our actual existing democracy, enabling academia to escape the strange and doleful paradox that both influential current democratic theories, deliberative democracy on the left and public choice/social choice on the right, are critical rather than supportive of American democracy. Neither provides any reason for preferring our system over a nondemocratic one. Both are excessively pessimistic.

I argued that Schumpeter's personal political and social views do not taint his theory of democracy. But this is not to deny an overlap. Both his personal views and his theory reflect a disbelief in equality, if by equality is meant not political or juridical equality ("equality before the law") but equality of personal ability. I think Schumpeter, like Aristotle and Nietzsche, and more immediately Mosca, Pareto, and Michels,[66] believed that the outstanding fact about human beings is their inequality. In particular there is in every society a class of (mostly) men who are far above average in ambition, courage, energy, toughness, ambition, personal magnetism, and intelligence (or cunning). In other words, society is composed of wolves and sheep. The wolves are the natural leaders. They rise to the top in every society. The challenge to politics is to provide routes to the top that deflect the wolves from resorting to violence, usurpation, conquest, and oppression to obtain their place in the sun. In our society dangerous sports and high-stakes business dealings are among the routes by which these natural leaders can achieve the success, distinction, and power that they crave without danger to the public weal. Politics is another route, maybe the most important, since the natural leaders who have political tal-

---

See generally Charles Ingrao, "The Problem of 'Enlightened Absolutism' and the German States," 58 *Journal of Modern History*, Dec. 1986 supplement, p. S161.

66. See, for example, Holmes, note 25 above, at 271 n. 36; Robert A. Dahl, *Democracy and Its Critics* 275–276 (1989); Alan Zuckerman, "The Concept 'Political Elite': Lessons from Mosca and Pareto," 39 *Journal of Politics* 324 (1977); Philip J. Cook, "Robert Michels's *Political Parties* in Perspective," 33 *Journal of Politics* 773 (1971); John D. May, "Democracy, Organization, Michels," 59 *American Political Science Review* 417 (1965). Michels's political theory is a particularly clear anticipation of Schumpeter's. See Robert Michels, *Political Parties: A Sociological Study of the Oligarchical Tendencies of Modern Democracy* (1915).

ents and aspirations are the ones that pose the greatest potential danger to civilized society. Schumpeter's theory of democracy is realistic in its recognition that these people exist, that they will be the rulers whatever the structure of government, and that democratic politics, by giving these natural leaders a competitive arena in which to strive for political power and attain it in a chastened, socially unthreatening, in fact socially responsible, form, performs an indispensable social function unacknowledged in the conventional pieties of democratic discourse. What Plato failed to recognize in urging that philosophers should be the kings, and what Plato's descendants among deliberative democrats fail to recognize in urging government by discussion, is that a political system that does not enable the natural rulers to rule cannot survive. Schumpeter, following Aristotle, realized that rule by natural rulers is consistent with democracy.

Pragmatism and Convergence

Schumpeter's concept of democracy should be attractive to pragmatists. This is not because they see elite democracy as the last barrier against socialism; the trend to socialism—the trend that Schumpeter so feared—has been stopped in its tracks. And it is not only because elite democracy, which, to repeat, is our democracy, has the essential virtue that everyday pragmatists look for in a social institution: it works better than the alternatives. It is also because a pragmatist prefers to start from what we have and evaluate proposals for change on the basis of their consequences than to start from an idealized conception and ask what measures would have to be taken to get there from where we are. It is the priority of the empirical over the theoretical. That American democracy does not much resemble Concept 1 democracy is at once inevitable, because Concept 1 democracy is unattainable, and reassuring, because it has unattractive features and if implemented might fail as badly as other inventions of armchair political theorists, such as Marxism, have failed. Madison, Jefferson, Adams, and the other authors of our Concept 2 democracy were theorists too, but more *engagé* ones than Plato, Aristotle, Hobbes, Locke, and Bentham (not to mention Rousseau, Kant, and Hegel), whose practical activities, though in some cases extensive, were neither as crucial nor as consuming as those in which the founders of the United States were involved.[67] The contrast

---

67. An example of the limitations of political theory is the constitution that Locke and

with modern academic political theorists is even more striking; and note that the most theoretical of our engaged theorists, Jefferson, was also the least sensible.

We can get a little more empirical here by asking whether America's Schumpeterian democracy produces better or worse outcomes on the whole than the parliamentary democracies of Western Europe. The parties in a parliamentary democracy tend to be more disciplined and professional than American parties, and most parliamentary democracies employ one form or another of proportional representation and have multiple parties, ideologically defined. These characteristics bring parliamentary democracy closer to the ideal of the deliberative democrats than presidential democracy does. And yet, glancing at the parliamentary democracies that we consider our peers, one does not sense that they are on the whole any better governed. They seem to have as much corruption, scandal, and misfeasance generally as American government does, and while they have more generous social safety nets,[68] which delights the vast majority of our deliberative democrats that is egalitarian, they pay a big price in heavy taxes, high unemployment, and sluggish economic growth. The parliamentary democracies are also less welcoming to immigrants—necessarily so, since a generous social safety net acts as a magnet to immigrants. Even a cosmopolitan liberal like Derek Bok acknowledges that "no other country enjoys more freedom or inspires greater loyalty in its citizens" than the United States.[69]

Shaftsbury drafted for the colony of Carolina in 1669—a notable flop. See Richard Middleton, *Colonial America: A History, 1585–1776*, at 138–142 (2d ed. 1996).

68. This may actually be a consequence of proportional representation. Proportional representation increases the demand for transfer payments by facilitating the rise of parties that consist of groups of voters having common characteristics regardless of where they live. In contrast, when representatives are selected by majority vote in specific geographical districts, they tend to focus on local interests, which tend to differ from the interests of a group defined by common characteristics rather than by location. See Gian Maria Milesi-Ferretti, Roberto Perotti, and Massimo Rostagno, "Electoral Systems and Public Spending," 117 *Quarterly Journal of Economics* 609 (2002).

69. Derek Bok, *The Trouble with Government* 18 (2001). Bok goes on, however, to accuse American government of myriad failures, and in a comparison of the United States to six other democracies (Britain, Canada, France, Germany, Japan, and Sweden) along 75(!) dimensions of social welfare, finds the United States to be below average (in progress since 1960) in two-thirds of them. See id. at 30–34 (tab. 2). Bok makes no effort, however, to correct for causal factors unrelated to government, such as differences in the size and composition of the national populations, or to weight the different welfare dimensions; so, for example, he gives growth in public and private support for the arts the same weight in the comparison as per capita income. Emphasis on growth is misleading, moreover, because the

In emphasizing the pragmatic character of Schumpeter's concept of democracy relative to Dewey's, I may seem to be indulging in paradox. Dewey's concept of democracy was a classic Concept 1 concept,[70] while Schumpeter was the leading theorist of Concept 2. Schumpeter is not generally regarded as a pragmatist, while Dewey is the archetypal pragmatist. Schumpeter's theory owes nothing so far as I am aware to pragmatic philosophy; Dewey's owes everything to it. Actually both men were pragmatists. The difference in their approaches to issues of political governance is the difference between everyday and philosophical pragmatism—and demonstrates that philosophical pragmatism can be just as theoretical, just as top-down, and just as divorced from reality as the Platonic philosophical tradition against which the pragmatists revolted.

The gap between Dewey and Schumpeter is wide indeed. But the gap between Concept 1 and Concept 2 democracy is not as wide as the discussion to this point has suggested. I have been using "Concept 1 democracy" and "deliberative democracy" almost interchangeably, and there is a potential for confusion in that equation that I now want to try to dispel in order to expose the surprising tendency of deliberative democracy to merge into elite democracy at the practical level—another pragmatic point.

Concept 1 democracy is deliberative democracy in a strong sense, but there is a weaker one. It is the sense in which the U.S. Constitution and its framers created or envisaged a democratic system, and that is a sense in which Schumpeter's concept of democracy is deliberative too. Joseph Bessette, who coined the term "deliberative democracy," affixes it not to a theory but to the system actually created by the Constitution,[71] whose framers, as we began to see in the last chapter, were assiduous in circumscribing the democratic principle. Their concept of democracy was closer

---

United States in 1960 was already ahead of the comparison countries along most dimensions, making it easier for the other countries to show progress since 1960. There are also a number of notable omissions from the comparison variables, such as disposable income, tax burden, property crime rates, and quality of higher education, in all of which the United States shines in comparisons with the other countries in Bok's sample.

70. "Dewey's philosophy was almost in principle antipathetic to the adversarial system in politics. The reason lay in Dewey's assimilation of political decision making and scientific inquiry. The idea that politics, like science, involved a cooperative and intelligent search for solutions to consensually defined problems consorts badly with the politics of 'winners and losers' that the party struggle involves." Alan Ryan, *John Dewey and the High Tide of American Liberalism* 245 (1995).

71. Joseph M. Bessette, *The Mild Voice of Reason: Deliberative Democracy and American National Government*, ch. 2 (1994).

to Concept 2 than to Concept 1—recall how often the Constitution of 1787 has been described as elitist. Can Concept 2 democracy be deliberative? If so, how different are the two concepts likely to be in practice?

Under the Constitution of 1787, most features of which have survived to this day, the people were to have no power to make or to execute laws except when serving on juries, though, granted, this was a significant exception at the time because eighteenth-century American juries were authorized to find law as well as fact. Direct democracy, whether in the form of referendums, initiatives, recalls, plebiscites, or town meetings, was not authorized. The people were not even authorized to issue binding instructions to their representatives[72]—an acknowledgment that the relation of an elected official to the citizenry would not be that of agent to principal. And unlike real fiduciaries the representatives were laid under no duty of fairly representing the *entire* electorate; they were free to play favorites.

In creating the Electoral College, the framers opted for an aristocratic mode of selecting the nation's chief executive.[73] The Senate was likewise envisioned as an elite body; its small membership, long term of office, and indirect election were expected to make it an effective check on popular passion. The life-tenured Supreme Court was even more elite, exclusive, and insulated from popular desires. The House of Representatives, the only democratic branch of the new federal government (and it was democratic only if the eighteenth-century limitations on the suffrage are ignored), was denied any role in the appointment of judges and executive officials or in the approval of treaties. The Constitution did create two deliberative institutions, the Senate and the Supreme Court; and a filtering mechanism, the Electoral College, for the appointment of the chief executive. But these were elitist devices superimposed on the democratic base rather than institutions for democratic deliberation like the Athenian Assembly. Their purpose was to make government more responsible and effective but less democratic. One reason the Constitution of 1787 does not mention the right to vote may be that voting is the antithesis of deliberation and the mark of its failure.

On Bessette's realistic understanding of "deliberative democracy," the

---

72. Sunstein, note 7 above, at 242.

73. "From a distance of two centuries, the idea that a group of provincial notables, called electors, might actually select a president seems like a quaint tribute to the limits of their imagination and their doubts about democracy." Jack N. Rakove, "The E-College in the E-Age," in *The Unfinished Election of 2000*, at 201, 207 (Jack N. Rakove ed. 2001).

term is an oxymoron as applied to the original design of the American federal government. Deliberation competed with democracy. The framers hoped that they had so designed the federal government that members of the elite would occupy the principal offices. Their understanding, which persists in those modern versions of deliberative democracy that emphasize expert administration and judicial review,[74] is closer to Concept 2 than to Concept 1. Perhaps, apart from the radical left, we are all Schumpeterians now.

And for another reason: although Concept 1 is aspirational, even utopian, maybe that aspect of it is just rhetorical overkill. The advocates of Concept 1 ask for the moon but, recognizing the problems of cost and feasibility that would beset a genuine effort at transforming our democracy into the Concept 1 ideal, would doubtless be content with modest increases in the deliberative capacities and motivations of voters and officials. Measures that would fall far short of achieving the ultimate goals of Concept 1 democrats, such as increasing the civics component in high school curricula, might at modest cost make our politics slightly more deliberative. The Concept 2 democrat could hardly complain.

An Economic Interpretation of Concept 2 Democracy

Schumpeter was a great economist; and though his theory of democracy is not formally economic, it bears the stamp of his profession.[75] Nothing comes more easily to an economist than doubt that democratic voting is deliberative in any serious sense and an inclination to regard political competition in a democracy (or any other polity, but it is democracy that highlights the nonviolent competitive element in politics, suggesting an analogy to economic competition) as a power struggle. The economist comes to the study of politics from the study of markets, where profit-seeking sellers compete for the favor of buyers.[76] It is natural for him to analogize political competition not to discussion in a faculty workshop but instead to economic competition, with votes taking the place of sales and power of

74. "From the left, we get 'deliberative democracy,' a philosophy that insists on stringent preconditions for self-rule, preconditions that it turns out can be satisfied only by small bodies as far removed from popular politics as possible." Larry D. Kramer, "The Supreme Court in Politics," in id. at 105, 152.

75. He did, however, though very briefly, compare political with economic competition. Schumpeter, note 45 above, at 271.

76. See id. at 258–260.

profits and with the two sides of the market sharply differentiated—the sellers (candidates) representing the active side, the buyers (voters) the passive.[77] In economic as in political markets the buyer does not design the product; he chooses from a menu presented to him by the sellers. Schooled in the economic advantages of the division of labor, the economist turned political scientist is alert to the advantages likely to flow from constituting a corps of specialists in governing, the representatives and other officials, thus freeing the rest of the citizenry to specialize in other pursuits. This salutary division of labor entails a separation in outlook and knowledge between governors and governed, but that is no different from the separation between sellers and buyers in economic markets.

The economist turned political scientist notices, however, that the electoral market is deficient in the conditions that would enable the "buyers," that is, the citizens, to make sound choices. The buyers in economic markets have strong financial or otherwise self-interested incentives to choose carefully between competing sellers, and usually they have enough knowledge to be able to determine which seller is offering the better value. The citizen, in contrast, the buyer in the political market, seems to have no incentive to vote at all, let alone to invest in learning which candidate offers the greatest value, since a single vote will not swing the election. And he is asked to buy a "product"—the candidate and the candidate's likely policies—the value of which is almost impossible to determine even if the voter irrationally invests a great deal of time and effort in studying the candidates and the issues.

Another way to state the difference between the economic marketplace and the political marketplace is that the "goods" in the latter are not priced. As Hayek emphasized (see Chapter 7), price is a cheap and accurate signal. It compacts enormous information. High-income consumers can use price as an index of quality; low-income consumers can use price to guide them to the cheapest goods consistent with minimum quality. There is no comparably economical and informative signal to guide the voter, though we'll see that there are some substitutes. It is neither a surprise, nor impressive evidence of altruism or public-spiritedness, that public opinion is often not strongly self-interested.[78] Since an individual's expression of his opinion on a political question, whether in the vote he casts or

77. Westbrook spotted, but too quickly dismissed, the analogy. See text at note 54 above.
78. See Jack Citrin and Donald Philip Green, "The Self-Interest Motive in American Public Opinion," 3 *Research in Micropolitics: A Research Annual* 1 (1990).

in the answer he gives to a pollster, is unlikely to have any effect on his welfare, there is no particular reason why considerations of personal welfare should determine his opinion.

Then too there are greater economies of scale in political than in most economic markets and therefore stronger monopolistic tendencies. The reason is the unusually serious information problems that beset political markets. "The scale of political activity is large . . . because many [political] offices tie together numerous activities . . . An electorate with a limited amount of political information finds it easier to place one person in charge of many activities than to choose one person for each activity."[79] As a result, the only important U.S. political parties are national, and there are only two of them, making political competition duopolistic. Duopolists often collude rather than compete vigorously with each other.

The economist who turns his eye to politics thus beholds an unedifying prospect from his professional standpoint. And yet his perspective offers reassurance as well. Many economic markets are oligopolistic rather than atomistic in their structure, yet still effectively competitive; this is true even of many duopolies, especially if there is a potential threat of new entry. Or consider voter apathy. If one looks at the buying side of a well-functioning consumer market, one sees there a good deal of—well, apathy. Another name for it is contentment. Buyers do not need to be alert, assiduous shoppers when they rightly believe that the market in which they are buying is competitive. They have reasonable assurance that the products offered them by the market will be of satisfactory price and quality.

Sellers in a competitive market, moreover, however vigorously they compete with one another, offer products similar in price and quality. Otherwise it would be not a competitive, but a monopolized, market. We can expect the same thing in the political marketplace. We should not take the Tweedledum-Tweedledee character of major-party competition as a sign that competition is not working. If the parties were highly dissimilar, one of them would probably be the permanent minority party.

And while what I am calling apathy and equating to contentment could signify alienation, studies of nonvoters suggest otherwise.[80] They find that

79. Gary S. Becker, "Competition and Democracy," 1 *Journal of Law and Economics* 105, 108 (1958). Becker later moved away from Schumpeter's theory, substituting "a definition of democracy as free competition among pressure groups for political favors in place of Schumpeter's definition of democracy as free competition for political leadership." Becker, note 32 above, at 141.

80. See, for example, Richard G. Niemi and Herbert F. Weisberg, "Is It Rational to Vote?"

nonvoters tend to have similar political views to voters[81] and that nonvoting is concentrated among the young and among people who move around a lot.[82] The young are less knowledgeable about political "commodities" and therefore "buy" fewer of them, while voting is more costly for people who change their state of residence and so must reregister. Turnout in close elections is higher not because voters irrationally believe that their vote may swing the election (the probability of an election's being swung by one vote is infinitesimal), but because the contestants spend more on political advertising and other promotional activities in a close election, thus stirring greater interest on the part of the electorate.[83]

Furthermore, in political as in economic markets, relatively uninformed "consumers," that is, the voters, can and do use information shortcuts to make up for their information deficits, as by inferring a candidate's suitability from the identity of his supporters and opponents.[84] Political parties reduce voters' information costs; a voter who knows a candidate's political affiliation (easy information to come by) knows something, and maybe a lot, about the policies the candidate is likely to support if elected. Party affiliation corresponds to a trademark in an ordinary market. A trademark is a low-cost signal of the quality of a product, and investment in a trademark is a commitment to maintain existing quality, since the investment will be lost if consumers defect because the producer has failed to maintain the promised quality. The broader point is that a consumer may

in *Classics in Voting Behavior* 13, 19–20 (Richard G. Niemi and Herbert F. Weisberg eds. 1993).

81. See Ruy A. Teixeira, *The Disappearing American Voter* 94–101 (1992); Arthur T. Hadley, *The Empty Polling Booth* 149 (1978) (tab. 1).

82. See id. at 150–151 (tab. 2). Very few of the nonvoters in Hadley's exhaustive study seem seriously disaffected.

83. See Ron Schachar and Barry Nalebuff, "Follow the Leader: Theory and Evidence on Political Participation," 89 *American Economic Review* 525 (1999); John H. Aldrich, "Rational Choice and Turnout," 37 *American Journal of Political Science* 246, 266–268 (1993).

84. See, for example, Donald A. Wittman, *The Myth of Democratic Failure: Why Political Institutions Are Efficient*, chs. 2–3, 5 (1995); Samuel L. Popkin, *The Reasoning Voter: Communication and Persuasion in Presidential Campaigns* (1991); Arthur Lupia, "Shortcuts versus Encyclopedias: Information and Voting Behavior in California Insurance Reform Elections," 88 *American Political Science Review* 63 (1994); James H. Kuklinski, Daniel S. Metlay, and W. D. Kay, "Citizen Knowledge and Choices on the Complex Issue of Nuclear Energy," 26 *American Journal of Political Science* 615 (1982). Cf. Paul Milgrom and John Roberts, "Relying on the Information of Interested Parties," 17 *Rand Journal of Economics* 18 (1986). Still, public ignorance about political matters is staggering; for a recent summary of the literature, see Samuel DeCanio, "Beyond Marxist State Theory: Autonomy in Democratic Societies," 14 *Critical Review* 215, 219–221 (2000). My favorite example: in 1964 only 38 percent of the American public knew that the Soviet Union was not a member of NATO. Id. at 220.

make the same decision on the basis of incomplete information as he would on the basis of complete information; there is empirical evidence that this is the case for most voters.[85]

There is even a respect in which information deficiencies are less serious in the electoral market than in ordinary markets. In an ordinary market, if 50 percent of the consumers are well informed and the other 50 percent are not, the latter group will make a lot of mistakes,[86] and thus incur a loss of utility. But in a political market, if only (say) 10 percent of the voters are well informed and the others vote randomly, the outcome will be the same within a small margin of error as if all 100 percent were well informed. The reason for the difference is that consumers get what they buy, but voters get what the majority "buys."

Although economists don't much stress the point, the apathy or, better, the rational inertia of consumers, besides economizing on precious time, serves to stabilize markets in important ways. The fact that most consumers are not actively shopping for most products at any given time (not that they're not buying, but that they're not considering changing their existing consumption pattern) minimizes the frequency and amplitude of fluctuations in demand and supply, averting the sudden gluts and shortages that would ensue if the entire consuming public flocked all at once to a new product. In the latter event, prices would change until equilibrium was restored, but changing prices is not costless and meanwhile there would be uncertainty, queuing, bankruptcies, and disemployment. The interest in stability is even greater in the political sphere because of the potentially disastrous consequences of sudden sharp changes in political governance. Imagine if all citizens were avid students of political theory and became mesmerized by the radically disinterested political theory of a charismatic political entrepreneur and as a result elected officials who wanted to change the course of the nation 180 degrees. That is a terrifying prospect, held at bay by many things but among them the fact that most citizens are interested not in what is best in some sense for the nation or the world but rather in what is best from the standpoint of their self-inter-

---

85. See Richard R. Lau and David P. Redlawsk, "Voting Correctly," 91 *American Political Science Review* 585 (1997). Besides reducing voter information costs, party affiliation creates economies of scale; by voting a straight ticket, the voter in effect produces many votes at the cost of one vote. John H. Aldrich, *Why Parties? The Origin and Transformation of Political Parties in America* 49–50 (1995).

86. Fewer than one might think, though, because the uninformed are protected to a certain extent by the informed, since sellers cannot easily discriminate between the two groups.

est. Except in circumstances of desperation, a concern with self creates resistance to radical social change.

Just the fact that sellers and consumers are assumed to be motivated wholly or at least very largely by self-interest rather than by concepts of the public good is reassuring. It shows that a market can serve the public good even if none of the participants is trying to serve it. The invisible hand of the economic market can be found at work in the political market as well. It doesn't operate as efficiently in the political market because it lacks that valuable tool, price. But this is not a criticism of democratic government. To government falls those tasks that the price system cannot perform well. It is not an accident, or some dumb socialist project, that national defense, judicial enforcement of contract, property, and other rights, crime control, regulation of pollution and other externalities, poor relief, and internal security are not provided by private enterprise.

Still another name for Concept 2 democracy, it should be clear by now, is "competitive democracy"—and the competitive element inherent in a system of representative democracy brings out still another problem with Concept 1 democracy. Concept 1 conceives of politics as ideally a cooperative search for truth—this is particularly clear in Dewey's conception— whereas representative democracy is inherently, quintessentially competitive.[87] Although scientists tend to be highly competitive people, the structure of scientific inquiry (Dewey's model for epistemic democracy) is cooperative rather than competitive; the "competitors" share information, "collude," pool results, and so forth in ways that would be illegal in an economic market and that are not found in political markets either. The major parties sometimes collude, for example to stifle third parties, as we'll see in the next chapter; but within each party there is fierce competition between factions and between rival candidates. Politics could not be reorganized along the lines of scientific inquiry yet remain workably democratic. Either Plato's rule of philosopher kings (undemocratic) or a town-meeting-style direct democracy (democratic but unworkable) makes a better fit with Concept 1 than representative democracy does because

87. See Russell Hardin, "Deliberation: Method, Not Theory," in *Deliberative Politics: Essays on Democracy and Disagreement* 103, 112 (Stephen Macedo ed. 1999); David Austen-Smith, "Rational Consumers and Irrational Voters: A Review Essay on *Black Hole Tariffs and Endogenous Policy Theory*, by Stephen Magee, William Brock and Leslie Young, Cambridge University Press 1989," 3 *Economics and Politics* 73, 82–83 (1991); Bernard Grofman and Barbara Norrander, "Efficient Use of Reference Group Cues in a Single Dimension," 64 *Public Choice* 213 (1990).

representative democracy is competitive, rather than cooperative, in the way that Schumpeter explained and the economic analogies bring out. Concept 1's endorsement of representative democracy is a bow in the direction of Concept 2, a bow to reality.

We tend to take for granted the competitive character of our politics. We should not. It was not that long ago that the southern states were one-party polities. This changed with Lyndon Johnson's support of the Civil Rights Act of 1964, Richard Nixon's "southern strategy," and the enfranchisement of southern blacks. The South was notoriously badly governed before its politics became competitive, as were northern cities that also had one-party governments (the same party, by the way). It is because the members of the Schumpeterian "elite," the governing class, can no more be trusted with power than other human beings that Schumpeterian democracy is *competitive* democracy.

The role of the politician in the Schumpeterian model is central and becomes clearer when the model is inflected by economics. Critics of American democracy deride politicians as panderers to the uninformed preferences of the average citizen. For the critics, the correct economic analogy is to sellers simply giving the consumer what he wants. The analogy is incomplete. There are sellers and there are sellers. The most interesting are those who seek to create (in order, of course, to then be able to satisfy—at a price) new desires of consumers. The consuming public did not know that it wanted automobiles, radios, frozen food, compact disks, e-mail, or laptop computers before these things were invented. The voting public did not know that it wanted social security, conscription, public education, an independent central bank, an interstate highway system, a Presidency open to a divorced or Catholic person, the North Atlantic Treaty Organization, or the auctioning of rights to the use of the electromagnetic spectrum before these things were proposed by political entrepreneurs, as distinct from run-of-the-mill politicians. Concept 2 democracy may not be edifying, but it need not be mediocre. This point is related to democracy's advantage as the system that diverts the energies of dangerously ambitious men into socially harmless, even beneficial, channels. Some of those men are practical-minded idealists (as opposed to mere dreamers)—which doesn't necessarily make them less dangerous.

The interesting sellers and the uninteresting sellers have something important in common: the profit motive. Without that, there would be no assurance that consumers were being well served. The interesting and the

uninteresting politicians also have something similar, and similarly important, in common: ambition to obtain and retain public office. Without
that, the voters would have no control over their representatives. "No
more irresponsible government is imaginable than one of high-minded
men unconcerned for their political futures."[88] Such government would be
irresponsible in the literal sense of not being responsible to the people.
This is another thing that many Concept 1 democrats do not understand.

The competitive process that is the heart of Concept 2 democracy does
not operate only at election time. In between elections, and quite apart
from the possibility of recalling or impeaching an elected official before
his term expires, elected officials from the different parties, and their adherents, compete vigorously, for example by pointing out the errors, over-
sights, and iniquities of the opposition. Campaigning, actual or latent, is
continuous. Compare that to a system in which the only check on officials
between elections is an ombudsman (the heir of the Roman tribune) or the
judiciary. Or a system, modeled on the representation of the workers in a
collective bargaining unit that has voted to make the union the exclusive
representative of the unit in bargaining with the employer over terms and
conditions of employment, in which representatives would have a fiduciary
obligation to represent all their constituents fairly, including those who
had voted for the losing candidate (which is the duty of an exclusive bargaining representative). Such a duty would inhibit representatives from
courting popular support between elections.

Competition provides stronger incentives for monitoring and criticism
than bureaucratic, including judicial, control mechanisms do. Schumpeter
overlooked the importance of between-elections competition because his
model democracy was Great Britain, which had (and still has) a highly centralized government. There were no traces of a federal system. The Cabinet had virtually unlimited power, since it controlled Parliament; thus the
legislative and executive branches were fused. The judges, though independent, had no power of constitutional review. The United States, with
its separation of powers, is in a constant competitive boil. The competition
between Jefferson and Marshall (see Chapter 2) did more to maintain a
competitive political system, by preserving Federalist institutions in a period of anti-Federalist electoral dominance, than the one-sided electoral
competition of that period did.

88. Joseph A. Schlesinger, *Ambition and Politics: Political Careers in the United States* 2
(1966).

American political competition is institutional as well as party competition.[89] The ferocity of turf wars is no joke, as I learned when I was chief judge of my court. Because it is difficult to compensate an agency for giving up some of its power to another agency—because there is no market in governmental property and power—turf wars are difficult to head off, ameliorate, or resolve by the normal economic methods of dispute resolution. These "wars" have many bad effects, not only in perpetuating archaic governmental structures and practices but also in discouraging cooperation among agencies having overlapping or complementary functions. But they are also an effective method of monitoring governmental performance from the inside, with outsiders enlisted when necessary by the insiders, by means of news leaks. In addition, institutional competition (what Peretti calls "pluralistic democracy" as opposed to "majoritarian democracy"),[90] as in the "capture" of different government agencies by different interest groups, offers minorities additional voice in government that they might not have in a majoritarian democracy.

Schumpeter not only slighted institutional competition as well as between-election competition generally; he also did not foresee the emergence of a shadow government of think-tank and academic operatives and the general rise of experts and expertise enabled by and driving a vast expansion in the staffs of elected officials. That is, he did not foresee the fuller, more effective exploitation of the division of labor to cope with the increased challenge of political governance posed by an expanding society characterized by rapidly increasing economic, technological, and social differentiation and complexity. (American government, in other words, has become more *professional* since he wrote.) When these omissions in his analysis are rectified, the case for Schumpeterian democracy is strengthened.

Schumpeter's implicit economic model of the democratic process was shortly made explicit by the economists Anthony Downs and Gary Becker,[91] and in succeeding decades a substantial economic literature on politics developed under the rubric of "public choice." The sources of

89. See, for example, M. Elizabeth Magill, "Beyond Powers and Branches in Separation of Powers Law," 150 *University of Pennsylvania Law Review* 603, 644–649 (2001).

90. See Terri Jennings Peretti, *In Defense of a Political Court*, ch. 7 (1999).

91. See Anthony Downs, *An Economic Theory of Democracy* (1957); Becker, note 79 above.

92. In the text, I emphasize George Stigler's interest-group theory of politics; in the next footnote, I mention Buchanan and Tullock's important contribution. Kenneth Arrow's im-

public-choice theory are various,[92] but few of the contributors to it have been significantly influenced by Schumpeter or for that matter have been much concerned with distinguishing among alternative conceptions of democracy.[93] The focus has been on the manifold ways in which a public-interest model of government, orthodox among economists until the 1970s, fails to explain policy. Public-choice theory is a theory of government failure designed to balance the theories of market failure that public-interest theorists trotted out to justify pervasive government regulation of the economy.[94] In George Stigler's version of public-choice theory, officials "sell" (in exchange for campaign contributions and other electoral sup-

---

possibility theorem, which denied that voting was a reliable method of aggregating individual preferences, and Mancur Olson's analysis of collective action, which asserted that free-rider problems would make it difficult for individuals as distinct from interest groups to influence public policy, are other important sources of public-choice scholarship, although their own contributions are often classified under the rubric "social choice." See Kenneth J. Arrow, *Social Choice and Individual Values* (2d ed. 1963); Mancur Olson, *The Logic of Collective Action: Public Goods and the Theory of Groups* (1965). The list goes on and on. But it does not include Schumpeter.

93. An early classic of public choice, James M. Buchanan and Gordon Tullock, *The Calculus of Consent: Logical Foundations of Constitutional Democracy* (1962), explicitly distinguishes its approach from that of Schumpeter and Downs by disclaiming focus on the *representative* character of democracy—the key to the Schumpeterian concept, see id. at 8, 335. (Later, however, Tullock discussed representative democracy from a Downsian standpoint in his book *Towards a Mathematics of Politics* 106–108 [1967].) An otherwise comprehensive recent survey of the economic literature on constitutionalism devotes only two pages to democracy and contains no reference to Schumpeter. See Stefan Voigt, "Positive Constitutional Economics: A Survey," 90 *Public Choice* 11 (1997). The principal exception to the neglect by economists of Schumpeter's democratic theory is Donald Wittman's book, *The Myth of Democratic Failure*, note 84 above, which argues that the political "market," understood in Schumpeterian terms, is as efficient as the conventional economic market. See also Wittman, "Comment on William Niskanen, 'On the Origin and Identification of Government Failure'" (forthcoming in *Political Economy and Public Finance*). Other recent applications of Schumpeter's approach may be found in *The Competitive State: Villa Colombella Papers on Competitive Politics* (Albert Breton et al. eds. 1991). See especially Robert A. Young, "Tectonic Politics and Political Competition," in id. at 129. Also in the spirit of Schumpeter, though he is not cited, are John E. Roemer, *Political Competition: Theory and Applications* (2001), and Timothy Beasley and Stephen Coate, "An Economic Model of Representative Democracy," 112 *Quarterly Journal of Economics* 85 (1997).

94. "With the emergence of public choice theory in the mid-1980s, academic analyses of public policy found both vehicle for and justification of a profound skepticism about the capacity of government to advance the public interest effectively." Cynthia R. Farina and Jeffrey J. Rachlinski, "Foreword: Post-Public Choice?" 87 *Cornell Law Review* 267, 267–268 (2002). Useful summaries of public-choice theory include Robert D. Cooter, *The Strategic Constitution* (2000); Daniel A. Farber and Philip P. Frickey, *Law and Public Choice: A Critical Introduction* (1991); and Jonathan R. Macey, "Public Choice and the Law," in *The New Palgrave Dictionary of Economics and the Law*, vol. 3, p. 171 (Peter Newman ed. 1998).

port) government aid and protection to interest groups that are able to overcome the free-rider problems that plague coalitions.[95] These interest groups function essentially as cartels, a traditional source of market failure. Diffuse interests, for example the consumer interest in competitive markets, are difficult to organize into effective "cartels" and therefore are underweighted in the political process. The result of the imbalance in the interest-group pressures that play upon politicians is that much of what government does reduces rather than increases economic efficiency without promoting competing conceptions of the social good, such as distributive justice.

Missing from the analysis, however, are the politicians and the voters—the sellers and the buyers in the political market and the focus of Schumpeter's theory. Instead interest groups are deemed the authors of public policy; politicians and voters are implicitly modeled as lackeys and dupes, respectively. The motivation for this approach is in part methodological. Rational-choice economics, which undergirds public-choice theory, has no very satisfactory explanation for why people vote at all, or if they do vote why they vote their self-interest, since their vote isn't going to swing the election. But if therefore the voter is to be ignored completely in analyzing public policy, the implication is that public policy will be the same (other things being equal) in dictatorships and democracies. And in fact there is evidence for this startling proposition, the core of what might be called "pure" public-choice theory, in a recent paper that finds, after correcting for demographic and economic variables, that the form of government has no effect on the amount of public spending on social security despite the fact that the elderly appear to wield disproportionate weight in a democratic (but presumably not a dictatorial) political system.[96] Even if the finding is correct (there is contrary evidence),[97] it cannot be the whole story.

What I am calling "pure" public-choice theory is fatally oversimpli-

95. George J. Stigler, *The Citizen and the State: Essays on Regulation* (1975); Stephen P. Magee, William A. Brock, and Leslie Young, *Black Hole Tariffs and Endogenous Political Theory: Political Economy in General Equilibrium* (1989); Richard A. Posner, "Theories of Economic Regulation," 5 *Bell Journal of Economics and Management Science* 335 (1974).

96. Casey B. Mulligan, Richard Gil, and Xavier Sala-i-Martin, "Social Security and Democracy," 39–40 (National Bureau of Economic Research, Working Paper No. w8958, May 2002).

97. See Peter H. Lindert, "The Rise of Social Spending, 1880–1930," 31 *Explorations in Economic History* 1, 17–21, 24, 34 (1994).

fied.[98] It cannot explain, for example, the well-attested generalization that democratic nations almost never go to war with each other[99] (because they know that other democracies also face domestic opposition to use of force, and so are less inclined to interpret the actions of another democracy as belligerent), the brittleness of autocracy, or the bizarre policies adopted by fascist and communist regimes. And it is vulnerable to criticisms by political scientists, notably that public-choice theory, at least in its original economic form, is unduly pessimistic.[100] But the criticisms do not draw on Schumpeter's concept of democracy, and public-choice theory remains generally pessimistic about the policy outputs of democratic government.

Concept 2 democrats acknowledge that interest-group pressures deform public policy. But as there is no evidence that nondemocratic regimes are less susceptible to those pressures, the frictions that interest groups create should be considered the ineliminable transaction costs of government, akin to transportation costs in ordinary markets. We accept the need for transportation and therefore the costs incident to it, and we should do likewise with respect to government. When public-choice theorists point to avoidable inefficiencies of government regulation they provide valid arguments for reform. These arguments have contributed to the deregulation and privatization movements, which have had some signal successes. The Schumpeterian, seeing politics as a kind of market but one that lacks the important information-generating and -compacting tool of price, is sympathetic to these movements in a way that few deliberative democrats are.[101] The danger of public-choice theory, as of deliberative democracy, is

98. See, for example, Sam Peltzman, *Political Participation and Government Regulation* (1998).

99. See, for example, Bruce Bueno de Mesquita and David Lalman, *War and Reason: Domestic and International Imperatives*, ch. 5 (1992).

100. See Tom Ginsburg, "Ways of Criticizing Public Choice: The Uses of Empiricism and Theory in Legal Scholarship" (forthcoming in *University of Illinois Law Review*). The optimistic and pessimistic versions are debated at length in Symposium, "Getting Beyond Criticism: New Theories of the Regulatory State," 87 *Cornell Law Review* 267 (2002).

101. "Whatever its other merits, imposing market organization on state agencies such as schools and other services designs away the need for cognizant citizens to act collectively. The question of what the state should do is answered by citizens in their capacity as consumers through prices and purchasing and not through any public deliberation." Archon Fung, "Creating Deliberative Publics: Governance after Devolution and Democratic Centralism," *The Good Society*, no. 1, 2002, pp. 66, 67. To which the Schumpeterian responds: "Precisely! And a very good thing!"

overstatement, contributing to the generally hostile attitude of the academy toward contemporary American democracy.

Whereas public-choice theorists tend to be implacably hostile to interest groups, Concept 2 democrats are friendlier to them because of the importance of interest groups to the operation of the democratic process. This greater friendliness creates a link to liberal interest-group theory, the pluralism of Arthur Bentley and David Truman,[102] which Stigler turned on its head. Not being economists, Bentley and Truman had missed the cartel analogy and with it the adverse effects of interest groups on economic efficiency. Concept 2 accepts that those effects are real; more broadly, accepts the public-choice theorists' skepticism that government officials can be trusted to promote the public interest. I shall use that skepticism in the next chapter to urge that our system of regulating the political process be modeled on the regulation of economic markets by antitrust law—specifically, and not surprisingly, Schumpeter's own (implicit) antitrust theory.

Another point at which Concept 2 diverges from public-choice theory concerns the need for channeling the energies of the ambitious. In Stigler's interest-group theory, officials are merely the supple tools of power. Agents, not principals, they are neither a distinct nor even an important stratum of the community, let alone a dangerous elite whose domestication is a major project and achievement of democracy. The passivity of officials assumed in public-choice models is the reason economic theorists of democracy devote little attention to the actual structure of a democratic system. If interest groups rule and officials merely broker the interest groups' deals, the structure of government is incidental.

The emphasis that Schumpeter's theory of democracy places on the existence of distinct tiers or classes of participants in the political process (voters and politicians, mass and elite) suggests a parallel to the long-running debate over "corporate democracy." Beginning in the 1930s with the work of Berle and Means, concern arose about the "separation of owner-

102. See Arthur F. Bentley, *The Process of Government: A Study of Social Pressures* (1908); David B. Truman, *The Government Process: Political Interests and Public Opinion* (1951). "Pluralism" in the Bentley-Truman sense of policy as shaped by interest groups should be distinguished from the more familiar sense of pluralism as the rejection of the idea, implicit in some versions of Concept 1 democracy, that it is possible to reason to a single conception of the common good. See Chantal Mouffe, "Citizenship," in *Political Philosophy: Theories Thinkers Concepts* 290, 293 (Seymour Martin Lipset ed. 2001); Jeffrey M. Berry, "Interest Groups," in id. at 398, 402. Pluralism in the second sense is an element of Concept 2 democracy.

ship and control" in the modern corporation.[103] The shareholders of a large publicly traded corporation are its nominal owners, corresponding to the electorate in the political system. They elect the board of directors, which in turn appoints the management. But like the politicians in Schumpeter's theory of political democracy, the directors and managers are the real "rulers" and have their own interests, which often diverge from those of the shareholders. The Securities and Exchange Commission has attempted to encourage greater shareholder participation in corporate management by requiring management to include shareholder proposals in the proxy materials distributed to the shareholders in advance of the corporation's annual meeting.[104] In effect, it has attempted to bring about Concept 1 corporate democracy.[105] It has failed.[106] Like voters, most shareholders of publicly traded corporations have only a small stake in the corporations whose shares they own—too small to give them an incentive to devote significant time and effort to monitoring the performance of corporate management. It is easier for them either to sell their shares if the corporation is doing badly, or, by holding a diversified portfolio, to offset unusually good performance by some of their stocks against unusually bad performance by others. Still, they do have the power to oust management, and the existence of this power both is a spur to management to perform well (or at least not too badly) and enables management to be replaced when it flounders disastrously. In practice, corporate democracy is Concept 2 democracy.[107]

The analogy is imperfect because corporate "citizens" have more options than political citizens. Expatriation is too costly an exit option to be

---

103. See Adolf A. Berle and Gardiner C. Means, *The Modern Corporation and Private Property* (1932). In the modern literature, this is described as a problem in "agency costs," that is, a problem arising from the fact that agents (such as corporate managers) have divergent objectives from their principals (the shareholders). See, for example, Andrei Shleifer and Robert W. Vishny, "A Survey of Corporate Governance," 52 *Journal of Finance* 737, 740–748 (1997).

104. See SEC Rule 14a-8; James D. Cox, Robert W. Hillman, and Donald P. Langevoort, *Securities Regulation: Cases and Materials* 1010–1012 (3d ed. 2001).

105. But this should be distinguished from the form of industrial democracy (see Introduction), also moribund, that seeks to alter the governance of the corporation to make it responsive to interests other than those of the shareholders. See, for example, Thomas M. Jones and Leonard D. Goldberg, "Governing the Large Corporation: More Arguments for Public Directors," 7 *Academy of Management Review* 603 (1982).

106. See, for example, Frank H. Easterbrook and Daniel R. Fischel, *The Economic Structure of Corporate Law* 85 (1991).

107. Cf. Richard A. Posner, *Economic Analysis of Law* § 14.7 (5th ed. 1998).

equated to selling one's shares; and it is impossible to hold a diversified portfolio of citizenships. On the other hand, there is more vigorous competition for political office than there generally is for corporate directorships; rarely in fact are shareholders asked to choose between rival slates. And while shareholders' legal rights against management are important to the welfare of investors,[108] citizens likewise have important rights against their "rulers" under the free-speech, just-compensation, equal-protection, and other clauses of the Constitution.

Still another economic perspective on Schumpeterian democracy is provided by the economics of rent-seeking. The term refers to the dissipation of resources in efforts to obtain pure profit (what economists call "rent"). Resources devoted solely to shifting wealth from one person's pocket to another's are wasted from a social standpoint. The expenditure of such resources moves wealth around without increasing it; and since real costs are being incurred, the social pie shrinks in the process of being redivided. Universal suffrage is a method of reducing political rent-seeking, since unrepresented people are a natural prey for rent-seekers who have their hands on the levers of governmental power. In addition, the larger the electorate the more difficult it is for the would-be rent-seekers to forge electoral coalitions for the exploitation of electoral minorities because the costs of organizing rise with the number of people who must be brought into the coalition for it to be effective. It used to be feared that democracy would encourage the plundering of the rich simply because they are a minority; and presumably they are a smaller minority the larger the electorate, since the electorate is expanded by the extension of the franchise to the members of previously marginalized groups. But the costs to the majority of thus killing the geese that lay the golden eggs discourage this form of exploitation. The more heavily the rich are taxed, the less taxable income they will generate, so that at sufficiently high rates of taxation the net transfer to the rest of the population will be negative.[109] And in fact we observe only moderate levels of wealth redistribution by government in modern democracies—especially the United States.[110]

The causality is complex; and reliance on the nonwealthy to recog-

108. The thesis of Shleifer and Vishny, note 103 above.
109. Casey B. Mulligan, "Economic Limits on 'Rational' Democratic Redistribution" (University of Chicago, George J. Stigler Center for the Study of the Economy and the State, Working Paper No. 171, March 2002).
110. Posner, note 8 above, at 103–104. See also Ian Shapiro, "Why the Poor Don't Soak the Rich," *Daedalus*, Winter 2002, p. 118.

nize the full costs to them of soaking the rich would be a risky strategy. Reflection on rent-seeking helps to explain and justify the limitations on democracy that are created by constitutional and other supermajority requirements for legislative action. Without such limitations (whose existence, by the way, complicates any effort to ascribe the failure of democratic governments to undertake ambitious schemes of wealth redistribution purely to the rational self-interest of the electorate), winning majority control of the legislature would be much more valuable to the winner, and so factions would expend greater resources on the struggle for that control.[111] The additional resources would be largely wasted from a social standpoint, especially if the goals of the contestants were to achieve maximum power by extinguishing democracy.

But Schumpeter's theory is a theory of democracy, not a theory of government. It does not inquire into the scope and goals of government. In this respect it differs dramatically from his fellow-Austrian Hayek's approach, examined in Chapter 7. A complete theory of pragmatic liberalism, which I do not attempt in this book, would specify the optimal limits on the scope and power of democratic government. I am content to describe pragmatic liberalism as the union of Schumpeterian democracy with a pragmatic concept of legality; there is literature enough on the principles that are necessary to protect people against illiberal and inefficient[112] government actions.

A Behavioralist Interpretation

Schumpeter's theory of democracy is indebted to psychology as well as to economics. He bolstered his unidealized vision of democracy by reference to a then-influential literature on "crowd psychology" by Le Bon, Pareto, and others (reactionaries all), who analogized the voting masses to mobs. Ironically in light of this provenance—but I repeat that a good idea should

111. Jack Hirshleifer, "The Paradox of Power," in Hirshleifer, *The Dark Side of the Force: Economic Foundations of Conflict Theory* 43, 63 (2001).

112. Shleifer and Vishny, note 103 above, at 767–768, for example, emphasize the inefficiency of state-owned business enterprises. As they explain, these firms are controlled by bureaucrats who lack the normal profit-maximizing incentives and constraints, as well as being buffeted by interest groups, such as labor unions, that lack those incentives and constraints as well. Only privatization, and not political democracy, Schumpeterian or otherwise, can solve these problems (though, as I have noted, a Schumpeterian should find privatization, where feasible, congenial). Although many Concept 1 democrats are social democrats, they no longer advocate public ownership of the means of production.

not be rejected because of its unsavory origins—a number of present-day psychologists and economists, joined by some notably liberal law professors, have questioned the accuracy of the conventional economic model of rationally self-interested behavior by invoking a variety of cognitive quirks that deflect people from rational behavior.[113] These behavioralists are in the line of descent from the crowd psychologists, but their critique is more encompassing and to the extent that it undermines faith in markets it undermines faith in the democratic electorate even more. Both the ability and the incentive to overcome one's cognitive deficiencies are weaker in political markets than in economic ones because the voter has a smaller stake and less information in choosing between candidates than the consumer has in choosing between sellers of ordinary goods and services. The idea that voting taps into some deep vein of civic responsibility and political intelligence in the average person is unrealistic—although it is of course possible that people are more easily bamboozled into voting against their self-interest than they are into abandoning self-interest when they are transacting in economic markets.

In Cass Sunstein's writings on the regulation of health, safety, television, and the Internet,[114] the cognitive quirks become a basis for arguing for a shift of regulatory authority from Congress to expert administrators—precisely in order to dilute irrational democratic influence. Neither the electorate nor even its representatives can be trusted.[115] Sunstein describes himself as a deliberative democrat, and he is, but in the same Bessettian sense in which the framers of the Constitution of 1787 were deliberative democrats and in which even Schumpeter, when shorn of his obnoxious personal political views, was a deliberative democrat. If the people are incapable of any political activity other than choosing between candidates, any intelligence in government will have to be the intelligence of an elite

---

113. See, for example, Richard H. Thaler, *Quasi Rational Economics* (1991); *Behavioral Law and Economics* (Cass R. Sunstein ed. 2000). The psychological literature is comprehensively reviewed in Eldar Shafir and Robyn A. LeBoeuf, "Rationality," 53 *Annual Review of Psychology* 491 (2002). The names, such as "behavioral decision theory" and "behavioralism," that are most commonly affixed to this literature are misleading because of the association of behavioralism with B. F. Skinner's antimentalist psychology, which is in fact remote from contemporary "behavioralism."

114. See, for example, Cass R. Sunstein, *Risk and Reason: Safety, Law, and the Environment* (2002); Sunstein, *Republic.com* (2001); Sunstein, *Free Markets and Social Justice* (1997).

115. See note 39 above; and, for pungent criticism of deliberative democrats' distrust of legislators, see Richard D. Parker, "Taking Politics Personally," 12 *Cardozo Studies in Law and Literature* 103, 114–117 (2000).

from which the candidates (and appointed officials, including judges and experts) are drawn. Schumpeter did not deny that there *is* such intelligence. He was counting on it to hold back the tide of democratic socialism. He himself had been minister of finance in Austria's first post–World War I government.

Sunstein's concept of democracy, if fully fleshed out and pushed to its logical limits, might end up resembling Schumpeter's, reinforcing my earlier convergence thesis. It might even end up to the right of Schumpeter's concept. Recall the distinction between deliberation over means and deliberation over ends. The former is far more likely to yield productive agreement. But it is also more amenable to expert treatment. Nothing is more natural or more common than to assign the design, formulation, and implementation of specific policies to experts. This makes it possible to envisage a two-step process of government reform the end result of which might be to asphyxiate democratic choice. First, efforts are made to instrumentalize political reasoning to the extent possible so that intractable issues of ends are transformed into issues of means. Second, the responsibility for the extensive instrumental reasoning now required of government is handed over to technical experts—instrumental reasoning is what technical expertise is good for. But if deliberation over means is professionalized in this manner and thus removed from democratic deliberation, and if deliberation over ends is interminable and more likely to irritate than to inform or edify, what exactly is left of deliberative democracy? What is left is the choice between candidates. What is left is a version of Concept 2 democracy.

But a truncated version. Remember that Concept 2 democracy is the democracy of interests. The two-step process just described of subjecting public policy to control by experts would severely curtail the representation of interests. Suppose for example that the regulation of abortion, or of assisted suicide, were consigned to medical professionals, and issues of school busing and school prayer to education professionals. Then the very people who feel most strongly about these things would not be represented in the decisionmaking process. Politics and public opinion would fall out of alignment. The Concept 2 democrat does not rhapsodize over democracy the way the Concept 1 democrat, or the populist or transformative democrat, does, but he *is* a democrat; and rule by experts, carried far enough, transforms democracy into oligarchy.

More is lost by swinging too far in the direction of the rule of experts than the representation of interests. Experts constitute a distinct class in society, with values and perspectives that differ systematically from those of "ordinary" people. Without supposing that the man in the street has any penetrating insights denied the expert, or is immune from demagoguery, we may nevertheless think it reassuring that political power is shared between experts and nonexperts rather than being a monopoly of the former. One reason that democracies tend to be more stable than authoritarian governments is that the latter are more susceptible to "vanguardism," the tendency to reckless social experimentation that rule by experts fosters.

This analysis casts "crowd psychology," "herd behavior," and related phenomena of imitative action in a different light from that of mere cognitive defects or limitations. The fact that voters tend to take their cues from others who are better informed, yet without blindly following either demagogues or experts, may increase rather than reduce the rationality of political action, as well as imparting to the political process a salutary inertia, impeding precipitate change. Indeed, what may appear to be cognitive quirks may actually be efficient mechanisms for coping rationally with uncertainty, including uncertainty about political candidates and issues.[116]

Speaking of voting, we can find help in the behavioralist literature, when inflected with the insights of evolutionary biology, in solving the puzzle of why people vote in political elections at all, when voting carries with it some costs but no instrumental benefits. As Paul Rubin explains, voters may overestimate their impact on the outcome of an election because human beings do not have a good intuitive sense for probabilities (there is much other evidence for this as well); in the ancestral environment, the term evolutionary biologists use for the period of prehistory in which man reached approximately his present biological state, the equivalent of a "vote" (the expression of a preference) would have been cast in a setting of very few people, where a single vote could well be decisive.[117]

But Is Concept 2 Democracy Legitimate?

Quite apart from the unloveliness of its inventor, might not Concept 2 democracy fail the test of legitimacy? The answer depends in the first in-

116. Lau and Redlawsk, note 85 above, at 586.
117. Paul H. Rubin, *Darwinian Politics: The Evolutionary Origins of Freedom* 163 (2001). See id. at 168 on the general difficulty people have in reasoning about probability.

stance on whether political legitimacy is considered a normative or a positive concept. If the former, and if, therefore, a theory of democracy is legitimate only if it is sound, then the issue of the legitimacy of Concept 2 does not require separate consideration from the issue, already considered, of its soundness. But if political legitimacy is understood in positive terms, as in Max Weber's pioneering analysis, in which a regime is legitimate if people comply with its laws and cooperate in social undertakings as a matter of acceptance rather than just of coerced obedience, then we do have to inquire into the legitimacy of Concept 2 democracy; and let us do so.

People are less likely to cooperate with a regime that they regard as usurpative, hopelessly corrupt, or deeply immoral than they are with one that they do not regard in so dismal a light. The illegitimate regime will have to accept the erosion of its authority or, at high cost, substitute forced submission for unforced cooperation. But quite apart from the affinities between the Schumpeterian concept and that of the framers of the U.S. Constitution, there are no indications that the perceived legitimacy of American democracy depends on a belief that it is deliberative. The conditions for that legitimacy are, rather, that the government conform to basic norms of legality, that it be subject to the control of at least formally democratic institutions, that the people adversely affected by government measures have an opportunity to protest, and that government deliver a certain range of services at an acceptable cost in the tax and other burdens that government places on the population. The satisfaction of these relatively undemanding conditions does not require Concept 1 democracy.

It would be unrealistic to attribute political apathy, if that is the right term (I have questioned whether it is) for the low turnout rate in recent elections, to a deficiency of deliberation. "Deliberative democracy" is an academic notion.[118] Debates over it have no spillover into the political arena or the popular culture. The practical advantages of our Concept 2 democracy and the lack of any solid evidence of the feasibility or desirability of moving to Concept 1 have persuaded the vast majority of the American people to accept, more or less cheerfully, the system we have. That system is Concept 2 democracy.

Legitimacy must not be confused with enthusiasm, so let us consider

---

118. A tip-off is the statement of the editor of a book of essays, by and for academics, on deliberative democracy, of his "hope that this volume is itself a contribution to the democratic deliberation that Gutmann and Thompson [note 20 above] have so ably championed and advanced." Stephen Macedo, Preface to *Deliberative Politics*, note 87 above, at v, vi.

whether Concept 2 democracy is—to dramatize the question—the sort of thing Americans are willing to die for. Viewed as ideology rather than as description, isn't it too thin, even too sordid, to inspire the kind of support required not just to soothe malcontents but to move the civic-minded to strenuous efforts on behalf of important national projects? Maybe; but I think Americans' primary allegiance is to more concrete objects—including in that category, however, vivid symbols such as the American flag— than to a particular democratic ideology. Abstractions such as liberalism, capitalism, and democracy are valued (though more often simply taken for granted) as components of a political and economic system that generates the things that people value and that invests symbols such as the American flag, American power, the freedom and diversity of Americans, and American citizenship with their emotional power. The specific conceptions of these political components, such as deliberative versus Schumpeterian versus populist versus transformative democracy—terms unknown to more than a handful of Americans—are not what most Americans think distinctive about their nation and worthy of support.[119]

We should consider the democratic legitimacy not only of American government in general when viewed from a pragmatic perspective but also of pragmatic adjudication in particular. The Concept 1 democrat can be expected to deny the legitimacy of pragmatic adjudication, at least in the uncompromising form advocated in this book—provided that he has faith in theory-generated constraints on judicial discretion. But he is likely to have such faith. He believes in the power of deliberation to generate agreement on principles that will guide the decisions of voters and officials—and why not the decisions of judges as well? Suppose our deliberative democrat is a formalist and thinks that what judges should do is translate broader commands (constitutional or legislative) into narrower ones (judicial decisions) or implement political principles declared by or implicit in the Constitution. In other words, suppose he thinks the proper judicial role is a purely interpretive one, with "interpretation" understood to be different from creation. Then judicial decisions could be given a democratic pedigree of sorts, being traceable back to a democratic enactment, whether the Constitution or a statute or the toleration by the democratic branches of the exercise of common law rulemaking powers by judges. But only the judicial decisions that could be traced in that way would have the

119. For a further discussion of political legitimacy, see Chapter 7.

pedigree and thus be legitimate. The deliberative democrat who is not a formalist will consider a broader range of decisions legitimate but will shy away from describing them as pragmatic, thinking pragmatic decisions lack either deliberative or democratic groundings.

The pragmatist does not justify decisions by reference to their antecedents, and so the arguments that Concept 1 democrats might make in an effort to domesticate and democratize the judicial process are not available to the advocate of pragmatic adjudication. Not that the latter denies that many, in fact most, judicial decisions are interpretive in the narrow sense that distinguishes interpretation from creation. But not the really important ones, the ones that shape the law and become the platform for subsequent, uncontroversially interpretive decisions.

No matter; the pragmatic adjudicator is naturally drawn anyway to the pragmatic concept of democracy and so feels no need to align his judicial theory with Concept 1. The Concept 2 democrat does not prate about self-rule or insist on a democratic or deliberative pedigree or grounding for official action. He wants judges like other officials to be responsive to durable public opinion and to this end he wants them to be subject to controls that prevent them from exercising wholly arbitrary power. But the controls need not be theories internalized by judges. Judges are not exempt from the pragmatist's unillusioned view of human nature. What prevents them from straying too far from their assigned role are such non-theoretical devices as making judgeships elective positions or, better (given the manifold drawbacks of an elected judiciary), the carrot of promotion, the stick of reprimand or impeachment, and careful screening of judicial candidates to exclude those who as judges would be unlikely to play the judicial "game," with its rule-of-law strictures, preferring to play other games, the politician's for example. That is a good reason why only lawyers are appointed to be federal judges, though there is no legal requirement.

Congress's control over the budget and jurisdiction of the federal courts is another factor of a practical rather than conceptual character that checks judicial discretion. Another is the feedback effect on judicial appointments of public opinion when it turns sharply hostile to the existing judges because of their decisions. Supreme Court Justices who buck public opinion too hard have to worry that by doing so they are making it unlikely that their future colleagues and their successors will be much like them; and, as I shall emphasize in Chapter 9, judges do care about the choice of their colleagues and successors. Another feedback effect that tends to hold judicial aggression in check derives from the fact that sudden overturnings of settled principles are likely to trigger avalanches of litigation that clog the courts and increase the workloads and criticisms of the judges, inviting legislative intervention.

Still another check is the judiciary's dependence on the executive branch to enforce its judgments if there is resistance to them. This is an example of the broader point that the judges don't have their hands on all the levers of power; Congress can for example check judicial expansion of civil liberties by increasing the severity of punishment, curtailing postconviction review of criminal judgments, and "defunding" legal representation of indigent criminals.

Finally, judges are at least somewhat sensitive to professional criticism for being willful, for acting like politicians rather than like judges. Criticism not backed by threats is a weak motivator in most settings, but since judges have no financial or other tangible personal stake in their decisions, the influence of criticism on their behavior should not be discounted entirely.[120]

Are these constraints on judicial discretion enough to obviate the danger of judicial monarchism, without the disciplining effect of a theory, of a commitment to judicial self-restraint? Probably not; and while Terri Peretti may be largely correct that a self-consciously political court would stay better aligned with the policies of the democratically elected politicians who nominated and confirmed the judges, would be more sensitive to public opinion, and would activate the many political checks (which I just summarized) on judges by dropping the mask of nonpolitics that judges like to wear[121]—in short, would cohere better with democracy than a mandarin court—this presupposes that the judges, even if not elected, are at least broadly representative. Whether one is a populist democrat like Peretti, or a Concept 2 democrat who being realistic about judicial as about other human nature[122] believes that theories of judicial self-restraint

120. It should be discounted heavily, however, as it is the judicial reflex to dismiss criticism as motivated by professional envy, politics, sour grapes, or lack of insight into the conditions and constraints of the judicial role.

121. Peretti, note 90 above, pt. 2.

122. There is increasing realism about judicial motivation in the scholarly literature on judging. See, for example, Stephen B. Burbank and Barry Friedman, "Reconsidering Judicial Independence," in *Judicial Independence at the Crossroads: An Interdisciplinary Approach* 9, 22–35 (Burbank and Friedman eds. 2002); Frederick Schauer, "Incentives, Reputation, and the Inglorious Determinants of Judicial Behavior," 68 *University of Cincinnati Law Review* 615 (2000).

are typically masks for judicial activists to don, one should embrace the idea of a diverse, a representative, judiciary, which I introduced in Chapter 3. The Justices of the Supreme Court are at once too insulated from political control and too powerful politically to be selected without regard to considerations of representation, if representation is the heart of democracy as Concept 2 democrats believe. Not that a court of only nine judges can be made fully representative of the American population; but if it represented only a tiny sliver, demographically, morally, and ideologically, of the population, its legitimacy would be in question. The people would not recognize it as their court. It would be making political decisions without having a secure claim to political legitimacy. The practical alternative to a diverse, representative judiciary is not a mandarin judiciary exercising political power but a mandarin judiciary confining itself to technical legal issues—a modestly, timidly interpretive judiciary.

The question of judicial legitimacy is most sharply posed by the aggressive deployment by judges of their essentially discretionary power to interpret the Constitution, the sort of behavior that gets denounced as "judicial activism." So we should consider how the Concept 1 democrat and the Concept 2 democrat stand with respect to judicial activism. Is one more comfortable with it than the other? Can it be thought legitimate under either concept?

The answers depend on what is meant by "judicial activism." Here are three possibilities. First, it could mean an inclination to enlarge the power of the courts at the expense of the other branches of government.[123] (In the case of federal judicial activism, the other branches include all departments of state government and thus state courts as well as state and federal legislative and executive officials.) Some Concept 1 democrats are activists in this sense because they consider the courts to be the most responsible, expert deliberators on political questions. But so are a number of adherents to the competing school of thought that is critical of American democracy—public choice.[124] It stands to reason that skeptics about the democratic process would be skeptical about its most characteristic products, namely legislation and executive decisions. Concept 2 democrats, being more comfortable with our actual existing democracy than either its left-

---

123. See Richard A. Posner, *The Federal Courts: Challenge and Reform* 314–334 (1996).

124. See, for example, William H. Riker and Barry R. Weingast, "Constitutional Regulation of Legislative Choice: The Political Consequences of Judicial Deference to Legislatures," 74 *Virginia Law Review* 373 (1988).

wing or right-wing critics, can be expected to be less activist than either wing.

Second, "judicial activism" is often used pejoratively to refer to all-round judicial aggressiveness. Concept 2 democrats might seem more prone to this vice, since as pragmatists they have no faith in the power of theory to cabin judges. But, if so, this tendency is counteracted by another: Concept 2 democrats value our democracy more than Concept 1 democrats do, and this should make them more reluctant to support the use of judicial power to checkmate democratic choice.

Third, "judicial activism" could just denote a frank recognition that since judges in our system do have a great deal of discretion, especially when they are Supreme Court Justices interpreting the Constitution, they necessarily are "active" participants in political governance. They are not at all like the oracle at Delphi, who merely transmitted Apollo's warnings and predictions. (Blackstone called the English judges the oracles of the law.) By being active participants in governance, the judges increase institutional competition, which Schumpeterians like. In this harmless and maybe even beneficial sense of "judicial activism," Concept 2 democrats are acknowledged activists, Concept 1 democrats covert ones.

Pragmatic adjudication assigns judges a role consistent with Concept 2 democracy. Any doubts about its legitimacy are not specific to pragmatic adjudication but place a cloud over the entire political system. The fire directed at pragmatic adjudication should be aimed elsewhere.

CHAPTER SIX

The Concepts Applied

❧

The two concepts of democracy that we have been exploring can help us think about the Clinton impeachment and the 2000 election deadlock, the laws regulating democracy more broadly, and the puzzling insouciance of judges and law professors about democratic theory.

The Impeachment of President Clinton

The Clinton impeachment brought out Concept 1 democrats in droves, almost all of them expressing indignant opposition to it.[1] Clinton had been reelected president in 1996, two years earlier. As the only official other than the Vice President elected by the American people as a whole (well, not really, because the Electoral College is interposed between the electorate and the candidates, but that detail, which loomed large in the 2000 election deadlock, was ignored by most critics of the impeachment), the President stands at the apex of American democracy. A Congress controlled by the President's enemies was trying to pull him down, which would have undone, his defenders argued, the result of the 1996 election. Indeed, they charged that Congress was attempting a coup d'état. The

---

1. For opposition to the impeachment by a prominent Concept 1 democrat, see Cass R. Sunstein, *Designing Democracy: What Constitutions Do*, ch. 5 (2001).

charge was imprecise.[2] The effect of removing Clinton would have been to install his loyal paladin, Vice President Al Gore, as President, giving Gore a leg up for the 2000 election campaign that, in retrospect, he could have used. Furthermore, the power to impeach and remove an official is not an undemocratic power. Some states permit the people to vote to "recall" their elected representatives, that is, to remove an elected official during his term; this power enhances democratic control over officials. The power to impeach and remove, a power vested in a democratically elected body (the United States Congress, in the case of federal impeachment), is a surrogate for the recall. It enables the legislature as the agent of the electorate to remove an official whom the electorate cannot itself remove because he has a definite term of office that has not yet expired (or an indefinite term, as in the case of federal judges, the principal targets, historically, of the impeachment power) and because the Constitution does not authorize recall. The fact that Congress can impeach the President and other officials *increases* democratic control over officialdom.

It is true that a legislature, like any other political organ, may not always act in conformity with majority opinion. Public-opinion polls and the outcome of the November 1998 midterm elections revealed that the House of Representatives was defying public opinion in impeaching Clinton. But ours is not a system of direct democracy, nor one in which policy is supposed to be made by public-opinion polling. The system is intended to align official action with public opinion, but not every official action with every fluctuation in the Gallup Poll. That would be direct democracy. So the willingness of the House to defy the polls did not make the impeachment of President Clinton undemocratic. Moreover, the fact that removal by the Senate of an impeached official requires a two-thirds vote limits antimajoritarian impeachments, though it limits majoritarian ones as well. But the disruptive and intimidating effect of impeachment is a compelling argument against relying entirely on the supermajority requirement to prevent abuses. The grounds for impeachment should be narrowly construed and the House of Representatives should satisfy itself that the President is guilty as charged, not just that he may be, before impeaching him.

The Constitution's list of impeachable offenses—"Treason, Bribery, or other high Crimes and Misdemeanors"[3]—is, or more precisely should be

2. For the details of what follows, see Richard A. Posner, *An Affair of State; The Investigation, Impeachment, and Trial of President Clinton* (1999).

3. U.S. Const. art. II, § 4.

interpreted to be, sufficiently general to cover any serious abuse of public office, whether criminal or not. Abandonment of office, though not a crime, is an impeachable offense so understood[4]—a good example, by the way, of pragmatic interpretation; abandonment of office is an impeachable "offense" not because it is comparable in iniquity to treason, bribery, or other criminal behavior, but because of its intolerably adverse consequences for the nation. From this perspective, abandonment of office can be a more serious offense than accepting a bribe, depending on what the official is bribed to do. Hence Clinton's defenders pleaded the David defense. King David, we recall from the Old Testament, coveted Bathsheba, the wife of one of his officers, Uriah. So David dispatched Uriah to battle with orders to the commanding officer that Uriah not survive the battle, and he did not. The Old Testament treats this as a grave sin but not an unforgivable one because it did not interfere significantly with David's discharge of his royal duties; losing Uriah's military services was not a serious loss to the kingdom. And likewise Clinton's affair with Monica Lewinsky and his subsequent efforts to cover it up, though the efforts involved perjury and other obstructions of justice effectuated in part through misuse of official powers, did not substantially interfere with Clinton's performance of his Presidential duties.

And yet one might have expected Concept 1 democrats, prominent though they were as Clinton defenders, to think his disgraceful behavior a threat to their concept of democracy. Remember that Concept 1 is premised on the idea that people have the moral capacity and the moral duty to perform their political roles, whether the humble one of voting or the exalted one of discharging the duties of the highest political office in the land, in a disinterested, civic-minded fashion. Clinton offered a blatant example of political selfishness, first in risking his political reputation, thus endangering his political party and embarrassing his political associates, by the affair with Lewinsky and then in subordinating civic to private interest by trying to lie his way out of the embarrassment caused by the exposure of the affair and to disrupt the orderly course of legal justice. Observing that Clinton seemed able to perform the duties of his office tolerably well despite the enormous distraction of the scandal and ensuing legal processes, pragmatists were inclined to doubt that his behavior, scandalous

---

4. See Charles L. Black, Jr., *Impeachment: A Handbook* 33 (1974); Posner, note 2 above, at 98–100. The first federal judge to be impeached and removed from office, John Pickering, was an alcoholic and a lunatic but not a criminal. Id. at 99.

and even criminal as it was, warranted his removal from office. The ideal-ists, however, had it not been for their divided loyalties—divided between loyalty to Concept 1 and egalitarian sympathies that incline them strongly to the Democratic Party, indeed that have made some of them downright party fanatics—might have been expected to regard Clinton's behavior as a blow to democratic morality and his removal from office as a necessary cleansing of the democratic temple. At least they might have been ex-pected to raise the issue, even if they ultimately concluded that on balance, all things considered, it would be better to retain Clinton as President. Of course, this would be thinking like a pragmatist.

Concept 1 democrats may reply that they want to purify political dis-course by replacing our current politics of personalities with a politics of issues. A sophisticated person realizes that public morality differs from pri-vate; scoundrels in their private life can be upstanding public servants, while individuals who lead unblemished private lives can be political *faitnéants* or even monsters. The deliberation that Concept 1 democrats seek to encourage is not deliberation over the private foibles and peccadil-loes of public figures. The only effect of such deliberation (gossip, really) is to thin the ranks of those who seek public office and to distract the pub-lic from the issues of public morality that should be central to the political process. These are valid points. But as long as many ordinary people react to revelations of private misconduct on the part of public officials by dis-missing politics as an unsavory business, it behooves Concept 1 democrats to take measures to cleanse political office of its most disreputable occu-pants, a category to which many people would have consigned Clinton even before the scandalous pardons that he granted in the final days of his Presidency. Notice, too, how in distinguishing between public and private morality the Concept 1 democrat plays into the hands of the Concept 2 democrat, who wishes to debunk the idea of politics as a "noble" calling.

More may have been involved in the cleaving of Concept 1 democrats to Clinton in his hour of need than loyalty to the Democratic Party or a de-sire to divorce the political from the personal. Remember that many delib-erative democrats distrust legislatures. They want to see governance dele-gated to expert administrators, who are found primarily in the executive branch. And they are more likely to find a sympathetic audience for their policy views among executive branch officials, including the White House staff (and sometimes the President himself), than among Congressmen and their staffs,[5] because legislators, being more responsive to interest-group and other electoral pressures, often local, tend to have a more parochial and less intellectual outlook than the appointed officials of the executive branch.

A precipitant of the obstructions of justice that almost cost Clinton the Presidency was the Supreme Court's decision in *Clinton v. Jones*.[6] The Court held that a President does not have even a temporary immunity from being sued civilly for conduct that occurred before he became President, such as Clinton's alleged sexual harassment of Paula Jones. The decision cleared the way for the deposition of Clinton in Jones's suit, in which he first perjured himself. The Supreme Court's decision was notably unpragmatic in failing to consider the potentially devastating effect of a trial of the President on a sex charge.[7] A pragmatist would want the Supreme Court in a case with national political implications to consider carefully the likely consequences of its decision and not be hobbled by abstractions and formalisms. Although the consequences the Court should take into account include systemic ones (the interest in legal predictability and the other rule-of-law values),[8] those consequences did not make a strong case for denying the immunity sought by Clinton. The Court was not being asked to establish immunity for a broad class of officials that included the President, but for the President alone. Had the immunity been granted, the rest of the legal landscape would have remained unchanged.[9]

Clinton v. Jones was not excoriated by Concept 1 democrats. They are not everyday pragmatists and so they are less likely to distrust formalistic legal reasoning (though Dewey, a Concept 1 democrat but also if inconsistently a pragmatist, did), the kind that likes to abstract from the particulars of a case, that prefers rules to loose standards, and that shudders at the thought of contaminating law by politics. Or maybe it is because Concept

5. See Richard D. Parker, "Taking Politics Personally," 12 *Cardozo Studies in Law and Literature* 103, 123 (2000).

6. 520 U.S. 681 (1997).

7. Posner, note 2 above, at 225–230.

8. Unless, as noted in Chapter 2, a case has been placed in the category of cases that are decided by balancing case-specific consequences.

9. It is interesting to note that the French supreme court of appeal granted Jacques Chirac, the President of the French Republic, the immunity sought by Clinton—and extended it to criminal as well as civil suits. See Editorial, "Immunity Is Accepted If It Is Temporary," *Guardian Weekly*, Oct. 18–24, 2001 (translated from *Le Monde*).

1 democrats tend to be political theorists that they are inclined to think that judicial decisionmaking should be theoretically guided and informed.

The 2000 Election Deadlock

I shall have more to say about the unpragmatic character of *Clinton v. Jones* in Chapter 8. Let me turn now to the 2000 election deadlock.[10] Once again we find most Concept 1 democrats firmly aligned with the Democratic Party, this time in the person of Vice President Gore. They make three points. The first is that Gore should have been awarded Florida's electoral votes and hence the Presidency because it is reasonably clear (I agree it is reasonably clear)[11] that a majority of Floridians who cast votes on November 7, 2000 thought they were voting for him. A disproportionate number of Gore's supporters were disenfranchised because of poor election equipment and administration that made it difficult for voters who are inexperienced or have reading difficulties to cast a valid vote—and a majority of those voters were Gore supporters. Second, the Electoral College is a democratic anomaly; in a Concept 1 democracy Gore, as the unquestioned winner of the popular vote nationwide, should have become President. Third, by terminating the recount ordered by the Florida supreme court, the United States Supreme Court, an unelected body, took away the choice of the President from Congress, an elected body. I say it took it away from Congress rather than from the people of Florida or the people of the United States because, had the recount given the lead to Gore,[12] the likeliest consequence would have been the appointment of rival slates of electors between which Congress, pursuant to the Twelfth Amendment, would have had to choose. (Notice the tension between Concept 1 democrats' criticism of the "undemocratic" impeachment of Clinton by the House of Representatives and their criticism of the Supreme Court for having seized the choice of the President in 2000 from the "democratic" House and Senate.)

10. For background, see Richard A. Posner, *Breaking the Deadlock: The 2000 Election, the Constitution, and the Courts* (2001).

11. See id., ch. 2; Ford Fessenden and John M. Broder, "Study of Disputed Ballots Finds Justices Did Not Cast the Deciding Vote," *New York Times* (national ed.), Nov. 12, 2001, p. A1.

12. As now appears unlikely, however. See id., summarizing the comprehensive nine-month study of the Florida ballots conducted by the University of Chicago's National Opinion Research Center for a consortium of newspapers.

Concept 2 democrats agree that inexperienced people and people who have trouble reading—even people who are downright illiterate—ought to be enabled to vote, which means that steps should be taken to make voting technology as user-friendly as possible. Illiterates have interests, like everybody else, and those interests are not likely to be taken into account by the educated, who have different interests and no surplus of altruism, let alone much feel for the unique problems of the very poorly educated. And in the age of television, illiterates can glean the minimum of information about issues and candidates that they require in order to be able to cast a vote not much more ill informed than that of the literate, most of whom also get their political information from television. The number of newspaper readers who skip the news sections of the newspaper is legion.

The economics of the ordinary marketplace reinforces this analysis. Most consumers are not very careful shoppers. Some are content to take price as a signal of quality. If all consumers were so insouciant, sellers would "compete" by raising price. But as long as a substantial minority of consumers are careful shoppers, the rest of us are protected unless the seller is able to discriminate between the informed and the uninformed, and usually he cannot. The situation is similar in the political market. There is a lot of dumb, careless voting, but it is probably distributed randomly between the parties and so has little effect on outcomes.

It is Concept 1 democrats who, despite their egalitarianism, should be troubled by the idea of facilitating voting by illiterates. Few Concept 1 democrats are so naive as to suppose that illiterates deliberate in an intelligent, knowledgeable, and civic-minded manner over the ends of politics. What, then, could illiterate voters contribute to *deliberative* democracy? The emphasis that deliberative democrats beginning with John Dewey have placed on education as a precondition to competent political deliberation[13] would be senseless if illiterates were conceded to have that competence. "It would be foolish . . . to deny that education enhances deliberation and also foolish to assert that everybody could be equally well educated."[14] Think back to James Fishkin's "deliberative polls" (Chapter 4). Would Fishkin wish to include illiterates among the citizens who deliberate on television in his experiments?

13. See, for example, Amy Gutmann, *Democratic Education* (rev. ed. 1999). Gutmann considers compulsory schooling for illiterate adults but rejects the idea on grounds unrelated to deliberative capacity. See id. at 273–281.

14. Jon Elster, "Introduction," in *Deliberative Democracy* 1, 13 (Jon Elster ed. 1998).

Notice the strange inversion here: the Concept 1 democrat, the "liberal," has (or should have, if he wants to be consistent) difficulty accepting the broadening of the franchise to include illiterates; the Concept 2 democrat, the conservative, the Schumpeterian, urges it without qualification. Not Schumpeter himself, of course; he would have been appalled at the thought of giving the suffrage to illiterates.[15] But my interest is in the implications of his concept, not in his personal views or even in the implications that, under the pressure of those views, he may erroneously have drawn.

The reason for the inversion is that Concept 1 emphasizes intelligence and Concept 2 interest. Illiterates have interests; they should, therefore, Concept 2 implies, be allowed to vote. They are not the best-informed voters, but we have gotten along for more than 200 years with a system in which most of the voting public is no more seriously engaged in the political process than the audience for a football game is engaged in playing football. In emphasizing ideas over interests, and hence cognitive skills over feelings and desires, deliberative democracy is actually more elitist than elite democracy is.

The analogy of football may help still concerns that we need the public rhetoric of Concept 1 democracy to secure the minimal civic-mindedness required for even Concept 2 democracy to work. The football audience is engaged, often passionately; it just isn't engaged in the same activity as the football players. The half of the eligible population that votes in Presidential elections is interested in the candidates and the issues (though only a fraction of that half passionately so), even though most of the people who bother to vote realize that their choices are severely truncated and their role closer to that of a consumer or a spectator than to that of a ruler.

The pervasiveness of Fourth of July rhetoric about self-government, the responsibilities of citizenship, and the importance of civic-mindedness does however raise a question about the implicit picture of the voter that Concept 2 paints. Why is high-minded rhetoric employed unless it connects with something inside us, some impulse to high-minded action? For a partial answer I refer the reader to the discussion of puffery in Chapter 1, but here I add three points. First, there is a social interest in people's taking some interest in public affairs and bothering to vote, and as the cost of voting to the voter is small, a rhetoric of civic-mindedness may have a

---

15. Cf. Joseph A. Schumpeter, *Capitalism, Socialism, and Democracy* 244–245 (1942).

modest effect in encouraging voting, even in encouraging informed voting. Shame is a motivator. If no one voted, democracy would collapse. Not that this is a real danger; as fewer and fewer persons voted, the instrumental value of a vote would grow, and eventually an equilibrium would be reached well short of zero voting. Nevertheless, a person who does not vote but prefers democracy to dictatorship or anarchy, as most nonvoters do, or would do if they thought about the issue, is a free rider. We dislike free riders and, when the benefits they derive from free riding are not great, can sometimes shame them into changing their behavior.

Second, a person may utter high-minded rhetoric in order to signal high-mindedness in the hope that people will think him a trustworthy person.[16] We may not be high-minded ourselves, but we would like other people to be high-minded and we would like to be thought high-minded ourselves so that people will want to transact with us, commercially or personally. The hope is often forlorn, but high-minded talk is cheap, and so the fact that the benefits are small does not make it an irrational tactic. If as a result most people talk the high-minded talk, one who does not becomes suspect; and so the talk spreads, without necessarily reflecting or influencing behavior.

Third, the vocabulary that a people employs in describing its nation is likely to depend on what is most distinctive about the nation. One of the most distinctive things about the United States, a nation not characterized by ethnic or religious homogeneity, ancient roots, rich cultural traditions, or common origins, is the large role that a written constitution, judicial interpretation of that constitution, an immense and powerful legal profession, a commitment to legality, and a democratic heritage have played and continue to play in molding a highly diverse people into a political community. These defining features of the American nation invite an abstract and cosmopolitan public rhetoric. The word "democracy" occupies center stage in the rhetorical drama because America reinvented democracy, becoming the first modern democracy of any significance. So distinctive was American government and civil society that until late in the nineteenth century "America" and "democracy" were virtually interchangeable. It is no surprise that, as I noted in the last chapter, "democracy" is an all-purpose term of approbation in our political vocabulary. It is part of the verbal façade of a thoroughly pragmatic liberalism. Its all-purposehood, however,

---

16. See Eric A. Posner, *Law and Social Norms*, ch. 7 (2000).

reflects another point I made there, that Americans' understanding of and commitment to democracy are not tied to any specific conception of democracy.

But how much effort should be invested in enlarging the suffrage to include everyone who has an interest that the democratic process might protect? The hard-headed Concept 2 democrat, while favoring the broadest possible suffrage for the reasons explained in Chapter 5, will want to point out that our democracy seems remarkably robust to flaws in the democratic process, including limited suffrage. Even some Concept 1 democrats look back with nostalgia to the nineteenth century (with an implicit exception, though, for the southern states)—with its higher turnout, its smaller federal government, and the smaller role that experts, judges, bureaucrats, and other unelected wielders of political power played—as the heyday of American democracy. Yet the suffrage was much more limited then (women, men under twenty-one, and, as a practical matter, most blacks were disfranchised) than it is today, and vote fraud and vote buying were more common. This implies that the details of the democratic process may be relatively unimportant in other than purely symbolic terms, the importance of which is itself uncertain. The flowery rhetoric intoned by the Florida supreme court about the importance of counting every vote (that is, of making every vote count—the complaint was not that the election boards had failed to tabulate the ballots), and the horror expressed at the idea that the candidate with some minutely fewer votes might be declared the winner of an essentially tied election, are merely the vapors of Concept 1 democracy. It is not as if blacks, say, or people with reading difficulties, are not represented in the political process at all. They are represented; and the court should therefore have balanced the social benefits of increasing their representation slightly against the costs of conducting a recount that would have employed highly subjective criteria, probably would have recovered only a small percentage of votes, and, as we shall see in Chapter 9, might well have precipitated a Presidential succession crisis.

Then too the Florida court's anxiety about the importance of making every vote count, even at the cost of precipitating a succession crisis, smacks more of populist than of deliberative democracy. Voting in a sense marks the failure of deliberative democracy, the failure to have achieved consensus through deliberation. To put a matter to the vote is to cut off discussion and thus to give up on reason as the method of resolving disagreement. Scientists do not use voting to determine what scientific findings to accept. And so from a deliberative standpoint the fact that one candidate has a few more votes than another says nothing about the relative quality of the candidates. In contrast, the Concept 2 democrat applauds the use of voting to resolve political disagreements because it is quick and nearly costless and because the most serious of those disagreements cannot be resolved by discussion anyway.

Let me give an example of Concept 1-Concept 2 inversion unrelated to the Florida election litigation. Controversy rages over "race-conscious" state legislative districting. This means configuring legislative districts in such a way that a group that is a minority in the state as a whole, blacks say, will be a majority of the electorate in some districts.[17] The idea is that otherwise the minority will be unable to elect representatives of its choosing. Concept 1 democrats should be, and some are, troubled by race-conscious districting because it may encourage "citizens and representatives to come to experience and define their political identities and interests in partial terms,"[18] rather than considering what is best for the nation as a whole. It is more difficult for a principled Concept 2 democrat to oppose race-conscious districting if he thinks it will enable the interests of the minority to be represented more effectively. True, such districting may impair effective representation of the majority (which is to say the local minority—for example, whites after a district has been gerrymandered to create a secure black majority). But if so, this suggests that race-conscious districting is unlikely to have a *net* effect on representation, and so the principled Concept 2 democrat will have no ground for opposing it. A more serious concern is that race-conscious districting may not actually improve the representation of blacks—may indeed impair it, because legislators who have fewer blacks in their districts because the blacks have been "packed" into a handful of minority districts have been found to be less sensitive to the interests of blacks.[19]

Returning to the 2000 election, let us consider, in light of the fact that

17. For a thoughtful discussion, see Richard H. Pildes, "Diffusion of Political Power and the Voting Rights Act," 24 *Harvard Journal of Law and Public Policy* 119 (2000).

18. Id. at 121.

19. See L. Marvin Overby and Kenneth M. Cosgrove, "Unintended Consequences? Racial Redistricting and the Representation of Minority Interests," 58 *Journal of Politics* 540 (1996); Charles Cameron, David Epstein, and Sharyn O'Halloran, "Do Majority-Minority Districts Maximize Substantive Black Representation in Congress?" 90 *American Political Science Review* 794 (1996); Kevin A. Hill, "Does the Creation of Majority Black Districts Aid Republicans? An Analysis of the 1992 Congressional Elections in Eight Southern States," 57 *Journal of Politics* 394 (1995).

Gore won the popular vote nationwide, how Concept 1 and Concept 2 democrats line up with respect to the question whether to abolish the "undemocratic" Electoral College. Most Concept 1 democrats favor abolition. The Electoral College is not a deliberative body (the Constitution requires the electors to cast their ballots without leaving their states),[20] and with trivial though potentially momentous exceptions electors vote robotically for the candidate to whom they are pledged rather than exercising an independent judgment. Concept 2 democrats see serious practical objections to abolition—mainly that it might impede an orderly Presidential succession by requiring contentious and time-consuming nationwide recounts in close elections—and even a theoretical objection to which Concept 1 democrats should feel obliged to attend: contrary to appearances, the Electoral College, though indeed malapportioned because each state gets as many electoral votes as it has Congressmen plus Senators, disproportionately favors populous states and thus tends to offset the malapportionment of the Senate.[21]

The Electoral College system may also reduce political polarization by requiring a Presidential candidate to have transregional appeal because no politically homogeneous region of the United States has enough electoral votes to elect a President. Concept 2 democrats will see this as a benefit. Concept 1 democrats may not. They may think that greater polarization would stimulate greater interest by the public in political issues as well as put a wider range of issues in play.[22] A better argument for abolition, at least from the standpoint of a Concept 2 democrat, is that once a candidate decides he has no chance to win a majority of a state's electoral votes, he has no further incentive to campaign there, and so he deprives the voters in that state of genuine electoral competition.

Regarding Gore's likely edge over Bush among those eligible to vote in the Florida Presidential election, Concept 2 democrats no more believe that the likely preferences of those Floridians whose votes were rejected

20. U.S. Const. amend. XII. "The fact that electors had to meet on a single day, cast their ballots, and then disperse, hardly suggests that the [Constitutional] Convention placed any great confidence in their deliberative abilities. If it had, it could have allowed the electors to meet as one faculty, at one campus, there to vote, deliberate, and vote again until a president was chosen." Jack N. Rakove, "The E-College in the E-Age," in *The Unfinished Election of 2000*, at 201, 213 (Jack N. Rakove ed. 2001).

21. See Posner, note 10 above, at 228–231.

22. These and other arguments for retaining the Electoral College, once naive conceptions of democracy are rejected, are well made in John O. McGinnis, "Popular Sovereignty and the Electoral College," 29 *Florida State University Law Review* 995 (2001).

because they failed to comply with the instructions for casting a valid vote should be a factor in evaluating the legitimacy of the 2000 election than they believe that elections should be replaced by scientifically designed and administered public-opinion polls. The traditional and on the whole salutary American distrust of officials makes it unacceptable to determine the winner of an election by analytical means, whether statistical inference from a sample (as in polling) or informed speculation about the intentions of voters who spoiled their ballots with the result that the tabulating machinery did not record them as votes. Only legally valid votes, which is to say votes cast in conformity with the requirements of the election code, not imputed votes, count in determining who won. This is an example of formalism in the service of pragmatism.

Whether the recount sought by Gore and ordered by the Florida supreme court would have produced a count more in conformity with Florida's election code than the count certified by Florida's secretary of state (the count that showed Bush 527 votes ahead of Gore, which eventually became Bush's official margin of victory), and if not whether nevertheless the U.S. Supreme Court should have kept its nose out of the matter, are questions taken up in Chapter 9. Here I want to consider the bearing of democratic theory on whether the Court should have resolved the dispute itself, as it did, or should have tossed it to Congress.

Congress is indeed a more democratic body than the Supreme Court, but the relevance of this point is not immediately apparent. Had the deadlock been handed to Congress for resolution, the question would, or rather should, have been not which candidate would make the better President but which was the legal winner of the popular election in Florida. The Constitution and federal statutory law do not authorize Congress to pick the President when there is a dispute over the outcome of the Electoral College vote; Congress's duty in such a case is to resolve the dispute, and it is a legal dispute, which casts Congress in the role of a legal decisionmaker, just as in the case of impeachment. Congress is not a judicial body, however, and Concept 1 democrats do not want judicial disputes resolved by nonjudicial bodies; and so it is unclear that Concept 1 democrats had any principled ground for wanting the deadlock resolved by Congress if it was justiciable by the courts, as it was.

If this point is set to one side, however, on the realistic ground that Congress would inevitably have made a political rather than a judicial decision, then the pragmatic grounds required to justify the Court's decision terminating the recount and thus handing the election to Bush[23] would not impress Concept 1 democrats as much as they impress Concept 2 democrats. This is true even though some Concept 1 democrats acknowledge that a congressional attempt to resolve the election deadlock would have been disorderly and might even have precipitated a national crisis.[24] For a Concept 1 democrat, the principle of having the President chosen, on whatever grounds, by an elected rather than an unelected body, even a radically malapportioned one,[25] would be likely to outweigh the practical consequences, unless those consequences seemed very bad indeed. Concept 2 democrats, in contrast, would be inclined to weight those bad consequences more heavily than an abstract democratic benefit. That it is indeed abstract is suggested by the previous Presidential elections that were decided by Congress, namely the elections of 1800 (Jefferson over Burr), 1824 (John Quincy Adams over Jackson), and 1876 (Hayes over Tilden). This history teaches that when the President is chosen by Congress (the House of Representatives in the first two examples, and Congress on the basis of the recommendation of an ad hoc commission appointed by it, in the third), he comes into office trailing poison. The fatal duel between Burr and Hamilton may have been a consequence of the 1800 election foul-up, when Hamilton vigorously supported Jefferson, his traditional foe, against Burr.[26]

Judges on Democracy

Here is an odd and remarkable fact: in none of the cases that I have discussed, and I think in none that I could discuss, can one find a clearly artic-

23. As a practical, not a formal, matter. Congress could have refused to count Florida's electoral votes. There is nothing in the Constitution to prevent such a refusal, high-handed though it might seem, and it is doubtful that the Supreme Court would intervene to prevent it.

24. "At this point [rival slates of Presidential electors submitted to Congress], a genuine constitutional crisis might have arisen. It is not clear how it would have been settled. No doubt the nation would have survived, but things would have gotten very messy. The Court's decision made all of these issues academic. It averted what would have been, at the very least, an intense partisan struggle, lacking a solution that is likely to have been minimally acceptable to all sides . . . What I hope to have shown is why the Court might have done the nation a big favor." Cass R. Sunstein, "Order without Law," in *The Vote: Bush, Gore, and the Supreme Court* 205, 218 (Cass R. Sunstein and Richard A. Epstein eds. 2001). He means, I think, "may have done."

25. If neither candidate had obtained a majority of the electoral votes, the House of Representatives would have elected the President—but with each state's congressional delegation casting a single vote. U.S. Const. amend. XII.

26. Joseph J. Ellis, *Founding Brothers: The Revolutionary Generation* 40–43 (2000).

ulated theory of democracy.[27] The word "democracy" is bandied about a great deal by judges but dramatic interventions in the democratic process are undertaken by them with astonishing casualness. The *Lucas* decision (see Chapters 4 and 5), which forbade states to model the upper house of their legislatures on the U.S. Senate, is typical. If state legislatures modeled on the federal legislature are undemocratic, then the federal legislature itself is undemocratic—a sufficiently startling claim to invite, but not receive, careful judicial consideration of the meaning of the word "democratic." We saw that a malapportioned upper house can actually enhance representation—a possibility that the opinion in *Lucas*, which is brief to the point of being perfunctory, did not consider.

Though *Bush v. Gore* involved a confrontation between polar concepts of democracy, with the majority implicitly adopting Concept 2 and the minority Concept 1, neither concept is articulated in any of the opinions and it is doubtful whether any of the Justices is familiar with the scholarly literature that develops and expounds the concepts. Empty, sometimes naive or even fatuous, judicial remarks about democracy abound.[28] Some judicial

27. That the Justices of the Supreme Court are unreflectively engaged in a program of subjecting democratic politics to ever more intrusive judicial regulation in the name of the Constitution is a steady theme in the scholarship of Richard Pildes. See, for example, Richard H. Pildes, "Constitutionalizing Democratic Politics," in *A Badly Flawed Election: Debating Bush v. Gore, the Supreme Court and American Democracy* 155 (Ronald Dworkin ed. 2002).

28. Here are a few examples: "Democracy works 'only if the people have faith in those who govern, and that faith is bound to be shattered when high officials and their appointees engage in activities which arouse suspicions of malfeasance and corruption.'" Nixon v. Shrink Missouri Government PAC, 528 U.S. 377, 390 (2000). "An informed public is the essence of working democracy." Minneapolis Star & Tribune Co. v. Minnesota Commissioner of Revenue, 460 U.S. 575, 585 (1983). "A self-supporting and self-respecting democracy can plead no justification for the existence of child labor." Western Union Telegraph Co. v. Lenroot, 323 U.S. 490, 510 (1945) (dissenting opinion). "Lobbying is the sine qua non of democracy." Kottle v. Northwest Kidney Centers, 146 F.3d 1056, 1062 (9th Cir. 1998). "Groups whose ideas or candidates do not obtain a majority of votes lose. That is not an unfortunate by-product of democracy, but is rather the *purpose* of democracy." Nixon v. Kent County, 76 F.3d 1381, 1392 (6th Cir. 1996) (en banc) (citation omitted; emphasis in original). "The public school is . . . the symbol of our democracy." Brown v. Gilmore, 258 F.3d 265, 292 (4th Cir. 2001) (dissenting opinion). *The Oxford Dictionary of American Legal Quotations* (Fred R. Shapiro ed. 1993) contains only six quotations on democracy—none by a judge. See id. at 108–109. The best-known treatise on constitutional law now has an index entry for "Democracy," but all the entry contains is a cross-reference to "Majoritarian Politics," and the page references in that entry are few, and very few of them are to discussions of democracy. The author's thoughts on the subject are summarized in the following brief, inconclusive, and unsatisfactory passage: "The democracy of legislative and executive politics is overstated. The point does not require much development: the ways in which representative democracy in practice diverges from the ideal are well-known. The result then is an imperfectly anti-democratic judicial process and an imperfectly democratic political process. And, in any event, the Constitution's premises cannot be reduced to the perfection of democracy," the last point being a reference to the limited suffrage at the time the Constitution was ratified.

decisions, it is true, vindicate pretty much anyone's concept of democracy, for example decisions enfranchising racial minorities or protecting freedom of political speech. But the issues that have been litigated in recent decades, such as reapportionment, campaign financing, political gerrymandering, race-conscious districting, blanket primaries, fusion candidacies, and candidates' access to publicly sponsored campaign debates, not to mention the constitutional issues in *Bush v. Gore*, cannot be assessed as democracy-promoting or democracy-limiting without some notion of what democracy means or should mean in the American constitutional framework.

That the conservative Justices who composed the majority in *Bush v. Gore* are implicit Schumpeterians is fine; but one of those Justices, O'Connor, wrote the decision in *Shaw v. Reno*,[29] the case that placed race-conscious districting under a deep constitutional cloud. Her opinion states that legislators are supposed to represent their constituency as a whole[30] rather than just the people who voted for them.[31] Actually, as I've remarked several times already, legislators have no duty of "fair representation" akin to that of a collective bargaining representative; to impose such a duty would be the equivalent of requiring the seller of one brand of a product to provide the same post-sale service to purchasers of a competing brand that he provides to his own customers, and thus would be anticompetitive. But notice that if legislators had such a duty and performed it, the principal objections to race-conscious districting would fall away—along with the principal advantages claimed for it. For then whites and blacks would be protected regardless of the race of their representative or the structure of legislative districts.

Three reasons for judicial insouciance concerning democratic theory can be conjectured. One is the inconclusiveness of political science and political theory, which makes it difficult both to assess the practical effect of specific democratic practices and to select from among the rival con-

---

Laurence H. Tribe, *American Constitutional Law* 309 (3d ed. 2000) (footnotes omitted). Only the first volume of a projected two-volume third edition of Tribe's treatise has been published, and maybe there will be a meatier discussion of democracy in the second volume, though one doubts that, because the second volume is to deal with individual rights; it is the first that deals with the structure of government and the principles of judicial review. The second edition of the treatise, published in 1988, contained no index entry for "Democracy."

29. 509 U.S. 630 (1993).

30. Id. at 648–650.

31. More precisely, who they *believe* voted for them. One of the overlooked side-effects of the secret ballot is to make it more difficult for representatives to identify their supporters and opponents and hence to discriminate against the latter and in favor of the former.

cepts of political democracy one to be normative and so guide the assessment. Second, judges are in the business of limiting democracy. Unelected judges especially—which means all federal and some state judges—instinctively incline to the belief that an important part of their job is to ride herd on politicians, whom judges tend to look down on as being less thoughtful and disinterested than they themselves are. Members of the governing class, they do not feel deep down that an important part of their job is to give free rein to the preferences of ordinary people or the people's representatives. Given this bent (or deformity), it does not much matter whether particular judges are instinctively Concept 1 democrats or instinctively Concept 2 democrats. There is not much difference at the operating level between, on the one hand, dissatisfaction with the democratic process because it is insufficiently informed, deliberative, and public-spirited, and, on the other hand, a realistic—shading into a cynical—acceptance of the democratic process as simply the least-bad method of controlling public officials. Either way the process is unedifying and to the fastidious distasteful. That is one reason why it is easy to imagine *Bush v. Gore* having come out the other way had the candidates' positions in the deadlock been reversed. Conservative judges were unlikely to take Gore's democratic rhetoric seriously, but, equally, had it been Bush rather than Gore who was intoning that rhetoric, liberal judges would not have taken it seriously.

Third, and this is related to the second point, the issue of how much weight judges should give democratic choice tends to arise most often, or at least most conspicuously, when government action is challenged as unconstitutional, a context that tends to smother discussion of what democracy means or should mean. A traditional sally in the battle to establish judicial supremacy has been to argue that since the Constitution was ratified by popularly elected conventions in all thirteen states, decisions enforcing the Constitution against state or federal legislation vindicate democracy rather than limit it. The argument contains three fallacies. The first, which may seem of least importance because it is merely terminological, but in fact looms large in what is essentially a rhetorical contest, is equating popular sovereignty to democracy—the former referring to popular determination of the form of government, which could as well be a dictatorship as a democracy, and the latter to the democratic form of government, which might or might not be the form established by the people.[32]

32. See Jeremy Waldron, "Judicial Power and Popular Sovereignty" (Columbia Law School, n.d., unpublished).

An elected dictator is still a dictator, not a democrat. The United States forced democracy on Germany and Japan at the end of World War II; the governments formed under this compulsion were genuine democracies notwithstanding their lack of roots in popular sovereignty.

Second, the "democratic" defense of judicial review works only if constitutional decisions are interpretive in rather a narrow sense (one inapplicable, by the way, to many of Marshall's own decisions); otherwise they could not realistically be thought to be actualizing the popular will embodied in the Constitution. How could anyone think that the voters (anyway a very narrow slice of the population) who ratified the Constitution in 1788 also ratified—approved, consented to, embraced—the body of constitutional law that the courts have evolved in the course of the more than two centuries that have elapsed since? Acquiescence is not consent. So did the ratifiers merely write a blank check to the Supreme Court to rule the nation? That would make the ratification the equivalent of the election of a dictator, a Napoleon or a Hitler, by plebiscite—a people's decision to renounce democratic government, the sort of thing only a Carl Schmitt could love.[33]

Third, quite apart from the limitations of the eighteenth-century suffrage, the idea that the Constitution was the expression of the general will of the American people cannot be taken seriously. It is no accident that when law professors and judges talk about the creators of the Constitution, they invariably say the framers rather than the people who voted for delegates to the state ratifying conventions. The people were not permitted to vote provision by provision, and even voters who disagreed violently with some or even many of the provisions of the proposed constitution may have supported ratification because they thought the alternatives, which included a possible breakup of the union, would be even worse.

A defense of judicial review that cuts it loose from any "democratic" decision made when the Constitution was originally ratified is that it's a good method of testing the strength and durability of the people's passions.[34] "Insulation and the marvelous mystery of time give courts the capacity to appeal to men's better natures, to call forth their aspirations, which may have been forgotten in the moment's hue and cry. This is what Justice

33. See David Dyzenhaus, *Legality and Legitimacy: Carl Schmitt, Hans Kelsen, and Hermann Heller in Weimar* 57–58 (1997).

34. This is a principal theme of Alexander M. Bickel, *The Least Dangerous Branch: The Supreme Court at the Bar of Politics* (1962).

Stone called the opportunity for 'the sober second thought.'"[35] On this pa-
tronizing view, the masses are intermittently whipped up by demagogues
or by their own ignorant and exaggerated fears to support foolish, even
barbarous, public measures. Judicial resistance to these measures in the
name of the Constitution creates a cooling-off period. If the people's passions do not cool, eventually the courts will yield. But in the meantime the
courts will have created an opportunity for sober second thought about
the necessity and propriety of the measures.

This rationale for judicial review, with its curious fusion of different levels of deliberation, the Supreme Court Justices being cast in the role of
"teachers" in a national "seminar,"[36] creates the paradox that the stronger
the people's support for an innovative governmental measure, the more
likely it is to be invalidated by the judges. The paradox in turn produces an
inversion of Bruce Ackerman's theory of dualist democracy (see Chapter
4). For him the democratic process is at its most authentic when people are
really interested in politics. But that is most likely to be when they are
afraid of things that they think government can, and should, do more than
it is doing to combat—afraid for example of crime, of subversion, of (what
they consider) immorality, of massive unemployment, of invasion, of terrorism. Their fears may be derided as hysterical by judges who either do
not share the fears or take pride in not yielding to them.

The elitism of Bickel's view is noteworthy. A handful of lawyers is
deemed wiser, more farseeing, more sober than the nation as a whole. Not
just when they are considering technical issues, the domain of specialists,
but when they are considering quintessentially political issues such as the
proper scope of free speech or of the right to bear arms or to withhold cooperation from criminal investigators. John Dewey would not have agreed
with Bickel's epistemological claim. Granted that the Supreme Court Justices, although neither political nor even legal geniuses, are better educated and informed than the average American, and obviously know more
constitutional law, do they really know more than the 300 million other
Americans concerning what is at stake in the great constitutional controversies? Some of the most important dimensions of constitutional adjudication, moreover, such as the effect of capacious construals of constitu-

35. Id. at 26, quoting Harlan F. Stone, "The Common Law in the United States," 50 *Harvard Law Review* 4, 25 (1936).

36. Bickel, note 34 above, at 26. This is the conception of deliberation embraced by the opinion in Planned Parenthood v. Casey that I quoted in Chapter 4.

tional rights on public safety, are, as we shall see in Chapter 8, matters that professional training and experience in law barely touch. None of the current Supreme Court Justices, for example, has had significant experience with the operation of the criminal justice system, whether as prosecutor, defense attorney, police officer, or trial judge. And as members of the upper middle class (most of them are millionaires, and three of the millionaires are *very* wealthy), living in safe neighborhoods where they are largely insulated from anxieties about crime that plague people who live in bad neighborhoods, they lack victim experience as well. Appellate judges learn some things from the briefs and arguments of the lawyers and the evidence collected in the earlier stages of the litigation, but not enough to make them specialists in education, crime control, zoning, sexual mores, religious practices, or any of the other myriad fields of human activity that the Justices regulate in the name—the name only, in many cases—of the Constitution.

Except in those instances emphasized by John Ely[37] in which the courts use the Constitution to knock down impediments to the democratic process, such as discrimination against electoral minorities, judicial enforcement of the Constitution truncates rather than vindicates democratic choice. Aware though untroubled by this fact, judges and law professors focus on whether specific interpretive theories and specific decisions go too far in displacing the authority of other branches of government into the courts. But by "going too far" they mean stretching constitutional rights beyond their (in some sense) intended boundaries, not damaging some concrete, positive value of democracy. "Undemocratic" in law talk is merely an epithet hurled by judges or professors who disagree with a decision invalidating government action. The basis of their disagreement will be a divergence in beliefs concerning the meaning or scope not of democracy but of the constitutional right that the action was held to infringe. Rarely is it pointed out that interpretations of the Constitution that limit the autonomy of the states are antidemocratic because the states are more democratic than the federal government and certainly more so than the judicial branch of the federal government.[38]

The giveaway is the label, invented by Alexander Bickel[39] and now stan-

---

37. See John Hart Ely, *Democracy and Distrust: A Theory of Judicial Review*, chs. 4–6 (1980).

38. Rarely, but not never. See John O. McGinnis, "Reviving Tocqueville's America: The Rehnquist Court's Jurisprudence of Social Discovery," 90 *California Law Review* 485, 507–526 (2002).

39. See Bickel, note 34 above, at 16.

dard,[40] that has been affixed to the tension between democracy and judicial review: "the counter-majoritarian difficulty." "Difficulty"? Obviously something to be gotten around. "Counter-majoritarian?" A euphemism for undemocratic. It would be more candid to say that the Constitution is a mixture of democratic, oligarchic, and autocratic government, with the House of Representatives being the democratic branch and the Senate quasi-democratic (basically democratic, but with a hint of oligarchy), the Presidency the autocratic branch, and the judiciary the oligarchic branch. Each is a check on the others, so that the system as a whole is not dominated by the democratic, the oligarchic, or the autocratic principle.

Even so sophisticated a treatment of the tension between democracy and constitutional adjudication as found in Ely's justly famous book—with "democracy" in its title—lacks a coherent theory of democracy. At one point Ely compares his "representation-reinforcing" theory of constitutional law to "an 'antitrust' as opposed to a 'regulatory' orientation to economic affairs . . . Rather than dictate substantive results it intervenes only when the 'market,' in our case the political market, is systematically malfunctioning."[41] This is a promising beginning, reassuringly Schumpeterian, as is the first type of "malfunctioning" that Ely identifies: when "the ins are choking off the channels of political change to ensure that they will stay in."[42] But Ely then veers into Concept 1 democracy by specifying a second type of malfunction, in which elected "representatives . . . systematically disadvantag[e] some minority out of simple hostility or a prejudiced refusal to recognize commonalities of interest."[43] The implication is that judges should use the Constitution to police the good faith, disinterest, and knowledge of elected officials. Elsewhere Ely seems to equate democracy with simple majoritarianism,[44] though, as Dahl pointed out in a passage that I quoted in Chapter 5, our existing—and, historically and comparatively speaking, very successful—democracy is more about appeasing strategically situated and clamoring electoral minorities than about aggregating preferences across the entire adult population. Majoritarianism can, as we have seen, actually thwart representation.

This discussion casts further light on the question of the legitimacy of pragmatic adjudication, discussed in the preceding chapter. The project of

40. See, for example, Barry Friedman, "The History of the Countermajoritarian Difficulty, Part Three: The Lesson of *Lochner*," 76 *New York University Law Review* 1383 (2001).
41. Ely, note 37 above, at 102–103.
42. Id. at 103.
43. Id.
44. See, e.g., id. at 7.

reconciling democracy with judicial review by somehow giving judicial review a democratic pedigree is hopeless. This doesn't show that judicial review is illegitimate, however. All it shows is that political theorists and constitutional lawyers are going about the legitimacy inquiry in the wrong way. Remember that legitimacy is acceptance, and acceptance is much more likely to be based on practical results—on delivering the goods— than on a "convincing" philosophical or otherwise theoretical rationale. Although it is impossible on the basis of existing knowledge actually to determine whether the net effect of judicial review on the things that most Americans value, such as freedom and prosperity, has been positive, the people obviously are not in revolt against the courts. There is no crisis of judicial legitimacy. Rightly or wrongly, people judge the results of judicial review to be good enough. Since the *arguments* for the legitimacy of an oligarchic court in a democratic system are weak, it seems that the legitimacy of judicial review does not require arguments to establish, but only results.

Schumpeter, Antitrust, and the Law of Democracy

In an effort to induce greater judicial and academic self-consciousness about the meaning of democracy in cases involving the regulation of the democratic process,[45] I want now to summarize and extend the implications for such cases of explicitly embracing Concept 2 democracy, something I would like to see the courts do (though I'm not holding my breath).

Concept 2 democrats believe that, subject to very minimal tests of competence, everyone should be entitled to vote, just as every person should be permitted to buy the goods or services that he wants and can afford to pay for in the economic market. The everyone includes people who lack property and thus can't afford to pay a poll tax. The traditional justification of the poll tax was, in the words of Justice Harlan dissenting in the case that invalidated it, "that people with some property have a deeper stake in community affairs, and are consequently more responsible, more educated, more knowledgeable, more worthy of confidence than those without means."[46] That is canonical Concept 1-speak.

The everyone who should be permitted to vote includes people who

---

45. See Samuel Issacharoff, Pamela S. Karlan, and Richard H. Pildes, *The Law of Democracy: Legal Structure of the Political Process* (2d ed. 2001); Daniel Hays Lowenstein and Richard L. Hasen, *Election Law: Cases and Materials* (2d ed. 2001).

46. Harper v. Virginia Board of Elections, 383 U.S. 663, 685 (1966).

have been convicted of a felony but have served their time and been released but whose civil rights have not been restored by pardon or otherwise. These felons have interests like everybody else. Indeed, they have rather more urgent interests than most people, given the (rational) discrimination that felons encounter when they try to rebuild their lives on legal lines, as they sometimes do. If disenfranchisement is somehow considered an important deterrent to crime (a rather ludicrous idea), the normal penalties can be jacked up to compensate for giving felons the vote.

It is not a good argument against allowing felons to vote that they are "bad people." The fact that they have been released from prison reflects a judgment that they are capable of reintegration into civil society. The "bad people" concern could be alleviated, moreover, by imposing a cooling-off period before a felon was allowed to vote. If he had been "clean" for five years after his release from prison, this might be considered sufficient evidence that he had gone straight and was now at least a minimally responsible citizen.

I would not, however, permit prisoners (other than pretrial detainees, who by definition have not been convicted yet) to vote. It would be inimical to prison discipline. Prisoners already are excessively conscious of their legal rights, a consciousness that expresses itself in a flood of largely frivolous prisoner civil-rights and habeas corpus litigation.

A related question is whether permanent resident aliens should be permitted to vote. The permanency of their status gives them an interest (in both senses) in the operation of the government that is similar to that of citizens. But before coming to a judgment on the question whether they should be allowed to vote, we should consider the typical motives of permanent resident aliens in *not* becoming U.S. citizens, for those motives may bear on the nature and intensity of their interests. Unfortunately the literature on this question is sparse. It appears, however, that aliens who live in their own, non-English-speaking ethnic communities in the United States, especially if they expect to relocate permanently at some time in the future to their country of origin, where they have retained citizenship, are least likely to naturalize despite the significant benefits of citizen status.[47] These aliens have a relatively loose attachment to the United States. Their stake in the nation is less, and so their incentive to vote responsibly

47. See Audrey Singer and Greta Gilbertson, "Naturalization in the Wake of Anti-Immigrant Legislation: Dominicans in New York City" (Carnegie Endowment for International Peace, Working Paper No. 10, Feb. 2000). See generally Nancy Morawetz, "Rethinking Ret-

is less than citizens',[48] and their access to good information about the political process is limited. It seems to me a toss-up whether they should be allowed to vote.

The most serious departure from the principle of universal suffrage is the denial of the vote to children, which in combination with the above-average propensity of the elderly to vote results in an irrational and offensive skewing of political power in favor of the old and against the young, indeed making the latter political orphans. Children do not know their own interests well enough to be even minimally competent voters, but their parents do and most parents are sufficiently altruistic toward their children to be trustworthy "virtual" representatives of them. It might make sense to give each parent additional votes equal to one-half the number of his or her children, so that, for example, in a family consisting of a married couple and their three children each parent would have 2.5 votes. But I acknowledge that this is as utopian a proposal as anything proposed by a Concept 1 democrat!

A more complicated issue of underrepresentation involves the poor. Turnout among poor people tends to be low, which reduces their political weight; and many poor are disenfranchised by reason of a felony record, alienage, or reading difficulties that make it more difficult to cast a valid ballot. Moreover, as poverty declines in a society, the remaining poor constitute an ever-diminishing electoral bloc and one likely to consist predominantly of the hard-core poor, who are less likely to engage the electorate's sympathy and may require heavier expenditures (per capita, not necessarily aggregate, since there are fewer of them) to lift out of poverty. Cutting the other way is the fact that, as we saw in the last chapter, a smaller interest group may be politically more effective than a larger one. And to the extent that the hard-core poor impose costs on the electorate that could be reduced by social measures to help them, the nonpoor may be willing to support those measures in their own interest. But at this point one of the limitations of the democratic process rears its head: the great weight it gives swing voters. If as in the United States today, the poor are solidly in the camp of one of the parties (the Democratic Party, as it happens), then neither party has much interest in helping them: the Republican Party because it has written off the poor as potential Republican vot-

---

roactive Deportation Laws and the Due Process Clause," 73 *New York University Law Review* 97, 106–107 (1998).

48. So maybe persons with dual citizenship should not be allowed to vote in either country.

ers, the Democratic Party because it doesn't have to do much for the poor to retain their allegiance. Poor children, then, along with felons and aliens, may be the least likely group to have political heft in our Schumpeterian democracy.

To continue with my positive proposals: electoral law, technologies, procedures, and personnel should be oriented toward producing swift and definitive resolution of elections and election controversies rather than toward pursuing the will-o'-the-wisp of actualizing the general will. Efforts should also be made to adopt voter-friendly election technologies and procedures in order to facilitate voting by people who have literacy problems.[49]

The institutions that support the two-party system, such as winner-take-all voting (in contrast to proportional representation, which encourages multiple parties),[50] should be retained, except that barriers to third parties, such as requiring huge numbers of signatures on petitions for a place on the ballot, should be viewed with suspicion and, when unreasonably burdensome, invalidated. The danger of collusion between competitors, including competing political parties, is acute when there are only two—unless collusion would invite the formation and rapid growth of a third party and would thus be self-correcting. The problem is not the Tweedledum-Tweedledee character of the major parties in two-party systems. That is all to the good because it diminishes ideological conflict. The problem is with the quality and responsiveness of the policies and the candidates that two ideologically similar parties are apt to serve up to the electorate if there is no meaningful threat of entry by a third party that can offer better policies and candidates. That the major parties might copy a third party's policies and even raid it for candidates is all to the good—indeed, historically these have been the principal social benefits of having third parties. And recall from the last chapter the role of the threat of new entry into the political market in inducing the two parties to take account of the interests of nonswing voters.

The most dangerous form that collusion between the two major parties takes is precisely the erection of legal barriers to the competition of third parties.[51] Between them the two parties control every state's political system and can pass whatever laws are in their joint interest. However vigor-

---

49. For details, see Posner, note 10 above, at 241–244.

50. For a summary of the empirical literature, see Rein Taagepera and Matthew Soberg Shugart, *Seats and Votes: The Effects and Determinants of Electoral Systems* 50–57 (1989).

51. See Michael J. Klarman, "Majoritarian Judicial Review: The Entrenchment Problem," 85 *Georgetown Law Journal* 491 (1997).

ously the parties compete against each other to win elections, they have a joint interest in killing any third party in its cradle unless one of the major parties is confident that the new party will draw more votes from the other major party than from itself.

Not that entry by additional parties should be made costless. Unless there are *some* barriers to third (and fourth, etc.) parties, ballots would list so many candidates that voters would be hopelessly confused. (Confusion is similarly an objection to allowing all candidates to participate in all pre-election debates sponsored by independent groups such as the League of Women Voters.) One of the things that made the "butterfly" ballot used in Palm Beach County, Florida, in the 2000 Presidential election so confusing was that ten Presidential candidates were listed. It was difficult to list them all in legible type in a format that would group all the competitors on facing pages in order to reduce the likelihood that the voter would over-vote, that is, vote for more than one candidate for the same office, perhaps thinking (if they appeared on different pages) that they must be candidates for different offices. The solution the Palm Beach election supervisor de-vised—a facing-page format with the chads (the places for marking one's votes) in the middle—was an invitation to voter error.[52] She could hardly have done worse. Nevertheless, the task of weighing the entry-retarding against the confusion-reducing effects of ballot access is inescapable. Also inescapable is a chicken-and-egg problem: the less popular support a can-didate has, the stronger the argument for excluding him from the ballot, but the exclusion will ensure that he lacks popular support.[53]

The presumption should be in favor of allowing third-party candidates a place on the ballot. The Supreme Court has tended to reverse the presumption. A majority of the current Justices, being conservatives and therefore inclined to Concept 2 democracy (even if they have never heard of Joseph Schumpeter, or at least have never associated him with a theory of democracy), explicitly favor the preservation of the two-party system.[54] That is fine with me. But it is not the limitations on ballot access that pre-serve the system; it is winner-take-all voting as opposed to proportional representation.[55] Winner-take-all voting makes it extremely difficult for a third party to elect any of its candidates and thus become a credible rival

52. See Posner, note 10 above, at 82–86.
53. See Jamin B. Raskin, "The Debate Gerrymander," 77 *Texas Law Review* 1943 (1999).
54. See, for example, Timmons v. Twin Cities Area New Party, 520 U.S. 351, 367 (1997). See also Storer v. Brown, 415 U.S. 724, 736 (1974).
55. As noted in Timmons v. Twin Cities Area New Party, note 54 above, 520 U.S. at 379 (dissenting opinion).

to the major parties. A party that obtained an average of 20 percent of the vote in every congressional district, but never more than 30 percent, would probably fail to elect a single Congressman. And even if it could elect a Congressman, it could never elect a President and so it could not attract the ablest politicians. There is a vicious circle. A new party cannot gain traction without winning elections, is unlikely to win elections without good candidates, but is unlikely to be able to attract good candidates because its chances of winning elections are dim quite apart from candidate quality; they are dim because it is difficult to pry a large fraction of the electorate loose from its adherence to the established parties.[56]

The significance of third parties is not in destabilizing the two-party system but in keeping the major parties on their toes and even, in an analogy to (economic) "competition for the market" (for example, competition to obtain an exclusive cable-television franchise that will confer monopoly power on the franchisee), in occasionally knocking out one of the major parties and replacing it with a minor one. The minor party then becomes a major party and the two-party system is preserved. The system is sufficiently stable that measures to discourage ballot access by third parties serve mainly just to protect the two parties from a threat of new entry that might make them more responsive to the electorate or might even replace one of them.

The Supreme Court's attitude is typified by its influential decision in *Jenness v. Fortson.*[57] Georgia's election law provided that to get on the ballot a candidate who was not supported by a party that had received at least 20 percent of the votes in the previous election had to have the signatures of at least 5 percent of all the registered voters in the district in which he was running (the whole state, if he was running for governor). There were all sorts of ancillary restrictions as well, such as that the necessary signatures be obtained by mid-June even though the election was not until November and that each signature must be notarized. The Court upheld the law. The effect on third parties was devastating; and with the law sustained, other states quickly ratcheted up their requirements for ballot access.[58] There is no reason to think that such high barriers to third parties are necessary to prevent ballot confusion. The reason there were ten Pres-

56. John H. Aldrich, *Why Parties? The Origin and Transformation of Political Parties in America* 56–57 (1995).

57. 403 U.S. 431 (1971). For criticism, see Richard Winger, "The Supreme Court and the Burial of Ballot Access: A Critical Review of *Jenness v. Fortson,*" 1 *Election Law Journal* 235 (2002).

58. Id. at 246–249.

idential candidates on Florida's butterfly ballot was that Florida had gone to the other extreme. No petition or fee was required for a listing on the ballot, only a certification that the candidate's party had held a national Presidential nominating convention.[59]

Measures that protect incumbents as distinct from protecting the major parties, and thus limit electoral competition even within the limited scope allowed by a two-party system, should also be scrutinized critically. To the extent that incumbents have strong natural advantages in that competition, akin to those of entrenched monopolists in economic markets, campaign-finance "reform" may be such a measure. A new entrant, whether in a political or in an economic market, will often have to spend more than the incumbents do in order to convince voters or consumers, as the case may be, to switch.[60] A limitation on campaign spending may therefore hurt him more than it hurts the incumbent whom he is challenging. The problem is particularly acute in political markets governed by winner take all. A new entrant in an economic market who obtains a 10 percent market share may be able to survive quite nicely; a candidate who obtains 10 percent of the vote is a loser, period.

Also, it is not obvious why people or institutions with the largest stakes in the outcome of an election should be denied the opportunity to spend more money on efforts to influence the voters. We do not think it a bad thing that litigants in cases in which they have large stakes spend more money on lawyers than litigants in cases with small stakes, or that large shareholders have more votes in corporate elections than small ones. This is another argument against certain types of campaign-finance reform, but it must not be carried to the point of permitting the sale of votes. Because a single vote cast in a general election has essentially no chance of changing the outcome, a vote has no instrumental value and therefore many people would be willing to sell their votes for very little—especially those people who are eligible to vote but do not intend to bother doing so, and especially if they thought that other people would be willing to sell their own votes for a modest price. One can imagine the political equivalent of a two-tier tender offer: an offer to purchase the first million votes tendered for $25, the next million for $20, and so on.

It is true that, regardless of people's reservation price (the minimum

59. Id. at 244.
60. See John R. Lott, Jr., "Brand Names and Barriers to Entry in Political Markets," 51 *Public Choice* 87 (1986).

price they would be willing to sell at), the market price of a vote would be higher the greater the political parties' demand for votes. But even if the price per vote were as high as $100, many institutions and for that matter even a significant number of individuals could afford to purchase millions of votes. Such purchases could open a huge wedge between public opinion and electoral outcomes, a wedge that would thwart Concept 2's goal of providing comprehensive representation of the people's multiform interests. Even if competition among vote buyers forced up the price per vote to the point at which no buyer could accumulate more than a few hundred thousand votes, still, if enough votes to swing the outcome were controlled by a relative handful of individuals and institutions that had been able in the aggregate to purchase millions of votes, we might no longer have an adequately representative system of government.

Concern with the entrenchment of incumbents powers the movement for term limits. But it is not clear that term limits actually increase democratic control over elected officials. Term limits create more lame ducks, and lame ducks are not subject to the forces of electoral competition. They illustrate what economists call the "last period" problem. A firm that is about to go out of business has no incentive to cater to consumers' desires, and so it is with the lame-duck politician. The problem is easily exaggerated, however. Many politicians subject to term limits will seek election to other offices after their last term in their current office expires;[61] politics is, after all, their profession. And if the electorate were seriously concerned about its loss of control over lame ducks it would never reelect someone ineligible to run at the end of his new term—yet a majority of Presidents have been reelected since the two-term limit was enacted, and those denied reelection were not denied it by fear of lame-duckhood. Moreover, candidates whose policy preferences differ markedly from those of the electorate will tend not to be elected in the first place. The policy preferences of those candidates who are elected are thus likely to mirror the policy preferences of the majority of the voters—and to continue doing so throughout the lame-duck period.[62]

So the last-period problem is not a compelling basis for term limits after

61. See Andrew Caffrey and Mitchel Benson, "Term Limits Have Unexpected Outcomes: Politicians Take Lower Offices, Try New Ways to Extend Careers," *Wall Street Journal*, Mar. 4, 2002, p. A16.

62. See John R. Lott, Jr. and W. Robert Reed, "Shirking and Sorting in a Political Market with Finite-Lived Politicians," 61 *Public Choice* 75 (1989).

all. And an objection to them is that they may reduce the quality of government. The shorter a legislator's expected term of office, the less likely he is to support legislation that involves future social benefits but present costs, even when the benefits, after being discounted to present value, exceed the costs.

Devices that entrench incumbents or dominant parties, such as gerrymandering and malapportionment (where the parties differ in regional appeal and malapportionment has given one of the regions a number of representatives that is disproportionate to the region's electoral strength), should receive careful judicial scrutiny. But we know that malapportionment should not automatically be equated with a denial of representation. If the electorate approves a departure from "one person one vote" on grounds not obviously related to entrenchment of incumbents or the dominant party, there is nothing in Concept 2 democracy to warrant judicial intervention. The federal government has gotten along quite well with a malapportioned Senate and with entrustment of large governmental responsibilities to unelected officials, many with either de jure or de facto lifetime tenure. Why such institutions should be thought likely to work less well at the state or local level is a mystery, since state and local governments are intrinsically more democratic than the federal government. Professor Hasen has pointed out that "the one person, one vote standard sometimes works to prevent the formation of regional governments to deal with problems that are appropriately handled on a regional, rather than local, basis," because an electoral minority may be unwilling to form such a government unless it is given protection against control by a simple majority.[63]

---

63. Richard L. Hasen, "The Benefits of 'Judicially *Un*manageable' Standards in Election Cases under the Equal Protection Clause," 80 *North Carolina Law Review* 1469, 1482 (2002). In light of Hasen's advocacy of allowing departures from the "one person one vote" rule, it is remarkable that he should assert, in criticism of the argument that *Bush v. Gore* was no more a constitutional stretch than the "Warren Court" decisions celebrated by liberals, that "the Warren court cases, such as *Reynolds v. Sims* (establishing a one-person, one-vote principle), operated to ensure that the political process would function normally. In other words . . . the Warren court sought to correct political market failure, so that voting and interest group competition could take place on a level playing field." Richard L. Hasen, "A 'Tincture of Justice': Judge Posner's Failed Rehabilitation of *Bush v. Gore*," 80 *Texas Law Review* 137, 148–149 (2001) (footnote omitted). "Function normally"? "Level playing field"? The use of such terms to characterize the one-person one-vote doctrine of the reapportionment cases is inconsistent with Professor Hasen's own more considered analysis of reapportionment in his article in the *North Carolina Law Review*. It is also inconsistent with the conclusion of his *Texas Law Review* piece, where he states that Reynolds v. Sims, 377 U.S. 533 (1964), the one-person

Referendums and especially initiatives, the principal devices of direct democracy in modern governments, serve the important purpose in a two-party system of enabling collusive deals between the parties to be broken.[64] They are a safety valve. And remember the *Jones* case that I discussed in Chapter 3, the case that outlawed the blanket primary? Statutes regulating the electoral process should receive careful and skeptical judicial review because the major parties control the process and can be expected to manipulate it in their favor, squelching competition from third parties. If, however, as was the situation in *Jones*, the statute is adopted by direct vote of the electorate rather than by the legislators, which is to say by the consumers rather than by the possibly colluding sellers, the inference that the statute is anticompetitive is attenuated.

Many Concept 1 democrats oppose any form of direct democracy, distrusting as they do the deliberative capacities of ordinary people.[65] Their criticisms[66] are further evidence that Concept 1 democracy is more elitist than Concept 2 ("elite") democracy. (It is also evidence of the political agenda that actuates many democratic theorists, and so we read that "the initiative is no longer serving the progressive purposes for which it was intended.")[67] The critics say: "The initiative power creates state policy by simple majorities of eligible lay-voters. These voters are unaccountable to the public, are free to cast their ballots in secret, and are under no obligation to inform themselves on the issue."[68] "The electorate lacks the competence of legislators . . . Unlike legislators, voters cast their ballots in private, which threatens unbiased decision-making . . . Voters have thus been

---

one-vote case, "whether it is good or bad politics, begets *Bush v. Gore.*" 80 *Texas Law Review* at 154.

64. See Bruno S. Frey, "Direct Democracy: Politico-Economic Lessons from Swiss Experience," 84 *American Economic Review Papers and Proceedings* 338 (May 1994); Stefan Voigt, "Positive Constitutional Economics: A Survey," 90 *Public Choice* 11, 44–45 (1997). For evidence that the initiative, a principal example of direct democracy in modern American government, tends to align public spending with the electorate's preferences, see John G. Matsusaka, "Fiscal Effects of the Voter Initiative in the First Half of the Twentieth Century," 43 *Journal of Law and Economics* 619, 641 (2000).

65. See, for example, James Bohman, *Public Deliberation: Pluralism, Complexity, and Democracy* 245 (1996); Julian N. Eule, "Judicial Review of Direct Democracy," 99 *Yale Law Journal* 1503 (1990).

66. Well summarized in Catherine Engberg, Note, "Taking the Initiative: May Congress Reform State Initiative Lawmaking to Guarantee a Republican Form of Government?" 54 *Stanford Law Review* 569 (2001). See also Richard J. Ellis, *Democratic Delusions: The Initiative Process in America* (2002).

67. Engberg, note 66 above, at 577.

68. Id. at 570. But they *are* the public!

described as the 'least accountable branch' . . . The initiative process is usurping the role of representative democracy. Unaccountable and largely uninformed voters are empowered by the initiative to control state fiscal policy and alter individual rights."[69]

It is ironic that Concept 1 democrats should turn so sharply against direct democracy. Initiatives engage the populace more directly in the political process than ordinary elections do and make issues salient rather than personalities—initiatives are *only* about issues. This should delight the Concept 1 democrat. It is Concept 2 democrats who should be queasy because they don't want people to become obsessed with politics, spend a lot of time in political disputation, or get hot under the collar because ideological issues are being sharply and publicly debated rather than being smothered in legislative compromises. But they believe that direct democracy, in moderation, does have a role in maintaining political competition, if only as a safety valve, though at best it is merely a band-aid solution to the problem of collusion between the major parties.

We have yet to consider the threat to competitive democracy posed by partisan (as distinct from race-conscious) gerrymandering.[70] This is gerrymandering designed to create "safe" seats for the party that controls the legislature and thus does the redistricting. When control of the legislature is split between the parties, the aim is to create safe seats for both parties; here major-party collusion reaches its apogee. But in either case electoral competition, the lifeblood of democracy in the Schumpeterian sense that I am defending, is undermined.

It is surprising, therefore, but illustrative of legal professionals' neglect of democratic theory, that except for a few specialists in election law,[71] constitutional scholars pay little attention to partisan gerrymandering in comparison to the attention they lavish on malapportionment, campaign-finance reform, term limits, and racial gerrymandering. Much of the neglect may be due to the greater difficulty of limiting partisan gerrymandering than limiting departures from interdistrict population equality.[72] There is an infinite number of configurations that will divide a state

69. Id. at 577, 595. Notice the implication in these passages that the secret ballot is a mistake even in normal elections and that the people are merely a "branch" of government, on a par with the judiciary, the executive, and the legislative branches.

70. See *Political Gerrymandering and the Courts* (Bernard Grofman ed. 1990).

71. See Issacharoff, Karlan, and Pildes, note 45 above, at 868–889.

72. For a powerful statement of the difficulties, see Peter Schuck, "Partisan Gerryman-

into a given number of geographical areas of equal population, and the choice among them can hardly be a blind one. The norms of compactness and political neutrality are much less manageable than the norm of mathematical equality. As a result, although partisan gerrymandering is rife, the courts have done virtually nothing to control it.[73]

Ironically, the problem of partisan gerrymandering is exacerbated by the principle of "one person one vote," which in effect requires states to reapportion their legislatures after each decennial census in order to maintain equality of population across legislative districts in the face of the inevitable population shifts since the last census. Every reapportionment is an occasion for gerrymandering. The combination of judicial zeal for equal-population districts with judicial insouciance toward partisan gerrymandering is another sign that the judiciary lacks a theory of democracy.

But maybe all is for the best, and the legal profession's neglect of partisan gerrymandering a benign neglect after all. Although such gerrymandering may undermine electoral competition,[74] this is not certain, because the creation of safe districts requires boundary shifting that is likely to make other districts less safe.[75] And while the requirement of decennial redistricting imposed by the "one person one vote" rule increases the opportunities for gerrymandering, it also hurts many incumbents, who find themselves forced to run for reelection in differently constituted districts; the net effect may be to increase electoral competition.[76] In our era of weak party loyalty, moreover, the attractiveness of a candidate may be much more important to his electability than the party affiliation of the voters in his gerrymandered district.[77]

It should be apparent by now that the model that I am proposing to guide judicial decisionmaking with respect to the democratic process is antitrust law, which polices duopolistic and other imperfectly competitive

---

dering: A Political Problem without a Judicial Solution," in *Political Gerrymandering and the Courts*, note 70 above, at 240.

73. See Issacharoff, Karlan, and Pildes, note 45 above, at 886.

74. See Andrew Gelman and Gary King, "Enhancing Democracy through Legislative Redistricting," 88 *American Political Science Review* 541, 543, 553 (1994), and references cited there.

75. See Donald Ostdiek, "Congressional Redistricting and District Typologies," 57 *Journal of Politics* 533 (1995).

76. The thesis of Gelman and King, note 74 above.

77. The thesis of Mark E. Rush, *Does Redistricting Make a Difference? Partisan Representation and Electoral Behavior* (1993).

economic markets. (Ely was on to something.) Political markets are not identical to economic ones, as we have seen. But the same basic incentives and constraints are operative, including the incentive to collude and the pressure for improved performance that a threat of entry can exert. Antitrust analogies abound. The initiative, for example, can be thought of as a method of "backward integration," by which customers break up supplier cartels by entering the cartelized market and competing with the existing suppliers.

Antitrust policy comes in different forms, and we should consider which one fits Concept 2 democracy best. Two in particular require consideration. One, a static economic model, emphasizes the beneficial effect on the allocation of resources of having a number of competing firms. The principal effect emphasized is that of forcing price down to marginal cost. The analogy in the political arena would be a system in which there were a number of political parties, each representing the interests of some segment of the population and all together representing all those interests and maximizing welfare (in the sense of interest-appeasement), at least cost, through compromise among the parties. The contrasting form of antitrust, the dynamic, originates in Schumpeter's famous concept of "the gale of creative destruction." He argued that economic welfare is maximized over time as a result of a succession of monopolies. Each monopolist wrests control of the market from his predecessor by cost-reducing or product-improving innovations that give him, in turn, a temporary monopoly that enables him to recoup the expense of his innovation with a sufficient profit to compensate for the risk of failure, which is considerable in the case of innovation.[78]

Dynamic antitrust theory, the antitrust approach implied by Schumpeter's dynamic theory of economic welfare, aims not at achieving static efficiency by maintaining a currently competitive market but instead at facilitating economic progress by permitting monopoly while assuring that would-be challengers of the current monopolist have a fair shot at entry. Compare a market in which marginal cost is $10 and price also $10 with a market in which marginal cost is $6 and price $8 because a firm with

78. See Schumpeter, note 15 above, at 81–106; Schumpeter, *The Theory of Economic Development: An Inquiry into Profits, Capital, Credit, Interest, and the Business Cycle*, ch. 4 (1934); Richard R. Nelson and Sidney G. Winter, *An Evolutionay Theory of Economic Change*, pt. 5 (1982); Albert N. Link, "Firm Size and Efficient Entrepreneurial Activity: A Reformulation of the Schumpeter Hypothesis," 88 *Journal of Political Economy* 771 (1980).

a new idea entered the market, knocked out the existing firms, and, having thus achieved monopoly, is obtaining a monopoly return and will continue to do so until knocked out of the box by a still more innovative firm. Consumers, and society as a whole, are better off under the second scenario, one in which monopoly profits serve the socially valuable function of creating incentives to risky, socially beneficial innovation. In that scenario what is important is not the number of competitors at any moment but that the existing ones not be able to entrench themselves against new entry, in other words that their position in the market be contestable.[79] That is what is important in political markets as well: not that there be a multiplicity of parties but that new parties (such as the Republican Party of Lincoln in 1860), or new coalitions within existing parties (such as the coalitions that gave Franklin Roosevelt his Presidential electoral victories and Ronald Reagan his), not be blocked by the existing political formations. Schumpeterian antitrust thinking provides the right framework for the legal regulation of a Schumpeterian democracy.

Of Human Nature

This largely completes my discussion of Concept 2 (Schumpeterian) democracy, though there will be some further discussion in subsequent chapters. But before moving on to other matters, let me address the most powerful objection to it. This is that while Concept 1 may be daft in assuming, as implicitly it does, the perfectibility of human nature, Concept 2 rests on an unduly bleak view of human nature. It just is not the case, critics will argue, that Americans, whether as voters or as officials, are as selfish, as unconcerned with public questions and the public interest, as scornful of moral and political theory, as impervious to noninstrumental reasoning, as devoid of moral ambition, as uneducable and unedifiable, as my exposition of Concept 2 in this and the preceding chapters has assumed and at times asserted. Certainly the view of human nature that undergirds the analysis, while plausible to some, cannot be proved to be correct. Maybe the sunnier view that gives deliberative democrats such hope as they have is closer to the mark. These are empirical questions but there are no answers to convince doubters. Indeed, the existence of deep and unbridgeable differ-

79. See, for example, William J. Baumol, *The Free-Market Innovation Machine: Analyzing the Growth Miracle of Capitalism* 163–165 (2002).

ences in conceptions of human nature is part of the point of this book; it is one of the things that make deliberative democracy quixotic.

Rather than try in contradiction of my thesis to bridge the gap, let me consider briefly how sensitive the analysis in these chapters is to the assumptions about human nature that underlie them. I think not very. Remember what I said in Chapter 5 about the tendency of Concept 1 and Concept 2 to converge notwithstanding the divergent conceptions of human nature that underlie them. Suppose that people have and are prepared to act on moral and political theory to a greater extent than I have assumed. Suppose, then, that encouraging greater deliberation among voters would have a positive payoff in more informed and public-interested voting, rather than a negative payoff in protracted, polarizing, polemical *Sturm und Drang*. Then "Deliberation Day" would not seem quite so absurd. But no one could be so naive as to suppose that the nostrums of the deliberative democrats would so far reform the old Adam that we would no longer have to worry about the two parties' colluding to stifle third parties, or about incumbents' raising barriers to insurgents, or about the other abuses to which the measures discussed in this chapter are addressed. The abuses might be fewer but they would not be negligible. The principal issues that would divide Concept 1 and Concept 2 would concern, first, the abolition of the Electoral College and, second, the wisdom of moving to a system of proportional representation, which the Concept 1 democrat favors for precisely the reason the Concept 2 democrat disfavors it—that it would increase the salience and influence of ideology in the political process. Since neither reform is remotely likely, pragmatists will doubt that much of any moment is involved in the debate between Concept 1 and Concept 2 democracy. The big difference is that Concept 2, because of its greater realism, provides a stronger framework for appraisal of practical improvements in our democratic system.

Concept 2, moreover, does not deny the possibility, even the occasional reality, of idealism in government, though Concept 2 democrats are apt to think that our opportunistic Presidents (such as FDR) have done better than our idealistic ones (such as Wilson and Carter). Remember what I said in the last chapter about the politician as a policy entrepreneur. The utility function of a politician as of other "noneconomic" actors is obscure and doubtless complex, but it needn't consist solely of basely self-interested ends. Paul Rubin's version of behavioralist psychology that I mentioned in the last chapter opens a space for a realistic assumption that many judges and other officials are altruistic;[80] our genes may fool us into thinking that complete strangers are like kin because in the ancestral environment most of the individuals with whom people interacted *were* kin. Some people are attracted to jobs that involve the exercise of political power because they really want to make life better for others and are deluded neither about their motives nor about their ideals and the difficulties of implementing their ideals. Concept 2 democracy gives these people full scope at the same time that it domesticates the purely power-hungry aspirants for public office.

80. See Lynn A. Stout, "Judges as Altruistic Hierarchs," 43 *William and Mary Law Review* 1605 (2002). Of course, this doesn't mean they are democratic.

CHAPTER SEVEN

Kelsen versus Hayek: Pragmatism, Economics, and Democracy

⚜

The origin of this chapter may merit a brief comment. While casting about for a suitable topic for a lecture that I had agreed to give at an annual meeting of the European Association of Law and Economics, which was to be held in Vienna, I was told that economic analysis of law hadn't made much headway in Austria because the academic legal profession there remained under the sway of Austria's (and Continental Europe's) most distinguished twentieth-century legal philosopher, Hans Kelsen. I had never read Kelsen, but his reputation as a Kantian, and the title of his most famous book, *Pure Theory of Law*, made it indeed plausible that followers of Kelsen would be unsympathetic to the application of economics to law. Then I remembered that another famous twentieth-century Austrian intellectual—indeed, one more famous than Kelsen—namely Friedrich Hayek, had been a distinguished economist who had studied law as well as economics in college[1] and had written extensively about law—had written in fact a trilogy entitled *Law, Legislation and Liberty*. Although I had read little of Hayek's work, I was confident that he could be placed in opposition to Kelsen as a model for the integration of law and economics. With that in mind I set about to read Kelsen and Hayek.

1. F. A. Hayek, *Hayek on Hayek: An Autobiographical Dialogue* 62–63 (Stephen Kresge and Leif Wenar eds. 1994). In fact, his first university degree was in law. Alan Ebenstein, *Friedrich Hayek: A Biography* 28 (2001).

I shortly made the surprising discovery that Kelsen's philosophy of law opens a space for economic analysis, and in particular for the use of economics by judges in a wide range of cases that come before them, but that Hayek's philosophy of law closes that space, forbids judges to have anything to do with economics. His general approach is pragmatic, as is (I shall argue) Kelsen's, for remember that empirical social sciences, such as economics, exemplify the type of theory that a pragmatist should like. But Hayek, illustrating a point I made in Chapter 2, believes that pragmatism requires judges to be formalists, while Kelsen's philosophy of law denies this and in so doing creates a space for economics in law and also forges an important link between legal pragmatism and legal positivism. Indeed, I shall argue that Kelsen's positivism is the law side of pragmatic liberalism, just as Schumpeter's theory of democracy is the democracy side.

Kelsen's Theory of Law

My text for discussing Kelsen will be *Pure Theory of Law*, the classic statement of his position.[2] Knowing that he considered himself a Kantian, reacting to the connotations of the word "pure," and supposing that a pure theory of law would draw more on Kant's moral and legal theories than on his epistemology, one expects to encounter in Kelsen's book a moralistic conception of law far removed from pragmatic considerations. That is not what one encounters. The intellectual style, the method, of *Pure Theory of Law* is closer to that of the Vienna Circle, and hence to logical positivism,[3]

---

2. My references are to Max Knight's translation, published in 1967, of the second (1960) edition of *Pure Theory of Law*. However, the much shorter first edition (translated into English by Bonnie Litschewski Paulson and Stanley L. Paulson in 1992 under the title *Introduction to the Problems of Legal Theory*) contains the essentials of the theory. In between the two editions, Kelsen published *General Theory of Law and State* (Anders Wedberg trans. 1961 [1945]), which expounds the pure theory, and discusses critical and competing views, at greater length. The Preface, id. at xiii, is a particularly clear statement of Kelsen's aspiration to formulate a "pure" theory of law in the sense that I try to explain in the next paragraph of the text.

There is an enormous secondary literature on Kelsen's theory of law. For sympathetic but penetrating criticisms by another prominent legal positivist, see Joseph Raz, *The Concept of a Legal System: An Introduction to the Theory of Legal System*, chs. 3–5 (1970); Raz, *The Authority of Law: Essays on Law and Morality*, ch. 7 (1979), and for a detailed summary of the theory, see Iain Stewart, "The Critical Legal Science of Hans Kelsen," 17 *Journal of Law and Society* 273 (1990).

3. On which see the reassessment in Michael Friedman, *Reconsidering Logical Positivism* (1999). The affinities of Kelsen's philosophical approach to that of the logical positivists have often been noted. See, for example, Jeffrey Brand-Ballard, "Kelsen's Unstable Alternative to

than to that of Kant; and logical positivism has, as we know, affinities with pragmatism. Logical positivism also takes science as the model of objective inquiry, as did Dewey; and economics prides itself on being scientific, at least in method and aspiration, which is one of the reasons for thinking that pragmatism and economics go hand in hand too.

The "pure" of Kelsen's pure theory of law has nothing to do with idealism or with hostility to the social sciences. It has to do with his aim of offering a *universal* definition of law. The parallel is to Newton's universal theory of gravitation. Newton asked (or can be imagined as asking) what a cannonball, the ocean's surface, a feather, a planet, and all other physical objects have in common and answering that they all behave in conformity with the same law (that is, regularity) of gravitation. Newton's inquiry was of course positive rather than normative; he was trying to discover, not change, universal "laws" of nature. But Kelsen too is engaged in positive, not normative, analysis. He is trying to discover what all law has in common. Although he is seeking a positive theory of a social rather than a natural phenomenon and the particular phenomenon that he is interested in is normative, his interest is positive. In that sense his inquiry is, as he says, scientific and not just systematic.[4] We might call it sociological or even linguistic, in the sense of the Oxford ordinary-language philosophers; he is excavating the meaning of, the way we use, the word "law."

But the Newtonian analogy is strained. Law cannot be identified and measured, as distance, mass, velocity, and acceleration can be. Suppose someone discovered a society whose members claimed to have "law" but its "law" did not meet Kelsen's definition. He might try to save his concept from empirical falsification by saying that what that society called "law" was not really "law." These dodges occur in science too. Recall the example of the swan in Chapter 1: if one part of the definition of "swan" is that

---

Natural Law: Recent Critiques," 41 *American Journal of Jurisprudence* 133, 139–141 (1996); Alan Gewirth, "The Quest for Specificity in Jurisprudence," 69 *Ethics* 155, 156 (1959). Kelsen's skepticism about "absolute justice," which I noted in Chapter 3, is related to the logical positivists' belief that ethical language was merely "emotive," that it had no truth content.

4. See Preface to *General Theory of Law and State*, note 2 above, at xiv–xv. The German word for science, *Wissenschaft*, is closer to the English "scholarship" than to the English "science." But Kelsen, who studied law only at his father's insistence and regretted not having become a scientist or a philosopher, Iain Stewart, "The Basic Norm as Fiction," 25 *Juridical Review* (n.s.) 199, 214 n. 70 (1980), aspired to create a theory of law that would be scientific in the English sense.

it's white, and someone discovers a bird that has every attribute of a swan except whiteness, scientists have a choice between treating the discovery as falsifying their definition of "swan" and declaring that the bird is not a swan because it does not satisfy the definition. But Kelsen doesn't have such a choice. If a non-English-speaking society has a practice that seems to occupy the approximate role that law occupies in our society but does not satisfy Kelsen's definition, there is no way to decide whether the word that denotes the practice in the language of the society should be translated by "law." This is not a problem with swans, because you don't need to know the local language to know that the bird that you're looking at is what you call a swan.

Another difference between Kelsen's concept of law and the concept of the swan is that a swan has many attributes; whiteness is only one and, if it is missing, there are still many others on which to base a judgment that this black bird is a swan. Kelsen's concept of law has, as we shall see, only three attributes and they are seemingly of equal importance; if one is missing from a culture, how can one say that the culture does, or does not, have law? So it seems that Kelsen's theory cannot be refuted empirically, which means it's not really a scientific hypothesis (or source of such hypotheses) but rather a definition useful if at all only as a sociological generalization.

No matter; sociological generalizations are interesting too; so let us consider what it is that Kelsen finds all law has in common. It is nothing to do with the *content* of law, with legal rules and principles. Those vary enormously across societies and over time, which rules out any possibility of basing a universal definition of law on natural law (or "justice")[5] conceived of as a body of universal principles found instantiated in every society's legal system.[6] Kelsen denies that "certain traits of man have appeared so compelling both factually and morally that to transgress them would render positive laws at once unjust and ineffective."[7] And he means it, making clear—this Jewish refugee from Hitler (Kelsen was teaching at a German university when Hitler came to power, and he was fired forthwith and left Germany within a few months)—that Nazi laws, including the racial and retroactive laws, were law within the meaning of his theory. For Kelsen there are no such things as *"mala in se"*—that is, crimes such as murder

5. Hans Kelsen, *Pure Theory of Law*, note 2 above, at 67–69.
6. See, for example, id. at 13.
7. Gewirth, note 3 above, at 171.

that are wrong in themselves rather than wrong simply by virtue of the law's declaring them to be wrong *(mala prohibita)*.[8] He won't even allow talk of "breaking" the law.[9] A law is a norm. Far from being "broken" by an act contrary to it, it exists only by virtue of the possibility of such an act. The wrongful act is not the negation of law but its trigger.

A few principles may *seem* universal in the relevant sense; every legal system forbids murder, for example. But this turns out to be little better than a tautology. Murder is the deliberate *unjustified* killing of a human being. The important question is what counts as justification, and the answer varies from epoch to epoch and from society to society. (Nor must it always be deliberate; nor is deliberateness understood the same way in all societies.) Genocidal and cannibalistic societies, and societies that believe in human sacrifice, blood feuds, capital punishment, infanticide, and abortion on demand, define murder differently from gentler societies. There is some tendency to convergence, but it is limited to a tiny handful of basic legal norms. A concept of law based on the substantive overlaps among different legal systems would explain only a small fraction of law. It would be like a gravitational theory that explained the rate of fall only of safety pins and cantaloupes.

So natural law is out as a positive theory of law and with it, by the way, any possibility of *equating* law to economics. Economic norms are substantive. It would be absurd to suggest that a legal system that did not require an injurer to pay damages even when the cost of avoiding the injury was less than the expected cost of the injury did not have law. But no one has ever tried to go that far in integrating the disciplines, and we shall see that Kelsen's concept of law leaves plenty of room for economic principles to inform adjudication—though it leaves plenty of room for other principles as well, for I am not suggesting that Kelsen was carrying the torch for economics.

What Kelsen finds that all legal systems have in common and thus what becomes his concept of law is the property of being a *normative* system backed by a *credible* threat of using *physical force* against a violator of the norms. Morals and etiquette are also normative systems but differ from law in not relying on physical force to secure compliance. Propaganda, persuasion, indoctrination, even brainwashing—yes, but not physical force

8. Kelsen, *Pure Theory of Law*, note 2 above, at 112.
9. See id. at 112–113.

(at least if we except parental beatings!). A criminal gang may also have a normative system—prohibiting, for example, defecting or informing—and may use physical force to enforce its norms. But the gang's system will lack credibility or, Kelsen's preferred term, effectiveness "if the coercive order regarded as the legal order is more effective than the coercive order constituting the gang."[10] This may seem a tenuous distinction, but it will become clearer and more persuasive when we consider the importance of the international-law concept of recognition to Kelsen's theory.

We must also distinguish between the gang's coercing its members and its coercing outsiders. The gang's norms are internal. A member of the gang can be punished for transgressing them, but a robbery victim is not "punished" for transgressing a gang norm when the gang robs him. Coerciveness and normativity are separate elements of Kelsen's theory of law.

The theory invites the objection that much law is facilitative rather than punitive, for example laws that authorize the making of contracts; where is the coercion there? But contract law is a delegation to private persons of authority to create norms backed by a credible threat of using physical force against the violator.[11] If A and B make a contract that B then breaks, A can sue B and if he wins a judgment can enlist the force of the state to seize B's property to satisfy it.

Notice that on this view there is no interesting difference between right and duty—the holder of a right is simply someone authorized to invoke the sanctioning power of the state. Nor is there any interesting difference between public law (law enforced by or against the state) and private law, since both either create or, as in the case of contract law, authorize the creation of legal norms, that is, norms backed by an effective threat of physical force if they are disobeyed.[12] But not everything an authorized creator of legal norms, such as a legislature or a court, does is norm-creating. Consider a legislature's resolution congratulating a foreign head of state on the anniversary of his accession to power.[13] The resolution is a valid enactment but not a valid legal norm. It is not prescriptive or backed by a threat of physical force if disobeyed; not being prescriptive, it cannot *be* disobeyed.

10. Id. at 48.
11. Id. at 147–148.
12. See id. at 281–283.
13. Id. at 52–53.

Notice also how in collapsing right into duty ("right" is merely the "reflex" of "obligation")[14] Kelsen jettisons a superfluous concept. This is a constant feature of his theory and lends it an attractive spareness. This cutting to the heart of the matter by translating meaning into consequence is also a pragmatic characteristic, as when Kelsen points out that a judicial determination that a statute is unconstitutional is simply an alternative mode of repeal to the enactment of a repealing statute.[15] Or when he explains, anent the question whether "free will" is a prerequisite to making a person legally responsible for his violations of the law, that we can do quite nicely without any concept of free will; it is enough that the threat of sanctions enters into the causal chain that determines a person's behavior.[16] Or when, regarding the corporation, he, like Dewey, rejects the concept of a juristic person along with all other personifications, stating "the law does not create persons."[17] A corporation's rights and liabilities are merely the collective rights and liabilities either of the individuals who, by virtue of their contractual relation with the corporation, in effect own the corporation's property, or—in the case of shareholders that are trusts, other corporations, or other nonhuman entities—of the individuals who own the property of those entities.

The question remains how to identify a norm as being a *legal* norm, that is, a part of the society's normative system that is backed up by a credible threat to use physical force against a violator. This is the same as asking how we know that a specific norm is a *valid* legal norm and thus creates a legal duty. Very much in the spirit of logical positivism, Kelsen denies that a prescriptive statement can be derived from a factual assertion—an ought from an is. So the validity of a norm must depend on its derivation from another norm that has been determined to be valid.

There are two methods of derivation. One, the more conventional, the more "legalistic," is logic in a broad or a narrow sense. For example, we might say that the doctrines of contract law (consideration, reliance, statute of frauds, duress, modification, the parol evidence rule, and so forth) are derived logically from the basic norms of that law, such as freedom of contract, perhaps supplemented by procedural norms concerned with accuracy and with the cost of adjudication.

14. See, for example, id. at 128.
15. Id. at 271.
16. Id. at 94.
17. Id. at 191.

The other mode of derivation is by jurisdictional assignment, or delega-tion (my terminology—Kelsen's terms for the two types of derivation, "static" and "dynamic," are not illuminating): the creation of a norm is au-thorized by another, a higher norm. Contract will again illustrate. The norm that is contract law authorizes private persons to create the norms to govern their commercial relations, but the content of those norms (the price and other terms of the contract) cannot be derived from the princi-ples of contract law. Similarly, it would be unrealistic to suppose the rule of *Roe v. Wade* derived logically from the U.S. Constitution. (This of course is not one of Kelsen's examples—and it is characteristic of the Continental style of jurisprudence that he gives very few examples.) The rule is not a deduction from, but an interpretation of, the Constitution, and Kelsen is realistic about interpretation. Rather than assimilating it to deduction he regards it as placing limits on judicial discretion. He claims that the typical interpretive issue presented to a court is one in which there are two equally plausible interpretations and the judges must appeal to noninterpretive considerations in order to make a choice between them.[18] This is an ex-treme position. There are easy interpretive cases, as I noted in Chapter 2. But *Roe v. Wade* was not one of them and the decision is more realistically understood as a reflection of the relative weight that seven Justices of the U.S. Supreme Court placed on fetal life and women's reproductive auton-omy than as a consequence of reading the Constitution carefully and find-ing in it or fairly implied by it a right to abortion on demand. Neverthe-less, the rule created by *Roe v. Wade* is a valid legal norm because Article III of the U.S. Constitution authorized the Supreme Court to decide the case.

Even when deducible from another norm, "a legal norm is not valid be-cause it has a certain content, that is, because its content is logically deduc-ible from a presupposed basic norm, but because it is created in a certain way—ultimately in a way determined by a presupposed basic norm."[19] Otherwise treatise writers would be making law whenever they correctly deduced one legal norm from another, even if their deduction was never adopted by a court. A "content norm" (what Kelsen, again unhelpfully, calls a "material norm") cannot determine the validity of the norms deduc-ible from it because it does not have the form "___ is a valid norm." What is needed is a norm that creates competences to create subordinate norms: a jurisdictional norm.

18. Id. at 351–353.
19. Id. at 198.

Because a legal norm is valid only by virtue of its derivation from a higher jurisdictional norm, its validity depends on the higher norm's being valid, and so on up the ladder. An infinite regress looms that Kelsen averts by positing a basic norm *(Grundnorm)* as the highest norm in every legal system.[20] "Basic" and "highest" rather clash, but we should understand "highest" in the sense of original, in the same way that "upstream" points toward the origin of a river. In the case of the U.S. (federal) legal system, the basic norm is that the U.S. Constitution creates valid legal norms. The basic norm certifies the authoritativeness of the Constitution as a source of law.

The validity of the basic norm is—must be, by definition—assumed rather than proved. It could be proved only by being derived from another norm, and then it would not be the basic norm. Kelsen makes this clear with a theological example. The norm that God's commands should be obeyed is a basic norm, not a derived norm, because it would be absurd to justify obedience to God's commands by arguing that someone had ordered you to obey those commands.[21]

The idea of the basic norm is transcendental in the sense of being a precondition to having a theory of law, as causation was to Kant a precondition of certain physical theories. And just as the self in Kantian metaphysics is not a part of the empirical world but is instead the foundation or precondition of our empirical understandings, so the basic norm grounds the legal system but is not itself a part of it.[22]

The Constitution of the United States is a compendium of jurisdictional and content norms. It both parcels out authority among the various branches of government and places limits on the types of content norm that are permissible. For example, the Constitution forbids Congress to pass ex post facto laws (though this has been interpreted to mean just ex post facto *criminal* laws). Yet this does not mean that such a law cannot be a valid legal norm. The authority to determine whether a statute violates a content norm in the Constitution has been given to (or taken by) the

20. See id. at 193–203. Kelsen's concept of the *Grundnorm* is similar to, as well as earlier than, H. L. A. Hart's concept of the "rule of recognition." On the differences, see Hart, *The Concept of Law* 292–293 (2d ed. 1994).

21. Kelsen, *Pure Theory of Law*, note 2 above, at 203.

22. There is more to Kelsen's transcendentalism, but the more is interesting mainly to professional philosophers. For a major recent contribution, see Michael Steven Green, "Hans Kelsen and the Logic of Legal Systems," pt. 5 *(Alabama Law Review,* forthcoming 2002).

courts. Until a court declares an ex post facto law unconstitutional, the government stands ready to enforce it, using force if necessary, because Congress is empowered by a chain of delegations from the basic norm of the federal legal system to enact statutes. It would be different if Congress, rather than enacting a statute, merely issued a press release purporting to authorize an ex post facto punishment; a press release is not an authorized mode of creating a legal norm.[23]

The fact that the basic norm cannot be defended, but merely accepted, does not block inquiry into its origin or into the reason it is accepted as the basic norm. We can ask why the basic norm in our system is the norm that deems the Constitution of 1787[24] (ratified in 1788 and operational from 1789) rather than the Articles of Confederation a fount of valid legal norms. The answer is that no one would pay any attention to a legal norm derived from the Articles of Confederation. (That was not true before the Civil War.)[25] Therefore it would not *be* a legal norm because it would lack minimum efficacy, which, remember, is one of the conditions of a valid legal norm.

One could challenge the proposition that the norm that places the Constitution of 1787 together with its amendments at the head of all the other federal legal norms really is our basic legal norm, but the challenge would not affect Kelsen's argument. One might argue, for example, that the validity of the Constitution derives from the fact that it was ratified by popular vote (more precisely by the popularly elected delegates to state conventions) in all the then states comprising the United States. But one would then have to defend the validity of popular elections as a method of establishing a nation's constitution, and so on ad infinitum.

There is a practical reason for stopping with the norm that certifies the normativity of a nation's constitution. It is related to the international-law

23. This means, as Kelsen usefully points out, that even an agency not authorized to declare a statute unconstitutional has to decide whether the "statute" really is a statute. Kelsen, *Pure Theory of Law*, note 2 above, at 271–273. I should note here the breadth of Kelsen's concept of a content norm. Anything that is not a jurisdictional norm is a content norm—it can be substantive, like the rule against ex post facto laws, or procedural, such as the right of a criminal defendant to confront the witnesses against him.

24. I am simplifying; the legal systems of the U.S. states, though constrained by the Constitution, do not derive from it.

25. Cf. Daniel A. Farber, "E Pluribus Unum?" 18 *Constitutional Commentary* 243 (2001). Interestingly, parts of the Articles of Confederation remained operative for a time after the ratification of the new Constitution. Gary Lawson and Guy Seidman, "When Did the Constitution Become Law?" 77 *Notre Dame Law Review* 1, 23–24 (2001).

doctrine of recognition.[26] When a government is overthrown and a new government installed, foreign nations have to decide whether to recognize the new government. The general rule is that they will do so if it establishes solid control, likely to be durable, over the nation, irrespective of the legitimacy of its seizure of that control.[27] Recognition is an acknowledgment that any constitution promulgated by the new government will be valid, and so recognition can be said to establish the basic norm of a nation's legal system. Of course to reason so is to imply that a nation's basic norm is not really basic, that it is derived from the international-law norm of recognition, and this creates a potential problem of circularity, since international law is often thought to be valid only by virtue of being accepted by national law. Nothing in Kelsen's theory enables a choice to be made between an international-law *Grundnorm* validating national law and a national-law *Grundnorm* validating international law. He deems it a purely political choice—with pacifists favoring the former and imperialists the latter![28] But notice the interesting implication of his approach that international law and national law constitute a single legal system, whether ultimately international or ultimately national in character—the choice Kelsen thinks arbitrary.

The important points for my purposes are only that, as a practical matter, the control of a nation establishes the *Grundnorm*, the indispensable foundation, of the nation's legal system and that there is no need to defend the validity of the *Grundnorm*.[29]

26. See Kelsen, *Pure Theory of Law*, note 2 above, at 50, 210, 212, 215.

27. See, for example, Matimak Trading Co. v. Khalily, 118 F.3d 76, 80 (2d Cir. 1997). To avoid any implication that "recognition" implies approval, the U.S. State Department has decided "to deemphasize and avoid the use of recognition in cases of changes of governments and to concern ourselves with the question whether we wish to have diplomatic relations with the new governments. The Administration's policy is that establishment of relations does not involve approval or disapproval but merely demonstrates a willingness on our part to conduct our affairs with other governments directly." "Diplomatic Recognition," 77 *Department of State Bulletin* 462 (1977). But that "willingness" then becomes the basis for treating the new government as a foreign sovereign entitled to the usual respect. See, for example, National Coalition Government of the Union of Burma v. Unocal, Inc., 176 F.R.D. 329, 351–352 (C.D. Cal. 1997). In fact, "recognition" no longer has a uniform meaning in law, see Stefan Talmon, *Recognition of Governments in International Law: With Particular Reference to Governments in Exile* 21–43 (1998), and my usage in the text is nontechnical; I mean by "recognition" only the willingness to acknowledge a foreign government as having sovereign powers, including the power to make laws.

28. Kelsen, *Pure Theory of Law*, note 2 above, at 343. See generally Ines Weyland, "The Application of Kelsen's Theory of the Legal System to European Community Law—the Supremacy Puzzle Resolved," 21 *Law and Philosophy* 1 (2002).

29. These points were not original with Kelsen; they were the stock in trade of pre–World

We should be able to see more clearly now what the criminal gang lacks. It lacks a *Grundnorm*. Its control is too weak to induce widespread acceptance of the validity of its norms. Even gang members are bound to harbor grave doubts about the normativity of the gang's rules because they know that those rules are in conflict with the rules of a much more powerful normative system. Not always; there are countries with such weak governments that gangs (warlords, the Mafia and its imitators, and so on) may operate with complete immunity from government control, and the norms promulgated by such a gang may have more characteristics of legal norms than the official laws of the country do.[30] And criminal gangs sometimes seize entire nations (a plausible characterization of the Bolsheviks' seizure of power in Russia in 1917) and when this happens and the gang's control is secure, a *Grundnorm* pops into existence that makes the gang's norms valid legal norms. The criminal gang is "recognized" as the lawful, and hence lawgiving, government. And this is actually the rule rather than the exception. "The original constitution of virtually every country was invalid. It was made by people who were not entitled to rule. They seized power by conquest, usurpation, or revolution."[31]

Tony Honoré, whom I'm quoting, criticizes this conception of the source of legal obligation as a version of "Might is Right."[32] And so it is, but with two important qualifications. In Kelsen's system, might makes *legal* right, not right *simpliciter*, or moral right. And it does so as a matter of fact rather than as a normative matter. It just is a fact that a group that has secure control over a nation will be able to enact laws that are obeyed by the population, not uniformly of course, but not purely as a direct consequence of coercion. Secure control will (not should) induce most people to accept that the laws made by the controllers impose a legal obligation on them. They may think the laws wicked, unjust, foolish, extortionate, enacted without their consent, even "illegitimate," but if they violate them they will not deny that it is *laws* they are violating. They will not deny that they have legal obligations, although some of them may deny that their le-

---

War I German legal positivism. See Ellen Kennedy, "Introduction: Carl Schmitt's *Parlamentarismus* in Its Historical Context," in Carl Schmitt, *The Crisis of Parliamentary Democracy* xiii, xxxv–xxxvi (Ellen Kennedy trans. 1988).

30. Economists have explored the structural parallels between gangs and governments. See Kai A. Konrad and Stergios Skaperdas, "Extortion," 65 *Economica* 461, 462 (1998), and references cited there.

31. Tony Honoré, *Making Law Bind: Essays Legal and Philosophical* 103 (1987).

32. Id.

gal obligations have any moral force. The bravest of them may even feel morally obligated to disobey the laws.

This discussion casts further light on the issue of the legitimacy of our political system, discussed in Chapter 5, and of the legitimacy of *Marbury v. Madison* (the principle of judicial review, that is, the power of the courts to override the decisions of the other branches of government, in the name of the Constitution), discussed in Chapter 2. The U.S. Constitution was adopted in the wake of a violent revolution against lawfully constituted authority, and in violation of the provisions of the Articles of Confederation. The electorate whose representatives ratified the Constitution was a small and unrepresentative sample of the population, the most notable exclusion from the electorate, though, oddly, it is little remarked, being the Indian population, the conquered aboriginal inhabitants of America. In three states "the delegates voting for ratification represented fewer people than those voting against it."[33] *Marbury* asserted rather than deduced the supremacy of the Supreme Court in the interpretation of the Constitution. And the post–Civil War amendments to the Constitution (the Thirteenth through Fifteenth Amendments) would not have been ratified had it not been for the subjugation of the Confederate states by force of arms. The legitimacy of American government derives not from an impeccable pedigree of legalities but from the brute fact that the American people accept the validity of the legal norms promulgated by this government.

The Mafia case, as we may term the case in which a gang is the de facto government of a part of a nation's territory, is more of an embarrassment for Kelsen's account than the case of the criminal gang that succeeds in wresting control of an entire nation. The Mafia's norms may actually be more law-like in his sense than the laws of the official government. But no one would call them "laws" even if, as sometimes happens, the official government connives in the exercise of law-like powers by the gang and may even, in effect, have delegated law-enforcement responsibility to it. By the same token, although the terms of a private contract are "law" in Kelsen's sense (they are norms backed by a credible threat to use physical force against a violator), no one calls them that. The word is likewise not applied to the rules that parents impose on their children, even though those

---

33. Patrick T. Conley, "Rhode Island: First in War, Last in Peace—Rhode Island and the Constitution, 1786–1790," in *The Constitution and the States: The Role of the Original Thirteen in the Framing and Adoption of the Federal Constitution* 269, 278 (Patrick T. Conley and John P. Kaminski eds. 1988).

rules are enforceable by (gentle) force. So if Kelsen's theory aims to map the usage of the word "law," it falls short. But it is better regarded as an effort to identify the features that all legal systems have in common; the fact that other systems may possess those features as well does not invalidate Kelsen's account, though it makes it incomplete.

Laws can cease to be valid even within a recognized legal system. This happens when they lose efficacy, a process that, when complete, Kelsen calls desuetude.[34] In the usual case, a statute or body of case law[35] ceases to be valid by repeal or overruling, respectively. But sometimes, and in fact rather often—even in a legal system such as the American, which has no formal doctrine of desuetude[36]—a statute or precedent ceases to be a valid legal norm simply because it has lost its coercive backing. The clearest example is a statute that has never been declared unconstitutional or repealed but is identical to a statute that has been declared unconstitutional. To recur to an earlier example, if a federal criminal statute were *obviously* an ex post facto law, it might so lack efficacy—because no one was willing to enforce it—as not to be a valid legal norm. Another example would be a precedent that, though never explicitly overruled, was so far forgotten because of its inconsistency with other, newer precedents that no competent legal professional would think it still "good law." This has been the fate of a number of antitrust cases decided by the Supreme Court in the 1960s.[37]

It is at this point that Kelsen's theory of law approaches closest to Holmes's theory that the "law" concerning a question is merely a prediction of how the judges will answer it should it arise in a case.[38] The theory is otherwise uncongenial to Kelsen because of his belief that a norm (what ought to happen) cannot be derived from a fact (what will happen).[39] His objection can be restated in less abstract terms. Suppose that the U.S. Supreme Court were even more polarized than it is, and consisted of five very conservative Justices and four very liberal ones. And suppose one of the conservative Justices died and was replaced by an extreme liberal. It might be obvious that several cases awaiting argument and decision would

34. Kelsen, *Pure Theory of Law*, note 2 above, at 213.

35. Despite his orientation to the Continental rather than Anglo-American legal system, Kelsen was well aware that case law can be a source of valid legal norms. See id. at 250–256.

36. But maybe it should. See Cass R. Sunstein, *Designing Democracy: What Constitutions Do* 89–92 (2001).

37. See Richard A. Posner, *Antitrust Law* 128–130, 152–153 (2001).

38. Oliver Wendell Holmes, "The Path of the Law," 10 *Harvard Law Review* 457, 461 (1897).

39. See Kelsen, *General Theory of Law and State*, note 2 above, at 168–169.

now be decided differently from how they would have been decided had the conservative Justice lived. On Holmes's construal of "law," the change in membership would have changed the law. This would strike most people as a misuse of the word "law." It would amount to saying that an appeal based on a precedent that the appellant's lawyer should know with certainty will be overruled because of a change in the Supreme Court's membership would be a frivolous appeal, for which the lawyer or his client should be sanctioned—something no one believes. The prediction theory is quintessentially pragmatic[40] in defining "law" in terms of people's concrete interests; but applied outside the context of legal counseling it conflates the lawyer's advice about what the law *is* with the lawyer's advice about what the law *will be* when his client's case is decided. For Kelsen, the change in the membership of a court may portend a change in law, but the change in law does not occur until cases are decided. A legal obligation is a norm, so it cannot, Kelsen believes, be derived from a fact, such as a change in the membership of a court. Hence the need for a *Grundnorm*.

Kelsen's response to Holmes is not entirely satisfactory. Remember that for Kelsen a legal norm is a norm backed up by a credible threat to use force against a violator. If it is certain that because of a change of membership in a legal system's supreme court an existing norm will not be enforced—so certain that people can violate it with impunity—has it not ceased to be a legal norm? Isn't there, on Kelsen's account, a legal vacuum in such a case, with the old norm dead but a new norm not yet declared? And isn't this as inconsistent with our normal understanding of the meaning of the word "law" as Holmes's prediction theory?

This is a real problem for Kelsen's theory. But that the basic norm of every legal system is derived, not logically but sociologically, from a fact, namely the lawmakers' secure control over the nation, is not a problem for him despite his insistence that a norm cannot be derived from a fact. There is no contradiction because the fact in question, effective control of the nation, operates merely to identify a precondition for the use of the word "law" to describe a normative system. The concept of law requires that there be a basic norm, but the fact that creates that norm is not itself a norm, just as the blueprint for a house is not the house.

Kelsen's concept of the *Grundnorm* was strongly attacked by Carl Schmitt when both were law professors in the Weimar Republic. Weimar

40. See Thomas C. Grey, "Holmes and Legal Pragmatism," 41 *Stanford Law Review* 787, 830, 836–837 (1989).

had a constitution, and a basic norm that made the constitution and the laws enacted in conformity with it sources of valid legal norms. But the legitimacy of the basic norm was strongly challenged by the Nazis, the Communists, and other extremists, and weakly defended. Schmitt pointed out that a basic norm that rests merely on force is fragile because it can't be used to criticize efforts to overthrow it by force.[41] He who lives by the sword risks perishing by it. The U.S. Constitution followed a popular revolution and was ratified by majority vote in popularly elected conventions in all thirteen states. These circumstances, though as we just saw they are not the whole picture of the founding, imparted to the basic norm that closed the federal legal system a solidity that the circumstances that brought the Weimar Republic into being—namely, defeat in war, an anarchic aftermath, and extreme political polarization—could not impart to the basic norm of Weimar's legal system. (And even our basic norm remained shaky until the outcome of the Civil War.) This point does not invalidate Kelsen's theory but it suggests a certain thinness in it, an inability to differentiate between stable and unstable basic norms. I shall come back to this point in connection with Friedrich Hayek's attack on Kelsen's theory.

Kelsen, Pragmatism, and Economics

My summary of Kelsen's theory of law was bare of significant reference to economics or any other social science. The reason is that these bodies of thought or practice play no role in Kelsen's theory. There was no law and economics movement in Europe, and none recognized as such in the United States (though there were harbingers and glimmerings of such a movement, at least in hindsight), when the first edition of *Pure Theory of Law* was published in 1934. Although Kelsen was teaching in the United States in 1960, when the second edition was published, by which time the *Journal of Law and Economics* had begun publication, he was an old man and would hardly have been conscious of a movement, still nascent,[42] concerning a legal system that must still have seemed quite alien to him.[43]

But what is significant in Kelsen's theory for law and economics, and for

41. See Kennedy, note 29 above, at xxxvi.
42. See Richard A. Posner, *Frontiers of Legal Theory* 32–34 (2001).
43. He left Germany, as I mentioned, in 1933, but only for Switzerland; he did not move to the United States until 1940, when he was almost sixty years old.

the social sciences and other extralegal (in a narrow sense of "legal") sources of knowledge generally, is the space it creates for drawing on those sources for aid in formulating legal doctrines. Law for Kelsen, as we have seen, is a series of delegations, for example from the federal legal system's *Grundnorm* to the U.S. Constitution, from the Constitution to Congress, from Congress to judges, from judges (in contract cases) to contracting parties. What judges do with their delegated powers is law just by virtue of the delegation, provided they do not stray outside the delegation's bounds—for example (to adapt an earlier illustration to the judicial context), by issuing press releases in lieu of decisions.[44] Law is an assignment of competences.[45] The congeniality to a pragmatist of such an approach, a conspicuous feature of the judicial practice of Holmes, should be apparent. Believing "that there is no viewpoint that can claim precedence on the basis of its presumed objectivity gives rise to the question of whose viewpoint is to prevail."[46] That is a question of jurisdiction: who decides.

We may sense here a weakness in Kelsen's theory. Remember that a valid legal norm has to be backed up by a credible threat to use physical force against the violator—and is this condition satisfied when a judge exceeds his jurisdiction? Has he not, by doing so, violated a jurisdictional norm with impunity? No. The judge in such a case is subject not only to the reversal of his decision but also to discipline backed up, if need be, by force. For we must imagine the judge not merely taking jurisdiction of a case mistakenly but acting so far outside the boundaries of his delegated authority as to make his actions lawless, as in my example of decision by

44. See Kelsen, *Pure Theory of Law*, note 2 above, at 140. Stanley Fish mentions a study of judges in which the investigator "tried to get the judges to talk about the distinction between a government of laws and a government of men as it related to the understanding they had of their own authority, but he found that they understood their authority to flow from the role the society authorized them to play and not from any of the abstract concepts they might employ in the course of playing that role." Stanley Fish, *There's No Such Thing as Free Speech and It's a Good Thing, Too* 198 (1994).

45. This feature of his theory "may have derived in part from confusions that affected Habsburg law . . . There existed so many levels of jurisdiction . . . that endless conflicts ensued." William M. Johnston, *The Austrian Mind: An Intellectual and Social History 1848–1938*, at 97 (1972). One is put in mind of Kelsen's contemporary and (until the collapse of the Austro-Hungarian Empire in 1918) co-national, Franz Kafka (both were born in Prague, though Kelsen moved to Vienna as a child). A striking feature of Kafka's novel *The Trial* is pervasive uncertainty concerning the jurisdiction of the mysterious unnamed court in which Joseph K's case is lodged, in relation to the other courts of the nation.

46. Catharine Wells Hantzis, "Legal Innovation within the Wider Intellectual Tradition: The Pragmatism of Oliver Wendell Holmes, Jr.," 82 *Northwestern University Law Review* 541 (1988).

press release. Likewise a judge who refused to enforce the law, thus abandoning his office. In the federal system the ultimate coercive power that validates the jurisdictional norms that empower but also constrain judges is wielded by Congress. As we saw in the preceding chapter, the Constitution authorizes the removal of federal judges for misconduct or for abandonment of office. All legal systems reserve the power to remove judges who act dramatically outside their jurisdiction or who refuse to exercise that jurisdiction.

Recall from Chapter 2 that the pragmatic judge's duty to weigh consequences is subject to constraints imposed by the character of the judicial role. He is not, for example, to weigh the consequence to his pocketbook of ruling for or against one of the parties. If he does, he may be punished. Nor is he to be swayed by base partisan considerations (the charge made against the Justices who voted in the majority in *Bush v. Gore*, discussed in Chapter 9). "Judicial role" is another name for the judge's jurisdiction. When acting within that jurisdiction, he may have prudential or other practical reasons to truncate consideration of consequences further even than the role itself requires. But what requires particular emphasis is that those reasons belong to the content of law rather than to the scope of judicial authority. The content of the legal norms that judges create by their decisions is not given by Kelsen's concept of law.[47] As one of his natural-law critics puts it, "How the judge arrives at his decision is [for Kelsen] a 'meta-legal' question without interest for the jurist."[48] Kelsen's rejection of natural law, his emphasis on jurisdictional at the expense of substantive norms, his repeated references to judicial discretion, his claim that applying law is not a mechanical process but often involves "the creation of a lower norm on the basis of a higher norm,"[49] his acknowledgment that sometimes the only preexisting law that a court can apply to decide a case is the law that confers the power of decision on the court,[50] and his concept of interpretation as a frame rather than an algorithm, delimit a broad range of judicial action that is free yet lawful.[51] The judges have to fill it with something, but while that something is lawful, it is not the law in the

47. See, for example, Kelsen, *General Theory of Law and State*, note 2 above, at 151.
48. Lon L. Fuller, *The Law in Quest of Itself* 89 (1940).
49. Kelsen, *Pure Theory of Law*, note 2 above, at 235.
50. Kelsen, *General Theory of Law and State*, note 2 above, at 152.
51. See, for example, Kelsen, *Pure Theory of Law*, note 2 above, at 353; Dhananjai Shivakumar, "Note: The Pure Theory as Ideal Type: Defending Kelsen on the Basis of Weberian Methodology," 105 *Yale Law Journal* 1383, 1410 (1996).

sense of a body of preexisting doctrines. Kelsen even uses the term "ideology" to describe what the judge must use to create the specific legal norms needed for deciding cases not ruled by preexisting law.[52]

The content-free "purity" of Kelsen's theory got him into trouble with his critics. But he was not suggesting that jurists should have no truck with anything that fell outside his theory. He wanted rather to demarcate the range of questions about the legal system that could be answered without recourse to any tools other than logic. That was the domain of *pure* legal theory. Other questions about law could not be answered intelligently without recourse to "sociology" or, as we would say today, the social sciences and other sources of empirical knowledge.

Thus his theory was actually a reminder of the importance to adjudication of considerations that are not part of the conventional lawyer's kitbag. What obscured and continues to obscure this point is an accidental institutional characteristic of legal scholarship. The division between law and sociology is a division between two university departments. It was natural to suppose that Kelsen, by assigning the content of the law to "sociology," was abjuring law professors to have nothing to do with social sciences. There is no reason to interpret him in this way, no reason to suppose that it would have troubled him to imagine legal theorists in his sense cohabiting with academic lawyers (or even nonlawyers) interested in the content of the law and its illumination by the social sciences.

Kelsen's Positivism Contrasted with the Positivist Theories of Hart and Easterbrook

I criticized H. L. A. Hart's version of legal positivism in Chapter 2, saying it was misleading to describe the exercise of judicial discretion, in the open area where no preexisting legal norm could be found that would determine the outcome, as not doing law but instead as legislating.[53] This criticism cannot be leveled against Kelsen. He pictures the judge as either deriving a specific legal norm to resolve the case before him from a higher norm or, if there is no higher substantive norm to guide decision in the particular case, creating such a norm, as judges are authorized to do by the jurisdictional norm that authorizes them to decide cases. In either situation the judge is doing law; it is just that in the second he creates rather than de-

52. See, for example, Kelsen, *Pure Theory of Law*, note 2 above, at 105.
53. See also Richard A. Posner, *The Problematics of Moral and Legal Theory* 92–98 (1999).

rives the legal norm that he applies to decide the case. It is not, as Hart's formulation suggests, that the judge is a judge when he derives a specific norm from some higher norm but turns into a politician when he creates a specific norm. Kelsen would never say, with Hart, that when a judge decides a case in which "no decision either way is dictated by the law" he is "step[ping] outside the law."[54] And despite Hart's emphasis on the "internal perspective" (how judges view their role), Kelsen's concept of law is closer to judges' conception of their role than Hart's is. Judges don't in their own mind divide what they do on the bench into "applying law" and "legislating." What they think they're doing is deciding cases using all the resources available to them (legislative texts, precedents, policy, moral intuitions, and so forth) without however exceeding their jurisdiction, broadly defined, as they would be doing if they decided a case that was not justiciable or if they decided it on the basis of a financial or familial or partisan political interest in the outcome. We shall see in Chapter 9 that at least one critic of the Supreme Court's decision in *Bush v. Gore*, which terminated the recount of ballots cast in Florida in the 2000 Presidential election, regards the decision as "corrupt" because of the motives he imputes to the Justices, a charge that if sustained would make the decision lawless in Kelsen's sense of law, not merely erroneous.

I said that Kelsen's positivism is closer to the judge's internal perspective than Hart's; but it is not identical with it. The obvious reason is that judges and scholars employ different vocabularies; we should not expect a judge to recognize himself in an account by a philosopher of law any more than we would expect a scientist to recognize himself in an account by a philosopher of science. Moreover, the judicial role is internalized and made unconscious, so that when, for example, the judge is deciding an easy case, he is not aware of making a pragmatic judgment. And finally, any person in authority is tempted to shift the responsibility for his unpopular or controversial decisions; the judge shifts it to "the law."

Kelsen's jurisdictional concept of positivism has another advantage over Hart's: it accounts for the large areas of explicit discretion in a legal system. Prosecutorial discretion, sentencing discretion, scheduling and other case-management discretion, the discretionary judgments made by juries, the discretionary jurisdiction of many appellate courts, such as the U.S. Supreme Court and most state supreme courts—these illustrate the vast

---

54. Hart, note 20 above, at 272.

area in which judges (including jurors, who are ad hoc judges) exercise lawful authority but neither "legislate" in any recognizable sense of the word nor apply legal principles. Their actions are lawful and done without embarrassment, without a sense of the judge's skating on thin legal ice, even though unruled by law, because they are done pursuant to a chain of delegated powers that can be referred ultimately to the legal system's basic norm. These actions are "law" in a jurisdictional sense, in Kelsen's sense, though not in a substantive one.

Because Kelsen's concept of law is content-free, he can be described as a *pragmatic* positivist. Being purely jurisdictional, his theory is not committed to the kind of legal reasoning that pragmatists deride as Platonic or formalistic. The judge's decisionmaking is lawful because he is a judge, not because he is engaged in a distinctive form of reasoning. Remember that Dewey's essential insight about law was that there is no such thing as legal reasoning; it is practical reasoning deployed on legal problems. Kelsen systematizes Dewey's insight, albeit in a characteristically abstract Continental form. And in doing so he implicitly licenses judges to use economics and other social sciences—and any other sources of insight into the practical consequences of rules and decisions—by making clear that law does not dictate the outcome of judicial decisions. Concocting novel legal norms from materials supplied by fields external to law in its narrow, professional sense is one of the things a judge does.

This account ignores, however, the possibility of a local concept of law narrower than the universal concept. Kelsen is concerned with what all legal systems have in common. A given legal system might have a much more specific notion of what shall count as law. It might, for example, regard all "law" that did not conform to some notion of natural law as not law at all, even if it satisfied Kelsen's criteria for law. That is one interpretation of the concept of law adopted by the Nuremberg Tribunal, which punished German officials for acts committed in conformity with the laws of Nazi Germany. A certain kind of positivist, one closer to Hart than to Kelsen, might think that natural law is inconsistent with the Anglo-American concept of law and that therefore the Nuremberg Tribunal acted lawlessly in punishing such people. Nothing in Kelsen's theory bears on such a disagreement.

As an example of a "local" theory of law far narrower than Kelsen's theory, consider my judicial colleague Frank Easterbrook's positivist theory of constitutional interpretation.[55] He deems judicial interpretations of the U.S. Constitution lawless unless the judges are merely "enforcing enacted words rather than unenacted (more likely, imagined) intents, purposes, and wills."[56] He derives this view from the proposition that "the fundamental theory of political legitimacy in the United States is contractarian." The Constitution is a contract and should be interpreted accordingly.[57] This claim is unconvincing on at least two grounds.[58] The first is the leap from contractarian to contractual. Social-contract theory can be found both in the historical background of the Constitution and in modern political theories of democracy. But social contractarians use the word "contract" in a loose, nontechnical sense either to emphasize the importance of consent in democratic theory or, what is closely related, to ground political legitimacy in some idea of what people might be expected to agree to were it feasible to negotiate anew the basic institutions of the society.

Second, judicial interpretation of contracts is not purely textualist. As I noted in Chapter 2, plain meaning is given a lot of weight but is sometimes disregarded, and often the language of a contract is not clear and so the contract's meaning is not plain. Speculation about intentions and purposes figures largely in contract litigation and there are all sorts of defenses and meliorative doctrines designed to avoid textual traps—doctrines of patent and latent ambiguity, the defenses of impossibility, impracticability, and frustration, implied duties of good faith and best efforts, the concept of contracts that are implied in fact, quantum meruit and restitution, the defenses of laches and of the statute of limitations, notions of estoppel, limitations on remedies, the need for flexibility in the interpretation of long-term contracts, and much else besides. Adapt these to judicial enforcement of the Constitution imagined as a contract having an exceptionally long term and being very difficult to modify and it is not at all clear that the results would be much different from what we have as a result of the interpretive notions that Easterbrook detests, such as that of "the liv-

55. Succinctly articulated in Frank H. Easterbrook, "Textualism and the Dead Hand," 66 *George Washington Law Review* 1119 (1998). He states there: "textualists are positivists." Id.
56. Id. at 1120.
57. Id. at 1121–1122.
58. For other objections to the contractarian interpretation of the Constitution, see Jed Rubenfeld, *Freedom and Time: A Theory of Constitutional Self-Government* 61–62 (2001). But I do not mean to deny that there are illuminating analogies between constitutions and contracts. See Richard A. Posner, *Economic Analysis of Law* § 23.1, pp. 676–677 (5th ed. 1998).

ing Constitution." It is not as if the sole doctrine of contract were the "four corners" (plain-meaning) rule of textual literalism and the only escape hatch voluntary modification by the parties, akin to amendment of the Constitution.

In defense of textualism as the only way of holding judges on a very short tether in constitutional cases, Easterbrook asks "why . . . should [federal] judges be obeyed?"[59] and answers that it is only because (and if) the Constitution has a single meaning, the textual meaning. Kelsen would have given a different answer. Federal judges should be obeyed by virtue of the basic norm of federal law when they are exercising the judicial power of the United States, conferred on judges by Article III of the Constitution. The fact that the Constitution can be interpreted to mean different things has nothing to do with judicial legitimacy, which does not depend on the existence of univocal substantive directives to judges. Remember that Kelsen thought it common for texts to be susceptible of equally good alternative interpretations. Far from debarring judges from choosing, the need for choice between the equally plausible interpretations of a legally operative document is one of the reasons we *have* judges. Were those documents clear there would be fewer legal disputes, so fewer judges, and in a sense less law. Were they perfectly clear maybe compliance would be perfect and we wouldn't need any judges. It is odd to think that the more judges, the less law. The basic norm tells us whose interpretation has the force of law: the judge's, because he *is* a judge, acting within the scope of his jurisdiction, not because he can point to a text-based command that he is repeating without creative embellishment.

Kelsen's theory is a better description of the concept of law actually regnant in the United States than Easterbrook's. This is not surprising, despite Kelsen's foreignness, because Kelsen wanted to explain the law as it is while Easterbrook wants to change our understanding of it. As Kelsen would have predicted, decisions of federal courts are obeyed even when the textual basis for a decision is exceedingly tenuous, as in such famous cases as *Roe v. Wade*. By way of an ironic contrast, consider one of the few cases in which a Supreme Court decision interpreting the Constitution has been openly defied by one of the other branches of the federal government. Early in the Civil War, Chief Justice Roger Taney granted an application for habeas corpus by a Maryland resident who was being detained

59. Easterbrook, note 55 above, at 1122.

by the Union Army on suspicion of being implicated in treason and rebel-lion.[60] The Constitution authorizes the suspension of habeas corpus in time of war or rebellion, but by Congress,[61] not by the President. Al-though Taney thus had a solid basis in the constitutional text for granting Merryman's petition for habeas corpus, the government refused to obey the Chief Justice's order—and got away with its defiance. The propensity to obey judges is unrelated to the textual basis for their decisions. It is a function simply of their jurisdiction, with *Ex parte Merryman* a rare excep-tion. A plausible interpretation of Lincoln's defiance of the Chief Justice is, in Martin Sheffer's words, that "during an emergency the law of necessity superseded the law of the Constitution."[62] (This is pragmatism; whether it is *legal* pragmatism I defer to the next chapter.)

It may be objected that I am taking Easterbrook's question about why judges should be obeyed in the wrong way, as a threat rather than as sim-ply a demand for a justification. But when critics of the judiciary ask why judges should be obeyed, invariably there is an implication that the fail-ure to give an intellectually convincing answer endangers judicial author-ity. Thus we find Robert Bork, whose jurisprudence is similar to Easter-brook's, stating ominously: "The man who prefers results to processes has no reason to say that the Court is more legitimate than any other institu-tion capable of wielding power. If the Court will not agree with him, why not argue his case to some other group, say the Joint Chiefs of Staff, a body with rather better means for enforcing its decisions? No answer exists."[63] The answer, banal but conclusive, is that the joint chiefs will

---

60. Ex parte Merryman, 17 Fed. Cas. 144 (Cir. Ct. D. Md. 1861). See Carl B. Swisher, *The Taney Period 1836–64* (vol. 5 of the *Oliver Wendell Holmes Devise History of the Supreme Court of the United States*) 844–854 (1974).

61. U.S. Const. art. I, § 9, cl. 2. The Constitution does not say this in so many words; it says that habeas corpus may be suspended in time of war or rebellion but not that *only* Con-gress may suspend it. However, Article I, where this provision is found, is an enumeration of congressional powers. Article II, which lists the President's powers, contains no reference to habeas corpus. It would be surprising for so awesome a power to be conferred on the Presi-dent by implication. Still, there is an argument that the President's role as commander in chief of the armed forces and his duty to see that the laws are faithfully executed, see U.S. Const. art. II, §§ 2, 3, empower him to suspend habeas corpus if urgently required by a genu-ine national emergency. See, for example, Martin S. Sheffer, "Presidential Power to Suspend Habeas Corpus: The Taney-Bates Dialogue and *Ex Parte Merryman*," 11 *Oklahoma City Uni-versity Law Review* 1 (1986); Kirk L. Davies, "The Imposition of Martial Law in the United States," 49 *Air Force Law Review* 67, 81–90 (2000).

62. Sheffer, note 61 above, at 23.

63. Robert H. Bork, *The Tempting of America: The Political Seduction of the Law* 265 (1990). As a pedantic detail I point out that the joint chiefs are merely advisers; they have no com-

not listen to someone who tells them that the Supreme Court is being usurpative.

Hayek's Theory of Adjudication

Friedrich Hayek, a generation younger than Kelsen (he was born in 1899, Kelsen in 1881), is famous for two ideas. The first, which builds on the work of the earlier Austrian economist Ludwig von Mises, is that socialism (in the sense of public ownership of the means of production) is unworkable because to make it work would require more information about the economy than could possibly be obtained and processed by a central planning board.[64] The information necessary for the operation of the economy is distributed among the many millions of individuals who engage in economic activity (billions, in the case of the global economy). Each has a tiny amount of the relevant information, and the price system is the only way in which the information possessed by each can be pooled and translated into an efficient schedule of economic outputs.

First advanced in the 1930s, when most economists considered socialism eminently feasible and many considered it superior to capitalism, which had seemed in that depression decade to have proved itself incapable of organizing a modern economy efficiently, Hayek's idea was prescient and is the basis of his celebrity as an economist.[65] His second famous idea, advanced in *The Road to Serfdom* (1944), is that socialism, even in the limited form advocated by the British Labour Party of the day, would if adopted lead inexorably to totalitarianism.[66] This idea has proved to be

---

mand authority. The line of command runs from the President to the Secretary of Defense to the generals and admirals heading the various operational commands, such as the Central Command and the Pacific Command. Bork can relax.

64. See, for example, Friedrich A. von Hayek, "Economics and Knowledge," 4 *Economica* 33 (1937); Hayek, "The Use of Knowledge in Society," 35 *American Economic Review* 519 (1945); Hayek, "Two Pages of Fiction: The Impossibility of Socialist Calculation," in *The Essence of Hayek* 53 (Chiaki Nishiyama and Kurt R. Leube eds. 1984); Sherwin Rosen, "Austrian and Neoclassical Economics: Any Gains from Trade?" *Journal of Economic Perspectives*, Fall 1997, p. 139; Steven Horwitz, "From Smith to Menger to Hayek: Liberalism in the Spontaneous-Order Tradition," *Independent Review*, Summer 2001, p. 81; Louis Makowski and Joseph M. Ostroy, "Perfect Competition and the Creativity of the Market," 39 *Journal of Economic Literature* 479, 487–489 (2001).

65. The idea is elaborated in a technical literature well illustrated by Sanford J. Grossman, "An Introduction to the Theory of Rational Expectations under Asymmetric Information," 48 *Review of Economic Studies* 541 (1981).

66. Friedrich A. Hayek, *The Road to Serfdom* (1944), esp. ch. 13. In fairness to Hayek, the program advocated by the Labour Party was more radical than the one it implemented when

false. Socialism in either the limited form advocated by social-democratic parties or the extreme form instituted in the communist countries leads, via Hayek's first point, the unworkability of socialism, to capitalism. The Soviet Union was totalitarian, but not because it was socialist. Nazi Germany was totalitarian but was not, contrary to Hayek and despite the name of Hitler's party (National Socialist German Workers' Party), socialist. Nor, as he thought, had socialist thought paved the way for the Nazis by assisting in the creation of a planned economy for Germany during World War I,[67] though that planned economy did give Lenin ideas for organizing a communist economy in Russia.[68]

I am not interested in Hayek's two famous ideas as such, but rather in his legal theory.[69] Both ideas, however, influenced the theory, the first decisively. The theory is simple and readily summarized.[70] There are two ways of establishing norms to guide human behavior. In one, which Hayek calls "constructivist rationalism,"[71] they are prescribed from the top down by a legislature, a bureaucracy, or a judiciary—in other words, by experts who

---

it took power in 1945. But as late as 1972, in a foreword to a reprinted edition of the book, he reaffirmed its main conclusions.

Steven Lukes has noted the basic fallacy in what he calls "the 'Road to Serfdom Argument.'" The argument "consists in linking, through a kind of guilt by association, thinkers and ideas one seeks to criticize with the most extreme thinkers and ideas said to be related to them and then claiming that the former, in the end, lead to the catastrophes held to result from the latter." Lukes, "Liberals on the Warpath," *Times Literary Supplement*, Sept. 14, 2001, p. 10.

67. See Hayek, note 66 above, ch. 12 ("The Socialist Roots of Naziism"). The book has little to say about communism because, as Hayek later acknowledged, he had been reluctant to criticize the Soviet Union, Britain's wartime ally. Hayek, "Foreword," in id. (1976 reprint edition) at iii–iv.

68. See, for example, Edward Hallett Carr, *A History of Soviet Russia*, vol. 2: *The Bolshevik Revolution 1917–1923*, at 363 (1952); G. D. H. Cole, "The Bolshevik Revolution," 4 *Soviet Studies* 139, 150 (1952).

69. Lucidly summarized in Charles Covell, *The Defence of Natural Law* 126–139 (1992).

70. The first volume of his trilogy *Law, Legislation and Liberty: A New Statement of the Liberal Principles of Justice and Political Economy*, entitled *Rules and Order* (1973), contains the fullest statement of his legal theory; indeed, virtually the entire book is devoted to expounding and defending it. But he discusses law at almost the same length in an earlier book, *The Constitution of Liberty*, pt. 2 (1960).

A virtually identical theory of law is propounded in Bruno Leoni, *Freedom and the Law* (3d ed. 1991). Leoni, an Italian lawyer who was a friend of Hayek, published the first edition of his book in 1961, the year after *The Constitution of Liberty* was published. Leoni is sometimes thought to have anticipated the claim (on which see, for example, Posner, note 58 above, pt. 1) that common law decisions tend to be more efficient than statutory ones. The attribution is incorrect. Leoni liked the common law for the same reason that Hayek did; he thought that common law judges enforced custom (with some tidying) rather than making law. See, for example, Leoni, above, at 86–87.

71. See, for example, Hayek, *Rules and Order*, note 70 above, at 95, 117.

gather the information necessary to formulate by the method of reason the best possible set of norms. This approach, as we might guess from Hayek's aversion to central planning, he rejects as requiring too much information to be feasible. In addition, it endangers liberty by enlarging the administrative powers of government and thus weakening the rule of law—the thesis of *The Road to Serfdom*.[72]

The alternative method of creating norms is that of custom and is based on the superiority of what Hayek calls "spontaneous order" to order brought about by plan or design. The word "spontaneous," with its connotation of suddenness, is not the happiest term for what he has in mind; "unplanned" or "undesigned" would be better and "evolved" would be best, given his emphasis on the analogy of natural selection. The natural world is an extraordinarily complex system, amazingly "well designed," but according to Darwinian theory there was no designer. Markets are another example of "spontaneous order" in Hayek's sense. They emerged thousands of years ago; they were not invented or designed; and their operation does not involve central planning. Consider the system by which New York City is supplied with paper towels. No towel czar decides how many towels are needed when and by whom and then obtains the necessary inputs, which include the raw materials used in the manufacture of towels, the workers involved in that manufacture, packaging equipment, accounting and other support activities, storage facilities, and means of delivery. And yet the interactions of millions of consumers and thousands of suppliers of inputs bring about an orderly supply. There is no coordinator—except price. A still larger spontaneous order, moreover, coordinates the New York towel market with other regional towel markets and ultimately with the entire national and world economy.

In the normative realm the spontaneous order that corresponds to the market is custom; indeed, the market itself could be thought a product of custom. So strong is Hayek's dislike of planning that at times he comes close to denying that legislatures have *any* business regulating private behavior. Regulation is the business of custom. Not that Hayek is an anarchist and wants to abolish government. But he thinks that virtually the only proper business of a legislature is to direct and control the government, for example by levying the taxes that are necessary to defray the cost

72. "A directed economy must be run on more or less dictatorial lines . . . Whoever controls all economic activity controls the means for all our ends and must therefore decide which are to be satisfied and which not." Hayek, note 66 above, at 88, 91.

of government and by appointing and monitoring government officials.[73] He points out that historically that *was* the primary function of the British Parliament and not the laying down of rules of conduct for private citizens. Most of those rules were laid down by the royal judges. Those are the rules and doctrines of the common law. Even crimes were declared and defined by judges. (The modern view, at least in the U.S. federal system, is that there are no common law crimes; declaring conduct criminal is a legislative prerogative.) But judges' traditional aversion to appearing to be creative led them to say that what they were doing in deciding common law cases was not making new rules or standards of conduct but merely enforcing immemorial custom. Hayek takes this claim literally. He thinks (and he thinks the English common law judges thought) that the only question a judge is entitled to decide is "whether the conduct under dispute conformed to recognized rules," that is, to "the established custom which they [the parties] ought to have known."[74] Alternatively but equivalently, the judges' duty is to enforce the expectations created by custom.[75] Judges who step outside this boundary are—and here we see the influence of Hayek's second master idea at work—stepping onto the slippery slope to totalitarianism: "a socialist judge would really be a contradiction in terms."[76]

But so, by Hayek's logic, would a capitalist judge be. The contradiction Hayek identifies has nothing to do with the content of the judge's policy views. It lies rather in the judge's allowing those views to influence his decisions. Hayek acknowledges that there are gaps in legal rules and, what amounts to the same thing, that "new situations in which the established rules are not adequate will constantly arise," requiring the "formulation of new rules" by the judges.[77] But they are to fill these gaps with custom. Their role remains a passive one. They are not to engage in a "balancing of the particular interests affected [by the rules] in the light of their importance" or to concern themselves "with the effects of [the rules'] applications in particular instances."[78] In fact, "neither the judges nor the parties

73. Hayek, *Rules and Order,* note 70 above, at 125–131. Elsewhere, however, as we shall see, he allows a significantly greater scope to legislation.

74. Id. at 87. Like his fellow Austrian conservative, Schumpeter, Hayek greatly admired the British political system—and in both cases the *limitations* on democracy were the aspect of the British system that particularly attracted them.

75. Id. at 97, 119.

76. Id. at 121.

77. Id. at 119.

78. Id. at 121.

involved need to know anything about the nature of the resulting overall order, or about any 'interest of society' which they serve."[79] The "overall order" that the judges are to serve is the market[80] but they needn't even know that. The Hayekian judge is a thoroughgoing formalist. "He is required to think only about the internal logic of the law."[81]

Hayek does not think that *all* customs should be made enforceable by legal sanctions—only those that are general or, the term he prefers, "abstract."[82] Contract law is the paradigm. It provides merely a framework for private action, leaving the identity of the parties, and the price and other terms of the contract, to private determination. That is, contract law "abstracts" from all the particulars of people's voluntary interactions and so maximizes their freedom, their "spontaneity."

Hayek does not explain who decides which customs shall have the backing of law. But presumably it is the judges, whom he would also permit to engage in "piecemeal tinkering . . . to make the whole [body of law] more consistent both internally as well as with the facts to which the rules are applied."[83] This is a bow in the direction of Kelsenian positivism. But the dearth of examples—a Germanic characteristic of his writing on law that Hayek shares with Kelsen—makes it difficult to discern how deep the bow is; a few pages later Hayek says that "impartial justice . . . is not concerned with the effects of their application [that is, the application of 'end-independent rules']."[84] And "the judge is not performing his function if he disappoints reasonable expectations created by earlier decisions."[85] As a detail, I note that Hayek's disapproval of law founded on "constructivist rationalism" rather than on custom is in tension with his great admiration for the Constitution of the United States.[86]

When Hayek is writing against lawgiving by legislatures and judges, any perception of externalities or other sources of market failure is occluded. Yet he is aware that the amount of pollution is not optimized, or cartels prevented from arising, by the spontaneous order of the market. The control of pollution and of monopoly requires government to intervene in the

79. Id. at 119.
80. Id. at 115.
81. Ludwig Van den Hauwe, "Friedrich August von Hayek (1899–1992)," in *The Elgar Companion to Law and Economics* 339, 344 (Jürgen G. Backhaus ed. 1999).
82. See, for example, Hayek, *The Constitution of Liberty*, note 70 above, at 151–154.
83. Hayek, *Rules and Order*, note 70 above, at 118.
84. Id. at 121.
85. Id. at 88. See Covell, note 69 above, at 133.
86. See Hayek, *The Constitution of Liberty*, note 70 above, ch. 12.

market.[87] Hayek thinks the scope of public intervention should be quite limited, but he acknowledges the necessity of it. He is not a doctrinaire adherent to the idea that the only proper functions of government are internal and external security, the functions of the "nightwatchman" state. *The Constitution of Liberty* countenances some surprising departures from laissez-faire,[88] though Hayek is skeptical that economists have much to contribute to the design of public regulation of the economy.[89]

Nevertheless, he is insufficiently critical of the limitations of custom as a normative order.[90] Much as pragmatists admire Darwin, they recognize that evolution, lacking a teleology, cannot be assumed to lead to normatively attractive results. Two limitations of custom as a source of social norms require particular emphasis. First, as in the pollution and monopoly examples, customs often support cooperative activities that are harmful to society as a whole. Competing firms might evolve a custom that price-cutting is unethical; that custom, encouraging an unwholesome degree of cooperation, obviously could not be made the basis of antitrust law—in fact, it has to be forbidden by that law. Similarly, manufacturers might, in fact would be bound to, evolve a custom of ignoring the pollution they create; that custom could not be made the basis of environmental law. Or consider, what is analytically the same as pollution, accidents to "strangers" in the sense of persons with whom the injurer has no actual or potential contractual relation. The customary level of safety in the injurers' industry could not be assumed to be socially optimal because, unless forced to do so by law, the injurers would not take into account the accident costs of their victims in deciding how safe to make their operations or products. Courts therefore refuse to make compliance with industry custom a defense to liability for negligence—an example of an economically sound judge-made rule of law that obviously is not based on custom.[91] The rejection of cus-

---

87. See, for example, volume 3 of *Law, Legislation and Liberty*, entitled *The Political Order of a Free People* 42–43, 86–87 (1979); Ebenstein, note 1 above, at 225.

88. Hayek, *The Constitution of Liberty*, note 70 above, at 224–231.

89. Id. at 229–230.

90. These are emphasized in Francesco Parisi, "Spontaneous Emergence of Law: Customary Law," in *Encyclopedia of Law and Economics*, vol. 5: *The Economics of Crime and Litigation* 603, 611–618 (Boudewijn Bouckaert and Gerrit De Geest eds. 2000), and in Richard A. Posner and Eric B. Rasmusen, "Creating and Enforcing Norms, with Special Reference to Sanctions," 19 *International Review of Law and Economics* 369 (1999).

91. See William M. Landes and Richard A. Posner, *The Economic Structure of Tort Law* 132–139 (1987). It is unsound, however, when applied to accidents arising out of a contractual relation between injurer and victim. See id. at 135–139.

tom as a defense to liability in such cases is consistent with Hayek's conception of economic efficiency, but it is inconsistent with the role he assigns to judges. They are not to upset customs.

Second, Hayek ignores the problems that arise from the fact that custom, being acephalous (there is no "custom-giver" analogous to a legislature, which is a lawgiver), tends to change very slowly. If economic or other social practices are changing rapidly, custom will often fail to keep up and will become a drag on progress. There are many dysfunctional customs; failure to recognize this fact is a parody of Burkean conservatism. Hayek rejected the label of conservative for himself but it is unclear how his veneration of custom can be squared with that rejection.

Limiting judicial discretion as tightly as Hayek wanted to do might be defended by arguing that legislatures have superior competence to judges when it comes to making rules of conduct. But the closest Hayek comes to making such an argument (which would have required him to acknowledge forthrightly the limitations of custom as a source of law, something he was unwilling to do) is in emphasizing that rules should be changed only prospectively, which is the method of legislation, in order to protect reasonable expectations.[92] This cannot be a complete theory of the respective competences of legislatures and courts, especially since Hayek is so distrustful of legislatures.

Valid or not, Hayek's position that the only thing a judge should do is enforce custom without regard to consequences, because custom is the only legitimate source of law and therefore a legal judgment that does not draw its essence from custom is not true law,[93] extinguishes any role for economic or other social-scientific analysis in adjudication. That is why I said at the outset of this chapter that Hayek, the economist, closes the space that economic analysis might occupy in adjudication, while Kelsen, the legal philosopher, opens that space wide.

Of course he opens it wide to other things besides economics, including very bad things. The Nazi and Soviet legal systems, though they flouted

92. Hayek, *Rules and Order,* note 70 above, at 88–89.

93. There is a resemblance here, as Hayek notes approvingly in *The Road to Serfdom,* note 66 above, at 22, 74, 152–153, to the German "historical school" of jurisprudence, founded by Friedrich Carl von Savigny, who, as Kelsen notes, thought that the only legitimate law was customary law. Kelsen, *General Theory of Law and State,* note 2 above, at 126. The customary law Savigny had in mind was Roman law. See Posner, note 42 above, at 195. This suggests certain difficulties in ascertaining what is to count as custom. Hayek does not discuss these difficulties; Leoni, however, writes admiringly of Roman law. See, for example, Leoni, note 70 above, at 9–10, 82–86.

the rule of law in a most shocking fashion, were true legal systems under Kelsen's concept of law, as his critics have been quick to note.[94] But the shock diminishes if we distinguish between "law" and "rule of law." These only sound like the same thing. The former is something that all societies have except the most ancient and the most primitive; the latter is one of the elements of a liberal polity, whether it is classical liberal or, though to a slightly lesser degree, modern welfare liberal or, my preferred version, pragmatically liberal. It is not paying a compliment to Nazi Germany or the Soviet Union to say they had law, but it is a justified condemnation of them that they did not have the rule of law, that is, did not require that the laws be general, generally prospective, reasonably clear, and administered rationally and impartially. The rule of law is a normative notion rather than a description of what all law has in common, but it is misleadingly named; it seems to imply that a society without it is lawless, whereas a society that lacks the rule of law is merely not a liberal society. Hayek falls into this verbal trap by using the term "true law" to denote legal doctrines, procedures, and so forth that conform to the rule of law.[95] This is a misleading usage because the opposite of "true law" in his sense is not false law or no law; it is bad law. One of H. L. A. Hart's strongest arguments for legal positivism is that it enables us to speak of bad law because, to a positivist, goodness is not part of the definition of "law."

Remember my example of a constitutional content norm, the rule against ex post facto criminal legislation? The requirement that a statute be promulgated in advance of its taking effect, so that people have a fair opportunity to comply with it, is one of the elements of the rule of law. (As an aside, notice how a requirement of publicness is implicit in a requirement of prospectivity, since as a practical matter a secret law operates retroactively—no one can know that he has violated it.) But if there were no such requirement (and there isn't, in the case of civil statutes), it would not make ours a lawless society. The rule of law is not part of Kelsen's definition of law because its various components are not found in all legal systems.

Not only is it no compliment in Kelsen's world to say that Nazi Ger-

94. See, for example, David Dyzenhaus, *Legality and Legitimacy: Carl Schmitt, Hans Kelsen and Hermann Heller in Weimar* 157–160 (1997); Franz Neumann, *Behemoth: The Structure and Practice of National Socialism, 1933–1944,* at 46–47 (1944).

95. See, for example, Hayek, *The Constitution of Liberty,* note 70 above, at 208–209. The confusion of "law" with "rule of law" is common. When judges or professors criticize a judicial decision as "lawless," what they mean is that they think it violates the rule of law.

many or the Soviet Union had law; his concept of law brings into sharp focus the divergence of these systems from the rule of law. If we ask what the
basic norm of the Nazi legal system was, the answer is that Hitler's oral
or written commands, express or implied—perhaps even his unexpressed
wishes—were the supreme law of Germany. The basic norm of the Soviet
Union was not that the Soviet constitution and laws promulgated in conformity with it were valid, but that what Stalin (who held no government
post for much of his reign) or, after his death, the Politburo (a party, not a
governmental, organ) ordered was valid.

It would be hasty to describe Hayek as an "enemy" of economic analysis
of law, for so far all I have said is that he rejects an economic analysis that
says that judges should use economics to help decide their cases; and to the
extent that this rejection is based on economic grounds, it just means that
his is a different economic theory of law from that of people like me. In
part at least, his antipathy to using economic analysis to guide adjudication
is clearly based on an economic ground: the superiority, as he sees it, of
spontaneous to planned order because of the costs of information. But one
cannot read Hayek with any care and think he has only economic reasons
for wanting judges not to meddle with economics. His passionate opposition to central planning in all its forms, even the attenuated form represented by a judiciary that pays some attention to externalities, is moral and
political as well as economic. To equate law to the rule of law[96] is to embrace a natural-law conception of law; law is not law if it lacks certain civilized features. And while natural law need be no more hostile to economics
than Kelsenian positivism is, since in a morally diverse society the concept
of "natural law" has no fixed content, Hayek's conception of the rule of
law—and hence of law itself, given his equation of the terms—necessarily
excludes a role for economics in adjudication because in his view any judge
whose aspirations rise above enforcing custom is a lawless judge.

Natural lawyers are forever in quest of substantive or procedural principles that shall be criterial of law everywhere and for all time. But nothing
of any use ever turns up. If there are universal principles of law, they are
too vague and abstract to resolve any concrete issues. Invariably, therefore,
natural-law theories are parochial; they would have no bite otherwise.
Catholics defend a version of natural law based on Catholic theology, free

96. Just as Lon Fuller did through his concept of the "internal morality" of the law. See
Lon L. Fuller, *The Morality of Law* (1964), and, for trenchant criticism, Lloyd L. Weinreb,
Natural Law and Justice 102–104, 295 n. 6 (1987).

marketers like Hayek a version of natural law based on the needs (as he saw it) of the free market. Whether Catholics are right that abortion is murder, and whether Hayek is right that property rights are sacred, are not put on the road to being answered by being cast as questions about natural law. What Hayek might *constructively* have argued is that the common law provides a better framework for economic development than the civil law does because judges in common law countries tend to have greater independence from the (more) political branches of government and so are more reliable enforcers of property rights. There is even evidence to support this view.[97] But Hayek, his head filled with philosophy, was riding a different horse, or rather a different team. His theory of law is a peculiar mixture of the pragmatic and the dogmatic. The fundamental orientation is pragmatic—his Darwinesque ruling concept of "spontaneous order" is pragmatic, his theory of knowledge echoes Dewey's concept of epistemic democracy, and his passionate commitment to the rule of law is based ultimately on a belief that even small departures from it put us on the road to ruin. The last belief is wrong, however, and gives Hayek's rule-of-law ideology its doctrinaire cast.

His position underscores the tension between liberalism and democracy. As one of his sympathetic commentators remarked, "Hayek is not opposed to democracy *as such*."[98] But in practice, much like his fellow Austrian economist Schumpeter, Hayek sees democracy as paving the way to socialism. They differ mainly in that Hayek thought Nazism a form of socialism, while Schumpeter, obnoxiously but perceptively, thought it a rearguard action against socialism. Believing as he did that Hitlerian tyranny "was the natural outcome of the replacement of the traditional rule of law and its liberal values by democratic legislation and administrative regulations on the basis of legislation,"[99] Hayek wanted to surround democracy with so many restrictions that all that the people would be able to do would be to pick the officials and all that the officials would be able to do would be to administer the government; they could not establish rules of private behavior.

97. See Paul G. Mahoney, "The Common Law and Economic Growth: Hayek Might Be Right," 30 *Journal of Legal Studies* 503 (2001); Simeon Djankov et al., "Legal Structure and Judicial Efficiency: The Lex Mundi Project" (World Bank, Oct. 2001); Edward Glaeser and Andrei Shleifer, "Legal Origins" (forthcoming in *Quarterly Journal of Economics*).

98. Gottfried Dietze, "Hayek on the Rule of Law," in *Essays on Hayek* 107, 130 (Fritz Machlup ed. 1976) (emphasis added).

99. Id. at 133.

But the picture that I have sketched so far of Hayek's take on law remains incomplete. It leaves out a way of construing "rule of law" that ties it in more closely than I have yet acknowledged to economic analysis of law, though I hinted at the tie in the discussion in Chapter 2 of the pragmatic virtues of legal formalism. It is an interpretation that places Hayek in a Continental jurisprudential tradition that begins with the *Nicomachean Ethics*, in which Aristotle set forth the theory of law that he called "corrective justice." He also discussed distributive and retributive justice, and equity, but these are to one side of my concerns.

The central tenet of Aristotle's concept of corrective justice is that if someone through wrongful behavior disturbs the preexisting balance between himself and another person to the injury of the latter, the victim is entitled to some form of redress that will, to the extent feasible, restore that preexisting balance—that will correct, in other words, the departure from equilibrium that was brought about by the wrongful act. The concept is highly abstract. What shall count as wrongful behavior is not specified, nor the forms of redress that shall be deemed appropriate. But all that is important here is the following corollary that Aristotle drew from his theory: law when it is doing corrective justice must abstract from the personal qualities, the merit or desert, of the wrongdoer and his victim. The victim may be seen to be a bad man and the wrongdoer a good one when we consider the character and entire course of a person's career, the summation of all his good and bad deeds, and not just the particular episode that resulted in the injury to the victim. The victim nevertheless is entitled to redress. The entitlement is a corollary of corrective justice rather than a separate principle of justice because corrective justice seeks to restore a preexisting equilibrium rather than to change it. The court doesn't use the occasion to enrich or impoverish either wrongdoer or victim on the basis of a judgment about either's merits or deserts apart from the circumstances of the injury itself.

This is what is called doing justice "without regard to persons" and it remains a cornerstone of law in all civilized societies. It is one of the features that *defines* a society as civilized. The reason is practical (Aristotle was a practical thinker). If obtaining redress for injuries depended on a person's reputation, people would invest inordinate resources in becoming well liked, well regarded. To the extent that such investment took the form of doing genuinely good things, it would enhance social welfare. But often a person would find it easier to obtain a good reputation by cultivating the friendship of the powerful, allying with the powerful through marriage, avoiding unpopular stands, and other methods unrelated, even antithetical, to the good of society. Furthermore, even when a person obtained a good reputation by good means, once he had that reputation he could use it to inflict wrongful injuries with impunity on persons who lacked a good reputation; so incentives to wrongful behavior would be created. The friendless would be an outlaw; the "good" could prey on them with impunity. Energies would be deflected from socially constructive activities into rent-seeking and clientalism.

So we want law to be "impersonal" in rather a literal sense. We want the judges to abstract from the personal characteristics of the parties to the litigation before them and treat them as representatives of classes of activity, such as drivers and pedestrians. This aspiration for legal justice received canonical expression in Max Weber's concept of formal rationality. Law engaged his interest as both an illustration of and as a causal agent in the process of modernization, the process by which instrumental rationality—the intelligent fitting of means to ends—implemented through such institutions and practices as bureaucracy, professionalism, and specialization comes to supplant older methods of social ordering. The older methods include family and clan ties, magic, charisma, intimidation, and other means of social control in which nonrational associations and influences predominate. Law, in Weber's analysis, participates in the modernizing process by shucking off its supernatural, charismatic, and discretionary elements and becoming increasingly cut-and-dried, rational, and bureaucratic—increasingly a system in which disinterested civil servants, constituting a professionalized judiciary, resolve disputes by applying clearly stated rules designed to promote rational economic planning by private and public actors to facts that these civil servants also ascertain rationally. The rules do not prescribe any private actions—do not tell people what contracts to make, what risks to take, what callings to follow. Instead they create the framework within which people can go about their business—acquiring and exploiting property, making contracts, investing and lending, engaging in risky activities, and so forth, confident that known, clear, substantively neutral rules provide the exclusive statement of their public rights and duties. To the extent that the legal system conforms to these criteria, it attains formal rationality—the optimal environment for capitalism.

With Weber we are already far beyond Aristotle. This is particularly clear when we consider Weber's argument that the efficacy of the law as a handmaiden of a capitalist economy depends on law's maintaining its professional autonomy. (Aristotle had written at a time when there were no professional judges and the economy was precapitalist.) Judges are not to be the cheerleaders for capitalism. They are to enforce the abstract norms of the law without regard to the consequences for the persons and activities encountered in the cases they are called on to decide. Neutrality not only as to personal worth as in Aristotle but also as to ideology is important for maximizing the predictability of law—and it is predictability, above all, that Weber thought capitalists require of the legal framework—and for reassuring the potentially restive classes in society that the law is not infected by class bias.

This is already close to Hayek but differs with regard to the optimal institutional framework for achieving the formal rationality of the law. The legal system that Weber had in mind as exemplary for modernization was the civil-law system found in Germany and other Continental nations, and eventually in Japan and much of the rest of the world as well. The legal codes of the Continental nations, beginning with the Code Napoléon, and the bureaucratic judiciaries that administered them, signified to Weber the triumph of formal rationality. Yet the earliest capitalist superpower, namely Great Britain, and the most advanced capitalist power of his day as of ours, namely the United States, were common law rather than code countries. The embarrassment that the common law posed for Weber's thesis was, however, slight. The Continental judiciary is (and was in Weber's time as well) more creative and less rule-bound, less "bureaucratic," than Weber believed, while the common law has always been more predictable than outsiders realize; and so in short the common law and civilian legal traditions are convergent, though differences remain. What capitalism *essentially* requires of law is the protection of property and political rights, the enforcement of contracts, and some regulation of markets, by reasonably disinterested judges, rather than the maximum clarity and coherence attainable by legal rules.

Hayek turned Weber upside down by arguing that the common law was a better institutional framework for achieving formal rationality than the civil law. But it was not better because common law made by English and American judges was more efficient than the rules of the civil law. As we have seen, Hayek thought the role of the common law judge had rightly been a passive one, one of identifying existing customs. The judges were not to create new rules, rules not founded on custom, or to bother their heads about efficiency (hostility to efficiency as a guide to public policy is a defining feature of "Austrian economics," the school of thought of which Hayek is the most illustrious exemplar). I have questioned the adequacy of this view. But it should be clear nevertheless that to describe Hayek as an "enemy" of economic analysis of law would be a mistake. Recall the economic construal I gave of Aristotle's theory of corrective justice. Hayek would surely have subscribed to that construal; a staunch opponent of socialism, he regarded legally enforceable contract and property rights as the bedrock of capitalism. Weber, an economist as well as a jurist, sociologist, philosopher, and political scientist, likewise regarded law's formal rationality as fundamental to capitalism. It would be anachronistic to describe Aristotle as an economic analyst of law; but Weber and Hayek are surely that.

Their economic analysis of law, however, goes only so far as to identify the economic functions of law's impersonality and formal rationality, the economic functions, in a word, of the "rule of law," a narrower concept than that of law itself. And in the case of Hayek, advocacy of the economic case for the rule of law—for the basic institutional framework of legal doctrine and decisionmaking—was conjoined with an implicit rejection of the Anglo-American approach to the economic analysis of law, an approach that, in contrast to Hayek's, assigns an active role to judges and legislators in formulating public policy called law.

I do not myself sense any essential tension between the Anglo-American and Continental traditions of economic analysis of law. The rule of law in approximately the form advocated by the notables of the Continental tradition beginning with Aristotle has important economizing effects. But if the concept of the rule of law is pressed to the extreme of stripping judges of any creative function, the sacrifice of efficiency is too great. Hayek failed to recognize the tradeoff between the efficiencies created by a formalist concept of law and the efficiencies obtainable only if judges or legislators formulate efficient legal doctrines. Custom can't be relied on to generate such doctrines, and therefore judges who adhere blindly to custom, as Hayek wanted them to do, will produce outcomes that frequently are inefficient. The danger of course, one to which Hayek was acutely sensitive—perhaps two sensitive—is that if judges are set at large to modify customs in line with the precepts of economics, they will see their role as that of central planners licensed to reshape the economy in accordance with whatever economic views they happen to hold.

The danger of judicial discretion run wild is a real one; Hayek's warnings against it remain timely. But it is timely primarily for Europe rather than for America. Europe is at the crossroads, where one path leads to discretionary adjudication on the Anglo-American model while the other is the continuation of the tradition of judicial modesty that (to an American) is the most striking feature of the European judiciary. But the second path is not open to judges in America. As I have emphasized throughout this book, the inability of political parties to control American legislatures, the tricameral character of the Congress and the state legislatures (the veto making the President or governor in essence a third branch of government), the heterogeneity of American society, including its legal culture, the method by which we choose our judges (the absence of a career judiciary), and the sheer complexity of American law (the Constitution layered on federal statutes and the whole of federal law laid over the laws of the fifty states) make the exercise of broad discretionary authority by American judges unavoidable. And thus the question, to which Hayek had no answer, is what shall guide that discretion. My answer is pragmatism flavored by economic analysis[100]—an answer compatible with Kelsen but not with Hayek. Kelsen, the "pure" theorist, was not a formalist; Hayek, the economist, was.

Hayek on Kelsen; Kelsen and Schumpeter

Hayek was a stern critic of Kelsen's theory of law (I am not aware that Kelsen ever wrote about Hayek's views of law, which were not published until late in Kelsen's life). *The Road to Serfdom* draws a straight line between Bismarck's social welfare legislation and Hitler[101]—and the line runs through Kelsen, whose pure theory of law, Hayek argued in a later book,

> signaled the definite eclipse of all traditions of limited government . . .
> There are no possible limits to the power of the legislator . . . Every
> single tenet of the traditional conception of the rule of law is repre-
> sented as a metaphysical superstition . . . The possibilities which this

100. See generally Elisabeth Krecké, "Economic Analysis and Legal Pragmatism" (Université d'Aix-Marseilles III, June 2002, unpublished).

101. Hayek, *The Road to Serfdom*, note 66 above, at 167–180. Hayek here fell into the common trap of thinking that Bismarck's social welfare legislation was redistributive. It was not: the cost was borne by the workers. Peter H. Lindert, "The Rise of Social Spending, 1880–1930," 31 *Explorations in Economic History* 1, 9–15 (1994).

state of opinion created for an unlimited dictatorship were already clearly seen by acute observers at the time Hitler was trying to gain power . . . But it was too late. The antilibertarian forces had learned too well the positivist doctrine that the state must not be bound by law.[102]

Hayek is right that Kelsen taught that despotic governments, including "unlimited dictatorships," have law. But Kelsen never said they had good law, or the rule of law. The suggestion that Hitler might have been prevented from gaining power if only despotic laws had been denied the label "true laws"[103] merely shows Hayek's exaggerated belief in the influence of philosophy on society.

Kelsen and Hayek are ships passing in the night. Kelsen's theory of law is content-neutral; Hayek is interested only in content. This is not to deny that Kelsen held definite views about the content of law—views that as it happens were far more liberal in the modern sense of the term than Hayek's. Kelsen had drafted Austria's post–World War I constitution, and a notable feature of it was the creation of a constitutional court (of which he became one of the first members!), that is, a court that places definite "limits to the power of the legislator." Kelsen repeatedly uses the example of a justiciable constitution to illustrate the highest legal norm beneath the *Grundnorm*. He thought the primary function of a constitution was to allocate powers among the various branches of government and otherwise prescribe the structure of government, but he did not think it improper that the constitution should include substantive norms such as freedom of speech and religion.[104] He would not have subscribed to Hayek's view of "true" (that is, good) law because he was not a Hayekian libertarian—not because he was a legal positivist.

David Dyzenhaus has a deeper understanding of Kelsen than Hayek did but shares Hayek's questionable belief that the Weimar Republic was weakened by Kelsen's failure to develop a theory of law that would have tied legality to democracy rather than allowing it to float free of the form of government. "Kelsen's legal positivism, while not exactly paving the way

102. Hayek, *The Constitution of Liberty*, note 70 above, at 238–239 (footnotes omitted). See also Dietze, note 98 above, at 131–133.

103. See Hayek, *The Constitution of Liberty*, note 70 above, at 238.

104. Hans Kelsen, "The Function of a Constitution," in *Essays on Kelsen* 110, 118–119 (Richard Tur and William Twining eds. 1986).

for Nazism, offered no legal resource which could be used to resist a fascist seizure of power in Germany."[105] By "legal resource" Dyzenhaus means a theory. It is fanciful to suppose that a theory of law propounded by a Jewish professor would have done anything to stop Hitler. Anyway, if as I believe Kelsen's was a genuinely positive theory of law, criticism based on its social consequences is misplaced. It is like criticizing atomic theory for having led to the destruction of Hiroshima and Nagasaki.

It remains to note the affinity between Kelsen's theory of law and his fellow-Austrian Schumpeter's theory of democracy. It is that affinity that led me to describe them as twin pillars of pragmatic liberalism. Both theories are in a sense formal (not formalistic) or jurisdictional rather than substantive or doctrinal. Both are skeptical about the motivational or behavioral effects of theory, and in that respect both are pragmatic. Kelsen's theory has judges ranging within their jurisdiction more or less freely, or at least free of tight constraints woven of theories of the judicial function, interpretation, stare decisis, and the like. The constraints that do operate on judges and channel their discretion, constraints that necessarily are material and psychological rather than conceptual because concepts do not constrain,[106] come from judges' training, selection, and personal values, and from the rules and practices governing judicial conduct, appeals, promotion, rewards, impeachment, and so on, not from commitment to jurisprudential theories. Similarly, in Schumpeter's concept of democracy the constraints on officials come not from high-minded deliberation on moral or political theory by voters or by the officials themselves but by competition within the governing class for political office, by competition ("turf wars") among officials and among overlapping branches of government, and by the various restrictions that the law places on official discretion. Kelsen's and Schumpeter's theories are realistic rather than edifying, and it is possible that under conditions of political instability such as afflicted Weimar a more normatively ambitious type of theory would have greater rhetorical force and hence political value. But their theories provide the appropriate framework not only for understanding American law and society but also for evaluating the piecemeal reforms that are the only type that are feasible or desirable in the present circumstances of the United States.

The connection between Kelsen's theory of law—more broadly, the

---

105. Dyzenhaus, note 94 above, at 5.
106. Directly; the significance of this qualification was explained in Chapter 2.

pragmatic theory of law—and Schumpeter's theory of democracy, which is also pragmatic, is highlighted by the equally tight connection between their opposites, which in the Preface I combined under the rubric of "deliberative liberalism." Whether talking about votes, about the actions of elected or appointed nonjudicial officials, or about judicial decisions, deliberativists want decisionmaking to be guided and constrained by disinterested principle. In contrast, Schumpeter and Kelsen saw that democratic and judicial action could be guided and constrained only by interests and institutions.

CHAPTER EIGHT

Legality and Necessity

❦

Freedom is a relative not an absolute value. It is cherished more or less depending on its consequences in the context at hand.[1]

In an emergency a government is entrusted with sweeping powers of legislation. In ordinary times it is the duty of the law-maker to find a just balance between the powers that should be granted to government and the freedom that should be left to the individual. The existence of an emergency does not absolve the government as law-maker altogether from this duty. The scales are altered: the power of the government will be much greater; but the need for a just balance still remains.[2]

In the remaining chapters I try to put more flesh on the bones of judicial pragmatism. The focus in this chapter and the next is on cases and issues that involved an actual or claimed national emergency. The usual understanding of the cases that I shall be discussing is that the emergency, rightly or wrongly, trumped the law. They were cases, in other words, in which the "law of necessity" (not a real law) was allowed to override real laws. This understanding is too simple. In this chapter I also consider, under the rubric of "lawyers' hubris," whether lawyers should have the whip hand in determining how public-safety concerns should be balanced against the values protected by existing legal doctrines.

---

1. Stephen Holmes, "Liberalism in the Mirror of Transnational Terror," *Tocqueville Review/La Revue Tocqueville*, no. 2, 2001, pp. 5, 6.

2. Patrick Devlin, unpublished ms., quoted in Brian Simpson, "The Devlin Commission (1959): Colonialism, Emergencies, and the Rule of Law," 22 *Oxford Journal of Legal Studies* 17, 36 (2002).

Crisis Prevention as Pragmatic Adjudication

The threat of a national crisis leagued *Bush v. Gore*, the subject of the next chapter, with a number of earlier Supreme Court cases in which an actual or impending national crisis had influenced the outcome. One is *Korematsu v. United States*,[3] the case that upheld the military order, issued a few months after the Japanese attack on Pearl Harbor, that excluded persons of Japanese ancestry from the west coast of the United States even if they were U.S. citizens. The Supreme Court held that the order, though unquestionably a species of racial discrimination,[4] was a permissible exercise of the warmaking powers that the Constitution grants to Congress and the President. The Court noted that the fear of possible sabotage by persons affected by the order was supported by the reported refusal of thousands of American citizens of Japanese ancestry to swear unqualified allegiance to the United States.[5]

Justice Jackson dissented in an opinion, surprising in one of the greatest pragmatic Justices, in which he said that because a court is in no position to determine the reasonableness of a military order, its reasonableness could not be a defense to a charge of racial discrimination: "a civil court cannot be made to enforce an order which violates constitutional limitations even if it is a reasonable exercise of military authority."[6] This is the same Justice who famously warned against treating the Bill of Rights as a national suicide pact.[7] That could well be the slogan of pragmatic Supreme

3. 323 U.S. 214 (1944). See also Hirabayashi v. United States, 320 U.S. 81 (1943).

4. It is now apparent that racial prejudice was a significant motivation for the exclusion order. See Greg Robinson, *By Order of the President: FDR and the Internment of Japanese Americans* (2001); Gil Gott, "A Tale of New Precedents: Japanese American Internment as Foreign Affairs Law," 40 *Boston College Law Review* 179, 226–232 (1998), and references cited there.

5. See also U.S. Department of War, *Japanese Evacuation from the West Coast: Final Report, 1942*, ch. 2 (1978).

6. 323 U.S. at 247.

7. Terminiello v. City of Chicago, 337 U.S. 1, 37 (1949) (dissenting opinion). This was repeated in the majority opinion in Kennedy v. Mendoza-Martinez, 372 U.S. 144, 160 (1963). In the wake of the September 11, 2001 terrorist attacks, we find even the notably liberal Laurence Tribe repeating the slogan. Laurence H. Tribe, "Trial by Fury: Why Congress Must Curb Bush's Military Courts," *New Republic*, Dec. 10, 2001, pp. 18, 20. Although Tribe believes that the President's order creating such tribunals is overbroad, he is not opposed to a limited use of them, remarking in quintessentially pragmatic vein that "we must not bind ourselves too tightly to a mast suited only for navigating peaceful seas." Id. Equally noteworthy is a similar comment by Ronald Dworkin, who, although disagreeing that military tribunals should be used at all, states: "What any nation can afford to provide, by way of protec-

Court Justices. While stating that "defense measures will not, and often should not, be held within the limits that bind civil authority in peace,"[8] Jackson would have forbidden the courts to back up the military order by convicting Korematsu for violating it, pursuant to a statute that made such violations criminal. But if the statute punishing violations of the order were unenforceable, the efficacy of the order, and of "defense measures" taken in time of war generally, would be weakened. If the Constitution is not to be treated as a suicide pact, why should military exigencies not influence the scope of the constitutional rights that the Supreme Court has manufactured from the Constitution's vague provisions? In fact, if the exclusion order was "reasonable," as Jackson said it was, why was it not constitutional? It did not violate any hard-edged rule of constitutional law.

Liberals detest *Korematsu*, just as they do *Bush v. Gore*. Yet they believe that the prohibition against racial discrimination can be bent, without violation of the Constitution, if the race discriminated against, under the rubric of affirmative action, is white rather than yellow. The cases are different, of course, though the net effect of the difference is unclear. Affirmative action is not stigmatizing; on the other hand, there was a greater perceived urgency to taking defensive measures in World War II than there is to perpetuating affirmative action today, always a highly controversial policy and now rather long in the tooth.[9] *Bush v. Gore* is similar to

---

tion for accused criminals, must at least partly depend on the consequences such protections would have for its own security. The terrorist threat to our security is very great, and perhaps unprecedented, and we cannot be as scrupulous in our concern for the rights of suspected terrorists as we are for the rights of people suspected of less dangerous crimes. As Justice Jackson put it in a now-often-quoted remark, we cannot allow our Constitution and our shared sense of decency to become a suicide pact." Ronald Dworkin, "The Threat to Patriotism," *New York Review of Books*, Feb. 28, 2002, pp. 44, 47. (What Jackson actually said was: "The choice is not between order and liberty. It is between liberty with order and anarchy without either. There is danger that, if the Court does not temper its doctrinaire logic with a little practical wisdom, it will convert the constitutional Bill of Rights into a suicide pact." 337 U.S. at 37.) For other notable acknowledgments by liberals, in the wake of the September 11 attacks, that the interest in public safety may justify some curtailment in the accepted scope of civil liberties, see Alan M. Dershowitz, *Why Terrorism Works* (2002); Paul Gewirtz, "Privacy and Speech," 2001 *Supreme Court Review* 139, 169 n. 104 (Dennis J. Hutchinson, David A. Strauss, and Geoffrey R. Stone eds. 2002).

8. 323 U.S. at 244.

9. A further distinction, though doctrinal, an anachronism, and to one side of the modern debate over *Korematsu*, is that at the time the case was decided the Supreme Court had not yet held that the principle of equal protection applied to the federal government; the equal protection clause itself is found only in the Fourteenth Amendment and is applicable only to the states. In Bolling v. Sharpe, 347 U.S. 497 (1954), the Supreme Court "discovered" an equal protection component in the due process clause of the Fifth Amendment. *Bolling* is another

Korematsu because of the sense of a crisis lurking in the background, while *Korematsu* is similar to cases allowing affirmative action, although only— but it is not a trivial respect—in showing that powerful norms of legal justice, such as the nondiscrimination principle, can bend to practical exigencies, whether it is winning a war or improving race relations. The point is not that law is suspended in times of emergency, though that can happen too, as when Lincoln suspended habeas corpus repeatedly during the early weeks of the Civil War.[10] The point rather is that law is usually flexible enough to allow judges to give controlling weight to the immediate consequences of decision if those consequences are sufficiently grave.

An even closer liberal counterpart to *Korematsu* than affirmative action, because it too involved a national emergency, is *Home Building & Loan Association v. Blaisdell*,[11] the case that filleted the Constitution's contracts clause. In 1933, in the depths of the Great Depression, Minnesota passed a law that gave relief to debtors by declaring a moratorium on foreclosures. Although Article I of the Constitution forbids states to pass laws impairing the obligation of contracts, and Minnesota's law did just that, the Supreme Court upheld the law. The Court reasoned ingeniously that "the policy of protecting contracts against impairment presupposes the maintenance of a government by virtue of which contractual relations are worth while—a government which retains adequate authority to secure the peace and good order of society."[12] This is a fancy way of saying that a state *can* impair the obligation of contracts, notwithstanding the constitutional provision (a provision aimed at debtor relief laws, which had flourished after the Revolution, frightening the commercial class and providing impetus to the enactment of the Constitution), provided it has a compelling reason to do so. The decision may have been wrong, but I would not call it usurpative. Most constitutional provisions have—or, more precisely, can be given, by judges exercising the elastic power of interpretation—enough wiggle room to accommodate an emergency.

---

example of quintessentially pragmatic adjudication. Its doctrinal grounding was weak, to say the least. The basis of the decision was simply the absurdity of outlawing segregation everywhere in the United States, as the Supreme Court had just done in *Brown v. Board of Education*, except the seat of government.

10. See Martin S. Sheffer, "Presidential Power to Suspend Habeas Corpus: The Taney-Bates Dialogue and *Ex Parte Merryman*," 11 *Oklahoma City University Law Review* 1, 7–8 (1986), and discussion in Chapter 7.

11. 290 U.S. 398 (1934).

12. Id. at 435.

The importance of pragmatic considerations in judicial decisionmaking is brought into sharp focus by the terrorist attacks on the United States of September 11, 2001. The attacks caused some people to rethink their criticisms of the defenders of *Bush v. Gore* who argued that a Presidential succession crisis would have been too high a price to pay for the abstract benefit to democratic theory of letting Congress, the more democratic branch, determine the succession. But the implications of September 11 for this book are broader.

In the wake of the attacks a number of measures, legislative and executive, were adopted with the aim of reducing the likelihood of a repetition. The concerns actuating these measures were pragmatic in the most fundamental sense. Civil libertarians, however, feared an erosion of civil liberties. They offered historical examples of supposed overreactions to threats to national security, treating our existing civil liberties—protections of privacy, of the freedom of the press, of the rights of criminal suspects, and the rest—as sacrosanct and insisting therefore that the battle against international terrorism must accommodate itself to them.

This approach to the balance between liberty and security is unsound. Its basic flaw is the prioritizing of liberty. The civil liberties of Americans—the right not to be arrested except upon probable cause to believe one has committed a crime, for example, or not to be prosecuted for violating a criminal statute enacted after the violation—have been made legally enforceable by the Constitution and by statutes. The statutes can be amended relatively easily but not the Constitution. That may be why the framers left most of its provisions that confer rights pretty vague—at any rate, vague they are. The courts have made them more definite in the course of deciding cases. The process has been basically a pragmatic one. The scope of the rights has been determined, through an interaction of constitutional text and judicial interpretation, by the judges' weighing the competing interests at stake—call them public safety and liberty. Neither interest should enjoy priority over the other in the balancing process. Both are important but their relative importance differs from time to time and situation to situation and so the law should be flexible. The safer the nation feels, the more weight judges will and should give to liberty. The greater the threat that some activity poses to the nation's safety, the stronger will seem—and will be—the grounds for seeking to repress that activity at some cost to liberty, and so the balance will tilt the other way. The present contours of the rights that the Constitution confers, having been shaped far more by judicial interpretation than by the literal text (which leaves undefined such critical terms as "freedom of speech, "due process of law" and "unreasonable" searches and seizures), are alterable in response to perceived changes in the risks to public safety. "Neglect of historical context as an all-important shaper of constitutional law has always been intellectually unwise. After 'historical context' crashed into our lives two months ago [that is, on September 11, 2001], ignoring it has become politically impossible."[13]

Concretely, the balance between liberty and safety should be struck at the point at which any further curtailment of civil liberties would create a greater expected harm to society by reducing liberty than it would create an expected benefit to society by increasing public safety while any further expansion of civil liberties would create a greater expected harm to society by reducing safety than it would create an expected benefit by increasing liberty. This is the point at which the marginal benefit of curtailing liberty equals the marginal cost; anywhere to either side of that point, social welfare is less. I use the terms "*expected* benefit" and "*expected* cost" (or "harm") to underscore the probabilistic nature of the required assessment.

In recognition of the pitfalls of delusive exactness, I offer "balancing" as a framework for analysis rather than as a formula to be solved quantitatively. One of the important things that it shows is that knowing how a change in the scope of liberties affects the public safety is as important as knowing how such a change affects liberty and knowing the statutes, the constitutional provisions, the international conventions, the cases, and the other conventional materials of legal analysis.

The parity between liberty and safety in the formulation of constitutional doctrine is obscured by a mistaken sense that because the Constitution creates no enforceable legal right to safety—you can't sue Congress for failing to pass effective laws to combat terrorism—any curtailment of liberty in the name of safety goes against the constitutional grain. "The semantic repertoire of our constitutional law—we tend to speak of constitutional 'claims' and 'rights' rather than constitutional 'principles' or 'rules'—subtly suggests that when a constitutional question arises, constitutional values are represented only by one side or another."[14] Actually, the values and concerns that fix the limits of constitutional rights are as consti-

13. Holmes, note 1 above, at 12. A dramatic example of Holmes's point is how attitudes toward the constitutionality of flag-burning are likely to change in the wake of September 11. See discussion in Chapter 10.

14. Paul M. Bator, "The State Courts and Federal Litigation," 22 *William and Mary Law Review* 605, 632 (1981).

tutionally significant as those that inform the rights. They limit rather than create rights for severely practical reasons having nothing to do with relative importance, such as the impracticability of asking judges to decide what fraction of the national income should go to defense and internal security and how that fraction should be allocated among the classes of persons seeking protection from foreign or domestic threats to personal safety. The judicially enforceable Constitution is primarily a charter of negative liberties, liberties from government.[15] The government's responsibility to secure citizens' positive liberties by providing protective and other social services is enforced by Congress and the President rather than by the courts. That doesn't make the positive liberties any less important than the negative ones (as liberals themselves are quick to point out when the positive liberty in question is the social safety net). It is therefore "misleading and simplistic to test a judge's fidelity to the Constitution in terms of supposed attitudes toward a narrow checklist of constitutional rules especially favored by enthusiastic partisans of an interventionist federal judiciary."[16]

The events of September 11 revealed the United States to be in greater jeopardy from international terrorism than had been believed by most people until then—revealed it to be threatened by a diffuse, shadowy, but very dangerous enemy that had to be fought with internal police measures as well as with military force. It stands to reason that such a revelation would lead to our civil liberties being curtailed. A pragmatist would say they *should* be curtailed to the extent that the beneficial consequences for the safety of the nation (which, remember, is a concern of constitutional dignity rather than a concern to be weighed *against* the Constitution) outweigh the adverse impact on liberty. All that can reasonably be asked of the responsible legislative and judicial officials in a grave national emergency is that they try to weigh both sorts of consequence equally carefully, without a thumb on the scale or a desire to shift the balance for extraneous reasons.

Against this it is argued that the lesson of history is that officials habitually exaggerate dangers to the nation's security. Actually, the lesson of history is the opposite. Officialdom has repeatedly and disastrously underestimated these dangers—whether it is the danger of secession that led to

---

15. See, for example, DeShaney v. Winnebago County Department of Social Services, 489 U.S. 189 (1989).

16. Bator, note 14 above, at 633 n. 65.

the Civil War, or the danger of a Japanese attack on the United States that led to the disaster at Pearl Harbor, or the danger of Soviet espionage in the 1940s that accelerated the Soviet Union's acquisition of nuclear weapons and by doing so emboldened Stalin to encourage North Korea to invade South Korea in 1950, or the installation in 1962 of Soviet missiles in Cuba that precipitated the Cuban missile crisis, or the outbreaks of urban violence and political assassinations in the 1960s, or the Tet Offensive of 1968 in the Vietnam War, or the Iranian Revolution of 1979 and subsequent taking of American diplomats hostage, or the catastrophe of September 11, 2001. What is true is that when a nation is surprised and hurt there is a danger that it will overreact—yet it is only with the benefit of hindsight that a reaction can be separated into its proper and excess layers. In hindsight we know that interning the Japanese-American residents of the West Coast did not shorten World War II. But was this known at the time? If not, should not the government have erred on the side of caution, as it did? Was the court wrong that later enjoined *Progressive* magazine from publishing an article that contained classified information about the design of the hydrogen bomb?[17] Was the Supreme Court wrong to say that government may "prevent actual obstruction to its recruiting service or the publication of the sailing dates of transports or the number and location of troops" in time of war?[18]

Even today one cannot say that President Lincoln was wrong to suspend habeas corpus at the outset of the Civil War, when the Union's prospects seemed bleak. The Constitution authorizes only Congress to suspend habeas corpus and thus allow people to be held indefinitely in federal custody without any legal protection against mistaken arrest and detention. But as Lincoln asked rhetorically in a message to Congress, "Are all the laws, *but one*, to go unexecuted, and the government itself go to pieces, lest that one be violated?"[19] Another of Lincoln's wartime measures, the Emancipa-

17. United States v. Progressive, Inc., 467 F. Supp. 990 (W.D. Wis.), appeal dismissed without opinion, 610 F.2d 819 (7th Cir. 1979). The current counterpart to the *Progressive* article is the *Encyclopedia of Jihad*, an eleven-volume manual of mayhem. See Rodney A. Smolla, "From *Hit Man* to *Encyclopedia of Jihad:* How to Distinguish Freedom of Speech from Terrorist Training," 22 *Loyola of Los Angeles Entertainment Law Review* 479 (2002). See also Rice v. Paladin Enterprises, Inc., 128 F.3d 233 (4th Cir. 1997).

18. Near v. Minnesota, 283 U.S. 697, 716 (1931).

19. Abraham Lincoln, "Message to Congress in Special Session," July 4, 1861, in *The Collected Works of Abraham Lincoln*, vol. 4, pp. 421, 430 (Roy P. Basler ed. 1953) (emphasis in original). Lincoln's suspension of habeas corpus is defended in William A. Galston, *Liberal Pluralism: The Implications of Value Pluralism for Political Theory and Practice* 87 (2002).

tion Proclamation, may well have been unconstitutional too.[20] Ronald Dworkin thinks we should be "ashamed" of the suspension of civil rights during the Civil War.[21] He ignores the possibility that suspension reasonably appeared necessary to avoid losing the war.

Yet Lincoln would have been wrong to cancel the 1864 Presidential election, as some urged. By November 1864 the North was close to victory; and canceling the election would have created a more dangerous precedent than the wartime suspension of habeas corpus. Civil liberties remain in the balance even in the most dangerous of times and even though their relative weight must be less then because of heightened concern for public safety. It is as misleading to say that "security comes before liberty"[22] as it is to say the reverse. The prioritizing of either security or liberty is unpragmatic.

The unconstitutional acts that Lincoln committed during the Civil War suggest that even legality must sometimes be traded off against other values. He argued that the United States government, "like all others, possessed an absolute power of self-defense, a power to be exerted by the President of the United States. And this power extended to the breaking of the fundamental laws of the nation, if such a step were unavoidable."[23] The United States is a nation under law, but first it is a nation. Would it have been worthwhile to lose the Civil War merely to prevent the violation of the Constitution? Was not Lincoln correct that to save the Constitution it might be necessary to violate it?[24] Is it not vital to morale in wartime that a nation's leaders show themselves resolute, and is not brushing aside legal niceties that might interfere with the determined prosecution of the war

20. See Phillip S. Paludan, *A Covenant with Death: The Constitution, Law and Equality in the Civil War Era* 85–197 (1975); George P. Fletcher, *Our Secret Constitution: How Lincoln Redefined American Democracy* 37 (2001); Jill Elaine Hasday, "Civil War as Paradigm: Reestablishing the Rule of Law at the End of the Cold War," 5 *Kansas Journal of Law and Public Policy* 129, 130 (1996); Sanford Levinson, "Was the Emancipation Proclamation Constitutional? Do We/Should We Care What the Answer Is?" 2001 *University of Illinois Law Review* 1135; Jay Winik, "Security Comes before Liberty," *Wall Street Journal*, Oct. 23, 2001, p. A26.

21. Dworkin, note 7 above, at 45.

22. Winik, note 20 above—a useful article; it is only the title that I am objecting to. And maybe he just meant that *survival* comes before liberty, which I would agree with.

23. Clinton L. Rossiter, *Constitutional Dictatorship: Crisis Government in the Modern Democracies* 229 (1948).

24. See Larry Alexander and Frederick Schauer, "On Extrajudicial Constitutional Interpretation," 110 *Harvard Law Review* 1359, 1382 (1997); William P. Marshall, "The Supreme Court, *Bush v. Gore*, and Rough Justice," 29 *Florida State University Law Review* 787, 790 (2001).

one way of showing this?[25] And would it really be worthwhile today to endanger thousands, maybe millions, of Americans merely to preserve *all* the
civil libertarian decisions of the Warren Court, decisions by no mean
firmly based on the constitutional text? Decisions expanding civil liberties
in safe times will be resisted, and rightly so, if they have a ratchet effect,
precluding retrenchment even in times of national crisis.

Months before the terrorist attacks, my court was asked to relax a decree
that tightly constrained investigations by the Chicago police department
of subversive activities. The decree had been entered many years earlier to
prevent a repetition of abusive police investigations of left-wing radicals
during the 1970s and earlier by the City's "Red Squad." We granted the
City's request to relax the decree, noting that

> in the heyday of the Red Squad, law enforcers from J. Edgar Hoover's
> FBI on down to the local level in Chicago focused to an unhealthy
> degree on political dissidents, whose primary activity was advocacy
> though it sometimes spilled over into violence. Today the concern,
> prudent and not paranoid, is with ideologically motivated terrorism.
> The City does not want to resurrect the Red Squad. It wants to
> be able to keep tabs on incipient terrorist groups. New groups of po-
> litical extremists, believers in and advocates of violence, form daily
> around the world. If one forms in or migrates to Chicago, the de-
> cree renders the police helpless to do anything to protect the public
> against the day when the group decides to commit a terrorist act. Un-
> til the group goes beyond the advocacy of violence and begins prepa-
> ratory actions that might create reasonable suspicion of imminent
> criminal activity, the hands of the police are tied. And if the police
> have been forbidden to investigate until then, if the investigation can-
> not begin until the group is well on its way toward the commission of
> terrorist acts, the investigation may come too late to prevent the acts
> or to identify the perpetrators. If police get wind that a group of peo-
> ple have begun meeting and discussing the desirability of committing
> acts of violence in pursuit of an ideological agenda, a due regard for
> the public safety counsels allowing the police department to monitor

25. As I argue, with reference to the severe measures that Britain took against suspected
subversives during the dark days of World War II, in Richard A. Posner, *Overcoming Law* 167
(1995).

the statements of the group's members, to build a file, perhaps to plant an undercover agent.

All this the First Amendment permits (unless the motives of the police are improper or the methods forbidden by the Fourth Amendment or other provisions of federal or state law), but the decree forbids. The decree impedes efforts by the police to cope with the problems of today because earlier generations of police coped improperly with the problems of yesterday. Because of what the Red Squad did many years ago, today's Chicago police are fated unless the decree is modified to labor indefinitely under severe handicaps that other American police are free from. First Amendment rights are secure. But under the decree as written and interpreted, the public safety is insecure and the prerogatives of local government scorned. To continue federal judicial micromanagement of local investigations of domestic and international terrorist activities in Chicago is to undermine the federal system and to trifle with the public safety.[26]

Legal justice is a human creation rather than a divine gift, an instrument for promoting social welfare rather than a mandarin mystery, and as the conditions essential to that welfare change, so must the law change. Judges must not lose sight of rule-of-law values, which weigh in favor of reading statutes and constitutional provisions the way they were written, and are themselves pragmatic. But rarely are such provisions so clear in terms of context and history as well as semantics that urgent practical concerns cannot be accommodated by interpretation but only by refusing to enforce the law.

The Fourth Amendment prohibits unreasonable searches and seizures (including arrests). This is conventionally understood to mean that arrests and searches cannot lawfully be made without probable cause (reasonable probability) to believe that the person arrested has committed a crime or that the premises to be searched will turn up contraband or evidence of

26. Alliance to End Repression v. City of Chicago, 237 F.3d 799, 802 (7th Cir. 2001) (citations omitted). See Jess Bravin, "In Fight against Terrorism, City Police Face Dilemma— Striking a Balance between Aggressive Policing and Privacy Protections," *Wall Street Journal*, Nov. 5, 2001, p. A22. Years earlier, and on the basis of similar concerns, we had relaxed the restrictions that the same decree imposed on the FBI. See Alliance to End Repression v. City of Chicago, 742 F.2d 1007 (7th Cir. 1984) (en banc). In effect, we anticipated the recently issued guidelines expanding the FBI's authority to investigate potential terrorist activities. See Neil Lewis, "Ashcroft Permits F.B.I. to Monitor Internet and Public Activities," *New York Times* (national ed.), May 31, 2002, p. A18.

crime. That understanding is flawed. The word "unreasonable" invites a wide-ranging comparison between the benefits and costs of a search or seizure. For example, the more costly the search is to the person searched, and the less likely it is to unearth contraband or evidence of crime, the likelier it is to be found unreasonable. Using this sliding-scale approach, the courts have held that since a brief stop of a suspect for minimum questioning and a pat-down search is less intrusive (costly) than a full arrest, stops are permissible upon mere reasonable suspicion, understood to be a weaker ground than probable cause.

A further implication of the sliding-scale approach is that if the cost of a search or seizure is held constant, the level of suspicion required to justify the search or seizure should fall (to zero, in the limit, as we are about to see) as the magnitude of the crime under investigation rises, since the harm to society of failing to detect a crime is greater the graver the crime.[27] There is enough case support for such an interpretation of the Fourth Amendment to have emboldened me to suggest in a pre–September 11, 2001 opinion that "if the Indianapolis police had a credible tip that a car loaded with dynamite and driven by an unidentified terrorist was en route to downtown Indianapolis, they would not be violating the Constitution if they blocked all the roads to the downtown area even though this would amount to stopping thousands of drivers without suspecting any one of them of criminal activity."[28] Affirming the decision (which did not involve dynamite or terrorism, but a drug roadblock, which both my court and the Supreme Court held was unconstitutional), the Supreme Court remarked that, "as the Court of Appeals noted, the Fourth Amendment would almost certainly permit an appropriately tailored roadblock set up to thwart an imminent terrorist attack."[29] This is an example of pragmatic

27. The point can be clarified for some readers by stating the test for a reasonable search in algebraic terms. If C is the cost (in inconvenience, disruption of privacy, and fear) of the search, P the probability that the search will be fruitful in uncovering evidence of crime (or even in preventing a crime from being committed), and G the gravity of the crime, so that PG is the expected benefit of the search, then the search should be allowed if C < PG. Hence the lower C is, the less P need be to justify a search or seizure; this is the rationale for allowing brief stops on the basis of merely a reasonable suspicion. But, similarly, the higher G is, the less P need be to justify the search or seizure.

28. Edmond v. Goldsmith, 183 F.3d 659, 663 (7th Cir. 1999), affirmed under the name City of Indianapolis v. Edmond, 531 U.S. 32 (2000). "O.J. Simpson could benefit from a reasonable-doubt standard and exclusionary rules; but that is because he was not likely to incinerate Los Angeles after he was released." Holmes, note 1 above, at 13.

29. City of Indianapolis v. Edmond, note 28 above, at 45. To similar effect, see Florida v. J.L., 529 U.S. 266, 273–274 (2000): "We do not say, for example, that a report of a person

constitutional reasoning and also illustrates the consilience of pragmatic and economic analysis.[30]

Civil libertarians do not like the scope of civil liberties to vary with practical exigencies even when they are the exigencies of wartime. They worry that if liberties are curtailed in time of war or other national emergency the curtailment will act as a precedent in time of peace. They fear, in other words, a ratchet that will cause a secular decline in liberties. Better, it might seem, to leave them untouched, the law unmodified, and instead authorize the President or Congress to suspend their operation only for the duration of an emergency. But history, a valuable though not infallible source of data for pragmatic judgments, casts doubt on both the premise and the conclusion. The curtailment of civil liberties in the Civil War, World War I (and the ensuing "Red Scare"), World War II, and the Cold War did not outlast the emergencies, real or imagined (imagined, in the case of World War I and the Red Scare),[31] that called them into existence. When the emergencies ended, civil liberties were restored, and later they were enlarged. There was no ratchet; the only ratchet under consideration derives from the contention by civil libertarians that an expansion of liberties must never be reversed.

It is argued that unlike a real war, the war against terrorism will never end because international terrorism is acephalous and so there is no one authorized to end it. But the Cold War lasted more than four decades without permanently reducing the scope of civil liberties; it is impossible to say at this time whether there will be a substantial threat of international terrorism forty years from now. "Permanent emergency" does sound like an oxymoron; "protracted emergency" does not.

The history of American civil liberties in and out of wartime suggests, moreover, that there is no need to create a general power—presumably lodged in the President because responding effectively to emergencies requires unity of command—to suspend constitutional protections. Those protections are flexible, as we have seen, and anyway in times of national emergency Presidents have done what they thought necessary to do to

---

carrying a bomb need bear the indicia of reliability we demand for a report of a person carrying a firearm before the police can constitutionally conduct a frisk."

30. See Richard A. Posner, *Economic Analysis of Law* § 28.1, p. 748 (5th ed. 1998).

31. See Robert K. Murray, *Red Scare: A Study in National Hysteria, 1919–1920* (1955). Not that World War I was a merely "imagined" emergency, but that the efforts of radicals to obstruct U.S. participation in it were pretty feeble. I discuss some of those efforts in Chapter 10 in connection with Justice Holmes's free-speech opinions.

protect the nation, with scant regard for legality. Amending the Constitution to confer explicit authority on the President to suspend constitutional protections in emergency circumstances might actually be dangerous. Article 48 of the Weimar constitution authorized the President of the German Republic to suspend certain constitutional rights temporarily "if the public safety and order of the German Reich is seriously disturbed or endangered."[32] The sad fate of the Weimar Republic, to which Article 48 apparently contributed,[33] suggests that it is more prudent to recognize the executive's de facto authority to suspend constitutional guarantees in desperate situations than, by codifying that authority, to invite tests of its limits. That is why, despite the compelling pragmatic justifications for President Lincoln's action in suspending habeas corpus at the outset of the Civil War (among them that Congress, which clearly could have suspended habeas corpus and later did so, was not in session when he first suspended it), I lean to the view that his action was unconstitutional; as Sheffer puts it, the law of necessity suspended the enforcement of the Constitution.[34]

A further reason not to codify the "law of necessity" is that a true emergency, the only situation in which overriding the Constitution and the laws is justifiable, is almost always unanticipated; if anticipated, it could probably have been prevented. The best response to an unanticipated crisis cannot be selected in advance. An emergency-powers provision in the Constitution would be either uselessly vague or, if precise, likely to be cast aside, in the event of a genuine national emergency, as inadequate.

The concept of a national emergency adds poignancy to the discussion in Chapter 6 of one of the notably undemocratic rationales for empower-

32. David Dyzenhaus, *Legality and Legitimacy: Carl Schmitt, Hans Kelsen and Hermann Heller in Weimar* 33 (1997). The roots of Article 48 are in the Roman Republic, in which the temporary appointment of a dictator was authorized in times of emergency.

33. See id., ch. 1; Hans Mommsen, *The Rise and Fall of Weimar Democracy* 57 (1996); Karl Dietrich Bracher, *The German Dictatorship: The Origins, Structure, and Effects of National Socialism* 193 (1970). No doubt, however, it would be "error to ascribe the demolition of the German Republic to this single defective institution of emergency government." Rossiter, note 23 above, at 73.

34. See Chapter 7. The issue of Presidential suspension of habeas corpus, bound up as it is with the power to declare martial law, remains unresolved, although the Supreme Court in Ex parte Milligan, 71 U.S. 2, 124–127 (1866), rejected a *general* power to suspend constitutional protections in wartime by declaring martial law. The Constitution does not expressly empower Congress or the President to declare martial law, but power to do so has been held to be implicit in the grants of warmaking powers in both Article I and Article II. Ex parte Quirin, 317 U.S. 1, 29 (1942). *Milligan* suggests, however, that the procedural provisions of the Bill of Rights can be suspended only if, as a result of war or rebellion, the courts are closed. 71 U.S. at 126–127.

ing judges to invalidate statutes and executive action in the name of the Constitution—the need to check the transient passions of an ignorantly aroused public. The idea is that resisting those passions is a test of their strength; if they prove durable, the courts eventually back down. The problem with applying this idea to national emergencies is latent in the word "emergency." There isn't time. When thousands of Americans are killed in minutes, courts asked to invalidate police measures that curtail civil liberties can't responsibly take the position that they will block the measures for years in order to be able to determine the durability of the public support for them.

An issue much discussed in the wake of the September 11 attacks is whether it is constitutional for the President to create military tribunals to try foreign terrorists.[35] It is, if we are at "war" with these terrorists and they are illegal combatants, akin to spies, who if captured can lawfully be tried by such tribunals. That is the teaching of the *Quirin* case.[36] But if they are merely criminals, then we cannot be at war with them. The insistence of so many legal experts on seeking to discover from legal texts whether the September 11 terrorist attacks were acts of "war" or mere "crimes" attests to the hold that formalist thinking continues to exert over the legal imagination. From the standpoint of conventional legal analysis the attacks can be classified with equal facility as either war or crime, or both, or neither. The fallacy that blocks recognition of this simple point is the assumption that the word "war" denotes a natural kind or some other antecedent reality to which law must conform. Because "war" is nothing of the sort, because for present purposes it is merely a legal conclusion, the relevant question is not whether the September 11 attacks *were* acts of war but whether they should be *deemed* acts of war. The answer should depend on the consequences of answering it one way rather than the other. It is the same type of question the Allies faced at the end of World War II— not, had the Nazi leaders committed criminal violations of international law punishable by an ad hoc international tribunal, but should they be deemed to have committed such acts. Would that be the best approach to preventing a recrudescence of Nazism, preserving Allied unity, and serving other important values, and if so would these benefits outweigh the costs in impairment of rule-of-law values, such as the requirement of an impar-

35. For an excellent discussion, see Curtis A. Bradley and Jack L. Goldsmith, "The Constitutional Validity of Military Commissions," 5 *Green Bag* (2d ser.) 249 (2002).

36. See note 34 aabove.

tial tribunal[37] and the prohibition of criminal punishment for acts that were not criminal when they were committed?

The protests of civil libertarians against a temporary curtailment of some constitutional doctrines in recognition that the balance between individual liberty and public safety shifted in the wake of September 11 have been largely ineffectual for a reason central to this book: they have not been couched in pragmatic terms. It is futile to oppose eminently pragmatic concerns for the personal safety, the property, the prosperity, and the tranquillity of Americans with abstractions about civil liberties or recitations of slogans from Supreme Court opinions. There are pragmatic benefits to civil liberties; if there were not, America would be a police state. By emphasizing those benefits—such as preventing disaffection by minorities likely to be the particular targets of draconian police measures, discouraging police practices that may be ineffectual as well as brutal and may be motivated by private or political agendas unrelated to national security (a factor in *Korematsu*), economizing on the costs of achieving reasonable security, avoiding a mindless militarization of society, and, most important of all perhaps, preventing the growth of a Weimaresque *habit* of suspending constitutional rights in times of stress or fear—civil libertarians might make headway against people who want to shift the balance too far toward increased security in an anxious era; and there are always some of those.

But, in addition, if civil libertarianism is not to degenerate into dogma—if the American Civil Liberties Union and other civil-liberties groups are not to be relegated to the status of knee-jerk, one-dimensional pressure groups, like the environmental extremists who refuse as a matter of principle to consider any tradeoffs—civil libertarians must recognize the costs as well as benefits of the liberties they defend. This was signally *not* done in a speech that Supreme Court Justice William Brennan gave some years ago[38] and that the Brennan Center for Justice at New York University Law

37. The fact that the Nuremberg Tribunal acquitted some of the defendants did not make it impartial. It was a trial of the losers of a war by the winners.

38. William J. Brennan, Jr., "The Quest to Develop a Jurisprudence of Civil Liberties in Times of Security Crises," 18 *Israel Yearbook on Human Rights* 11 (1988). A careful study of the opinions, both majority and dissenting, of Justice Brennan and his faithful ally on the Supreme Court, Justice Thurgood Marshall, concludes that had they had their way, the government's ability to cope with crime would have been severely and unreasonably impaired. Craig M. Bradley and Joseph L. Hoffman, "'Be Careful What You Ask For': The 2000 Presidential Election, the U.S. Supreme Court, and the Law of Criminal Procedure," 76 *Indiana Law Journal* 889 (2001). Of particular note is Bradley and Hoffman's argument that the views of

School distributed in the wake of the September 11 attacks, mistakenly thinking the speech timely. The speech does not acknowledge that there has *ever* been a problem of national security in the United States that would have warranted the slightest modification in the expansive concept of civil liberties defended by Brennan. No distinction is made between the suspension of habeas corpus early in the Civil War, when the rebellion of the southern states was on the verge of success, or measures taken early in World War II, when again the nation seemed seriously endangered, from the measures taken during World War I and the Red Scare that followed, measures that should have been perceived as hysterical, or basely political, or both, at the time. Brennan's speech ignorantly derides the concern with Communist espionage and subversion in the early days of the Cold War as hysterical.[39] It evades the need to balance civil liberties against the public safety by refusing to acknowledge that the public safety has ever been threatened. As even the liberal journalist Nicholas Kristof acknowledges, "civil libertarians are . . . dishonest in refusing to acknowledge the trade-off between public security and individual freedom . . . as risks change, we who care about civil liberties need to realign balances between security and freedom.[40]

Lawyers' Hubris

I have been complaining that the lawyers who have expressed concern about the curtailment of civil liberties in response to the newly perceived dangers of international terrorism are failing to give due weight to the public-safety concerns that, along with considerations of liberty, determine the extent of our civil liberties. There is an even deeper problem,

---

these Justices concerning criminal procedure failed to evolve in light of relevant social changes, such as the increased professionalization of, and the increased minority representation in, the nation's police forces. Id. at 930–931.

39. "The Soviet Union's unrestrained espionage against the United States from 1942 to 1945 was of the type that a nation directs at any enemy state." John Earl Haynes and Harvey Klehr, *Venona: Decoding Soviet Espionage in America* 22 (1999). See also Allen Weinstein and Alexander Vassiliev, *The Haunted Wood: Soviet Espionage in America—The Stalin Era* (1999). The Communist Party of the U.S.A. was "a conspiracy financed by a hostile foreign power that recruited members for clandestine work, developed an elaborate underground apparatus, and used that apparatus to collaborate with espionage services of that power." Harvey Klehr, John Earl Haynes, and Fridrick Igorevich Firsov, *The Secret World of American Communism* 326 (1995).

40. Nicholas D. Kristof, "Liberal Reality Check," *New York Times* (national ed.), May 31, 2002, p. A25.

linked to lawyers' age-old assumption of omnicompetence, to what might be termed "lawyers' hubris." It is the idea—a residue of legal formalism and guild professionalism and the antithesis of legal pragmatism—that lawyers' training and experience equip them to determine what weight should be given to *any* factors, however arcane, technical, or otherwise remote from the knowledge and experience of a lawyer, that bear upon the optimal scope of legal rights and duties—equip them, therefore, to balance the liberty and security concerns that determine the extent of legally protected civil liberties. Legal professionals have much to say about the content of the legal doctrines that protect civil liberties, about the practical administration of those doctrines, about the values that are promoted by our current civil liberties, and about the costs of curtailing those liberties, but they cannot responsibly make *recommendations* concerning the appropriate scope of those liberties in the face of international terrorism because they have no expertise with regard to the other side of the balance, the security side. At most they may be able to make some purely procedural recommendations—for example, recommending sunset provisions for draconian laws or requirements of congressional concurrence with certain executive acts; these probably would not be very big sticks in the spokes. Judges have a greater but still limited capacity to strike the balance between liberty and security.

The problem is that of partial perspective and limited knowledge. Recall that one of the considerations bearing on the reasonableness of a search or seizure is the gravity of the crime under investigation. Anyone who is not a fanatic will acknowledge that if a terrorist with an atomic bomb in his knapsack were known to be at large in Manhattan, the permissible scope for searching and seizing would be very broad indeed. This is no longer a fanciful hypothetical. As Professor Ackerman, not one to exaggerate threats to national security, has written, next time the terrorists may strike with "an atomic bomb in a suitcase or a biotoxin in the water supply."[41] It is only a possibility, which distinguishes it from the case in which a terrorist is *known* to be at large with an atomic bomb. But in either case, the scope of lawful investigative activity depends on a balancing of the costs to liberty against the benefits in averting a disastrous attack. The benefits depend on the probability and consequences of the various possible forms of attack and on the likely efficacy of particular investigative efforts in reduc-

41. Bruce Ackerman, "Don't Panic," *London Review of Books*, Feb. 7, 2002, p. 15.

ing that probability. Legal thinkers can tell us about the costs, but unless they double as experts in national security they can tell us nothing about the benefits.

One can imagine a conference in which civil-liberties lawyers would explain the social costs of curtailing Fourth Amendment freedoms while experts on terrorism and national security would explain the benefits; and perhaps both groups would agree on where the balance should be struck. If not, at least the opposing views would be on the table and could be put before the courts, though one can imagine the judges throwing up their hands and pronouncing the question a "political" one.[42] One can also imagine the President refusing to be bound by a judicial decision that he thought seriously endangered national security.

The Fourth Amendment may seem the easiest case for my thesis because the word "unreasonable" fairly invites a balancing of liberty against security. It is merely the clearest case. Balancing pervades constitutional law. Freedom of speech, as we shall see in more detail in Chapter 10, is simply the point at which the benefits of such freedom are believed to equal the costs; and so we observe that all sorts of speech are lawfully punished, including defamation, incitement, unauthorized disclosure of military plans and movements, and blueprints for manufacturing weapons of mass destruction. Consider the Fifth Amendment's self-incrimination clause: stretched to the breaking point by judicial interpretation in order to encompass incriminating statements made out of court, it has also been arbitrarily narrowed to allow prosecutors to force criminal defendants to give voice exemplars and blood samples.[43] It could be further narrowed by interpretation to permit relay questioning, the administration of truth serums, sleep deprivation, and other third-degree methods of interrogation in emergency situations. Habeas corpus can be suspended by Congress in times of war, as we know; and we know too that whether what the nation is in today counts as "war" cannot be answered by looking in a book somewhere but only by balancing the pros and cons of such a classification. The right to a jury trial in a federal criminal case is guaranteed by both Article III of the Constitution and the Sixth Amendment. There are no exceptions in the text, but the Supreme Court has read in exceptions for petty of-

---

42. On the "political questions" doctrine of judicial abstention, see the next chapter.

43. See Michael Green, "The Paradox of Auxiliary Rights: The Privilege against Self-Incrimination and the Right to Keep and Bear Arms" (forthcoming in *Duke Law Journal*), discussed in the next chapter.

fenses, as well as for courts-martial and other military trials. The exceptions have a historical warrant; they reflect practice when the Constitution and Bill of Rights were written and ratified, and hence the likely understanding of the meaning that the framers and ratifiers ascribed to the constitutional guarantee of jury trial. But fidelity to original understandings of eighteenth-century terms is not the only or even the dominant method of interpreting the Constitution. If it were, the Bill of Rights would be construed much more narrowly than it is—all but the Second Amendment (the right to bear arms).

Korematsu and *Quirin* have never been overruled, and they can be dusted off and used as precedents for what could amount to a wholesale suspension of civil liberties. *Milligan* tugs the other way; but is that century-and-a-half-old precedent sacrosanct? George Fletcher says that "if the Supreme Court reads its own cases faithfully, it will uphold the rule in *Ex parte Milligan* and strike down the conviction [by a military tribunal] of anyone who should have been tried in federal court."[44] That is carrying stare decisis awfully far. Those nineteenth-century Justices did not anticipate suitcase atomic bombs; are we to be imprisoned by the limitations of human foresight? Professor Fletcher probably approves of the Supreme Court's having responded to technological innovation, in the form of the telephone, by reinterpreting "seizure" to include wiretapping even when it is done without committing a trespass.[45] Might not the Court with equal propriety reinterpret its precedents in response to the technological innovation represented by a suitcase atomic bomb?

Bruce Ackerman, while rightly warning against "pedantic respect for civil liberties,"[46] seeks to distinguish our security situation today from that in World War II. He says that "Hitler did not merely rail against Western decadence in propaganda films in the manner of Osama bin Laden," but "stood at the head of multimillion-man armies aiming for total conquest."[47] Even if this were accurate (it is not; Hitler had a multimillion-man military establishment but he did not have multimillion-man "armies," and bin Laden is not merely a propagandist), terrorists who succeeded, as Ackerman believes they might, in detonating an atomic bomb in

44. George Fletcher, "War and the Constitution: Bush's Military Tribunals Haven't Got a Leg to Stand On," *American Prospect*, Jan. 1, 2002, p. 26.

45. Katz v. United States, 389 U.S. 347 (1967).

46. Ackerman, note 41 above, at 15.

47. Id.

New York would be inflicting a loss comparable to what Hitler might have inflicted on the United States. Ackerman says that the measures taken to curtail civil liberties in the wake of September 11, measures he describes as "secret detentions; the destruction of attorney-client confidentiality; [and] military tribunals," are "utterly disproportionate to the limited state of emergency created by 11 September."[48] How can he be confident that they are disproportionate, or that the emergency is limited, when he considers the risk of a suitcase atomic bomb nontrivial?

Jack Balkin attributes the security measures criticized by his colleague Ackerman to "paranoia."[49] He ends with a flourish: "For what profit has a country if it shall control the whole world and lose its democratic soul?" This is rhetoric to make the pragmatist gag. Does Balkin think that there is no danger to the nation that would justify curtailing civil liberties, or just that the present danger is insufficient to justify any such curtailment? If the latter, on what basis has he made that judgment? He is a law professor not known for expertise in security matters.

Balkin's rhetorical question sounds another questionable theme. It is the idea that even the gravest threats to public safety do not justify curtailing civil liberties. What is meant is not that such threats do not justify establishing a police state, but that they do not even justify curtailing the civil liberties that the Supreme Court made up pretty much out of whole cloth in the 1960s and 1970s. It amounts to saying that America would not have been worth defending in the 1950s. In like vein, philosopher Judith Lichtenberg says that "if we abandon the moral high ground, we risk corrupting the standards that render our country worth defending."[50] Many things make our nation worth defending, such as the fact that we live here and want to continue living.

Compare Michael Dorf's argument that if it is true that terrorists imprisoned at our military base at Guantanamo Bay can never be repatriated without endangering the security of the United States, because unlike ordinary soldiers they do not cease to be dangerous when their country makes peace (they have no country, or even leader whom they are bound to obey), this is an argument for either treating them as unlawful combat-

48. Id.
49. Jack M. Balkin, "Using Our Fears to Justify a Power Grab," *Los Angeles Times*, Nov. 29, 2001, pt. 2, p. 15.
50. Judith Lichtenberg, "The Ethics of Retaliation," *Philosophy and Public Opinion Quarterly*, Fall 2001, pp. 4, 8.

ants who can be detained indefinitely or, if instead they are classified as prisoners of war, for narrowly defining "cessation of active hostilities."[51] Dorf makes no claim to be an expert on Islamic fanaticism, so if such an expert told him that he was wrong about the detainees—that if released they would abandon al Qaeda—and no other expert dissented, he probably would surrender his premise quickly enough. Similarly, one could hardly quarrel with Balkin if he said, "*If* the danger from refusing to curtail our civil liberties however slightly is as slight as I think, though I admit I have no expertise in the matter, then the Administration is indeed reacting in a paranoid manner to September 11." But that is not the tone of his article.

Harold Koh argues for trying bin Laden, should he ever be caught, in a regular U.S. criminal court.[52] He makes a number of points in support of his argument. They're fine as far as they go. What is missing is any discussion of the arguments against, arguments the evaluation of which requires expertise that law professors lack, such as that if you try an enemy leader in a regular civilian court before the enemy has been defeated, you deliver to your enemy a propaganda platform as well as invite the taking of hostages in an effort to spring the defendant. These and other points are made by a colleague of Koh, Ruth Wedgwood.[53] I do not know whether she is right, but she may be and I do not see on what basis Professor Koh could think his own view more likely to be correct than hers.

Koh and Wedgwood at least are specialists in international law; they have a handle on a significant part of the problem of how to respond to international terrorism, if not on the entirety of it. Jeffrey Rosen, who lacks their expertise, is nevertheless outspokenly critical of the government's detention of some 1,100 aliens suspected of connections with the terrorists.[54] He does not discuss the possible benefits of such detentions. Concerning eavesdropping on conversations between suspected terrorists and their lawyers, he does say that it will "bring little in the way of increased security" because "lawyers already can't help their clients commit new crimes, and they have an ethical obligation to report threats of terrorism or vio-

51. Michael Dorf, "What Is an 'Unlawful' Combatant and Why Does It Matter?" *Findlaw's Legal Commentary*, Jan. 23, 2002, http://writ.news.findlaw.com/dorf/20020123.html.

52. See, for example, Harold Hongju Koh, "We Have the Right Courts for Bin Laden," *New York Times* (late ed.), Nov. 23, 2001, p. A39; Koh, "The U.S. Can't Allow Justice to Be Another War Casualty," *Los Angeles Times*, Dec. 17, 2001, pt. 2, p. 11.

53. See Ruth Wedgwood, "The Case for Military Tribunals," *Wall Street Journal*, Dec. 3, 2001, p. A18.

54. Jeffrey Rosen, "Holding Pattern: Why Congress Must Stop Ashcroft's Alien Detentions," *New Republic*, Dec. 10, 2001, p. 16.

lence."[55] Yet he immediately backtracks, pointing to the "crime/fraud" exception to the attorney-client privilege: "if the government has probable cause to believe that a client is using a lawyer to advance an illegal scheme, it can get a court order or even set up a sting operation."[56] So apparently lawyers aren't that trustworthy after all. What Rosen's disagreement with the government comes down to is the difference between the criterion for eavesdropping in the new rule, which is "reasonable suspicion," and the criterion in the existing law, which is "probable cause." This is a shift (recall the discussion of the application of the Fourth Amendment to brief stops versus full arrests), but a slight one. Might it not be justified by the fact that terrorists are a more dangerous type of criminal than the types that the framers of the existing law had in mind?

Anne-Marie Slaughter is one of the relatively few lawyers who believe that al Qaeda terrorists should be tried before international tribunals. She says that "if the public relations war is as important as the military war, as our allies and the administration insist, such trials [trials before military tribunals] would give the enemy a victory of enormous proportions."[57] Despite the "if," one senses no real doubt on her part. She adds that "military executions of convicted terrorists after such trials will create a new generation of martyrs."[58] They will "dignify terrorists as soldiers in Islam's war against America."[59] These are not legal points. They are hypotheses about foreign, primarily Muslim, public opinion—not an area of Professor Slaughter's expertise.[60]

And yet, anent martyrs, one good argument against criminalizing the burning of the American flag is that to do so would create "martyrs" (figurative not literal)—people who by risking prison to burn the American flag demonstrated the depth of their anti-Americanism. To say it's a good argument is to say one knows something about martyrs, after all. But

55. Id. at 17.
56. Id.
57. Anne-Marie Slaughter, "Al Qaeda Should Be Tried before the World," *New York Times* (national ed.), Nov. 17, 2001, p. A23. See also Anne-Marie Slaughter, "Tougher Than Terror: To Fight Criminal Terrorism, We Need to Strengthen Our Domestic and Global System of Criminal Justice, Not Terrorize It," *American Prospect*, Jan. 28, 2002, p. 22.
58. Slaughter, "Al Qaeda Should Be Tried before the World," note 57 above, at A23.
59. Id.
60. In her article in *American Prospect*, note 57 above, Slaughter instances the international collaboration in combating the illegal trade in drugs, women and children, arms, and money laundering as a model for how to deal with international terrorism. But all are examples of signal failures.

it is one thing for American lawyers to make a judgment about American "martyrs" in America, another for them to make a judgment about Islamic martyrs. Not that such a judgment is impossible; but it requires knowing a great deal about an alien culture.

Ronald Dworkin, in opposing military tribunals, notes that they are opposed not only by liberals but also by some conservatives. The only ones he mentions, however, are William Safire, the columnist, and Bob Barr, a Congressman, neither an expert on the terrorist threat.[61] Dworkin rejects the idea that the scope of Americans' civil liberties should be determined by balancing the competing interests. Yet as we know he acknowledges that the consequences of those liberties for public safety cannot be ignored.[62] But he proceeds to ignore them when he urges that "no conversations between a prisoner and his lawyer be monitored unless not only the attorney general but an independent judge has been satisfied that allowing such conversations to be private would jeopardize the lives of others."[63] This could not be shown without the evidence of the conversations themselves. Dworkin to his credit does not claim to know anything more than the average newspaper reader about the magnitude of the terrorist threat and the best methods of meeting it. But not knowing more, he is in no position to justify his opposition to the measures proposed or adopted by the government.

It would be nice if one could economize on the costs of decision by substituting a decisional method that did not require judges and lawyers to know so much. That is not feasible in the present context, given the fearful consequences that may ensue from underestimating the dangers that rigid adherence to the existing scope of our civil liberties poses to public safety. Suppose there were a 100 percent probability that unless prevented, a terrorist known to be at loose in Manhattan would explode a nuclear bomb. No sane person would balk at abandonment of the conventional limitations on the power to search and seize and the power to extract information from suspects and even bystanders. Would he refuse to countenance an exception for a lesser threat to public safety? If the probability were 99 percent rather than 100 percent, could he sanely adhere to that position? Eventually a rule and exception approach would dissolve into balancing,

61. Dworkin, note 7 above, at 44.
62. Id. at 47, quoted in note 7 above.
63. Id. at 49.

and disagreement would shrink to differing assessments of the risks and harms.

But isn't it *always* the case that law is a balancing act involving interests or consequences many of which are beyond the scope of a lawyer's training or experience? Isn't that as true of the law of medical malpractice, say, as of the law of criminal rights and military tribunals? The law is ultimately public policy and policy should be based on facts rather than on points of law, so lawyers and judges have to balance concrete interests drawn from the real world, as indeed I have been arguing that they should. This is hardly a counsel of complacency. It implies, rather, that lawyers' hubris is a menace in *many* fields of law, not just in those that abut on national security. Legal thinkers have to pay more attention to the facts and to other practical, empirical considerations bearing on legal policy than they do. This insight has powered the growth of interdisciplinary legal studies.

But there are differences across areas of the law in (1) the difficulty of estimating consequences and (2) the risk of erroneous estimation. Let me take the second point first. Risks of legal error need not be symmetrically distributed. The requirement of proving guilt of a crime beyond a reasonable doubt implicitly weights the risk of erroneous conviction more heavily than the risk of erroneous acquittal. Since no one is yet proposing a wholesale abrogation of civil liberties in response to the terrorist threat, the risk to the public safety of refusing to consider even the slightest curtailment of civil liberties probably outweighs the risk to liberty of curtailing civil liberties slightly.

The difficulty lawyers have estimating the dangers posed by international terrorism (the first point) is great for two reasons. One is the novelty of the particular dangers posed by the Islamicist terror movement. We do not have a rich body of experience to draw upon in deciding how to respond to those dangers. The other reason is the almost complete ignorance on the part of American lawyers of the culture, languages, politics, religion, and public opinion of the Muslim world.

But if lawyers are not equipped to formulate sound legal policy regarding international terrorism, who is? The President is, virtually by default. The relevant expertise, on which he can draw, is widely distributed both within and outside government, but often in a form that cannot easily be presented in a legal forum, and not only because of the need for secrecy. The President has unimpeded access to this expertise, has a wider range of advisers than any court, and can act much more rapidly than the courts and deploy a much greater array of weapons (in a quite literal sense). In times of crisis, moreover, it is natural to look to elected officials rather than to judges to choose the response. That is the democratic approach as well as the practical one.

Clinton v. Jones

A national emergency of a lesser but not trivial kind was presented by *Clinton v. Jones*,[64] where, the reader will recall from Chapter 6, the Supreme Court refused to give the President immunity during his term of office from being sued civilly for acts committed before he became President. The Court's notably unpragmatic decision overlooked the potentially disastrous effect of making the President defend himself in a sex case prosecuted by his political enemies. Not only is the decision increasingly criticized as being out of touch with reality; it has incited calls for appointing to the Court, the next time there is a vacancy, someone with more political experience than any of the present Justices has. The criticism and proposal attest to the importance of pragmatic thinking in American law.

"No man is above the law," the subtext of *Clinton v. Jones*, is a good example of the inadequacy of substituting a legal abstraction for pragmatic analysis. It also provides an apt vehicle for the elaboration of my comments in Chapter 1 about the difference between pragmatic behavior and a pragmatic vocabulary. Read literally, the phrase seems to mean that no man, even the President, is exempt from any law; and this invites the question, why? When the phrase is read in light of its background and purpose, however, a different meaning emerges—that the President of the United States, although the head of state, is not the sovereign and so enjoys no *general* exemption from law.[65] This interpretation does not preclude such selective exemptions as may be necessary to enable the President to perform his duties effectively. In fact, the President already enjoys a selective exemption from the law—it is called official immunity and it exempts officials, not limited to the President, from liability to pay damages for wrongful acts, committed in the performance of their official duties, of a kind that nonofficials are fully liable for. The President's immunity is even more extensive than that of other federal officials because it is not forfeited even if the President is acting in bad faith.[66] The President is above the law

---

64. 520 U.S. 681 (1997).
65. See id. at 697 n. 24.
66. See id. at 692–694.

in another sense as well: he has plenary power to pardon federal crimi-nals,[67] probably including himself.[68] The issue in *Clinton v. Jones* was not whether the President is above the law but whether the temporary immu-nity that he sought was a sensible extension of the immunity that he al-ready had. That was a question that invited but did not receive a sensible, pragmatic answer.

"No man is above the law" is useless in a case like *Clinton v. Jones* but it is a perfectly good slogan, expressing as it does a fundamental difference be-tween our kind of republic and a monarchy or dictatorship. Like much else in our political vocabulary it is not couched in the language of pragmatism. It is abstract, aspirational, and makes no reference to consequences. Its meaning, however, is consistent with a pragmatic approach to the question of what legal privileges public officials should enjoy that private persons do not. It also illustrates the downside to moralistic rhetoric—the danger of being misled if one takes it literally.

The Court in *Clinton v. Jones* was not *entirely* blind to pragmatic issues. It considered the possibility that rejection of the immunity sought by Clinton would incite a flood of politically motivated suits against Presi-dents. It rejected the possibility on the unsatisfactory ground that there had been very few suits against Presidents in the past based on acts com-mitted before they took office. This overlooked both the fact that Ameri-can society is increasingly litigious and increasingly disrespectful of of-ficials and the effect of *Clinton v. Jones* itself in encouraging future litigation, since it removed a legal uncertainty that might have discouraged such suits.

What is worse is that in focusing on the effect of the decision on future litigation the Court overlooked the likely effect on the then-current Presi-dent. The everyday pragmatist, while concerned, as I have emphasized, with systemic consequences, such as the effect of a decision on the incen-tive for future litigation, is also concerned with immediate consequences and inclined therefore to consider carefully the unique features of the indi-vidual case. What was unique about the suit by Paula Jones that the Presi-dent sought to shelve until his term was over was that it was a sex case (and moreover a sex case incited by the President's political enemies, some of whom could fairly be described as rabid), and the defendant's sex life is

---

67. U.S. Const. art. II, § 2, cl. 1.

68. See Richard A. Posner, *An Affair of State: The Investigation, Impeachment, and Trial of President Clinton* 108 (1999).

quite likely to be explored in such a case. A President's extramarital sex life is a politically explosive subject. Recognition of this fact should have been at the center of the Court's consideration, even though it was a fact without orthodox legal significance.

Clinton v. Jones and *Bush v. Gore* make a nice pair of bookends. In hindsight it is apparent that the Court failed to decide *Clinton v. Jones* pragmatically and as a result condemned the nation to a political crisis, the kind of thing that, as we shall see in the next chapter, *Bush v. Gore* may have (we shall never know for sure) headed off. Had the Court given Clinton the temporary immunity that he sought, he would not have been deposed by Paula Jones's lawyers; he therefore would not have had occasion to commit perjury and other obstructions of justice; the independent counsel would not have investigated the President's affair with Monica Lewinsky; there would have been no impeachment by the House of Representatives, no trial in the Senate, and no repercussions from the impeachment and trial in the 1998 midterm election and the 2000 Presidential election. The nation would have been spared a riveting but distracting political drama that impaired (though, I argued, not critically) Clinton's ability to govern effectively for the last two years of his term as well as subjecting a number of persons to enormous embarrassment and staggering legal expenses.

But to give Clinton his immunity the Court might have had to embrace pragmatic jurisprudence explicitly. The immunity he was seeking had no constitutional, statutory, or case-law pedigree; it had nothing going for it except pragmatic considerations. The creation of the immunity might have been perceived, though erroneously I have argued, as an offense against one of the most powerful formalist slogans—that no man is above the law. And it would have required treating seemingly like cases unlike, another dig in the ribs of the rule of law. For a *blanket* immunity would have made little sense. Suppose the President had had business dealings before he became President and at the outset of his term was sued by a former partner for breach of contract. It would be hard to argue with a straight face that permitting the suit to go forward, rather than freezing it for as long as eight years, would interfere seriously with the President's ability to do his job. To be persuasive, a decision in favor of Clinton would have had to distinguish between an ordinary civil case and a sex case and confine the immunity to the latter kind of case, somehow defined. Such a distinction would have been criticized as making sexual-harassment plaintiffs second-class legal citizens.

A defensible pragmatic opinion could have been written granting the President a temporary immunity limited to cases likely to interfere with his performance of his role as President, a category illustrated by but not necessarily exhausted in cases of sexual harassment. But it would have been a difficult opinion to write because the current Supreme Court Justices are wedded to formalist rhetoric, are afraid that their publicly embracing pragmatic adjudication would erode their authority, and as a result have failed to develop the rhetorical tools required for articulating a pragmatic approach. (And they got no help from the President's lawyers, whose arguments were formalistic.) This failure got them into trouble in *Bush v. Gore*, a pragmatic decision lacking an expressed pragmatic rationale.

Another alternative in *Clinton v. Jones* would have been to reject the President's claim of immunity but instruct the district court to try to resolve the case before making Clinton submit to being deposed. For later it turned out that the case could be, and it was, decided on the ground that even if Clinton had done all that Jones alleged, she had not suffered a sufficient injury to maintain a suit. To that ground Clinton's deposition was irrelevant. However, for the Supreme Court to have instructed the district judge on how to manage the proceeding before her would have violated another shibboleth, that trial judges possess a broad discretion in the management of litigation; that appellate judges, especially the lofty Justices of the Supreme Court, do not meddle in the details of such management.

Clinton v. Jones might not have assumed the importance that it did, as a way station toward the impeachment of the President, had it not been for an earlier blunder (as it would seem to a pragmatist, at any rate) by the Supreme Court. In *Morrison v. Olson*,[69] the Court had upheld the constitutionality of the independent-counsel law under which Kenneth Starr would later use Clinton's perjury in Paula Jones's case as the fulcrum of the investigation that led eventually to the impeachment. The official under investigation by an independent counsel in the *Morrison* case was a subordinate official (an assistant attorney general), not the President. Had the Court confined its decision to subordinate officials, leaving for another day the question whether the independent-counsel statute could constitutionally be applied to the President, Starr might have backed off from enlarging the Whitewater investigation to encompass perjury and other obstructions of justice growing out of a sexual escapade. Indeed, there might

69. 487 U.S. 654 (1988).

have been no Whitewater investigation by an independent counsel had the constitutionality of such investigations been left open by the Court in the *Morrison* case. This is an illustration of the wisdom of the pragmatic principle suggested in Chapter 2 that cases should be decided on narrow grounds at the outset of the development of a new body of law.

CHAPTER NINE

Pragmatic Adjudication:
The Case of *Bush v. Gore*

❧

It is important not how people vote, but who counts the votes.[1]

I undertake a tough brief in this chapter—to defend pragmatic adjudication in the context of the most execrated modern decision of the Supreme Court, a decision widely and I think correctly regarded as defensible, if at all (which most critics of *Bush v. Gore* deny, some considering the decision not only manifestly unsound but actually corrupt),[2] as a pragmatic solution to a looming national crisis. *Bush v. Gore* is a perfect example of the class of cases, discussed in the preceding chapter, in which pragmatic considerations either have or should have determined the outcome.[3]

The Case[4]

Early in the morning of November 8, 2000, it became clear that the Presidential election would be determined by the winner of the popular vote in Florida and that the vote was so close that the Florida election statute re-

1. Joseph Stalin, as reported by Andrei Shleifer and Robert W. Vishny, "A Survey of Corporate Governance," 52 *Journal of Finance* 737, 751 (1997).

2. The charge of corruption is elaborated in Alan M. Dershowitz, *Supreme Injustice: How the High Court Hijacked Election 2000* (2001). Dershowitz and I debated this charge in "Dialogue: The Supreme Court and the 2000 Election," *Slate*, July 2–4, 6, 2001, http://slate.msn.com/?id=111313.

3. For background and commentary, see, for example, Richard A. Posner, *Breaking the Deadlock: The 2000 Election, the Constitution, and the Courts* (2001); Samuel Issacharoff, Pamela S. Karlan, and Richard H. Pildes, *When Elections Go Bad: The Law of Democracy and the Presidential Election of 2000* (rev. ed. 2001); *The Vote: Bush, Gore, and the Supreme Court* (Cass R. Sunstein and Richard A. Epstein eds. 2001).

4. Much detail is omitted from my summary of the case; it can be found in Posner, note 3 above, chs. 3–4.

quired a machine recount unless the loser didn't want it; and Gore did want it. So the ballots were run through the tabulating machinery again and when the recount was completed Bush's lead had shrunk from 1,782 votes to 327, though overseas absentee ballots had yet to be counted.

Florida's election statute entitles a candidate, after the machine recount, to demand that a county's election board recount by hand a sample of the ballots cast in the county. If the hand recount reveals an "error in the vote tabulation" that may have affected the outcome of the election, the board is authorized to undertake various remedial measures, including a hand recount of all the ballots cast in the county. Gore demanded the sample recount in four heavily Democratic counties (Miami-Dade, Palm Beach, Broward, and Volusia). These recounts revealed numerous instances in which voters, by not punching cleanly through the chad of a Presidential candidate,[5] had failed to cast a vote for the candidate that the tabulating machines would record. Gore then requested a full hand recount in each of the four counties. The request was granted by each county's election board and the full hand recounts began.

The election statute requires final submission of the county vote totals to the state division of elections within seven days of the election (with an exception for overseas ballots). Only Volusia County completed a full hand recount by then and so was able to include the results in the final vote totals that it submitted to the state election division. Katherine Harris, who as Florida's secretary of state was the state's highest election official, refused to extend the statutory deadline to enable the other three counties to submit their totals. She ruled that the deadline could be extended only in exigent circumstances, such as a natural disaster that interfered with vote counting or recounting, that were not present in the 2000 election.

The election statute neither sets forth grounds for an extension of the statutory deadline nor defines the key statutory phrase "error in the vote tabulation." Nor does it specify the criteria to be used in a hand recount to recover votes from ballots spoiled by voter error, although it does say that in the case of "damaged" or "defective" ballots a vote shall be recorded if

5. All but Volusia County (the smallest) used the much-criticized punchcard voting technology. The "chad" is the perforated area (usually rectangular) on the punchcard ballot, adjacent to each candidate's name, that the voter uses a stylus to punch out. The ballot is tabulated by being run through a computer that trains a light or other electromagnetic beam on the ballot and records a vote for the candidate whose chad has been punched out, permitting the beam to pass through the chad hole to the sensor that records the vote. See id., Introduction and ch. 2.

there is a "clear indication of the intent of the voter."[6] What the statute does do is authorize the state election officials both to interpret and to apply the statute. The head of the division of elections, Katherine Harris's subordinate Clayton Roberts, used his interpretive authority to rule that voter errors are not errors in the vote *tabulation* (just as Harris herself had used the interpretive authority conferred on her by the statute to limit the grounds for extending the statutory deadline for recounts). As a result, there was no legal basis for a full hand recount in any of the four counties, none of the county election boards having based its request for a waiver of the statutory deadline on a defect in the design, maintenance, or operation of the tabulating machines.

Had these rulings stood, Bush would on November 18, 2000, after the addition of the late-arriving overseas ballots to the total, have been declared the winner of the popular vote in Florida by 930 votes. But before this happened, Gore brought suit to extend the statutory deadline for counting the votes. He lost in the lower court. The judge ruled that Harris had not abused her discretion (the canonical standard for judicial review of administrative action—and a good example of Hans Kelsen's concept of law as a ladder of delegations) by refusing to extend the deadline. But on November 21 the Florida supreme court reversed the trial court and ordered the deadline extended to November 26. The court relied in significant part on a provision of the Florida constitution that states, though without mention of voting, that "all political power is inherent in the people." The court not only extended the deadline to a date of its choosing but ruled that in any recount conducted during the enlarged period ballots spoiled by voters should nevertheless be counted as valid votes as long as the voter's intended choice of candidate was discernible.

Within the extended deadline Broward County completed a full hand recount that produced many new votes for Gore. After inclusion of Broward's results, and other adjustments, Harris on November 26 proclaimed Bush the winner of the Florida popular vote by a meager 527 votes.

Florida's election statute authorizes the bringing of a suit to contest the election result certified by the secretary of state. One of the grounds for such a suit, and the only one relevant to the 2000 Presidential election, is that not all "legal votes," a term characteristically left undefined by the

6. Citations to these and other statutory (and constitutional) provisions, as well as to the various judicial decisions, may be found in id., ch. 3.

statute, had been recorded. Gore brought a contest suit, complaining principally about the Miami-Dade election board's having abandoned its hand recount because unable to complete it within even the court-extended deadline of November 26. He also contended that the results of the recount by the Palm Beach election board (which showed a net gain of either 176 or 215 votes for Gore—probably the former, but this has never been determined), which was completed only hours after the extended deadline expired, should have been included in the final vote totals. He further complained that the Palm Beach board had used too stringent a standard for recovering votes from voter-spoiled ballots. It had refused to count "dimpled" ballots[7] as votes unless the ballot showed at least three dimples, a pattern the board thought indicated that the voter had been trying to vote in this fashion, as distinguished from having dimpled a chad inadvertently or having failed to punch it all the way through because of a last-minute change of mind about voting for that candidate.

The trial judge found that the Miami-Dade board had not abused its discretion in deciding to abandon the recount, because there was no reason to think a fair hand recount would produce a large enough gain for Gore to make him the winner of the popular vote in the state. (In hindsight, the judge appears to have been correct.) The Palm Beach board's choice of criteria to use in its recount was not an abuse of discretion either. The trial had confirmed that the spoiled ballots were due to voter errors, or to errors in which the voter was at least complicit (for example, for failing to seek assistance from polling-place personnel if unable to punch through a chad because of chad buildup in the tray of the punchcard voting machine), rather than to errors in the design, maintenance, or operation of the tabulating machinery. The trial had also revealed that there was no agreed-upon standard in Florida law for when to record dimples as votes. Dimples had never previously been recorded as votes in a Florida election.

Meanwhile the Florida supreme court's decision of November 21 extending the deadline for submission of final county vote totals had been appealed to the U.S. Supreme Court. The Court agreed to hear the appeal and on December 4 handed down a unanimous decision vacating the Florida court's decision and sending the case back to that court for further consideration. The Court relied on Article II of the U.S. Constitution,

7. A dimpled ballot is one in which the chad, though indented or pierced, remains attached to the ballot at all four of the chad's corners.

which in section 1, clause 2 provides that a state shall appoint its Presidential electors in the manner directed by the state's legislature. The Court said it would violate this "manner directed" clause for a state court to usurp the legislature's prerogative of determining the criteria of appointment. The Court thought the Florida court might have done this in using the "all political power is inherent in the people" provision of the state constitution to support its decision overriding the judgments of the state election officials. But the Court wasn't sure and so it sent the case back to the Florida court for clarification that was not immediately forthcoming.

Eventually, on December 11, the Florida court issued its "clarifying" opinion. The opinion states that the decision of November 21 had actually been based on the "plain language" of the election statute, but does not explain why, if so, it had placed so much weight on the "people power" provision of the state constitution. Moreover, what the court seems to have meant by its reference to "plain language" was not, as in the usual understanding of the plain-meaning standard of statutory interpretation (see Chapter 2), that the language of the statute unequivocally supported its decision. What it meant rather was that the decision did no violence to the statute's language because the language was vague. If it was vague, however—and it *was* vague—the court should have deferred to the interpretation of the state election officials. The fact that they were partisan Republicans did not disentitle them to the usual deference that reviewing courts grant to administrative decisions interpreting vague statutes that the administrative agency is responsible for enforcing. The Florida legislature had decided to make the secretary of state an elected official; elected officials are entitled to at least as much judicial deference as bureaucrats, and probably, because of their greater democratic legitimacy, more. And the election board in Miami-Dade County, which had decided to abandon its hand recount, was dominated by Democrats, not Republicans.

The trial judge's decision throwing out Gore's contest suit had also been issued on December 4 and on the 8th the Florida supreme court reversed, though this time by a vote of four to three (the November 21 decision had been unanimous). The court (which was rather jumping the gun, since it had not yet responded to the Supreme Court's request for clarification of its position) rejected the central thesis of the trial judge's decision. This was that the determination of whether the certified vote totals had excluded enough "legal votes" to change the outcome of the election was one for the state and local election officials to make, subject to judicial review only for abuse of discretion. The court ruled that the judgments of the election officials were entitled to *no* weight. This meant that the election outcome certified by the secretary of the state, even though it was the outcome produced by the court's own extension of the statutory deadline, had not been entitled to even a presumption of correctness in the contest proceeding. But if so, why had the court bothered to extend the deadline, thereby compressing the period for completion of the contest, including any further recount that a judgment in the contest suit might direct?

Unsatisfied that all "legal votes" had been counted, the state supreme court in its December 8 opinion (1) directed that the Palm Beach recount results, along with the partial results of the interrupted Miami-Dade recount, be added to the candidates' totals, a step that pushed Bush's lead below 200 votes; (2) ordered that all the undervoted ballots in the state, some 60,000, be recounted by hand, including the balance of the Miami-Dade ballots; but (3) directed that the recounting be done by judicial personnel throughout the state rather than by the county election boards or state election officials; (4) refused to establish criteria for recovering votes from spoiled ballots more specific than the intent of the voter; and (5) refused to authorize a recount of overvoted ballots. Those are ballots that contain votes or markings interpreted or interpretable as votes for more than one candidate for the same office. There were about 110,000 overvotes.

This decision the U.S. Supreme Court stayed the next day and reversed on December 12 in *Bush v. Gore*. A five-Justice majority (Rehnquist, O'Connor, Scalia, Kennedy, and Thomas) held that the recount order was a denial of the equal protection of the laws. The decision held that rulings (1), (2), (4), and (5) created arbitrary differences in the treatment of different voters' ballots. The normal remedy in such a case would be a remand to the lower court with instructions to purge its order of the unconstitutional features. Alternatively the Court might have specified the terms of a recount order that would satisfy the requirements of equal protection. Instead it declared that Florida law forbade resumption of the recount because it could not be completed by December 12. Of course not—the U.S. Supreme Court's decision was not issued until the night of December 12. With the recount killed, Bush's lead of 527 votes stood, making him the winner of Florida's electoral votes, and so, when the votes of the Electoral College were counted in January, of the Presidential election.

The significance of December 12 was that it was the "safe harbor" deadline under Title III of the U.S. Code, the Electoral Count Act, which is the statute that specifies the procedures for counting the electoral votes. Each state is to vote on December 18 and the votes are to be counted on January 6.[8] If a state appoints its electors by December 12, they cannot be challenged when Congress meets to count the electoral votes. The Florida supreme court's opinions in the election litigation had seemed to treat December 12 as the deadline for picking the state's electors, lest the pick be rejected by Congress. These intimations were the basis for the five-Justice majority's ruling in *Bush v. Gore* that as a matter of Florida law the recount could not resume.

Two Justices, Souter and Breyer, agreed that the recount order raised problems of equal protection that required a remedy but thought the proper remedy would be to send the case back to the Florida court for the design and conduct of a proper recount. Three of the Justices in the majority (Rehnquist, Scalia, and Thomas) opined that in addition to violating equal protection the recount order violated the "manner directed" clause of Article II of the Constitution. Souter and Breyer disagreed. The remaining Justices, Stevens and Ginsburg, disagreed that the recount order violated any constitutional provision.

A Potential Crisis Averted

What would have happened had the Supreme Court not resolved the election deadlock on December 12, 2000? This was and is unclear; but it is of vital concern to a pragmatic evaluation of the decision in *Bush v. Gore*. Here is a worst-case scenario that is by no means fantastic, or even highly improbable:

The recount is resumed on December 13, the Supreme Court having affirmed the Florida supreme court's order, and it results in a determination that Gore is the winner of the Florida popular vote. True, as I noted in Chapter 6, it now looks as if the recount would have confirmed Bush's victory. But that is on the assumption that it would have been conducted in as neutral and careful a fashion as the recount conducted by the National Opinion Research Center for a consortium of newspapers over a period of nine months. That is a heroic assumption, if only because of the extreme haste with which the real recount would have had to be conducted. That recount might well have given Gore the lead.

8. These dates are not specified in the Act. They happen to be the dates in 2000 picked out by the provisions of the Act that set forth the timetable for the decision stages specified in it.

Next in the worst-case scenario that I am sketching, the state supreme court holds that Gore has indeed won the election and directs Jeb Bush, the Governor of Florida, to certify that the votes of the electors pledged to Gore are the votes to be submitted to Congress. By now, however, because the statewide recount and judicial review of it could not be completed within a week, December 18 has come and gone. It is unclear whether electoral votes cast after that day can be counted at all, because the Constitution provides that all the electoral votes are to be cast on the same day, which in 2000 was December 18. Meanwhile the Florida legislature, dominated by Republicans, has appointed a slate of electors pledged to Bush. It has done that in reliance on a provision of the Electoral Count Act that authorizes the state legislature to select the electors if the normal state procedure (the popular election held on November 7) has failed to do so.

The Act provides that the newly elected Congress shall on its first day (January 6, in 2001) meet in joint session for the counting of the electoral votes, but that the two houses shall then meet separately to resolve any challenges to any of the electoral votes that the states have cast. (That is the nature of a bicameral legislature; the two houses vote separately.) The House is Republican, but the Senate is divided 50–50 and until January 20 the Democrats control it by virtue of the Vice President's authority to vote to break ties; for Gore retains his office until then. The Electoral Count Act provides that if the two houses cannot agree on the resolution of a dispute involving rival slates of electors—given the split control of Congress, a likely outcome in January 2001 had it not been for the Supreme Court's intervention—the electoral votes certified by the state governor shall be the ones counted. The Florida supreme court has ordered Jeb Bush to certify the Gore slate but he has balked and certified the George W. Bush slate instead. The court has responded by holding him in contempt and declaring his certification a nullity and the Gore slate the one legally certified by the governor. The governor remains defiant, so two slates of electors attempt to cast Florida's electoral votes.

The houses of Congress, being controlled by different parties, cannot agree on which slate to accept. Nor can the houses agree on what happens if *no* electoral votes from Florida are counted because the impasse remains unresolved. Does Gore win because he has a majority of the electoral votes that are counted, or does the fact that neither candidate has an absolute majority of those votes throw the election into the House of Representatives, where Bush would win? The Constitution is unclear, and the

Electoral Count Act silent, on the question. The U.S. Supreme Court refuses to intervene, invoking the "political questions" doctrine, pursuant to
which courts will refuse to resolve an issue if its resolution has been con-
fided to another branch of government and if it lacks the characteristics of
a justiciable controversy.[9] The Constitution puts the counting of electoral
votes in the hands of Congress with no hint of a judicial role and with no
indication of a standard that a court might use to resolve a dispute over
those votes.

On January 20, the deadlock still unresolved, an Acting President is appointed, probably Lawrence Summers, the Secretary of the Treasury.[10]
The order of appointment is Speaker of the House, President pro Tempore of the Senate, Secretary of State, and Secretary of the Treasury (there
is no need to dip further into the list, which goes on and on). But anyone
who accepts the appointment must resign his office, including membership in Congress in the case of the Speaker and the President pro Tempore. Neither the Speaker of the House (Hastert) nor the President pro
Tempore of the Senate (Thurmond) would be likely to accept the appointment under these conditions, the latter because his resignation from the
Senate would give control of the Senate to the Democrats. Madeleine
Albright, the Secretary of State, is ineligible for the appointment because
foreign-born.[11]

It is true that the scenario that leads to the appointment of Summers assumes that a Vice President has not been selected, since, if he has been, he
becomes Acting President.[12] But it is unlikely that a Vice President would
have been picked by January 20. The Twelfth Amendment provides that if
no candidate for Vice President receives a majority of electoral votes, the
Senate shall choose the Vice President—but to win, a candidate must receive a majority of the entire Senate, and the 50–50 split in the Senate
would prevent this. (The Vice President is not a member of the Senate,
and so he could not vote to break this tie.) And this is on the assumption
that it has somehow been resolved that neither candidate obtained a majority of the electoral votes, an issue itself likely to be deadlocked.

9. See Alexander M. Bickel, *The Least Dangerous Branch: The Supreme Court at the Bar of
Politics* 185–186 (2d ed. 1986); Posner, note 3 above, at 182–184.

10. See id. at 137–139.

11. In my book I expressed uncertainty over whether her ineligibility for the Presidency
would carry over to the position of Acting President, see id. at 138 n. 83, but I was wrong to
be uncertain. I had overlooked 3 U.S.C. § 19(e).

12. U.S. Const. amend. XX, § 3.

Who becomes Acting President is actually a detail from the standpoint of deciding who shall become President. No constitutional or statutory provision authorizes the appointment of an Acting Vice President, and so there would be no one to break Senate ties, making it unclear, therefore, how, or when, the deadlock over the Presidency would be resolved. Not a happy situation, all agree; and the significance of this fact for *Bush v. Gore* is at the heart of the issue of pragmatic adjudication raised by the Court's decision. Had the worst-case scenario that the decision averted come to pass, the forty-third President would have taken office after long delay, with no transition, with greatly impaired authority, perhaps amid unprecedented partisan bickering and bitterness, leaving a trail of poisonous suspicion of covert deals and corrupt maneuvers, and after an interregnum unsettling to the global and the U.S. domestic economy and possibly threatening to world peace.[13] How would the crisis over the Chinese seizure of our surveillance plane have been resolved by Acting President Summers? And would other hostile foreign powers or groups have tried to test us during the interregnum? Imagine if the terrorist attacks on the United States that occurred on September 11, 2001 had occurred on January 11 instead, amid acrimonious debate in Congress over who would be the next President.

The events of September 11 have another significance for the evaluation of *Bush v. Gore*. They show that bizarre catastrophes really can occur. A Presidential succession crisis may well have been as likely an occurrence, had the Supreme Court not intervened, as a terrorist attack that killed thousands of Americans in a matter of minutes.

A Pragmatic Donnybrook

The potential harm to the nation from allowing the 2000 Presidential election deadlock to drag on into and maybe even after January 2001 was the most arresting feature of *Bush v. Gore* from a pragmatic standpoint, but there were two other such features as well. One was the conflict of interest that all the Supreme Court Justices had in participating in the decision of

13. On essentially these grounds, William P. Marshall, "The Supreme Court, *Bush v. Gore*, and Rough Justice," 29 *Florida State University Law Review* 787, 796–809 (2001), concludes that the Supreme Court was right to take the case, though he argues that the Court should have affirmed the Florida supreme court. Yet an affirmance would have perpetuated the deadlock.

the case. Judges are not indifferent to who their colleagues and successors are likely to be, and the identity of the President is bound to make a difference—nowadays, given the dependence of Presidential candidates on the good will of the extremists in their parties, especially in appointments matters, probably a big difference—in the kind of person chosen to fill a vacancy on the Supreme Court. Presidents tend to propose and promulgate centrist policies but to throw a bone to the extreme wing of their party when it comes to appointments. The other feature of the litigation that posed a challenge to the pragmatist was the lack of an obvious handle in the Constitution for stopping the recount. These two features turn out to be related and I shall discuss them together.[14]

What significance should the Justices have given to the conflict of interest inherent in their deciding, in effect, who would be making, though subject of course to Senate confirmation, appointments to the Supreme Court during the next four years if any vacancies occurred? If the conservative Justices threw their weight behind Bush, as they did, they would be accused of partisanship, as they were, and the prestige and hence authority of the Supreme Court would suffer, as they have, though the damage seems unlikely to be great in the long run.

The damage would have been less had the conservative Justices managed to write a convincing opinion in defense of their position. Neither the per curiam majority opinion nor the concurring opinion of Chief Justice Rehnquist (joined by Scalia and Thomas) is convincing. The majority opinion adopts a ground (the equal protection clause of the Fourteenth Amendment) that is neither persuasive in itself nor consistent with the judicial philosophy of the conservative Justices, particularly the three just named, who joined the majority opinion without stated reservation while writing separately. Neither opinion discusses the pragmatic benefit of ending the deadlock, though without that benefit it is hard to see why the Supreme Court agreed to take the case (the Court's jurisdiction is discretionary), let alone why it decided it as it did. The Court's self-inflicted wound was deepened by Justice Scalia's action in writing an unconvincing opinion in support of the stay of the Florida supreme court's December 8 decision.[15] That action cast Scalia, the Justice praised by name along with

14. For a pragmatic analysis of *Bush v. Gore* that reaches a different conclusion from mine, see Ward Farnsworth, "'To Do a Great Right, Do a Little Wrong': A User's Guide to Judicial Lawlessness," 86 *Minnesota Law Review* 227 (2001).

15. It has been conjectured that Scalia was trying "to raise the costs to the median Jus-

Thomas during the Presidential campaign by Bush and denounced by name, again along with Thomas, by Gore as a "code word" for opposition to abortion rights, in the role of the ringleader of a conservative cabal determined to elect Bush. The wound was also deepened by the tone of the dissents, particularly Stevens's. Scalia should have realized that if there was no explanation accompanying the grant of the stay, the punches in Stevens's dissent would have landed on air. Observers would have assumed that the Court had reasons for what it did, and in time plausible reasons would have been conjectured.

Should the Justices have worried that future controversies over appointments to the Court would be embittered by the perceived partisanship of the decision? Probably not, if only because bitter confirmation battles are likely for other reasons—reasons connected to the inescapably pragmatic character of the Supreme Court's constitutional decisions. Pragmatic adjudication is concerned with consequences but does not in itself determine their weight or valence. It accepts that each judge will, within the bounds of permissible judicial discretion (that is, with due but not slavish regard for the rule-of-law virtues), cast his vote on the basis of personal values, temperament, unique life experiences, and ideology. Long before *Bush v. Gore*, it was understood that the law crafted by the Supreme Court, especially but not only when the Court is interpreting vague provisions of the Constitution, is not stabilized by text or precedent or the other tools of formalist judging. Supreme Court Justices have and exercise broad discretion, however much they deny it and pretend to be following the dictates of antecedently established principles traceable back to the constitutional text. *Bush v. Gore*, a notably pragmatic decision joined by several Justices of distinctly formalist pretensions (particularly Scalia and Thomas), is just a reminder of what we should have known all along: that pragmatism is the secret story of our courts, as it is of our entire political system. That is why ideology rather than competence is the focus of confirmation hearings for nominees to the Supreme Court.

Suppose that in deliberating over *Bush v. Gore* the conservative Justices,

---

tices—O'Connor and Kennedy—of defecting [from a tentative majority in favor of reversing the Florida supreme court] by publicizing that the stay had the support of five Justices." Michael Abramowicz and Maxwell L. Stearns, "Beyond Counting Votes: The Political Economy of *Bush v. Gore*," 54 *Vanderbilt Law Review* 1849, 1947 (2001). This is not a persuasive conjecture, as it was obvious that the stay, since it was issued by the Court rather than by an individual Justice, had the support of a majority of the Justices.

first setting aside as improper or trivial their interest in who might be filling any vacancy in the Court in the next four years, had decided that the
damage to the Court from a decision perceived as partisan would exceed
the damage to the nation from leaving the deadlock unresolved; would
that determination have justified them in refusing to intervene? I think it
would have, provided, however, that one distinguishes between the decision to grant certiorari, that is, to hear a case, and the decision of the case
on the merits. The Court's appellate jurisdiction is discretionary and by
tradition it gives no reasons for granting or denying certiorari; nor is there
a statute or regulation that limits or guides the Court's exercise of that discretion. The absence of legal standards fairly invites a pragmatic approach,
as Alexander Bickel argued.[16] Had the Court ducked the election crisis by
simply refusing to grant any of the petitions for certiorari that were filed in
the election litigation, it would not have been criticized as lawless or partisan, especially since—and this brings me to the third pragmatic issue presented by *Bush v. Gore*—the Constitution had to be stretched to provide a
remedy for Bush.

Once certiorari is granted, however, the Court should proceed to decide
a case without regard for the likely popularity of its decision. Not that
public opinion is irrelevant to law. The moral concerns that influence
many decisions are, at root, merely expressions of durable public opinion.
And no doubt in extreme cases, for example when the Court's very survival
is at stake, discretion may be the better part of valor and the correct pragmatic course to follow. But in general the courting of popularity by judges
is rightly destructive of public confidence in the courts. Ours is not a system of popular justice.

A hyperpragmatic question about *Bush v. Gore* may cast further light on
the degree to which pragmatic adjudication is open-ended. Had one of the
conservative Justices believed that Bush would be a much better President
than Gore, would that have justified him or her in voting to stop the
Florida recount? The answer is no.[17] The systemic consequences of allowing partisan politics to influence Supreme Court decisions would be worse
than the harm of having to put up with a bad President, of whom we have

16. Bickel, note 9 above, at 126–127, 132. He did not use the word "pragmatic," preferring
instead to speak of principle leavened with prudence, but it comes to much the same thing as
pragmatism.
17. Under *American* conditions—for the answer might have been different in Germany in
January 1933, if judicial intervention could have prevented Hitler's being appointed Chancellor.

had many. Justices who thought it a part of their job description to over-turn an election in order to annul a bad choice by the electorate would be deranging the balance of powers among the branches of government.

If this analysis is correct, it suggests that a sound theory of pragmatic adjudication will incorporate elements of "rule pragmatism," that is, will rule *completely* out of bounds for judges certain consequential consider-ations. This is implicit in the rules forbidding judges to sit in cases in which they have a financial interest: the financial implications of a decision for the judge are among the consequences of adjudication that judges are—rightly—*never* permitted to consider.[18]

But that is too easy a case; for we must distinguish between the personal and the social consequences of a judicial decision. Allowing the judge to base decision on the financial consequences for himself, his family, or his friends could not possibly have beneficial social (that is, overall) conse-quences. It would be inconsistent, therefore, with a judicial goal of so de-ciding cases as to bring about the best such consequences. But the possibil-ity that a decision based on political considerations, such as a preference for one Presidential candidate over another, could have beneficial social consequences cannot be excluded. Ronald Dworkin argues that this ac-knowledgment makes pragmatic adjudication "a hybrid process in which judges decide by assessing consequences, case by case, but adopt a rule that requires them to leave the most important consequences out."[19] By "the most important consequences" he means, with reference to *Bush v. Gore*, which of the candidates would make the better President.

There are differences, however, between judges' weighing that conse-quence and judges' weighing the claims of an orderly Presidential succes-sion. For one thing, judges do not have the information they would need in order to be able to predict with any confidence which candidate would make the better President. Probably no one has. (Think of how many Gore voters were relieved after the terrorist attacks of September 11, 2001, that Bush rather than Gore was President; or how often Presidents

18. Well, almost never—which is a warning against legal generalizations, few of which hold without exception. Under the "rule of necessity," judges may sit in cases from which they would otherwise be disqualified if no other judges are available to decide the case. The preceding footnote provides another reason for thinking that "almost never" rather than "never" is the correct answer to any proposal for limiting the considerations to which a prag-matic judge can attend.

19. Ronald Dworkin, "Introduction," in *A Badly Flawed Election: Debating* Bush v. Gore, *the Supreme Court and American Democracy* 1, 40 (Ronald Dworkin ed. 2002).

with splendid credentials, like the Adamses, Grant, Wilson, and Hoover, fizzle, while those of modest promise, such as Truman and Reagan, perform with unexpected success and distinction.) Knowing the absurdity of the Justices' setting themselves up as President pickers, the public would be understandably outraged to discover that judges had based their decision in *Bush v. Gore* on their view of which candidate would make the better President.[20] And anyway if the Presidential election is a toss-up, which is the only situation in which a decision by the Supreme Court would be likely to determine the outcome, this probably means that there isn't much to choose between the two candidates, ex ante. In contrast, judges can make a responsible though not precise assessment of the likelihood and gravity of a Presidential succession crisis, since these things depend in significant part on the complex legal rules applicable to a Presidential electoral deadlock.

More important is the point stressed in Chapter 2—the division of labor among the different institutions of government. Judges interpret and apply (and sometimes create) law, but the electorate, through its selection of the Presidential electors, picks the President. There is nothing unpragmatic in an official's staying within the bounds of his authority—quite the contrary—unless the consequences are catastrophic.

Another way to put this is that the adverse consequences of taking account of a particular *type* of consequence, such as which candidate might make the better President, are among the consequences that a pragmatic judge will weigh in deciding a case. Even so, it can be argued that before deciding that those consequences outweigh the consequences of the inferior candidate's becoming President, the judge must estimate the latter consequences as well. Suppose the socially beneficial consequences of deciding *Bush v. Gore* in a way that eliminates a potential Presidential succession crisis (that is, deciding for Bush) are 10, the adverse consequences of allowing the judges' preferences between the candidates to determine the outcome of a case are 12, but the adverse consequences of having Bush as President would be 25. Then a decision in favor of Gore, though partisan in motivation, would have the best overall consequences (because 25 is greater than 10 plus 12).

20. Notice that I do not say that the people would be outraged by the undemocratic character of the Court's choosing the President, since I am assuming that the Court would be making the choice only in a case in which the electoral process had produced what was, for all intents and purposes, a tie.

Such an approach might have made sense in the Weimar Republic on the eve of Hitler's appointment as Chancellor, but in our situation it would be a mistake for the reasons I have indicated. It is better that the judges deem the candidates of equal merit. Of course, any Supreme Court Justice who voted for President in 2000 must have had *some* preference for one of the candidates, but it is possible to have a preference yet not think it's the sort of thing one should act on.

Dworkin wants to fit pragmatic adjudication into a philosophical framework, thus blurring the distinction central to this book between philosophical and everyday pragmatism. Pragmatism for Dworkin is a species of consequentialism, like utilitarianism: a judicial decision is justified on pragmatic grounds by being shown to have the best overall consequences, and so all the consequences must somehow be considered and weighed. But everyday pragmatism, as we saw in Chapter 2, is not consequentialist. (Neither are most versions of philosophical pragmatism, but that is a story for another day.) It has regard for consequences, because they are important to any practical decision, but it is not bound to a norm of consequentialism. A judge, as I explained in that chapter, might reject an outcome that he thought would produce the best consequences because he thought it would so outrage public sensibilities that it would not be accepted as valid law. His decision could be redescribed in consequentialist terms, with the outrage one of the consequences, but no purpose would be served by such a redescription; it would just make the judge's decision seem more mechanical than it was. The everyday pragmatist's criterion of a sound decision is that it be the most reasonable decision that the judges can come up with in the circumstances; and truncating inquiry can be eminently reasonable.

Another reason not to equate pragmatism to consequentialism is that judges must decide cases even when the consequences are incommensurable in the sense that weights cannot be attached to them. A paper by Michael Green underscores this point.[21] He points out that the privilege against self-incrimination, the purpose of which is to enable a criminal suspect to refuse to cooperate with the inquiry into his guilt, has no logical stopping point; it would with equal logic support a refusal to provide a blood sample as to support a refusal to confess. The courts, however, have drawn a line between these two cases, holding that the blood sample can

21. Michael Green, "The Paradox of Auxiliary Rights: The Privilege against Self-Incrimination and the Right to Keep and Bear Arms" (forthcoming in *Duke Law Journal*).

be compelled but not the confession. The reason, Green argues persuasively, is simply that the judges don't want to make it too difficult to catch criminals. This is a pragmatic judgment, but only metaphorically can it be described as the product of a "weighing" of consequences, since the value of allowing people to refuse to cooperate with criminal investigations of them cannot be determined even approximately.

It is curious that Dworkin, who is well known for believing that judges should engage in moral and philosophical deliberation—that they should base decisions on principles, which he regards as having an entirely different character from policies, which he regards as the domain of utilitarian thinking (and thus of consequentialism)—insists that pragmatic decision-making must always be consequentialist in character. As I have been at pains to explain, nothing in pragmatism decrees that cost-benefit analysis or utility maximization or other consequentialist methods shall be the only legitimate method of making decisions. Practical deliberation, as Dworkin himself well knows, and indeed insists, cannot be so confined.[22] The classical pragmatic philosophers were not consequentialists; there is no reason their present-day avatars must be.

But now let me further complicate the issue of candidate preference in *Bush v. Gore* by supposing that the Justices, reasonably preferring one Presidential candidate to another, throw the decision that candidate's way but conceal their motives, thereby deflecting public indignation at the partisan character of the decision. If the concealment is effective, not only will there be no public indignation, thus removing one weight from the scales, but if the Justices are right about which candidate is superior and the other factors bearing on their decision are evenly balanced, the relative merit of the candidates may seem to tip the scales decisively in favor of the candidate whom the Justices prefer. But I think they would still be unpragmatic to base decision on their opinion of the candidates. The affront to the principle of corrective justice, a central tenet of which, as seen in Chapter 7, is that a litigant's personal deservingness is not a permissible ground for a decision in his favor, would be too great. The use of personal factors even just as tie-breakers would invite judges to stray far outside the boundaries of warranted confidence in their judgments. It would complicate litigation, dangerously enlarge judicial discretion, foster nepotism and clientalism, and undermine the law's predictability. It would also destroy the public's

---

22. For an excellent treatment, see D. Wiggins, "Deliberation and Practical Reason," in *Practical Reasoning* 144 (Joseph Raz ed. 1978).

trust in the judges' neutrality, if we assume realistically that the secret would eventually out—the secret that the judges had based decision on partisan considerations and then tried to conceal what they had done.

Pragmatic adjudication is on surer ground, moreover, the less controversial the nondoctrinal values brought to bear on the adjudicative process are. It is one thing to decide a case on the basis of the public safety, or even the public concern with an unsettled Presidential succession—for both are concerns that are very widely shared—and another to decide the case on the basis that Bush would be a better President than Gore.

Rule application can be a pragmatic method of legal decisionmaking. Compare a standard that requires a judge to recuse himself from a case in which his impartiality could reasonably be questioned with a rule that he *must* recuse himself if he has a financial interest in the case, however slight. It would not be unpragmatic to prefer the rule to the standard, even though the consequence might be that an able and in fact impartial judge had to recuse himself in favor of a less able and no more impartial one. Similarly, it would not be unpragmatic—in fact for all the reasons that I have given it would be eminently pragmatic—to prefer a rule that judges are not to consider who would be the better President in deciding a legal dispute over a deadlocked Presidential election to a standard that would permit judges to factor in that consideration. Nor would it be unpragmatic to refuse to recognize any but the most excruciatingly narrow exception to the rule, the kind of exception that might have spared Germany and the world from Hitler had a dispute arisen over the legality of his appointment as Chancellor in 1933.

But doesn't it miss the point to offer an elaborate pragmatic justification for not deciding cases on partisan grounds—the point simply being that it is *wrong* for judges to decide cases on such grounds? This is like the argument, to which I am actually sympathetic, that it misses the point to try to justify a rule against killing innocent people even when doing so would actually increase overall social welfare, on the ground that it would not *really* be a utility-maximizing policy because no official could be trusted with the power to make such tradeoffs. In both cases, and in many others that could be given, the moral repugnance to some course of action seems to precede, as it were, any utilitarian or pragmatic reason that can be given for it. And at this point pragmatism begins to seem scary, lacking any anchors in normal human feelings. But this is just another example of parallel vocabularies, the moralistic and the realistic. Neither has any priority; my goal is not to displace the former but to show that the basic rules and institutions of the American legal and political system are explicable in pragmatic terms. I am not interested in *why* we think it wrong for judges to base their decisions on partisan grounds; whether the origins are pragmatic or otherwise, there are consequences that can be evaluated pragmatically. I only want to show that it is not unpragmatic to disapprove of such decisions—provided that a tiny escape hatch remains (my Weimar example).

Between purely personal or partisan considerations on the one hand and the pragmatic concern with a looming national crisis on the other lies something that may help explain the outcome of *Bush v. Gore:* the choice between rival conceptions of democracy. The invocation by the Florida supreme court of the declaration in the state's constitution that "all political power is inherent in the people" in support of a desperate effort to make every vote count was redolent of Concept 1 democracy, with its strong emphasis on participation and the general will, and in a particularly uncompromising, almost Rousseauan form, while the Republicans' emphasis on procedural formality in voting was redolent of Concept 2 democracy. Remember that for Schumpeterians democracy is not an ideology of popular rule but simply the set of ground rules governing the competition for votes. Not that the Schumpeterian is indifferent to the content of those rules. But thinking of the electoral process on the model of a game or other contest, he has a lively sense of the importance of the rules being set *before* the game is played. In our political system the rules governing both federal and state electoral contests are fixed by state legislatures in advance of the election and administered by state officials. If the particular rules happen not to sort well with the ideological strivings of Concept 1 democrats and, specifically, fail to actualize the general will, that's too bad, or rather, to the dyed-in-the-wool Schumpeterian, that's fine. The essential point is that they be adhered to. So one can imagine conservative Justices siding with the Republicans not because they preferred Bush to Gore as President (though doubtless they did) but because of an instinctive aversion to Concept 1 democracy—an aversion that we have already observed in the reaction of these Justices to the ballot-access cases discussed in Chapter 6.

But how was that aversion to be translated into grounds of decision that would be accepted as legal grounds? Legal pragmatism doesn't permit a court to say that it is deciding a case one way rather than another because it is better so. That would be to ignore the constraints on judicial discretion that cluster under the rubric of the rule of law. There were two possible approaches the Court could take. The first, which was the one the majority embraced, was to reason that the recount ordered by the Florida supreme court would if carried out deny the equal protection of the laws, in violation of the Fourteenth Amendment, by making arbitrary distinctions among voters in the Florida Presidential election. Undervoted ballots would be recounted but not overvoted ones—the Florida court did not even try to give a reason for making *that* distinction among voters. And undervoters in Broward County (and perhaps other counties) would be treated more favorably than undervoters in Palm Beach County (and perhaps other counties) because the election board in Broward County had used a more liberal standard for recovering votes from undervoted ballots than the Palm Beach board had used. The recounts in those two counties had at least been completed. But the Florida supreme court declined to specify a uniform standard for the recount of the other 60,000 undervotes throughout the state that it was ordering, except the "voter's intent" standard, which is hopelessly vague when it comes to counting dimpled chads. The court made additional disparities inevitable by assigning the recounting to inexperienced personnel, by truncating the right of the candidates to make objections to the counters' decisions, and by imposing unrealistic deadlines, though understandably so in light of the looming December 12 safe-harbor deadline.

The recount order was farcical. But did it violate equal protection? The objection to supposing that it did is that while the recount would have been a farce, the election itself had been a farce in the same sense. It had been administered in an arbitrary manner that had produced large differences across and probably within counties in the percentage of ballots actually recorded as votes. The recount would probably not have produced a result closer to what a well-administered election would have produced; but it is difficult to say that it would have produced a worse result than the actual election produced. The underlying problem is the decentralization of election administration to the county and even the precinct level, which, along with a generally insouciant attitude on the part of election officials toward the details of election administration, causes arbitrary disparities in the likelihood that a person's vote will actually count. This problem had not previously been thought to rise to the level of a denial of equal protection, and, as I have said, the recount would not have aggravated the problem though it probably would not have ameliorated it either.

So if the recount was a denial of equal protection, the implication is that our system of decentralized election administration is a denial of equal protection too. Unwilling to embrace this far-reaching implication of its decision, the majority as much as said that the decision would have no precedential significance in future election litigation.[23] This made the opinion seem thoroughly unprincipled—and remember that pragmatists, too, believe in the value of the rule of law, one element of which is that rules, including rules laid down by courts in the course of deciding cases, should be general in application in order to minimize subjectivity, bias, and oppression. Likewise unprincipled was the remedy of stopping the recount. If the vice of the recount order was that its terms denied equal protection, the natural remedy would have been to direct the Florida supreme court to redo the order. To rule that Florida law, implicitly Florida case law (for there was nothing in the election statute on this point), forbade a recount after safe-harbor day was unprincipled too, because there was no relevant case law. There were, it is true, hints by the Florida supreme court that December 12 was indeed the deadline for any recounting, but these hints alluded not to any rule of Florida law but merely to judicial discretion to formulate an appropriate, and therefore a timely, remedy for the botched election.

The majority opinion must have been a particular embarrassment to the three most conservative Justices (Rehnquist, Scalia, and Thomas). For while it is not true that these Justices *never* support claims of denial of equal protection, they could not be expected to be sympathetic to a ground of decision that implied that the nation's traditionally decentralized election administration is unconstitutional. But here pragmatic considerations, though of a distinctly unedifying character, come into play again. Had these Justices refused to join the majority opinion, there would still have been a majority to stop the recount because these three Justices in their concurring opinion stated that the recount would violate Article

23. "Our consideration is limited to the present circumstances, for the problem of equal protection in election processes generally presents many complexities." Bush v. Gore, 531 U.S. 98, 109 (2000) (per curiam). It would be more precise to say that the particular Justices who joined the majority opinion do not intend to treat it as a precedent; they cannot prevent other Justices, including their successors, from doing so.

II. But now there would have been majorities to reject both grounds for stopping the recount. The three most conservative Justices plus Stevens and Ginsburg would have been voting to reject the equal protection ground, and all but the three most conservative Justices would have been voting to reject the Article II ground. The moral authority of the decision, at best limited because of the Justices' conflict of interest, would have been further weakened by the fact that a majority of the Justices had rejected the only available grounds for the decision.[24]

So did those three conservative Justices join an opinion they actually disagreed with? If they did, it would bring to the fore a disturbing feature of pragmatism, the "end justifies the means" sense that flavors some of the popular uses of the word. If the only things that matter to a decision are its consequences, then dishonesty—which might seem the right word for subscribing to a judicial opinion that one thinks all wrong—while no doubt regrettable, becomes just another factor in the decision calculus. But maybe this *is* the right way to think about judicial honesty or, more precisely, candor (for "honesty" has irrelevant financial connotations). A judge will often join an opinion with which he doesn't actually agree. He will do so because he doesn't think a dissent (or, what is functionally the same, a concurrence in the result but not in the majority opinion) will have any effect, or because he thinks a dissent would merely draw attention to a majority opinion otherwise likely to be ignored, or because, recognizing law's frequent indeterminacy, he lacks confidence that his view is sounder than that of his colleagues, or because he does not think the issue important enough to warrant the bother of writing a dissent and doesn't want to encourage other judges to dissent at the drop of a hat, or because he used the threat of dissent to obtain changes that made the majority opinion more palatable to him. These are pragmatic judgments, ones that I have made unapologetically a number of times in my own judicial career, and such judgments suffuse the writing of a judicial opinion as well, where tact and candor are frequent opponents. Are these bows to the practical to be regarded as tokens of a subtle form of corruption brought about by yielding to the pragmatic Sirens? If not, maybe the decision of the conservative Justices to join the majority opinion in *Bush v. Gore* is defensible even if they had to hold their noses to do so.

The Article II ground for stopping the recount was far stronger than the

24. See Abramowicz and Stearns, note 15 above, at 1933–1940.

equal protection ground, and the refusal of Justices O'Connor and Kennedy to adopt it strikes me as a failure of judicial statesmanship. Article II is explicit that the setting of the ground rules for the selection of a state's Presidential electors is the prerogative of the state's *legislature*. Granted, there is no indication that the choice of this word in lieu of "state" was deliberate or that the framers of the Constitution foresaw the use of Article II to limit the scope of state judicial intervention in the selection of a state's electors. But ever since the time of John Marshall, constitutional provisions have been treated more as resources than as commands, resources that judges use to craft solutions to problems the framers did not foresee. The problem at hand was a state court's intervening to (possibly) change the result of an election of the state's Presidential electors by changing the ground rules under which the election had been held. The intervention set the stage for an interbranch struggle within the state over the choice of the electors, and such a struggle would be likely to lead to the appointment of rival slates and hence to the kind of crisis that *Bush v. Gore* headed off. Article II interpreted as confirming the state legislature's prerogative in the determination of the ground rules for selecting a state's Presidential electors establishes a clear line of demarcation between the judicial and the legislative roles. By doing so it prevents state courts from hijacking an election by changing the rules after the outcome of the election is known.

The Article II ground has been criticized as implying that state courts have no power to interpret their state's election statute so far as bears on Presidential elections no matter how ambiguous or riddled with gaps the statute is, and no power to declare it unconstitutional no matter how blatantly its terms violate settled constitutional principles, whether federal or state. But that is not what the ground implies. The state courts retain their ordinary powers but the U.S. Supreme Court is authorized to intervene if, in the guise of interpretation, the state courts rewrite the state election law, usurping the legislature's authority. The difference between interpretive and usurpative judicial "work" on statutes is subtle, but is illuminated by comparison to the settled distinction in the law of labor arbitration between an arbitrator's interpreting a collective bargaining agreement, on the one hand, and, on the other, importing his own views of industrial justice in disregard of the agreement. The former is legitimate interpretation and is insulated from judicial review; the latter is usurpative and is forbidden. The distinction is not between interpretation and invention. Interpretation in the law is a spectrum running from narrow, literal, or strict at one end to broad, loose, or freewheeling at the other. Contracts are interpreted narrowly, vague constitutional provisions broadly. An arbitrator is constrained to narrow interpretation. He is not allowed to bring to bear his notions of industrial justice. Not because such background notions are foreign to interpretation, but because the scope of *his* interpretive authority is limited. Article II, section 1, clause 2 can reasonably be understood to constrain state courts similarly.

The interpretation that I have just sketched seemed to command the support of all nine Justices in the first opinion in the election litigation, that of December 4.[25] A unanimous decision by the Supreme Court may well be wrong, but it is unlikely to be so far wrong as to impair the Court's authority by making the Court a laughingstock. The issue that later divided the Justices was whether the Florida supreme court had stepped so far out of the line of the statute as to bring down the bar of Article II. That is a difficult issue, but, as I have argued elsewhere,[26] resolving it in favor of

25. "As a general rule, this Court defers to a state court's interpretation of a state statute. But in the case of a law enacted by a state legislature applicable not only to elections to state offices, but also to the election of Presidential electors, the legislature is not acting solely under the authority given it by the people of the State, but by virtue of a direct grant of authority made under Art. II, § 1, cl. 2, of the United States Constitution. That provision reads: 'Each State shall appoint, in such Manner as the Legislature thereof may direct, a Number of Electors, equal to the whole Number of Senators and Representatives to which the State may be entitled in the Congress . . .' Although we did not address the same question petitioner raises here, in *McPherson v. Blacker,* 146 U.S. 1, 25 (1892), we said: '[Art. II, § 1, cl. 2] does not read that the people or the citizens shall appoint, but that "each State shall"; and if the words "in such manner as the legislature thereof may direct," had been omitted, it would seem that the legislative power of appointment could not have been successfully questioned in the absence of any provision in the state constitution in that regard. Hence the insertion of those words, while operating as a limitation upon the State in respect of any attempt to circumscribe the legislative power, cannot be held to operate as a limitation on that power itself.' There are expressions in the opinion of the Supreme Court of Florida that may be read to indicate that it construed the Florida Election Code without regard to the extent to which the Florida Constitution could, consistent with Art. II, § 1, cl. 2, 'circumscribe the legislative power.' The opinion states, for example, that '[t]o the extent that the Legislature may enact laws regulating the electoral process, those laws are valid only if they impose no "unreasonable or unnecessary" restraints on the right of suffrage' guaranteed by the State Constitution. The opinion also states that 'because election laws are intended to facilitate the right of suffrage, such laws must be liberally construed in favor of the citizens' right to vote . . .'. . . After reviewing the opinion of the Florida Supreme Court, we find that there is considerable uncertainty as to the precise grounds for the decision . . . Specifically, we are unclear as to the extent to which the Florida Supreme Court saw the Florida Constitution as circumscribing the legislature's authority under Art. II, § 1, cl. 2." Bush v. Palm Beach County Canvassing Board, 531 U.S. 70, 76–78 (2000) (per curiam) (citations omitted).

26. Posner, note 3 above, chs. 2–3. For further elaboration of my views, see Richard A. Posner, "*Bush v. Gore*—Reply to Friedman," 29 *Florida State University Law Review* 871 (2001).

invalidating the Florida court's rulings and hence stopping the recount would have been a plausible application of Article II. A majority opinion so finding with emphasis on pragmatic factors would have been a defensible specimen of pragmatic adjudication.[27] Such an opinion could have been structured as follows: (1) a full description of the danger of a Presidential succession crisis, a danger inherent in the fact that neither the Constitution nor federal statutory or common law provides a mechanism for resolving a dispute over Presidential electors when the House and the Senate are controlled by different parties; (2) an explanation that the danger is particularly likely to materialize when a branch of state government, such as the judicial, changes the ground rules of the election after the election has been conducted, thus inciting another branch (the Florida legislature) to appoint its own slate of electors; and (3) a conclusion that Article II, section 1, clause 2 is a resource available to avert the succession crisis by preventing state courts (or, for that matter, other branches of state government) from revising the state's electoral code, whether in the guise of "interpretation" or otherwise, after the election.[28]

Such an opinion would have deprived critics of the Court of much of their ammunition. The Justices could not have been accused of betraying their settled convictions, because none of them had ever written or joined an opinion dealing with the "manner directed" clause of Article II, which was last (and first) before the Supreme Court in 1892,[29] and because views of the clause do not divide along "liberal" and "conservative" lines, as views of equal protection do. The Justices would have eluded other criticisms as well. The majority opinion would not have had to say that the decision had no precedential effect, because the ground of the decision would have had no implications for election administration generally. The Article II ground, being esoteric, would not have provided a handle for criticisms that the general public could understand. Formalists would have had to acknowledge that the ground had a textual basis in the word "legislature" in Article II. The ground could be persuasively related to the avoidance of the looming crisis. Overriding the Florida supreme court on the basis of Article II would not have been an affront to states' rights

27. See Posner, note 3 above, at 156–161.

28. The due process clause would provide an alternative constitutional grounding for this argument. "Stealing" an election by revising the rules after the election has taken place would be the equivalent of stuffing the ballot box and of other election frauds that deprive people of their right to vote.

29. McPherson v. Blacker, cited in note 25 above.

(which conservative Supreme Court Justices have tended to favor in recent years), since it would have been vindicating the authority of state legislatures. And there would have been no awkwardness in the remedy of stopping the recount, because if the recount order should never have been issued, rather than merely should have been configured differently, there would have been no occasion for a remand of the case to the Florida court rather than an outright reversal.

A decision based on Article II would have had the further advantage, just as giving Clinton the temporary immunity that he sought in the Paula Jones suit would have, of being unlikely to generate many consequences beyond the specific case. This is not only because Article II, section 1, clause 2 has a limited scope, but also because the problem to which it is addressed occurs so rarely. Virtually the only consequence of a decision based on that clause would have been to head off a looming national crisis. The decision could have been the poster child for pragmatic adjudication. A great opportunity was missed.

The Perils of Formalism

The failure of the majority in *Bush v. Gore* to adopt the Article II ground was a particular embarrassment for the Court's two most conservative Justices, Scalia and Thomas. For they had gone out of their way in opinions and (in Scalia's case) in speeches and articles to urge a concept of adjudication that is inconsistent with the majority opinion that they joined. *Bush v. Gore*'s severest critic, Alan Dershowitz, revels in being able to quote Scalia's statement that when he writes a majority opinion, he limits his freedom of action:

> If the next case should have such different facts that my political or policy preferences regarding the outcome are quite the opposite, I will be unable to indulge those preferences; I have committed myself to the governing principle. In the real world of appellate judging, it displays more judicial restraint to adopt such a course than to announce that, "on balance," we think the law was violated here—leaving ourselves free to say in the next case that, "on balance," it was not . . . Only by announcing rules do we hedge ourselves in.[30]

30. Antonin Scalia, "The Rule of Law as a Law of Rules," 56 *University of Chicago Law Review* 1175, 1179–1180 (1989), quoted in Dershowitz, note 2 above, at 123–124.

How does this square with the statement in the majority opinion in *Bush v. Gore*, which Scalia joined however reluctantly, that "our consideration is limited to the present circumstances, for the problem of equal protection in election processes generally presents many complexities?" It does not, thus inviting charges of hypocrisy, or worse—the charge of rank partisanship leveled against Scalia by Dershowitz on insufficient evidence but plausible enough to resonate with those Americans who already distrust the good faith of government officials.

The trouble Scalia got into with the passage I have just quoted illustrates the perils of formalism. Few American judges, especially at the higher levels of the judiciary, where indeterminacy characterizes so many of the important cases, are practicing formalists; and Scalia is not one of them. A judge who is not a formalist yet describes himself as one, who commits himself to principled adjudication and then joins an unprincipled opinion, opens himself to charges of hypocrisy. And if one thinks about it, the passage I quoted from Scalia shows formalism at its worst. He seems to be saying that a court should always adopt an inflexible rule in the first case to present an issue, refusing to modify the rule in the light of subsequent cases that involve new facts that may show that the rule was unsound, overbroad, too narrow, or premature. That doesn't sound like a sensible procedure, or one remotely descriptive of any actual Supreme Court Justice's practice.

One reason *Bush v. Gore* is so controversial in legal academic circles is that it suggests that at bottom *all* the Justices of the Supreme Court are pragmatists, albeit closeted ones. Pragmatism, especially of the everyday variety, the sense in which I am using the word to describe the Justices—not one of whom, I am pretty certain, has the slightest interest in philosophical pragmatism—is unpopular among legal academics because it implies that there is really nothing very special about legal reasoning. It is just practical reasoning applied to a particular class of disputes and dressed up in a special jargon. Law professors have to know the cases and statutes and other canonical materials that lawyers and judges refer to, have to know in other words how to talk the talk and walk the walk. But their knowledge and their rhetoric do not yield an understanding of how novel cases should be decided; for that, a pragmatic enterprise, the law professors would have to know a lot about the facts and politics of the particular case. They resist this conclusion, of course. Whether the majority and dissenting Justices in *Bush v. Gore* were motivated by partisan concerns, rival conceptions of democracy, or practical concerns about the consequences either of a botched Presidential succession or of the Supreme Court's deciding the election, none of their opinions can be explained by reference to "the law" in a sense that a conventional legal academic, as distinct from a committed Kelsenian, would recognize.

The Democratic Legitimacy of Pragmatic Adjudication Revisited

A crude but not entirely inaccurate description of *Bush v. Gore* is that the Supreme Court decided that the Court and not Congress, an elected body, should decide which Presidential candidate should become President. What a shocking idea—unelected, life-tenured judges selecting the President and doing so on pragmatic rather than doctrinal or interpretive or precedent-driven grounds! For while Article II supplied a plausible ground for stopping the Florida recount and thus in effect giving the Presidency to George W. Bush, it is persuasive only if great weight is given to pragmatic concerns with the consequences for political order and stability of allowing the selection of the President to be dragged out to the point where Congress would have to make the selection.

This defense of the result in *Bush v. Gore* should make us queasy, however, only if we think that Concept 1 democracy is the theory that should guide the Supreme Court in deciding election-law issues. Schumpeterians will challenge this proposition, and I have suggested that the conservative Justices may be unwitting Schumpeterians, though not consistently. The precise form in which the officials who rule the country are made responsive to public opinion and subjected to the forces of competition is not dictated by the theory of democracy. All that really matters is that the interests of the people be effectively represented in the councils of government and as a result that no official have anything like the power, discretion, and immunity enjoyed by old-fashioned monarchs and today by dictators. That the Supreme Court gets to pick the President every 200 years or so (the 2000 election was the first time this had happened) does not establish a dangerous divergence between public opinion and official will. (See the Gallup Poll figures cited below.)

The stakes in *Bush v. Gore* were as important to Concept 2 democrats as to Concept 1 democrats; they just pointed to the opposite result. Concept 2 democrats emphasize the very values of order, stability, and a smooth succession of officials that the decision in Bush's favor secured. And they doubt that Congress's selection of Gore, had it occurred, would have advanced democratic principles in other than an abstract, nonpragmatic sense. The popular vote and the Electoral College vote were alike too close to make a Bush victory undemocratic in a meaningful practical sense.

In criticism of *Bush v. Gore* and pragmatic adjudication more broadly, Ronald Dworkin states:

> Judges do not gain legitimacy from God or election or the will of the governed or their supposed pragmatic skill or inspired reasonableness. The sole ground of their legitimacy—the *sole* ground—is the discipline of argument: their institutional commitment to do nothing that they are not prepared to justify through arguments that satisfy, at once, two basic conditions. The first is sincerity. They must themselves believe, after searching self-examination, that these arguments justify what they do, and they must stand ready to do what the arguments justify in later, perhaps very different, cases as well, when their own personal preferences or politics are differently engaged. The second condition is transparency. The arguments they themselves find convincing must be exactly the arguments that they present to the professional and lay public in their opinions, in as much detail as is necessary to allow that public to judge the adequacy and future promise of those arguments for themselves.[31]

There is much that is questionable in this statement (which is a kind of bookend to the statement I quoted from Scalia), beginning with its failure to explain what is meant by "legitimacy." The word could mean public acceptance of judicial decisions or it could mean the conditions under which judicial decisions *should* be accepted by the public. Next one wonders why in a democratic culture the election of judges (many state judges are elected) would not confer legitimacy; and why, in a society the culture of which is pragmatic, the pragmatic reasonableness of the judges' decisions would not confer legitimacy either. If pragmatic reasonableness is what the people want of the judiciary, why is it illegitimate for the judiciary to give it to them?

As for sincerity and transparency, Dworkin must be aware of the consid-

---

31. Dworkin, note 19 above, at 54–55 (emphasis in original).

erable disingenuousness of many of the judicial opinions that he most admires, such as *Brown v. Board of Education*, which in order to spare the feelings of southerners pretended to pivot not on the evil of apartheid but on the supposed educational consequences of segregated schools as shown by inconclusive social-science research. If utter candor is a duty of judges as of no other public officials and if disingenuous judicial opinions are illegitimate, we have had a crisis of judicial legitimacy since *Marbury v. Madison*.

Where did we hear last about transparency? Why from Justice Scalia, when he said that a judge's public commitment to a principle announced in a case would make the judge unable to indulge his personal or political preferences in the next case. Scalia was talking in the first person. But we saw that in *Bush v. Gore* he slipped the reins of principle without comment. Judges whose decisions are subject to review by a higher court feel themselves bound by the principles announced by that court. These judges will often differ on how they interpret a principle and therefore on how tightly they are bound; but that the threat of reversal has some disciplining effect is undeniable. The Supreme Court is not subject to review by a higher court, and this greatly weakens its commitment to principles. This is the answer to those critics of pragmatism, like Dworkin, who fear that acknowledgment of the pragmatic character of adjudication would leave judges at large, permitting and indeed encouraging a wide-ranging discretion that would make law unpredictable and endanger unpopular litigants. That particular horse escaped from the barn long ago. Legal doctrine is something a court of last resort can always (well, almost always) get around and it will do so if the judges' feelings are sufficiently engaged. In this respect the pragmatist is no "worse" than the formalist, especially since, as I have emphasized throughout this book, the good pragmatic judge considers the maintenance of law's generality, neutrality, and predictability to be considerable social goods, rich in the pragmatic virtues. He may indeed give them greater weight than would a judge bent on doing "justice" come what may.

At least the pragmatic judge will not fool himself that he is the master of an esoteric art that enables judges to reason their way to the resolution of even the most difficult legal issues. He will recognize his ordinariness—will recognize that he has no pipeline to truth, that he is not Apollo's oracle and thus is not merely a transmitting medium relaying to the public decisions made elsewhere, and that he must take personal responsibility for his decisions rather than suppose them made in a heaven of Platonic legal forms. Who is more cocky—the dogmatist or the skeptic? Deprived of the self-confidence that comes from believing oneself in possession of truth-revealing expertise, the pragmatic judge will hesitate to wield his judicial authority with the true believer's relish and abandon. He will not always be a timid adjudicator. John Marshall was not. Circumstances configure the judicial role, and circumstances change. Formalism will be a pragmatic strategy in some circumstances, activism in others.

Coping with Indeterminacy

If law turns indeterminate in the pinch, as *Bush v. Gore* shows may happen, what if anything can be done to stabilize it? Legal thinkers as diverse as Carl Schmitt, Brian Simpson, and Stanley Fish have recognized, and the tension between Scalia's ostensible and actual judicial practice under-scores, that the quest for stability must focus on the judge, more particu-larly the judicial candidate, rather than on doctrine, interpretive theory, or judicial "philosophies." Schmitt, bizarrely and offensively by our stan-dards, thought that what German law needed was an ethnically homoge-neous legal profession, to be achieved by expelling all Jews from the pro-fession.[32] Echoing Savigny's concept of the *Volksgeist*, he claimed that every nation had a distinctive legal spirit, something that could not be cabined by rules; compliance with it required that the judges and the other mem-bers of the legal profession internalize it, so that it breathed through them. (He considered German Jews to be foreigners.) Simpson attributes the coherence of the English common law to the cultural homogeneity of the judges who created and administered it,[33] and Fish attributes such coherence as our law has to lawyers' professional culture.[34] The traits emphasized are distinct from professional competence. It is appropriate, therefore, for Senators who care about judicial outcomes to orient the confirmation process to nominees' ideology rather than just to their pro-fessional competence.

32. See William E. Scheuerman, *Carl Schmitt: The End of Law* 17, 126–128, 131 (1999).

33. Brian Simpson, "The Common Law and Legal Theory," in *Legal Theory and Common Law* 8 (William Twining ed. 1986).

34. Stanley Fish, *The Trouble with Principle* 295, 301–305 (1999); Fish, *There's No Such Thing as Free Speech and It's a Good Thing, Too* 225–230 (1994); Fish, "Almost Pragma-tism: Richard Posner's Jurisprudence," 57 *University of Chicago Law Review* 1447, 1463, 1473 (1990). But I do not agree with Fish's understanding of the professional culture. Richard A. Posner, *The Problematics of Moral and Legal Theory* 275–280 (1999).

Against the pragmatists Scalia has argued that "if the people come to believe that the Constitution is *not* a text like other texts; that it means, not what it says or what it was understood to mean, but what it *should* mean ... well, then, they will look for qualifications other than impartiality, judgment, and lawyerly acumen in those whom they select to interpret it."[35] I take issue with this argument in two respects. First, it describes as a future possibility what is a present reality and one to which Scalia's vote in *Bush v. Gore* and his opinion in support of the stay of the Florida supreme court's recount order contributed. Second, it assumes that a judge's allowing his ideology to influence his judicial behavior is inconsistent with impartiality, judgment, and lawyerly acumen. Obviously it is not inconsistent with the latter two attributes; but it is not inconsistent with impartiality either. Judicial impartiality is not the maintenance of a tabula rasa. It is the ability and willingness to set aside illegitimate considerations such as the personal attractiveness of the parties, their financial or familial relationship to the judge, or his own partisan preference. Ideology, in the sense of moral and political values that transcend the merely personal or partisan, is not an illegitimate, but an inescapable, feature of legal judgment, especially in the case of appellate courts, above all the Supreme Court. Does Justice Scalia think that his appointment to the Supreme Court by President Reagan was due *solely* to the opinion that the appointing authorities held of his impartiality, judgment, and lawyerly acumen, and not at all to his ideology?[36]

Although consideration of a judicial candidate's ideology by the appointing and confirming authorities is proper, the goal should not be to create a homogeneous judiciary, and not only for Deweyan reasons. Paradoxically, diversity is a surer route to stability in the conditions prevailing

35. Antonin Scalia, "Common-Law Courts in a Civil-Law System: The Role of United States Federal Courts in Interpreting the Constitution and Laws," in Antonin Scalia et al., *A Matter of Interpretation: Federal Courts and the Law* 3, 46–47 (1997) (emphases in original).

36. This is not intended as criticism. I consider Scalia's to have been a distinguished appointment. Nevertheless, I am in broad agreement with Terri Peretti's statement that "the ideological views anchoring and guiding [Scalia's] decisions were chosen by the elected politicians who selected him. President Reagan and a cooperative Senate knew precisely what they were getting with Scalia's appointment, and he has rarely surprised or disappointed them." Terri Jennings Peretti, "Does Judicial Independence Exist? The Lessons of Social Science Research," in *Judicial Independence at the Crossroads: An Interdisciplinary Approach* 103, 114 (Stephen B. Burbank and Barry Friedman eds. 2002). Peretti acknowledges that "Scalia's libertarian streak has revealed itself in some First Amendment cases. Probably topping the list of disappointments for conservatives are his opinions in the flag-burning cases." Id. at 126 n. 6. Other examples of "Scalia's libertarian streak" could be given, for example cases involving the Fourth Amendment (search and seizure) and the Sixth Amendment right of criminal defendants to confront the witnesses against them.

in the American legal system than homogeneity. American society is not homogeneous, and we are not about to make it so, as Schmitt might have wanted us to do. Nor are we about to strip the courts of their power to decide cases that are political rather than merely technical. In these circumstances a judiciary homogeneous in background, gender, ethnicity, and other factors that, realistically speaking, influence judgment on issues of high policy would be a disaster. It would be unrepresentative, blind to many important issues, adrift from the general culture, quite possibly extreme, and on all four counts deficient in authority and even legitimacy. The only practical means of stabilizing law in our system is, as I suggested in Chapter 3, to maintain a diverse judiciary, by analogy to stabilizing one's investment portfolio through diversification. This approach entails being realistic at the time of judicial nomination and confirmation about the likely course of the candidate's judging, a course that cannot be predicted from the disclaimers of "activism" that have become a routine part of the confirmation ritual. A diverse judiciary promises a degree of stability, predictability, and moderation—though the maintenance of judicial diversity depends on a regular alternation of Democratic and Republic Presidents, which of course cannot be assured.

Let me add that a diverse judiciary would *not* be a judiciary composed entirely of judges committed to legal pragmatism! The formalist (or quasi-formalist—I don't think full-bore formalism is remotely feasible at the level of the Supreme Court) brings something of value to the judicial table, namely a commitment to the rule-of-law virtues that is likely to be stronger than that of his pragmatic counterpart, a commitment that will help the court as a whole give proper weight to the systemic consequences of judicial decisions. Likely to be stronger but not certain to be so because the formalist's zeal to correct legal error, the concept of legal error being more vivid to him than to a pragmatist, may exceed his commitment to stare decisis and other continuity-enhancing dimensions of the rule of law. But even that zeal enlarges and diversifies the portfolio of judicial approaches.

Coming back for the last time to *Bush v. Gore*, I consider it at best a questionable decision, and at worst, especially if one focuses on the actual opinions and not on the best possible rationale for the decision, a very bad decision. But so what? Can't a bad decision be good? If these rhetorical questions sound paradoxical to the point of absurdity, consider Professor Sanford Levinson's recent avowal that "Marshall's opinion in *Marbury* [v.

Madison] is not more defensible than is the per curiam (or the concurrence) in *Bush v. Gore*," and he goes on to note very pertinently the elements of conflict of interest in Marshall's participation in *Marbury*.[37] But *Marbury* is a great decision, and Marshall the greatest Chief Justice in our history. As Levinson's deliberately provocative comparison brings out, the legal professoriat's criteria for good and bad decisions do not fit novel decisions, yet American law is to a great extent the residue of such decisions.

Could it be that constitutional law (and much other law as well) exists beyond right or wrong? Here is Professor Levinson again:

> Constitutional lawyers, whether practitioners, academics, or judges, seem to feel relatively few genuine constraints in [*sic*—he means "on"] the kinds of arguments they are willing to make or endorse. It is, I am confident, harder to recognize a "frivolous argument" in constitutional law than in any other area of legal analysis. Almost all constitutional analysts, as a matter of brute fact, seem committed to a de facto theory of "happy endings," whereby one's skills as a rhetorical manipulator of . . . the "modalities" of legal argument are devoted to achieving satisfying results.[38]

The Constitution's vagueness and age (now, not when *Marbury* was decided), and the political and social consequences and controversies that constitutional disputes produce, exert a pressure on judges that overwhelms their commitment to the mandarin values that shape professional as distinct from political critique of judicial behavior. It seems that a bad judge can be a great Justice of the Supreme Court, and a good judge an indifferent Justice.

I said that pragmatism is the secret story of our courts as of our political system in general and I shall end this chapter by noting that it is also the secret story of how Americans view the courts—which is not surprising if pragmatism in the everyday sense of the term that I am emphasizing is indeed the fundamental American political ideology. One might have sup-

---

37. Sanford Levinson, "*Bush v. Gore* and the French Revolution: A Tentative List of Some Early Lessons," *Law and Contemporary Problems*, Summer 2002, pp. 7, 19–20. Levinson notes "the absolutely remarkable conflict of interest presented by the spectacle of Marshall deciding on the legal status of a commission that he himself had signed, but failed to deliver to Marbury, while serving as John Adams' Secretary of State, the very office now occupied by James Madison." Id. at 20.

38. Id. at 11 (footnote omitted).

posed that the botch that the Supreme Court made of the election litigation—the choice of the wrong ground of decision, Scalia's defense of the
stay, and the shrill tone of some of the dissents[39]—the botch that armed
Dershowitz and other critics—would have lowered the Court in the eyes
of the people. Not so. In June of 2000 only 47 percent of the population
had "a great deal" or "quite a lot" of confidence in the Supreme Court. A
year later, six months after *Bush v. Gore*, that figure had risen to 50 percent,
putting the Court behind only the military, organized religion, and the police in the list of institutions that the respondents were asked about in the
survey, and ahead of the Presidency (47 percent), the medical system, the
media, business, labor, and Congress (26 percent).[40] The Court averted a
possible Presidential succession crisis. The fact that it did so with a notable
lack of juristic finesse, arousing the rage of the keepers of the legal flame,
has bothered few real people. "The [empirical] evidence . . . fails to support the claim that support for the [Supreme] Court is dependent on the
public's belief in judicial impartiality and independence. It is rare to find
even a majority of Americans agreeing that the Court is unbiased or that it
simply follows the law."[41] The public response to *Bush v. Gore* is one more
bit of confirming empirical evidence.

39. A strong critic of the decision nevertheless aptly characterizes the dissents by Stevens
and Ginsburg as "choleric" and a failure of self-restraint. Larry D. Kramer, "The Supreme
Court in Politics," in *The Unfinished Election of 2000*, at 105, 146 (Jack N. Rakove ed. 2001).

40. Gallup Organization, "Confidence in Institutions," June 8–10, 2001.

41. Peretti, note 36 above, at 118. See also Terri Jennings Peretti, *In Defense of a Political
Court*, ch. 6 (1999).

CHAPTER TEN

Purposes versus Consequences in First Amendment Analysis

✺

I have noted in previous chapters that many constitutional cases employ a "balancing" test in which the case-specific consequences that favor one outcome are weighed against the case-specific consequences that favor the opposite outcome. One of the areas in which this is a fruitful approach is the constitutional law of free speech.[1] Jed Rubenfeld disagrees.[2] He sets against the "cost-benefit, balancing" approach to free-speech issues,[3] with me as spokesman,[4] an approach that forswears balancing in favor of inquiry into legislative or regulatory purpose ("purposivism"). From certain "paradigm cases"[5]—by which he means constitutional interpretations today uniformly accepted as valid—he infers three things: the First Amendment forbids all regulation intended to limit the expression of opinion ("no one can be punished for expressing himself on a matter of opinion"),[6] regardless of consequences; it allows regulation of expression, again regardless of consequences, that is not so intended; and it also allows all false *factual* assertions to be punished.

The contrast between Rubenfeld's approach and the pragmatic ap-

1. See, for example, Richard A. Posner, *Frontiers of Legal Theory*, ch. 2 (2001).
2. Jed Rubenfeld, "The First Amendment's Purpose," 53 *Stanford Law Review* 767 (2001).
3. Id. at 785; see also id. at (for example) 768, 781, 791.
4. See, for example, id. at 779–781.
5. Id. at 821–822.
6. Id. at 770.

proach is stark and provides both the stimulus for this chapter and an opportunity to continue with the project begun in Chapters 6 and 7 of relating legal pragmatism to economic analysis of law[7] and to play a few more variations on some of the themes of the book.

The American concept of freedom of speech poses a challenge to the pragmatist because, like "democracy," it is the repository of a great deal of unpragmatic rhetoric. It is at the heart of the American "civil religion," a term well chosen to convey the moralistic fervor in which free speech is celebrated. Freedom of speech is frequently described as "absolute," even as "sacred," as the most important right in the Constitution, as the foundation of all other political rights, as prior to security, as not to be balanced against other interests, and so on. All this is wormwood to the pragmatist, whose approach to free speech has now to be described.

The Pragmatic Approach to Free Speech

The natural approach for a pragmatic judge to take to a novel free-speech case is to compare the social pluses and minuses of the restriction on speech that the plaintiff is challenging. Not that it would be pragmatic to ignore the relevant language of the First Amendment ("Congress shall make no law . . . abridging the freedom of speech, or of the press"); remember that pragmatic adjudication does not imply disregard of the conventional materials of judicial decision. But he will find nothing in that language to help him decide the kind of case that arises nowadays. ("Nowadays" is an important qualification, to which I'll return: there is a core of settled meaning to the First Amendment, but settled principles are rarely litigated.) The key terms in the free-speech clause, now that the reference to "Congress" in it has been interpreted to mean "any public agency or official, state or federal," are *abridging, freedom, speech,* and *press,* and none of these words is either defined or self-explanatory. So the pragmatist goes foraging in the history of the Constitution and again finds nothing that will resolve the modern cases. He then examines the rich case law interpreting the speech and press clauses and finds that it owes little to their

7. See also Elisabeth Krecké, "Economic Analysis and Legal Pragmatism" (Université d'Aix-Marseilles III, June 2002, unpublished); Daniel T. Ostas, "Postmodern Economic Analysis of Law: Extending the Pragmatic Vision of Richard A. Posner," 36 *American Business Law Journal* 193 (1998); Thomas F. Cotter, "Legal Pragmatism and the Law and Economics Movement," 84 *Georgetown Law Journal* 2071 (1996).

language or background or to the various theories that political philosophers and others have advanced concerning the proper scope of freedom of expression. Instead the constitutional law of free speech seems on
the whole, though certainly not in every respect, to be a product of the
judges' (mainly they are U.S. Supreme Court Justices) evaluation of consequences. So he is led back to the balancing approach that is the pragmatist's natural starting point.

He is reassured to find that approach instantiated in two famous opinions by Justice Holmes that set the law of free speech on its modern
course. The first is *Schenck v. United States.*[8] After the United States entered World War I, Schenck, the general secretary of the Socialist Party,
arranged for the distribution of 15,000 leaflets to draftees, denouncing the
war and urging opposition to the draft. The leaflets did not advocate illegal measures, such as refusing to serve, but Schenck conceded that a reasonable jury could have found that the intent of the mailing had been to
"influence [persons subject to the draft] to obstruct the carrying of it out."[9]
In upholding the convictions of Schenck and his associates, Holmes wrote
that "in ordinary times" the Socialist Party might have had a First Amendment right to distribute these leaflets. "But the character of every act depends upon the circumstances in which it is done. The most stringent protection of free speech would not protect a man in falsely shouting fire in a
theater, and causing a panic."[10] Speech may be punished when "the words
used are used in such circumstances and are of such a nature as to create a
clear and present danger that they will bring about the substantive evils
that Congress has a right to prevent."[11] With the country at war, Congress
had a legitimate and indeed urgent interest in preventing the recruitment
of soldiers from being obstructed, and the defendants' conduct was both
intended and likely to obstruct that recruitment, though probably to only
a small degree, as socialism didn't have a large following in the United
States.

In the case of falsely shouting fire in a crowded theater, the harm is immediate, palpable, grave, and nearly certain to occur. In the case of mailing
antiwar propaganda to draftees, the harm (obstruction of recruitment)
may be significant if it occurs, though I have just expressed doubt that

8. 249 U.S. 47 (1919).
9. Id. at 51.
10. Id. at 52.
11. Id.

Schenck's leafletting did much harm; but it is in any event much less certain to occur than in the case of shouting fire in a crowded theater. The
probabilistic character of most types of harm caused by speech thus was a salient feature of *Schenck*, and Holmes's "clear and present danger" test requires that the probability be high (though not necessarily as high as in the
fire case) and the harm imminent; stated differently, the *danger* of harm
must be great. The greater the probability of harm, the greater the *expected*
harm and therefore the greater the pragmatic justification for preventing
or punishing the speech that creates the danger. The probability is greater
the more certain and more immediate the danger is.

Immediacy has an additional significance, again illustrated by falsely
shouting fire in a crowded theater: the more immediate the harm brought
about by the speech, the less feasible it is to rely on competition among
speakers and on other sources of information to avert the harm without
need for public intervention. In economic terms, "market failure" is more
likely when counterspeech, a form of competition that protects the interests of the audience in much the same way that competition in ordinary
markets protects consumers, is infeasible. It does not follow that speech
should be regulable *only* when the harm is immediate. That would deny
the existence of a tradeoff between immediacy and gravity, as would requiring that the harm be *both* likely and grave. If it is grave enough, it
should be regulable even though unlikely, and if likely enough, it should be
regulable even though not particularly grave. The analysis is similar to
that of search and seizure (Chapter 8); and this is important in showing
that legal pragmatism need not imply deciding every case on its own bottom, unconnected with the rest of the legal universe. Legal pragmatism
has or can be given (especially with the aid of economic analysis) its own
disciplining structure.

In the second opinion, *Abrams v. United States*, a dissent written just
months after *Schenck*, Holmes introduced the market metaphor for freedom of speech: an idea is true (more precisely, as close to true as it is possible for us to come) only if it prevails in competition with other ideas in the
marketplace of ideas.[12] Hence government disserves truth by suppressing
competition in ideas. In thus identifying a benefit of freedom of speech,
Holmes, who in *Schenck* had discussed just the costs of free speech, in
Abrams can be seen sketching in the other side of a cost-benefit formula.

12. 250 U.S. 616, 630 (1919).

The different emphases are natural because in the earlier case Holmes was rejecting the First Amendment claim and in the later one urging its acceptance. And though in both cases leftists were agitating against U.S. participation in World War I, there was an important difference. The defendants in *Schenck* were actually trying to obstruct the draft, by mailing leaflets to draftees. The defendants in *Abrams* were distributing the leaflets at large; although some draftees and munitions workers may have been recipients, no evidence was presented that the defendants had tried to get the leaflets into the hands of either group.[13] The danger of an actual obstruction of the war effort thus was less in *Abrams*.

Holmes's analysis of the costs of speech was incomplete in *Schenck* because he focused only on the probability of harm if the speech was allowed and not on the magnitude of the harm if it occurred; he was looking only at one determinant of the expected harm of free speech. And the *Abrams* dissent does not examine the possibility, an implicit premise of *Schenck*, that competition between ideas will not always yield truth—in *Schenck*, the truth that the draftees ought to fight and in the theater hypothetical the truth that there is no fire. Indeed, it may be doubted whether "truth" was even involved in *Schenck*. The government's concern was not that the defendants were lying but that they were imperiling an important national project—the analogy would be to disseminating a truthful formula for making poison gas. These are cases in which competition in ideas is undesired even, or perhaps especially, if it produces truth.

Still, these two opinions of Holmes's, though imperfect like all legal innovations, are the germ of modern free-speech law. Their prestige and influence suggest that pragmatic balancing is part of the First Amendment interpretive tradition, and this is reassuring because, as I have insisted repeatedly throughout this book, one of the systemic consequences of legal decisionmaking to which a good pragmatist judge will attend is the unsettling effect on people's legal rights and duties, and the stimulus to cynicism about the judicial process, produced by judges who make scant effort to maintain continuity with established understandings of the law and to observe correlative limits on judicial creativity. Not (to sound once more another major note in this book) that the judge has a duty to abide by constitutional or statutory text, or by precedent. That would be the idea rejected by John Dewey that law is entirely a matter of applying rules laid down in

13. See Richard Polenberg, *Fighting Faiths: The Abrams Case, the Supreme Court, and Free Speech* 104 (1987).

the past. It would be a pedigree approach to adjudication, requiring that legal decisions be derivable by deduction or similarly "logical" processes from established legal norms, in contrast to Kelsen's ladder of delegations, which leaves open the reasoning process used by judges to decide cases within the scope of their delegated authority. My point is rather that continuity and restraint in the performance of the judicial function are important social goods, the goods summarized in the term "rule of law," and any judge proposing to innovate must consider not only the benefits of the innovation in making the law better adapted to its social environment (the Darwinian analogue) but also the costs in injury to those goods.

Judges also have to worry that if they buck public opinion too vigorously, the political (more precisely, the more political) branches of government will rear up and clip the judicial wings. Sheer prudence is thus likely to rein in the most aggressive assertions of judicial power. Judges are most aggressive when they are fulminating in dissent, because dissenters do not have to live with the consequences of the positions they are asserting—there are no consequences. But prudence in a judge interpreting the Constitution is not *merely* William Blake's definition of "prudence"—an ugly old maid courted by incapacity. It is also deference to democratic preferences and modesty about the power of legal reasoning to put judges in touch with the truth. The pragmatic judge will not fool himself into thinking that the sheer power of legal logic will or ought to carry the country with him on matters on which it feels strongly.

But if balancing is, as I am arguing, the pragmatic method of deciding free-speech cases, and if good consequences are relabeled "benefits" and bad ones "costs," as seems natural to do and as I have already done in discussing Holmes's free-speech opinions, then pragmatic adjudication is a form of cost-benefit analysis and Rubenfeld has labeled me correctly. Several qualifications are necessary, however, to prevent misunderstandings both of pragmatism and of the economic approach to law.

1. "Costs" and "benefits" in the First Amendment setting must not be understood primarily in monetary terms. Indeed, because the image of balancing costs and benefits exaggerates the precision attainable in the First Amendment area and tends to suppress the other qualifications that I have indicated, it might be better to avoid the "cost-benefit" label. It is more apt in areas of explicit economic regulation, such as antitrust law or the law of secured lending, where economic values in a narrow sense are the law's primary concern.

2. A related point: quantification is rarely feasible and even more rarely attempted when courts consider the consequences of free speech and its regulation.

3. Long-run rather than short-run costs and benefits are the proper focus; but this is consistent with placing the primary emphasis in the free-speech context on case-specific rather than systemic consequences. The Constitution is so difficult to amend that the consequences of a bad decision are bound to be worse on average than those of bad decisions in areas of the law where the legislature has the last word. The bad case-specific consequences of a constitutional decision are therefore more likely to outweigh any systemic virtues of such a decision than if it were a statutory case.

4. The pragmatic judge does not embrace cost-benefit analysis, or any other aspect of economics, as dogma ("welfare economics," derived for example from utilitarianism). He uses it only insofar as it helps him to identify and weigh the consequences of alternative decisions.

5. Costs and benefits need not be balanced anew in every case if the cost-benefit analysis of a class of cases has crystallized in a rule that the judges have merely to apply. This is related to the distinction between the systemic and the immediate consequences of a decision, and in philosophy between direct and indirect consequentialism (though remember that legal pragmatism is not consequentialism), for example act and rule utilitarianism. The distinction implies that a balancing test rarely will be the only decisionmaking method employed in an area of law. Judicial balancing of costs and benefits takes place at the margin, that is, outside the core of settled doctrine. Not everything is up for grabs in every case. It would not do for the Supreme Court to say, "While we recognize that freedom of speech has great social value, we cannot find any convincing evidence that the value added of having judges enforce it justifies the costs entailed, since we observe that peer nations like the United Kingdom have a reasonable amount of free speech without constitutional limitations on the government's power to censor. Therefore we shall no longer consider First Amendment claims justiciable." The pragmatic judge is constrained in his consideration of the case-specific consequences of decision by the settled features of the legal framework, whatever he thinks of them. The constraint is itself pragmatic: the judge keeps within self-imposed limits to avoid the erosion of his authority and to acknowledge the limitations of his own ability to rethink long-settled issues from the ground up.

6. There is no reason to expect the scope of the First Amendment freedoms to remain constant. As we saw in Chapter 8 in reference to international terrorism, that scope can contract or expand in tandem with changes in social conditions that bear on how much freedom to allow.

7. Recognizing that pragmatism and consequentialism are not synonyms, the pragmatic judge will be sensitive to other considerations, besides consequences, that are important to people (and to judges!), including deep, durable emotional reactions to practices such as child pornography, the bad consequences of which (at least when children are not used in the manufacture of the pornography) have not been demonstrated.

Point 5—that pragmatism does not necessarily imply balancing at retail and that any such case-by-case balancing takes place only outside the settled core of doctrine—is a warning against a too-quick collapse of pragmatism into case-by-case balancing. A pragmatist might reject the use of balancing tests in First Amendment cases because he thought the net consequences of using them bad, maybe by giving judges too much discretion; for recall that formalism can sometimes be the pragmatic strategy for judges to adopt. Although I think the balancing approach has great merit in First Amendment cases outside the heartland of settled law, this is not an entailment of the pragmatic approach. It is merely a pragmatic judgment related to a point made back in Chapter 3—the undesirability of freezing experimentation by casually invalidating governmental action on constitutional grounds.

Pragmatic adjudication in free-speech cases is illustrated by the behavior of those judges who believed the nation endangered by Communist advocacy of violent revolution. They did not think themselves compelled by the vague language of the First Amendment—remember that "freedom of speech" is not a defined term—to prevent Congress from punishing that advocacy (more precisely, conspiracy to advocate) in the 1950s when the Communist menace seemed acute.[14] The value of such advocacy seemed a good deal less than the danger it posed. And while the country may have exaggerated that danger, and a number of judges may have sensed this, the

14. See, for example, Dennis v. United States, 341 U.S. 494 (1951), affirming 183 F.2d 201 (2d Cir. 1950) (L. Hand, J.). Hand's opinion for the court of appeals vividly evokes the Communist menace as then perceived. With the wisdom of hindsight, it is apparent that nothing very terrible would have happened had the Smith Act, the statute criminalizing conspiracy to advocate the overthrow of the U.S. government by force or violence upheld in *Dennis*, been invalidated. But that was not clear at the time.

fear of Communism was a brute fact that judges had to consider—for recall that pragmatic adjudication is not exhausted in the judge's own view of the social consequences of a decision.

The Supreme Court's response to Communist subversion should engender skepticism about Rubenfeld's claim that "at its historical core" free speech forbids censoring political dissent "even where such dissent could genuinely lead to violence."[15] It is not as if *Dennis* was a detour from a history of judicial privileging of dangerous dissent. Quite the contrary; up to that time most judicial opinions in support of free speech had been dissents. (Both Schenck and Abrams lost their cases.) Speeches or writings advocating violent revolution can convey information, force people to think, and in other ways as well contribute to the marketplace of ideas and opinions. But whether such advocacy will be tolerated should in a pragmatic analysis depend to a significant extent on how much violence such advocacy is likely to engender and how great that likelihood is. These factors vary over time. When the danger posed by subversive speech passes, the judges become stricter in their scrutiny of legislation punishing such speech. They know that such legislation may curtail worthwhile public debate over political issues and they consider this too high a price to pay when the country is safe. Until September 11, 2001, the country felt very safe from subversion, so the Justices of the Supreme Court could without incurring a large political cost plume themselves on their fearless devotion to freedom of speech and professors could deride the cowardice of the *Dennis* decision, just as they did with regard to *Korematsu* (see Chapter 8). They may change their tune now in light of new fears for the nation's safety.

Similarly, if "respectable" society is united in being deeply offended by pornography, the judges are unlikely to try to thwart the government's efforts to suppress it, even if they privately scoff at Comstockery. Granted, offensiveness is not the only consequence that pragmatic judges will or should consider in deciding how far the First Amendment protects pornography. Nor is offensiveness a constant. As people become more blasé about sexual expression, judges who value the arts and feel incompetent to make qualitative distinctions, or are unwilling to allow legislatures to place tighter restrictions on popular than on elite culture, or are hostile to the

---

15. Rubenfeld, note 2 above, at 792. Though he emphasizes prior restraints (that is, censorship), his reference in this discussion to seditious libel and to nuisance laws indicates that he anathematizes ex post punishment as well.

moralistic or religious motivations for suppressing pornography, will invoke the First Amendment to curtail public regulation of pornography. They will permit the government to prohibit outright only its *most* offensive forms (today that is mainly child pornography); the less offensive ones they will permit the government to regulate, but not prohibit, by such means as zoning restrictions,[16] restrictions on live performances ("nude dancing"), and restrictions on access by children.[17]

The ostensible justification for permitting any restrictions on sexually expressive speech is the "secondary effects" generated by establishments that offer erotic materials or entertainment, such as prostitution and disorderly conduct, rather than their offensiveness. This cannot be taken completely seriously. Politically unpopular speech has secondary effects as well, in particular a heightened risk of public disorder; yet the Supreme Court has made clear that government cannot, by banning unpopular speakers in order to prevent disorder, allow a "heckler's veto."[18] To permit such a veto would just encourage the hecklers and allow free speech to be drowned out. The proper response is to punish the hecklers. Similarly, one might suppose that the proper response to illegal conduct, such as soliciting a nude dancer for sex, stimulated by erotic displays would be to punish the illegal conduct rather than to ban the displays and thus deprive the innocent audience of its access to the particular type of expression.

The main point is that freedom of speech is not absolute but is and should be relative to changes in circumstances, and not just changed perceptions of public safety and moral health but also changes in value perceptions. Some years ago the Supreme Court held that a person cannot be punished for burning the American flag so long as it is his own property

16. Rubenfeld's statement that "with the arguable exception of commercial speech, *all* protected speech, from pornography to political dissent, is treated formally alike in First Amendment law," id. at 824 (emphasis in original), is incorrect. Pornographic theaters and bookstores can be zoned into special "red light" districts. See, for example, City of Renton v. Playtime Theaters, Inc., 475 U.S. 41, 49–52 (1986). Similar "content-based" zoning of purveyors of political speech would be unconstitutional.

17. Rubenfeld, note 2 above, at 830, would allow government to keep sexually explicit material from children but doesn't explain how this position squares with his overall approach.

18. Forsyth County v. The Nationalist Movement, 505 U.S. 123, 134–135, 140 (1992); Terminiello v. Chicago, 337 U.S. 1, 4–5 (1949). I take it that Rubenfeld would agree, since, while the motive in banning speakers who are likely to provoke a violent reaction by members of their audience need not be to restrict the expression of unpopular views but may merely be to economize on police expense, the purpose is to restrict speech; economy is merely a desirable consequence, as well as the ultimate motive, of the ban. The distinction is a fragile one, however, as I'll suggest later.

and the fire does not risk a wider conflagration;[19] flag-burning is constitutionally protected speech. Some of the Justices dissented on the ground, which failed to persuade most students of constitutional law (myself included), that the flag is a unique national symbol, which the government should be empowered to protect from being desecrated. To a pragmatist the dissenters' argument is stronger today in the wake of the September 11, 2001 terrorist attacks and the extraordinary displays of the American flag that ensued. The social importance of the flag is suddenly much greater than it seemed to be, or perhaps was, a decade ago. The dangers that beset the nation today make it harder than ever to take topless dancing seriously as a threat to the nation's moral fiber, but at the same time they make the burning of the American flag seem obscene. This is not because burning the flag is likely to increase the terrorist threat; not at all. The issue is offensiveness, not danger. But offensiveness is, as I have said, a common basis for permitted restrictions of freedom of speech, and like danger it is relative to circumstances. This "relativism" has, I contend, constitutional significance for the pragmatist. But a better word than relativism would be empiricism. The aftermath of the September 11 attacks revealed something we didn't know about the social significance of the American flag. What it revealed has altered the perspective of many of us.

Moreover, the Schumpeterian democrat, at least, will be skeptical that every retrenchment from the broadest possible scope of First Amendment rights must constitute a threat to democracy. Antidemocratic speech (such as Nazi or Communist propaganda) and mute symbolism (such as flag-burning) are elements of political debate, to be sure. But nothing in history suggests that modest curtailments of these forms of expression interfere with or threaten "democracy" understood realistically not as the activity of a debating society but as a competition among members of the political elite for electoral support.

Yet if Congress again passed a law against flag-burning, I think the Supreme Court would again strike it down. Not out of devotion to stare decisis—the right to burn the flag is not the sort of thing on which strong claims of justifiable reliance are built—but simply to demonstrate that the Court doesn't buckle under pressure. If this conjecture is right, it suggests an essential *arbitrariness* to law that formalists should find intensely disquieting and that supports the pragmatist's belief that logic is indeed not the

19. Texas v. Johnson, 491 U.S. 397 (1989); United States v. Eichman, 496 U.S. 310 (1990).

life of the law. Much of law seems to depend on accidents of timing, of sequence; that is, it seems to be, as economists say, "path dependent"—where you start is where you end, though it was an accident that you started where you did and if you had started somewhere else you would have ended somewhere else. If the first flag-burning case had not come to the Court until the autumn of 2001, there might today be no constitutional right to burn the flag.

The "Purposivist" Critique of the Pragmatic Approach

Jed Rubenfeld defends his approach to free-speech issues in part by criticizing balancing as unworkable. He puts the hypothetical case of a speeder who seeks to justify speeding as a protest against a speed limit that he thinks too low. From the fact that, as he points out[20] and flag-burning illustrates, conduct can be expressive, he infers that the balancer "would have to try to measure the value of driving at high speed as an expressive activity, then balance this value against the pertinent harms, and then ask whether the state could successfully address these harms while letting some or all people drive a little faster on some or all highways at some or all times."[21] In this example Rubenfeld has committed the fallacy of making simple decisions seem difficult by decomposing them into their elements (as in Zeno's Paradox). The pragmatist's response to the speeding case is that to recognize a justification based on the speeder's alleged desire to protest the speed limit would emasculate speed limits while doing little to promote the expression of useful ideas, since there are plenty of other ways of expressing disagreement with a speed limit. The analytically similar case of conscientious objection to military service is stronger for a defense of freedom of conscience. Not only do we know that some people really do have strong feelings against participating in a war, however just; in addition, few people actually claim such exemptions—the stigma that attached to "draft dodgers" (whatever their motives) when the United States had a draft was a potent deterrent.

Rubenfeld further contends "that no one can pretend to know whether *the freedom of speech itself is worth its costs*,"[22] so that if we were serious about costs and benefits we would have to be agnostic about whether there

20. See also Posner, note 1 above, at 88.
21. Rubenfeld, note 2 above, at 787.
22. Id. at 793 (emphasis in original).

should be any right of free speech at all. An absurdly overextended concept of freedom of speech might indeed not be worth its costs. But something like the existing concept, applied in the conditions that obtain in the United States today, is clearly worth its modest costs (though in any event it is far too entrenched to be challenged by judges). If pragmatism endorses what may seem an unbecomingly timid judicial response to public concern with offensive or dangerous speech, at the same time it provides support for our national commitment to freedom of speech by rejecting the Platonic view that government can establish a pipeline to truth and, having done so, censor with a good conscience. But pragmatic philosophy is not needed to show that a democratic political system, a scientific and technological culture, college and university education, electronic media, a diverse religious culture, and a diverse popular and elite artistic culture cannot prosper without considerable freedom of inquiry and expression. The dependence of political democracy on freedom of the press (the media, we would now say) is particularly clear, as Tocqueville remarked.[23] But there is no evidence that such freedom must be absolute for democracy to be secure.

More difficult is the question whether balancing can be taken seriously as a method for deciding free-speech cases when the courts regularly ignore measures that have really big adverse effects on speech while pouncing on measures that have tiny effects. The price of third-class mail, which is set by the federal government, has a significant effect on the costs and hence circulation of magazines; entertainment taxes have a profound effect on the film and theater markets; the telephone excise tax affects the frequency of phone calls, some of which involve the exchange of ideas and opinions; the deductions from income tax allowed to authors affect the number of books—so for that matter does the fact that authors' royalties are subject to income tax at all. In contrast, most of the cases that have vindicated freedom of speech in the modern era have been faintly ridiculous, or at least distinctly marginal, involving as they have pornographic art and entertainment, old-fashioned street demonstrations, scatological insults, commercial billboards and other commercial advertising, violent video games, and indecent websites. But this pattern is not a refutation of pragmatism or a vindication of purposivism. The government has to tax. To force it in the name of the First Amendment to exempt from taxation all

23. Alexis de Tocqueville, *Democracy in America* 172–180 (Harvey C. Mansfield and Delba Winthrop eds. 2000).

activities that involve the production or dissemination of ideas and opinions would constitute an enormous subsidy to those activities. Imagine exempting authors and journalists from income tax on the ground that the exemption would lead to an increase in expressive activity—though it would. The direct regulations of speech that are struck down often have a smaller effect on the speech market, but the adverse consequences of prohibiting such regulations are immensely smaller.

A danger of the balancing approach to free speech is that the costs of freedom of expression are often more salient than the benefits, and their salience may cause the balance to shift too far toward suppression. People are deeply offended by hearing their religious, moral, political, or even aesthetic beliefs challenged; and offense is a cost. But as Mill said,

> the beliefs which we have most warrant for have no safeguard to rest on, but a standing invitation to the whole world to prove them unfounded. If the challenge is not accepted, or is accepted and the attempt fails, we are far enough from certainty still; but we have done the best that the existing state of human reason admits of; we have neglected nothing that could give the truth a chance of reaching us . . . This is the amount of certainty attainable by a fallible being, and this the sole way of attaining it.[24]

Peirce made the related point that only doubt leads people to question their beliefs.[25] Doubt is the engine of progress, but because people hate being in a state of doubt they may prefer to silence the doubters than to alter their beliefs. And because the costs of heterodox speech are immediate and the benefits deferred, the benefits may be slighted. All this must be kept steadily in mind by judges called upon to uphold the suppression of expression in the name of protecting people from being offended. To put this differently, suppressing speech because it is "shocking" is a good deal more questionable than suppressing it because it inflicts demonstrable harm or creates a palpable danger of future harm.

But the judicial finger must not rest too heavily on the constitutional

24. John Stuart Mill, *On Liberty* 22 (David Spitz ed. 1975). He makes the related point that without confronting objections to an idea its holder cannot understand and defend it. "He who knows only his own side of the case, knows little of that." Id. at 36.

25. See Charles Sanders Peirce, "The Fixation of Belief," in *Collected Papers of Charles Sanders Peirce* 223 (Charles Hartshorne and Paul Weiss eds. 1934).

trigger. Decisions invalidating regulation have the consequence very disturbing to a pragmatist of stifling experimentation and so depriving society of experience with alternative methods of dealing with perceived social problems. As this is true even when the regulation is of speech, the pragmatist is troubled by an approach to free speech that would banish from judicial consideration the likely consequences of the judges' decisions, shutting their minds to an argument that some novel regulation of expression might on balance have highly desirable consequences but we would have to try it to see. If the First Amendment commanded judges not to consider effects, then a proper respect for the pragmatic benefit of judicial self-restraint might counsel the judges to swallow hard and ignore them. But the amendment does not command abstention from reality; and the case law, far from treating free speech as an "absolute," recognizes a host of permissible restrictions of it (I list a few later). And while the risk of judges exaggerating the costs of free speech is a real one, as I have indicated, because the costs tend to be immediate and the benefits remote, on what basis can this risk be pronounced greater than that of stifling potentially beneficial government regulation?

This discussion may help to show why the mushiness inherent in a pragmatic approach to free-speech law is less troubling than would be a ruleless law of contracts. Free-speech law is constitutional law, and the interest in experimentation argues for resolving close cases against invalidation of government actions on constitutional grounds. First Amendment *rules* inevitably place many considerations that might favor a particular regulation of speech out of bounds, for it is the nature of rules to narrow the scope of inquiry more than standards do. The result is to create large, blanket exclusions from democratic choice and experimentation. Compare the rules set forth by the Supreme Court in *New York Times Co. v. Sullivan*[26] limiting defamation suits in the name of free speech with a standard that would forbid such suits only if the defendant proved, as the *Times* did prove, that the suit was a device for harassing a political opponent. Instead the rules laid down in *Sullivan* and subsequent decisions have greatly curtailed the permissible scope of defamation law across the board.

The *level* at which speech is regulated is important to a pragmatist. The more local the regulation, the lighter should be the judicial hand, because the effect of the regulation on the speech market will be smaller yet its

---

26. 376 U.S. 254 (1964).

value as experimentation may be great. The optimal level of regulation also depends on where the regulatory responsibility is lodged. In the case of national defense, that responsibility is national. It would make no sense to allow cities or states to impose military censorship. But neither would it make sense to accept the claim of the press and other media to be the responsible organ to decide whether to publicize military secrets. The media are responsible only to their shareholders, and, given the pressures of competition, cannot be trusted to give due weight to the public interest in limiting the dissemination of information when necessary to protect national security. (The *Progressive* case mentioned in Chapter 8 furnishes a striking illustration of this point.) Attention to the incentives of the persons involved either in expression or in its regulation explains the courts' hostility to "prior restraints" when they take the form that Blackstone discussed of censorship by boards of censors. Being in the business of suppression, censors are likely to be too skeptical of the social benefits of freedom of expression. Their career incentives push them to the opposite extreme from those of publishers. Neither extreme is likely to be the social optimum.

In linking Mill and Peirce to free-speech doctrine, I am acknowledging that pragmatic philosophy, and not merely everyday pragmatism, may have a payoff for the law after all. Holmes's dissent in the *Abrams* case echoed Peirce's famous essay "The Fixation of Belief."[27] And we recall that Holmes consorted with Peirce and the other pragmatists (he was, for example, a friend from childhood of William James) and had serious philosophical interests. In *Abrams* he describes freedom of speech as an experiment, and we recall from Chapter 3 that he thought the states should be permitted to experiment with social legislation. The metaphor of the marketplace of ideas that Holmes introduced in *Abrams* is pragmatic in analogizing inquiry to Darwinian natural selection: competing ideas are put forth and the "market" chooses, presumably by consulting its practical needs rather than by subjecting the competitors to criteria of validity. But whether Holmes was really "doing" philosophy in these cases must remain uncertain. Philosophical pragmatism, especially of the recusant variety, and everyday pragmatism reflect a similar mindset. This makes it impossible (or at least beyond my powers) to say whether Holmes's tough-minded rejection of conventional pieties in favor of commercial and Darwinian

27. See note 25 above.

analogies reflected or inspired his philosophical speculations. It is not as if philosophers *invented* free speech, or the market, or the theory of natural selection, any more than they invented democracy.

Holmes's competitive theory of free speech complements Schumpeter's competitive theory of democracy. Schumpeter's theory ascribes greater social importance to freedom of political speech than deliberative democracy does. For Schumpeter, democracy is a competition within the political class for the favor of the voters. The principal competitive weapon is language. Advertising, in the broadest sense of the word, is more important in the political than in the economic marketplace because the voter usually can't sample or inspect the policies that politicians advocate; so more rides on the persuasiveness of their plans and intentions than in the usual commercial competition. Not only are free speech and a free press indispensable to political competition, but the government cannot be trusted to regulate this market because the people in temporary control of the government are competitors of the people they would be regulating.[28] These obvious points are obscured when too much emphasis is placed, as in some versions of deliberative democracy, on rule by neutral experts rather than on the competitive process by which our rulers are actually chosen. If you think you have a handle on truth, which you are likely to think if you are an expert on the matter in issue, you're not likely to be interested in hearing a cacophony of competing views, many advanced by ignoramuses. What is less obvious is a point touched on in Chapter 6, that some regulation of the market in political speech is necessary to prevent confusion and drowning out, a simple example being regulation of the decibel level of sound trucks used to amplify political speeches. This concern has particular resonance for deliberative democrats because of the incompatibility of noise with genteel deliberation.[29]

Too much harping on the importance of freedom of political speech to democracy, however, threatens to obliterate the highly pertinent distinc-

28. For a helpful discussion, see Albert Breton and Ronald Wintrobe, "Freedom of Speech vs. Efficient Regulation in Markets for Ideas," 17 *Journal of Economic Behavior and Organization* 217, 233–237 (1992).

29. "The men whose labors brought forth the Constitution of the United States had the street outside Independence Hall covered with earth so that their deliberations might not be disturbed by passing traffic. Our democracy presupposes the deliberative process as a condition of thought and of responsible choice by the electorate. To the Founding Fathers it would hardly seem a proof of progress in the development of our democracy that the blare of sound trucks must be treated as a necessary medium in the deliberative process." Saia v. New York, 334 U.S. 558, 565 (1948) (Frankfurter, J., dissenting).

tion between total and marginal utility. Water is more important to life than wine is, but it does not follow that if offered a choice between a glass of water and a glass of wine, you should always choose the water. And similarly it does not follow from the greater importance of political than artistic speech to a society such as that of the United States that forbidding some crazy form of hate speech would impose a greater cost on society than burning all abstract art.

Jed Rubenfeld wants to use the purpose of a challenged regulation of expressive activity as the criterion of the regulation's legality. If the purpose is to limit expression, the regulation is invalid. Period.[30] There is nothing unpragmatic about using purposes in making judgments. We often infer the probable consequences of an action from evidence of a desire to produce them. This is a sensible procedure because people rarely undertake a course of action without having *some* reason to believe it will accomplish their purpose in undertaking it. Mixed motives and multiple purposes can bedevil an inquiry into purpose, as we'll see later, but it is not true that collective action is often, let alone characteristically, without discernible purposes; "collective purpose" is not an oxymoron.

Nor is it unpragmatic to worry, as Rubenfeld does in proposing his "purposivist" approach, about constitutional doctrines that are so loose that they give judges carte blanche to decide cases any way they want without inviting criticism that the judge is deviating from the previous course of decisions. Rules, as we know, can be a pragmatically superior method of regulation to an "all facts and circumstances" standard. The danger that censors will ban the expression of opinions they happen not to like is great enough to justify forbidding them to use a freewheeling balancing test to decide what to censor. But there is a difference between a presumption against censoring or punishing speech and a blanket rule, such as that "in the eyes of the Constitution, there is no such thing as a low-value opinion."[31] There are indeed valueless, noxious, and dangerous opinions, such as the opinion of a madman, which he disseminates over the Internet, that it is the duty of all true believers to kill prostitutes, or the opinion of Islamic extremists that it is a holy duty to kill Jews and Americans; why

30. See Elena Kagan, "Private Speech, Public Purpose: The Role of Governmental Motive in First Amendment Doctrine," 63 *University of Chicago Law Review* 413 (1996), for an earlier and more tempered version of Rubenfeld's argument.
31. Rubenfeld, note 2 above, at 826.

should the law be helpless against opinions known to incite violence? Holmes knew better.

After more than two centuries of Supreme Court decisions, moreover, it is difficult to argue with a straight face that categorical rules of constitutional law occasionally laid down by the Court constrain judicial discretion (especially the discretion of the Justices themselves, who cannot be prevented from overruling, or distinguishing to death, precedents they don't want to follow) more tightly than the explicit balancing approach that the Court has often used instead. It has used balancing, for example, to determine when the right to a fair trial should give way to the media's interest in reporting on trials and to evaluate time, place, and manner restrictions on speech and expressive conduct.[32] A common effect of substituting a rule for a standard is that considerations that the standard required to be weighed become sub rosa factors determining the scope of the rule and its exceptions. Think of the different layers of scrutiny that the Supreme Court requires courts to give restrictions on freedom of expression in traditional public forums (such as the streets and sidewalks), designated public forums (such as parts of a public university that are open to the public), limited public forums (such as a theater, which is dedicated to a particular kind of expressive activity), and nonpublic forums (such as government offices); would the results be significantly different had the Court been content with a standard directing judicial attention to the successively greater costs, as one proceeds down the forum chain, of allowing unrestricted access to public property for expressive activity?[33] And as often happens when a range of activities is subjected to governance by rules, the attempt to sort all forums in which expressive activity does or can take place into a handful of categories creates exquisite classification problems and thus great uncertainty.[34]

Delusive exactness is a traditional pitfall in the design of legal doctrines.

32. See, for example, Clark v. Community for Creative Non-Violence, 468 U.S. 288 (1984). A requirement that the organizer of a protest march obtain a permit specifying the time at which the march may be held, its duration, the route that may be followed, and the maximum electronic amplification permitted of the chants of the marchers, would be an illustration of such restrictions.

33. See Posner, note 1 above, at 71; Chicago Acorn v. Metropolitan Pier & Exposition Authority, 150 F.3d 695 (7th Cir. 1998).

34. See, for example, International Society for Krishna Consciousness, Inc. v. Lee (ISKCON), 505 U.S. 672 (1992), in which the Supreme Court struggled inconclusively with the question of how to classify an airport.

Consider Rubenfeld's argument that a city ordinance forbidding begging should have been deemed unconstitutional because it "target[ed] certain speech acts," namely requests for handouts.[35] "Speech acts" cannot be targeted? Does this mean that threats cannot be punished? How about offers to fix prices? To sell illegal drugs? Promises to commit murder for hire? Harassing phone calls by importunate creditors? Phone calls by heavy-breathing sexual harassers? Rubenfeld would allow punishment of some conspiratorial speech, speech that is part and parcel of forbidden conduct,[36] and this may take care of some of these examples, but not the last two. Although he says that telephone harassment laws can be upheld by analogy to laws forbidding breaking and entering, the analogy could also be used to forbid begging when it is perceived, as it so often is, as harassment. Rubenfeld contrasts the solicitation of handouts with the solicitation of votes, which he thinks a paradigmatic case of privileged conduct. It is not; soliciting votes at the entrance to polling places on election day is illegal.

Suppose that a major city, concerned solely with traffic congestion, noise, and the crowding of sidewalks and public parks, bans from the streets, sidewalks, and parks all activities that involve accosting strangers or interfering with their freedom of movement, including vending, picketing, begging, parading, demonstrating, soliciting, and haranguing. So long as there was no purpose to suppress or discourage the expression of opinions, such a ban would present no issue of free speech for Rubenfeld. Or suppose a law was passed forbidding false statements of fact in Presidential campaigns. The effect on political free speech would be devastating. But if the law really was intended just to eliminate demonstrable falsehoods and not to stifle the expression of opinions, it would pass constitutional muster with Rubenfeld. He flinches at one point, however, when he suggests that a ceiling on all forms of campaign spending, not just spending on advertising and other forms of communication, though aimed at spending, not at communicating, might well be unconstitutional because most campaign spending is on communication rather than, for example, security or transporation.[37] In fact, virtually all campaign expenditures are directly or indirectly for communication.

And flinch he should. Noting the analogy between a law that restricts

35. Rubenfeld, note 2 above, at 799.
36. Id. at 828.
37. Id. at 806.

freedom of expression though aimed at something else and a law that restricts religion though aimed at something else, he refers approvingly to *Employment Division v. Smith*.[38] That case purports to hold that the free-exercise clause of the First Amendment is not infringed by a law of general applicability not aimed at religion, even if the effect is to cripple religious observance. The logical implication is that a state that decided to forbid the sale or consumption of alcoholic beverages could, without violating the free-exercise clause, refuse to make an exception for the use of wine in communions. *Smith*, however, involved the use of peyote by an Indian tribe in an Indian religious service, and I have trouble imagining the Court upholding a law that inflicted equivalent damage on a major religion.[39]

What *Smith* really stands for is pragmatic disdain for formalist reasoning. As I said in the last chapter, Justice Scalia, the author of *Smith*, is not really a formalist, at least not a consistent one. His opinion in *Smith* points out, with refreshing realism, that the major religions have enough political muscle to obtain whatever exemptions from generally applicable laws are necessary to enable them to continue their principal observances. Why then should judges trouble their heads, when deciding a case involving a minor religion, about what to do with a similar law involving the practices or observances of a major religion? There will never be such a law. Slippery-slope reasoning has no practical role to play when the slope is not slippery.

The *Smith* analogy to one side, Rubenfeld wishes to expand the scope of freedom of speech in several directions. His approach implies that child pornography, even if it satisfies the demanding criteria of obscenity, cannot be banned from prime-time television, although pornographers could be forbidden to use actual children in making the pornography. Racist speech in prisons would be privileged. Military censorship in wartime, if intended not only to prevent the spilling of military secrets but also to protect morale against defeatist enemy propaganda, would be forbidden. Cabinet officers could not be fired for expressing opinions at variance with the President's. A racist employer, while he might be forced to hire blacks despite a sincere, ideologically grounded hostility to them, would be free to make the workplace unbearable for them by subjecting them to his racist views.

And Nazis could not be forbidden to send postcards to Jewish survivors

38. 494 U.S. 872 (1990).
39. Id. at 890.

of Nazi concentration camps expressing regret that the addressee had survived and promising to do better next time. Yet a similar postcard, denying that the Holocaust had occurred, could on the logic of Rubenfeld's approach be forbidden as a demonstrably false statement of fact. Nazis believed that Germans, Jews, and Slavs were separate races in a meaningful biological sense; this was false, and so the assertion of these beliefs could, under Rubenfeld's construal of the First Amendment, be punished. Yet after striking all errors of fact from Nazi propaganda, very little is left; the dichotomy between fact and opinion that Rubenfeld embraces[40] is devastating to continents of speech and empties of any practical meaning his contention that Nazi opinion is privileged.[41] Political speech is suffused with falsehoods. To use law to cleanse it of them would be a quixotic undertaking—or if it did succeed, it could only be by stifling political speech. Politicians do not have the discipline or the education that they would need to avoid making false factual assertions, especially but not only when they are speaking extemporaneously.

I am not suggesting that Rubenfeld would embrace all the implications of his position that I have listed. But I do not see how he could reject them yet still keep faith with his overall approach. He says the approach "is not intended to apply to the special contexts of government-owned property (for example, military bases) where the full set of ordinary First Amendment protections does not apply."[42] But on his account, there is nothing to distinguish government-owned property, including military bases, from streets and sidewalks—which, incidentally, are also owned by government. Likewise unexplained is the distinction he suggests between "managerial" and "regulatory" functions of government, the former illustrated by the courts, in which speech is properly restricted[43]—on pragmatic grounds, I would argue. Those grounds are not available to Rubenfeld, who is en-

---

40. See Rubenfeld, note 2 above, at 819–821. The Supreme Court has rejected the dichotomy for defamation cases, holding that a defamatory statement is not rendered privileged by being expressed as an opinion. Milkovich v. Lorain Journal Co., 497 U.S. 1, 17–21 (1990). The Court pointed out that an expression of opinion often implies a factual assertion. The point is not limited to defamation. If, as Rubenfeld's analysis suggests, factual implications always rendered an opinion punishable, the First Amendment would provide little protection for political speech.

41. "Nazi opinions cannot be banned." Rubenfeld, note 2 above, at 826. But what about expressions of the factual assumptions on which those opinions rest?

42. Id. at 798.

43. Id. at 819.

gaged here in adding epicycles in an attempt to stave off the collapse of his system.

Most interesting and difficult of the illustrations that I have used to exhibit the logic of Rubenfeld's approach are those involving the expression of Nazi views. Since Nazi ideology today poses no threat to American institutions and since it is difficult to demarcate Nazi or "fascist" expression from other, more meritorious forms of reactionary or Romantic thought, it ought to be allowed, crazy factual claims and all, without which the Nazi would be quite speechless. But I would draw the line at targeted abuse, my example of sending taunting postcards to Holocaust survivors, where the quantum of offensiveness shoots up and a prohibition would not significantly inhibit Nazi expressive activity. The intermediate case is that of the Nazi march in Skokie, a largely Jewish suburb of Chicago that contained a number of Holocaust survivors for whom the march revived bitter memories and may have seemed an ominous portent of what might someday happen here. My court (before I was appointed to it) held that the march was protected by the First Amendment.[44] I have no quarrel with the decision. It was easy enough for Jews to avoid the march (though not to avoid knowing that it was taking place); avoidance was easier than in my postcard hypothetical. And where was the line to be drawn—could the Nazis march only in neighborhoods in which the percentage of Jews in the population was below a specified level? How would that level be determined?

The pattern of prohibitions and permissions implied by Rubenfeld's theory could not be made to sound sensible to a person who was not a lawyer. That is a pretty reliable way of identifying a legal doctrine or proposal that is unpragmatic in an everyday sense. It lends a note of irony to Rubenfeld's description of his approach as "purposivism." The only purposes he considers are those of legislatures and other government agencies that want to restrict expressive activity. He never quizzes his own purposes and thus leaves unclear *why* he wants to create the pattern of permissions and prohibitions that his approach implies. The pattern makes no common sense but maybe it makes some special *legal* sense, something pragmatists just are blind to. Rubenfeld evidently thinks so, arguing that his theory is not imposed by him, as it appears to be, but rather wells up from

44. Collin v. Smith, 578 F.2d 1197 (7th Cir. 1978).

three case-created doctrines that he regards as paradigmatic. The pattern *is* the law, or at least is in the law, constituting a central tradition from which the Supreme Court has from time to time strayed.

This is to equivocate between positive and normative analysis. And someone who is permitted to choose, from the multitude of free-speech doctrines and decisions, three to be the fixed stars in the free-speech firmament can have no difficulty justifying whatever doctrinal structure he likes. The technique of picking your best friends in a large disorderly body of case law is facile. Someone who wanted to argue for a more limited right of free speech could take as paradigmatic not only *Dennis* but also the cases that allow punishment of nonobscene nude dancing, libel and slander, breach of a settlement agreement (in a lawsuit) that provides that its terms shall be kept confidential, copyright infringement, plagiarism, threats, speech by prison inmates and soldiers, criminal solicitations, advertising by casinos, publicity that casts a person in a false light or invades his privacy, verbal harassment, disclosure of privileged communications, political disagreements between a policymaking or confidential employee and his superior, obscenity, and foul language on prime-time television.

Rubenfeld's three paradigmatic cases (not cases actually, but judge-made doctrines inferred from or expressed in cases) are the absolute protection of political dissent, of religious speech, and of art. But cases privileging expression cannot support the half of his theory that says that the government has plenary authority to regulate expression when the purpose is not to suppress opinions. And the First Amendment has *not* been interpreted to protect political dissent, religious speech, and art absolutely. Hard-core pornographic art is regulable; and likewise political or religious speech that constitutes incitement, as when someone announces that it is his political or religious duty to kill the President. Political and religious speech, along with artistic expression, can also be limited in particular settings—prisons and military bases and a multitude of other nonpublic forums. And what has political, religious, or artistic expression to do with begging, or for that matter commercial advertising, both forms of expression that Rubenfeld thinks protected by the First Amendment from government regulation?

Rubenfeld defends his choice of paradigmatic cases by reference to a questionable philosophical theory about the triumph of science in the domain of fact. By a logic that he does not explain and that is not transparent, the fact that science has accustomed us to draw a sharp distinction between verifiable fact and unverifiable political, religious, moral, and aesthetic opinion has, he believes, led judges to give greater constitutional protection to the latter domain, that of unverifiable opinion, than they did *before* its hopelessly unscientific character was recognized. There is an echo of logical positivism, which, we recall from Chapter 1, divides assertions into tautologies (such as "no bachelors are married"), which are true by definition; verifiable facts, the truth value of which can be determined empirically; and everything else. Tautologies are the province of logic, dictionaries, and mathematics; verifiable facts the province of science; and everything else the province of emotion. The logical positivist regards religious, moral, and aesthetic statements as being emotive and thus as having no truth value at all.[45] The implication for First Amendment doctrine—the implication that Holmes, who, among his other philosophical insights, anticipated logical positivism, drew—is that censorship makes no sense. Censorship, as Plato in defending it clearly understood, presupposes the ability of the censor to distinguish true from false political, religious, moral, and aesthetic opinions.

Logical positivism in the strong form implied by Holmes's analysis of free speech is rejected by most philosophers today.[46] But Holmes can be reinterpreted as having made a simple, everyday-pragmatic point: censorship works best if there are objective criteria that the censor can use, as with the Food and Drug Administration's censorship of claims for the safety or efficacy of drugs, or the Securities and Exchange Commission's censorship of prospectuses for new issues of securities. But it does not matter, as Rubenfeld seems to believe, whether the criteria are "objective" because they are scientific in the sense of observer-independent or objective merely in the sense of resting on a consensus of the relevant community of inquirers. No scientific method is available to prove that movies of people engaging in sexual intercourse with children or animals are "wrong." But everyone in American society whose opinion counts believes

45. The classic statements remain A. J. Ayer, *Language, Truth, and Logic* (rev. ed. 1946), and, before him, David Hume, *An Enquiry concerning Human Understanding* 165 (3d ed., P. H. Nedditch ed. 1975) (§ 12, pt. 3).

46. Including pragmatists; indeed, within philosophy pragmatism is considered to have knocked science off the perch on which logical positivism had placed it. But, as I noted in Chapter 1, this is an intramural battle. The outsider to philosophy is more likely to be struck by the affinities between logical positivism and pragmatism, especially in their shared skepticism about moral absolutes and other products of the kind of rationalism that one associates with Plato and Kant and, in law, with natural-law theories.

these things are wrong and should be prohibited, which is all that is necessary to create an "objective" basis for prohibiting them, notwithstanding the First Amendment. Rubenfeld wants to banish these beliefs from First Amendment law, but he will not be able to do that until someone weans people from them.

In the aftermath of the September 11 terrorist attacks on the United States, we have renewed respect for the power of ideas to incite violent actions. The greater that power, the greater the need for some regulation. But the consequences of speech are precisely what Rubenfeld places beyond the reach of governmental action. He is impervious to the dangers of free speech.

Finally, Rubenfeld's approach underestimates the difficulty of discerning legislative motive.[47] That difficulty would be even greater if his approach were adopted by the courts because legislators would then "game" it by peppering legislative history with assurances that their motives were pure and their purposes innocent of reference to the opinions of the persons whose expression they were curtailing.[48] But the difficulty is great enough without regard to that possibility, as shown by Rubenfeld's argument that so long as bullfighting is banned out of concern for the welfare of the bulls rather than out of hostility to the "message" conveyed by bullfighting (approval of *macho* values, perhaps), the fact that it *has* a message that the ban therefore blocks is unproblematic under his approach. But in the real world a ban on bullfighting would be supported by some legislators who wanted to kill the message,[49] by others who wanted to save the bulls, by others who had both objectives, and by others who had no view of the matter but were simply logrolling with the antibullfighting legislators.

Rubenfeld believes that a regulation the purpose of which is to restrict expressive activity is not saved by the fact that the motive behind it is to accomplish some innocent end, such as saving money on police or saving the lives of bulls. The bullfighting case *seems* to be a purpose case rather than a

47. The objection cannot be elided, as Kagan, note 30 above, at 439, believes, by shifting the focus to the question whether, but for the impermissible motive, the legislation would have been enacted. My example in the text that follows illustrates the potential indeterminacy of the answer to that question.

48. Cf. Adrian Vermeule, "The Cycles of Statutory Interpretation," 68 *University of Chicago Law Review* 149 (2001).

49. This point was made by Judge Easterbrook, discussing the same hypothetical, in his dissenting opinion in Miller v. Civil City of South Bend, 904 F.2d 1081, 1127 (7th Cir. 1990), reversed under the name Barnes v. Glen Theatre, Inc., 501 U.S. 560 (1991).

motive case because the ban on bullfighting can be stated without any reference to expressive activity: "don't kill bulls." But this cannot be right, because there is no law against killing a bull (provided you own it). The ban is on killing bulls for a particular purpose, namely their use in an expressive activity that depends upon the killing. This seems like purposive discrimination against a disfavored expressive activity. Unless I am mistaken, purposivism implies that prohibiting bullfighting in the United States is unconstitutional. Animal-rights advocates will shudder—democrats, and pragmatists, as well.

Conclusion

❦

This book has argued for approaching law and politics from the perspective that I call "everyday pragmatism," which is distinct from though related to philosophical pragmatism. More specifically, I have tried to make the case for two legs of the pragmatic-liberal tripod: legal pragmatism and pragmatic democracy. The third leg is liberty in the sense of the rights that the people of a nation have against its government. These are rights to be left alone in such pursuits as speaking and earning, though they are subject to limitations necessary to prevent violence, fraud, and other unwarranted interferences with people's freedom of action and to enable the creation of important public goods—things such as education and national defense that people want but that a private market will not supply in the desired quantity. The issue of liberty is thus the issue of the optimal scope of government. I have argued elsewhere for a libertarian delimitation of that scope similar to what John Stuart Mill proposed in *On Liberty*.[1] I do not pursue that argument here, but I do think it worth noting the essentially pragmatic cast of Mill's position. (And remember that Mill—to whom William James dedicated his book *Pragmatism*—was a proto-pragmatist.) The libertarian position for which Mill argued in *On Liberty* is independent of moral theory, including his own utilitarianism. It is grounded in sensible practical observations, such as that people are gen-

1. See, for example, Richard A. Posner, *Overcoming Law* 23–29 (1995).

erally the best judges of what is in their own self-interest, that experimentation is important to material and intellectual progress, and that beliefs that are not subjected to challenge lack robustness.[2]

But pragmatists cannot just go on repeating or elaborating Mill. To complete the case for pragmatic liberalism requires adding to the pragmatic analysis of liberty pragmatic analyses of adjudication and of democracy; that has been the undertaking of this book. I have tried to show that these pragmatic analyses are connected by their common origin in an unillusioned conception of the character, motives, and competence of the participants in the governmental process, whether judges, politicians, other officials, or ordinary voters. If, as pragmatists (who among their other characteristics take Darwinism *very* seriously) believe, people are monkeys with big brains rather than aspiring quasi-angels, some of the most influential conceptions both of law and of democracy must be discarded.

Take law first. Legal formalists believe that it is a feasible project to subject even American judges to the discipline of legal doctrine. They are wrong; it is not feasible under the social and political conditions prevailing in the United States. Doctrine has an indirectly constraining effect on our judges because judicial adherence to settled principles promotes practical goods that society values, such as the knowability of legal rights and obligations. A degree of adherence to well-settled doctrine is thus a pragmatic good. But this acknowledgment situates the underlying cause of the constraining force of doctrine in the practical, not the theoretical, concerns of judges, concerns that stem from the material, psychological, and institutional constraints on them. Society could alter those constraints if it wanted to make law more predictable, for example (as I noted briefly in Chapter 2) by substituting courts of specialists for courts of generalists. What is futile is to suppose that by preaching a theology of judicial self-restraint or legal formalism we (don't ask who "we" are exactly) can alter judicial behavior significantly in the same way that the performance of a computer can be altered by inputting revised commands. And what is alarmist is to think that an absence of theoretical constraints leaves judges free to roam untethered, irresponsible, throughout legal space. A pragmatic approach to adjudication, which the influences operating on American judges nudge them toward, has considerably more structure than com-

2. See Richard A. Posner, *Public Intellectuals: A Study of Decline* 353–355 (2001).

monly believed. It is not ad hoc; it is not antihistoricist; it is not neglectful of rule-of-law values; it is not a synonym for utilitarianism or any other consequentialism; and it does not advocate deciding every case on the basis of loose standards rather than tight rules.

Even more important than defending pragmatic adjudication from its detractors is demonstrating, as I have tried to do, the urgent need for taking a pragmatic approach to cases that arise out of national emergencies—cases involving war, terrorism, economic depression, a botched national election, a Presidential scandal. Such cases are not infrequent in our dynamic, even turbulent, society, and they are among the most important cases that judges decide.

One's conception of the optimal scope and freedom of judges depends, to a degree largely unrecognized by the legal profession, including its academic and judicial branches, on one's conception of American democracy. I have endeavored in this book to revitalize and extend Joseph Schumpeter's democratic theory, a theory that has lost considerable ground in recent decades to deliberative democracy on the left and public-choice theory on the right. Deliberative democrats share with legal formalists (and often they are the same people) a misplaced faith in the power of theory to constrain directly the behavior of the participants, both high and low, in the political process. They believe that voters and officials alike can be induced to become well-informed and public-spirited collaborators in a continuous national debate over the policies that are in the best interest of the nation as a whole or that conform to some other conception of the Good. This belief seems to me quixotic, and, more interesting, wrongheaded in suggesting that we would be better off if we reallocated time and emotion from private activities, both personal and commercial, to the public realm. One of the merits of Schumpeter's democratic theory is its recognition that a considerable virtue of modern representative democracy is its enabling people to delegate most political responsibility to specialists in politics, leaving the rest of us free to pursue our private interests. Delegation is not abdication. The political process is competitive, like the market. Voters correspond to consumers in an ordinary market and politicians to sellers. The voter is sovereign in the same sense, imperfect but not trivial, as the consumer.

At the other end of the democracy spectrum, public-choice theorists, with their emphasis on interest groups to the virtual exclusion of the other participants in the political process, give too little weight to the independent role of the politician in that process. To continue the market analogy, the politician is a seller, not just, as interest-group theory assumes, merely a broker. And both the deliberativists and the public-choice theorists, by giving up too soon on American democratic politics, tend to assign too large a goverance role to judges, overlooking the extent to which they share the infirmities of the other participants in the political process.

The appeal of Schumpeterian democracy to a pragmatist is not its theoretical cogency but its consistency with what I have called the pragmatic mood to distinguish everyday pragmatism—the untheorized outlook of most Americans—from pragmatic philosophy, which is increasingly academized and as a result remote from practical concerns, belying its pragmatic character. The pragmatic mood is the outlook of ordinary people under conditions, such as democracy and free markets, that push them to focus on their material concerns, personal interests, and opinions rather than on spiritual concerns, group interests, and the quest for truth—that, indeed, induce the bracketing or marginalizing of most ideological debate. The pragmatic mood induces a willingness to delegate political rule to a specialist class of ambitious, rivalrous politicians, leaving a reduced but essential checking role to the people. The relation of officials to voters resembles that between sellers and consumers and between corporate managers and shareholders rather than either the relation among the members of a scientific team or the relation between a charismatic religious leader and his flock.

Representative democracy interpreted along the lines suggested by Schumpeter and further developed in the chapters of this book that deal with democratic theory depicts elected officials as constrained by material and institutional factors rather than by ideology—the same sorts of constraints that legal pragmatism finds operating on judges. Recurring for a moment to that undiscussed third leg of pragmatic liberalism, liberty, we can see that the theme common to all three legs is distrust of officials, though liberty adds distrust of democratic majorities as well. Whether as judges, voters, or elected or appointed officials, people are not at all like angels, either actually or prospectively. We do well to model their behavior, and evaluate the constraints on that behavior, in realistic rather than idealistic terms. When that is done, a program of reform emerges, one that I have sketched especially in Chapter 6 and with particular reference to the composition of the judiciary (great emphasis, I argue, should be placed on judicial diversity) and to the legal rules and principles governing the political process itself. Pragmatic liberalism is clear-eyed; it is not complacent.

Index

❦